Advance Praise for Mobile Marketing: An Hour a Day

"Nothing gets you closer to your consumer than mobile. And nothing gets to closer to mobile marketing perfection than Mobile Marketing: An Hour a Day."

— Greg Stuart, CEO, Mobile Marketing Association and Co-Author of *What Sticks*

"Noah and Rachel have crafted a book that is filled with clear, well thought out strategic guidance on all things mobile. As you read, you can tell how passionate and knowledgeable they are on the topic, but more importantly, how experienced they are in guiding clients through strategic decisions. They don't offer one-size-fits all approaches, but instead present readers with information and expert perspectives to help customize the strategy on an individual business (and budget) level. This is an excellent go-to guide for mobile novices as well as mobile maestros."

— Joy Liuzzo, President, Wave Collapse

"In an industry where the only constant is change, Elkin and Pasqua expertly detail the mobile landscape, tactics, and tools available to today's mobile marketer. This is a must-read for those who seek to avoid shiny new object syndrome to develop long-term mobile strategies with tangible business outcome."

— Sara Holoubek, CEO, Luminary Labs

"I have known and worked with Rachel and Noah for many years, and they have always provided the last word for me on all things mobile. I found myself getting immersed in the book as I read - just as I did when I listened to them talk about mobile marketing and strategy in person. There is no doubt that this is now my go-to book for mobile. Not only does it have the brain trust going for it, but it also has the data to back it up."

— Rob Garner, VP Strategy, iCrossing and Author of *Search and Social: The Definitive Guide to Real-Time Content Marketing*

"Mobile is so important - more important than many realize - but so often not properly understood. If you ever wished that one or two levelheaded types would sit you down and take you through the whole thing, step-by-step, this is your lucky day.

"Rachel and Noah are two of the cleverest, best informed people in mobile. You need to see things the way they see them, if you want a mobile strategy that's more than hit-and-hope wrapped up in fancy buzzwords.

"Where a lot of books in this field will treat you like an idiot or an expert, Mobile Marketing: An Hour a Day *gives it you straight, explaining the jargon and marking out a clear path to developing a useful mobile strategy. Unless you are a bona fide mobile expert already, you should read this - it is on the required reading list for me, my colleagues and clients as of now."*

— Antony Mayfield, Founding Partner, Brilliant Noise and Author of *Me and My Web Shadow*

"Mobile has become what we all are. Noah and Rachel have done marketers a huge service in producing a knowledge resource that will equip them to ride the tide of change rather than be crushed by it. Think of this book as an essential read and a starting point to a roadmap, one that will allow you to plot the path for your mobile marketing strategy to succeed."

— Peggy Anne Salz, Mobile Industry Author and Founder, MobileGroove

"There are two meaningful misconceptions about mobile: one is that it is about devices, and the other is that it is a single, homogenous thing. Mobility is a consumer context: you are mobile whether you're in the office on your phone, in the living room watching television, or on a plane on a tablet. What you're doing and what mobility means to you are very different things in each of those contexts, and for marketers, the applications in each of those settings can vary greatly. Refreshingly, Noah and Rachel deeply understand this and offer practical advice to help you successfully take advantage of the most personal and measurable medium ever available to a marketer."

— Eric Litman, Chairman and CEO, Medialets

"This is a crucial read for anyone trying to make sense of the mobile space and understand how to best leverage mobile for marketing. Easy-to-follow principles make it simple to develop your strategy and help you stay ahead of your competition."

— Maria Mandel Dunsche, Vice President, Marketing & Media Innovation, AT&T AdWorks

"Between the two of them, Noah Elkin and Rachel Pasqua have put together the quintessential academic tome on mobile marketing. Not only is it rich with data, but its detailed emphasis on sound mobile strategy and tactics will benefit mobile first-timers as well as marketers with experience in the medium."

— Mickey Alam Khan, Editor in Chief, *Mobile Marketer* and *Mobile Commerce Daily*

"An indispensable guide to capitalizing on the mobile revolution, from two of the brightest minds in the business."

— Rick Mathieson, Author of *The On-Demand Brand* and *Branding Unbound*

Mobile Marketing:

An Hour a Day

Mobile Marketing:

An Hour a Day

Rachel Pasqua

Noah Elkin

WILEY

John Wiley & Sons, Inc.

Senior Acquisitions Editor: Willem Knibbe
Development Editor: Me Schutz
Technical Editor: Mac Ling
Production Editor: Christine O'Connor
Copy Editor: Kathy Grider Carlyle
Editorial Manager: Pete Gaughan
Production Manager: Tim Tate
Vice President and Executive Group Publisher: Richard Swadley
Vice President and Publisher: Neil Edde
Book Designer: Franz Baumhackl
Proofreader: Gillian McGarvey, Word One New York
Indexer: Robert Swanson
Project Coordinator, Cover: Katherine Crocker
Cover Designer: Ryan Sneed
Cover Photo: © TommL / iStockPhoto

Published simultaneously in Canada

ISBN: 978-1-118-38844-0
ISBN: 978-1-118-58829-1 (ebk.)
ISBN: 978-1-118-46240-9 (ebk.)
ISBN: 978-1-118-58837-6 (ebk.)

Library of Congress Control Number: 2012949804

10 9 8 7 6 5 4 3 2 1

Dear Reader,

Thank you for choosing *Mobile Marketing: An Hour a Day*. This book is part of a family of premium-quality Sybex books, all of which are written by outstanding authors who combine practical experience with a gift for teaching.

Sybex was founded in 1976. More than 30 years later, we're still committed to producing consistently exceptional books. With each of our titles, we're working hard to set a new standard for the industry. From the paper we print on, to the authors we work with, our goal is to bring you the best books available.

I hope you see all that reflected in these pages. I'd be very interested to hear your comments and get your feedback on how we're doing. Feel free to let me know what you think about this or any other Sybex book by sending me an email at `nedde@wiley.com`. If you think you've found a technical error in this book, please visit `http://sybex.custhelp.com`. Customer feedback is critical to our efforts at Sybex.

Best regards,

Neil Edde
Vice President and Publisher
Sybex, an Imprint of Wiley

To Richard, Nico, and Ava, my inspirations in all things. –rp

To Barbara, for giving everything meaning, and to Max and Zora, for providing a glimpse of the mobile future. –ne

Acknowledgments

We had talked about writing a book together for several years but only began to make progress thanks to our friend and coworker Rob Garner, who introduced us to Willem Knibbe and the team at Sybex. Without Willem's forbearance and guidance as we plodded our way through the early development of the book, it never would have made it to the shelves.

Thanks are also due to our intrepid editorial team, including Mary Ellen Schutz, Pete Gaughan, Christine O'Connor, Kathy Grider-Carlyle, Gillian McGarvey, proofreader, and indexer Robert Swanson who assisted us at all hours of the day (and night) and kept us on schedule. Special thanks go to Mac Ling, who served as our outside technical editor with uncompromising precision. His encyclopedic knowledge of all things mobile helped clarify more points throughout the book than we care to count. Any errors that remain are, of course, purely our responsibility.

Many friends and industry colleagues lent us their time and thoughts over the course of writing this book, including Adam Broitman, Alan Siegel, Alistair Goodman, Collin Cornwell, David Berkowitz, Greg Sterling, Jack Philbin, Jason Spero, Jeff Hasen, Jim Lecinski (who merits a special heartfelt thanks for not only providing his considerable insights on how marketing is evolving, but also for writing the foreword to this book), Johnny Vulkan, Joy Liuzzo, Nick Roshon, Nihal Mehta, Nikao Yang, Nussar Ahmad, Peter Farago, Sasha Sklar, Shiva Vannavada, Steve Smith, and Tom Daly. To say we could not have done it without your inspiration, wisdom, and contributions is a severe understatement.

We are likewise deeply indebted to our respective companies and coworkers for their generosity of time and spirit.

Noah Elkin At eMarketer, I would like to single out Dana Hill, who always managed to find the time to convert the eMarketer charts used in this book to the proper production format; Allison Smith, for ensuring many of those charts got created when we needed them; fellow mobile analyst Catherine Boyle, whose writing on geo-location helped give shape to Chapter 7; and Nicole Perrin, for her at-the-drop-of-a-hat editorial feedback. I feel lucky to work with such wonderful, supportive colleagues! In addition, I am grateful to eMarketer chairman Geoff Ramsey and CEO Terry Chabrowe for the encouragement I received to work on this project. Geoff also deserves a shout-out for paving the way with his own Wiley book, *Digital Impact: The Two Secrets of Online Marketing Success.*

Rachel Pasqua At iCrossing, I am deeply indebted to my wonderful colleagues on the marketing team without whose support over the years this book never would have materialized. Special thanks go out to our brilliant chief marketing officer, Tari Haro, marketing mavens extraordinaire Christiana Henry, Katie Lamkin, Kristen Kalupski, Rachel Klein, Ryan Utter, and the amazing and talented David Deal. Profound thanks also go to iCrossing's senior executive team for their support over the years, especially Dave Johnson, Don Scales, Brian Powley, Mike Jackson, Adam Lavelle, and, of course, to the countless talented colleagues past and present from whom I've had the good fortune to learn, including but by no means limited to Dana Mellecker, Yoav Ilan, Mark Frieser, Sasha Sklar, and Paramjeet Sanghera.

Last but definitely not in any way least, our families bore the brunt of our absence at night and on weekends while we sequestered ourselves to write this book. And it was not just our spouses' seemingly inexhaustible supply of patience that helped us persevere, but also the inspiration our young children provided—they epitomize the "pinch-and-zoom" generation and the experience of growing up mobile. Someday soon, every screen they use will indeed be touch-sensitive. Without all of their love, support, understanding, and encouragement, we never would have made it to the finish line. This book is for them.

About the Authors

Rachel Pasqua and Noah Elkin were colleagues at iCrossing from 2005 to 2008, where they focused on bringing best-of-breed emerging technology strategy to the company's roster of A-list clients. Rachel and Noah have since collaborated in various settings, including founding the Emerging Technologies Committee for the Search Engine Marketing Professional Organization (SEMPO), chairing panels at industry conferences, and co-teaching courses on mobile marketing at Rutgers University's Center for Management Development.

Rachel Pasqua

Rachel Pasqua is a digital strategist, analyst, and speaker with extensive expertise in mobile, social, and ambient marketing. She joined iCrossing (`www.icrossing.com`), a global digital marketing agency owned by the Hearst Corporation, in 2005 to build out its emerging media group and she continues to serve as vice president of mobile, helping iCrossing's many Fortune 500 clients connect successfully with their audiences in a multiplatform, always–on world. A digital industry veteran, she has more than 15 years of experience spanning from content strategy to native mobile app development to near field communications. Prior to her online career, she worked for several years in the film industry in New York City as a writer and producer and holds a B.A. in Filmmaking from Boston University.

Rachel is a frequent and often-quoted speaker on digital trends at industry conferences, including OMMA, MediaPost, L2 Forum, and Digiday, and she has judged numerous media events including the Communication Arts 2010 Interactive Design Annual. She writes regularly about digital innovation on iCrossing's blog, Great Finds (`http://greatfinds.icrossing.com/`), on Twitter at `twitter.com/rachelpasqua`, and on her personal blog, Mobile, Social, Ambient (`www.rachelpasqua.com`). When she's not hard at work helping iCrossing clients figure out their mobile strategy, she's busy collaborating on digital art projects with her husband, noted artist and creative director Richard Pasqua, and being a mom to their four-year-old twins at their home on Long Island's south shore.

Noah Elkin, Ph.D.

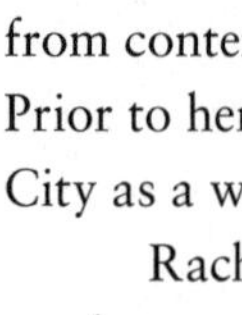

Noah is Principal Analyst at eMarketer (`www.emarketer.com`), where he helps clients understand the latest developments in mobile marketing, usage, content, devices, and commerce. He is quoted frequently in leading business publications, including the *New York Times*, *The Wall Street Journal*, *Bloomberg BusinessWeek*, *Forbes*, *Ad Age* and NPR's "Marketplace," and speaks regularly at industry events and conferences such as ad:tech, iMedia Summits, Mobile World Congress, Mobile Marketing Forum, Digiday, and OMMA.

Prior to his work at eMarketer, Noah helped launch the U.S. arm of international digital agency Steak, where he served as managing partner, and before that, worked with Rachel as iCrossing's vice president of corporate strategy. Noah has consulted for organizations as diverse as the Inter-American Development Bank, Oxford Analytica, and the United Nations Conference on Trade and Development (UNCTAD), for which he was appointed to chair the first ministerial meeting on information and communication technology (ICT) for development organized at the regional level by UNCTAD. Noah holds a Ph.D. in Latin American History from Rutgers University and was awarded a Fulbright Fellowship to Brazil. He lives in Columbia County, NY, with his wife and two children, who have perfected the art of reimagining every remote control as an iPhone and every Etch-a-Sketch as an iPad. An avid distance runner, Noah has completed four marathons. He actively shares his insights on mobile, social, and digital media trends on Twitter at `twitter.com/noahelkin`.

Contents

Foreword

Holiday Shopping. Relax, this is just a thought-experiment — you have an entire year before you need to really worry about it again...

For now though, take a moment to think about the last holiday shopping season that's now comfortably in your rearview mirror. As you checked names and gifts off of your list, how did you decide you wanted to buy one tablet instead of another, one brand's mountain bike or its competitor's, or one bottle of cabernet as opposed to a different one?

If you're like me — and millions of shoppers everywhere around the world — you probably did your homework before, and during, the shopping process. You likely searched the web to find product reviews of those different tablets. You probably took pictures of different bikes with your smartphone and read reviews online while you walked around the sporting-goods store. And I bet you discussed your holiday wine options with some aficionados on your social network of choice to get some input and feedback.

Shopping sure isn't what it used to be. In fact, it's a whole new ballgame.

What does this mean for businesses, and marketers, in particular? A lot. The ubiquity of the web, and most recently, the explosion of smartphones and tablets, have enabled us to become more informed, and all-around better shoppers, wherever we may be. Sometimes we use these devices to identify the best brand that meets our need, sometimes we use them to find the best deal — often it's both.

As marketers, we need to recognize this tectonic shift that has happened in consumer behavior and adapt — fast. At Google, we've called these steps towards a purchase 'Zero Moments of Truth', a play on P&G's famous 'First Moment of Truth'. Marketers need to pivot and connect with consumers during these 'zero' moments, while they read reviews online, connect with friends via social media, and do so in a largely mobile context. Marketers who do stand to gain a competitive advantage. Those who don't? Well...

This is a watershed moment for marketers, and the beginning of a new era for business as a whole. That's why I'm so excited about Rachel and Noah's book — not only do they get it, but they've provided a series of excellent, concrete steps to help businesses connect with the increasingly mobile, increasingly informed, and increasingly savvy shoppers, that we've become.

Theirs is a guide for modern marketing, in the ZMOT era. I hope you enjoy it and act on it.

Best,

JIM LECINSKI,

Vice President US Sales & Service, Google

Introduction

*We'd like to start out by telling you that we don't think that 2013 is the year of mobile. We're both asked this question on an almost daily basis and we've been giving the same standard answer for a while now—*every year *is the year of mobile. With each passing year, mobile (like the Web before it) becomes more indispensable in our daily lives and more and more crucial to the way we do business. However, because you've picked up this book, you've most likely decided that 2013* is *the year of mobile, at least as far as you're concerned. So, we're here to help.*

In all honesty though, we don't believe in mobile media—or social media for that matter. As we see it, the way we use digital media to interact with brands and each other is inherently social. We're social creatures, after all. The platforms through which we interact are increasingly diverse. It's simply the natural evolution of the Web.

As marketers and human beings, we tend to be resistant to change. When we encounter a new tool or technology, it's our natural inclination to try to frame it in the context of what we already know. Here are some cases in point: think of the many websites in the early 1990s that were simply digitized versions of print brochures, or similarly, the early mobile websites that were just shrunken versions of their .com counterparts. It takes time for us to accept that something has disturbed the status quo and even more time for us to adapt to the change and let it alter the way we function—but inevitably, it does.

Based on our observation of clients, we estimate the majority of household name brands received roughly 10 percent of their overall site traffic from mobile devices in 2011. By early 2012, that number was closer to 15 percent. By the time this book is published, it will be more like 20 to 25 percent. Those numbers should be enough to dispel any lingering illusion that you can still wait to figure out your mobile strategy. Even if we haven't yet reached critical mass, the inevitable is looming large on the horizon. The way you market, advertise, build your brand, and engage with your customers has changed for good. Again. That's the bad news. The good news is that this opens up a whole new world of opportunity to do it all better.

Everything evolves. Change is good. You just have to be prepared.

Why We Wrote This Book

We've been friends, colleagues, and frequent collaborators for years, and between us, we've written countless blog posts, white papers, and articles examining every aspect of the mobile industry, from apps to augmented reality (AR). When the opportunity to write *Mobile Marketing: An Hour a Day* came along, we were skeptical at first: can we really explain everything you need to know in one book? We spend our day-to-day professional lives helping brands figure out their mobile strategies, and if there is one thing we've learned in the process, it's that there is a mobile aspect to everything you do as a brand. From marketing to customer relationship management (CRM), the opportunities are endless. It's also a fast-changing, endlessly complex ecosystem and navigating it is no small undertaking.

Last year, all the marketers we knew wanted to develop an iPad app. This year, the question shifted to "How do I develop a *mobile strategy*?" That persistent question made us realize that this book is timelier than ever. Marketers are realizing that mobile plays a role in every step of the customer journey, from awareness to advocacy. As a result, there's a real need in our industry to understand all the touchpoints involved and how they connect. In the end, you will only truly learn what is right for your brand and business through hands-on effort, but we can give you the benefit of our experience in crafting a mobile strategy and teach you the key things you need to know to support it.

Throughout this book, we'll continually remind you that it's important to maintain a strategic mindset, even as you drill down into tactics. Mobile is rife with shiny objects, and building that iPad app or developing that AR campaign before you've thought through all the variables can be extremely tempting.

However, the results are almost always disappointing when you go this route. People—and strategy—should always come before technology and tactics. In this book, we'll give you a framework for assessing the needs of your customers and your own goals, and a strategic methodology for satisfying both. Of course, we'll also provide a comprehensive explanation of what the opportunities are and how to capitalize on them. In the process, we'll ask you to keep a few key things in mind:

Mobile is about people—not devices. It's not about the iPad or Android; it's about getting your brand in front of the right people, in the right place, and at the right time. It's a state of being, not a collection of technologies. The technologies are just the tools that help us create the kinds of real-time, hyper-relevant experiences that will resonate with our audience.

Mobile is social. Marketing is about conversations, and those conversations are no longer confined to the desktop. Mobile devices are fast becoming a primary means of accessing and sharing digital information. Understanding this symbiotic relationship enhances your ability to create successful mobile programs and user experiences.

Mobile is ambient. Mobile is about more than just smartphones and tablets. Interactive signage, augmented reality, Bluetooth, near field communications, and surface technologies all have a role to play in your brand's ability to connect with consumers. The "Internet of Things" is very much a reality and offers us the opportunity to integrate digital interaction into the physical world.

In essence, it's not about the hardware, but about the context. Smartphones, tablets, and other mobile devices give us a richer, more meaningful array of contextual information than the desktop ever could. Our goal is to help you use that data to create richer, more meaningful user experiences that bring you closer to your customers every step of the way.

In the process of putting this book together, we interviewed a great number of people in the industry, from senior marketing executives of household name brands to some of the smartest engineers, strategists, and entrepreneurs in the business. They all had invaluable perspectives to share, many of which are threaded throughout the chapters that follow.

The conversation that stands out the most was the one we had with Alan Siegel, founder of iconic branding firm, Siegel+Gale (`www.siegelgale.com`). One of the original mad men, he started out in the advertising business in the early 1960s and worked for some of the best known agencies on Madison Avenue before founding his eponymous shop in 1969. Now, 44 years later, when most of his contemporaries have retired, he's started a new branding firm, Siegel Vision (`www.siegelvision.com`), and is more excited than ever about the possibilities we have as brand builders and marketers. He spoke to us over lunch when we were writing the very first chapter about innovation, change, and the industry he's seen evolve across a career of over 50 years.

"Mobile should be a natural extension of everything you do, but don't get too preoccupied with the platforms. Be preoccupied with the *content*. It's not new media, it's *just media*. The platform is just the delivery system—you have to understand it, of course, but don't make it the focal point. It's a tool to create great experiences, nothing more."

Wise words from one of advertising's elder statesmen, who has seen the industry evolve from TV, radio, and print to today's *splinternet*.

Who Should Read This Book

Given the increasingly prominent role mobile devices play in our personal and professional lives, virtually anyone can benefit from reading this book. But, it will be most useful for people who want to understand the full spectrum of the mobile landscape and use it to build their business. Most of these readers will fall into one of three groups:

- Agency-side marketers
- Brand-side marketers
- Small- and medium-sized business owners

The size and scope of your business and your specific role within it are practically extraneous; sooner or later (but most likely sooner), you're going to need to know how to reach your audience on mobile devices. So, whether you are a sole proprietor or a member of a large team within a Fortune 500 corporation, *Mobile Marketing: An Hour a Day* is designed for you. The roadmap we've laid out and the examples we've supplied will get you up to speed on what you need to know now and give you tools to keep your education up-to-date.

Even if mobile marketing ends up being a small portion of what you do or if your responsibilities only comprise a slice of a broader mobile marketing campaign, we believe the more you know about the strategy, development, monitoring, and measurement efforts that go into getting a mobile campaign up and running, the better able you'll be to do your job. You may not be *in* mobile marketing today, but the day is fast approaching when all of us will be in mobile, whether by design or simply by necessity.

What You Will Learn

Mobile devices provide many people with their first digital experience. For them, their mobile device *is* the Web. That adds up to a significant marketing opportunity. How significant, you might ask? Just consider that by eMarketer's estimate, 4.2 billion people will own a mobile phone in 2013—nearly 60 percent of the world's population! Within that vast group of *mobile phone users*, there is tremendous variation in the types of devices they carry, how people use them, and, by extension, how you can market to them and what kinds of outcomes you can reasonably expect to achieve.

We firmly believe that the best way for you to get started in mobile marketing is by gaining a firm understanding of the current mobile landscape in all of its wonderful complexity, and by grounding your thinking in a comprehensive strategic framework that you can then use to decide which of the many tactics and channels we discuss in this book are right for your brand and your business. We can't do this groundwork for you (unless you hire us, of course), but we can delineate the steps you need to take and equip you with the tools to undertake this journey. With mobile marketing, as with so many other things, "look before you leap" will be your watchwords.

We encourage you not to be distracted by the many shiny objects (devices, marketing techniques, and otherwise) that revolve around the mobile universe. Instead, remember that mobile is primarily about creating and fostering real-time relationships with your customers. The devices will change, and change rapidly, so it is the concept of enabling real-time relationships that should remain at the core of everything you do. This book will teach you how to harness the devices and marketing techniques to achieve that goal.

Note: Throughout this book, we include tips, examples, and use cases designed to help you hone your skills and improve your business's mobile presence and the effectiveness of your mobile marketing programs.

What You Need

We cover the basics of mobile strategy and marketing throughout the book, but the more general marketing knowledge you bring to the table, the more of a head start you'll have. There are many facets of mobile marketing that are specific to the discipline, as you'll see as you read on, but much of it is also inextricably tied to basic marketing principles.

In particular, a working comprehension of search engine optimization, paid search, social media marketing, online advertising, analytics, website development, and content marketing will come in handy, especially if you're developing mobile content or building an app. The reason why? As much as your app is designed to market your business, the app itself needs to be marketed or it risks getting lost amidst a sea of hundreds of thousands of other options. You'll need to marshal your paid, owned, and earned media to ensure your app and your content find their desired audience.

Depending on your audience and your marketing objectives, having access to recent, if not the latest, versions of devices (smartphones and tablets) on at least the top-two platforms (Apple's iOS and Android) is a must. You can use online simulators for many aspects of mobile app and ad development, but having a real feel and affinity for the devices your audience will use to engage with your mobile marketing program is the preferred route. A passing familiarity with the app stores that accompany each of these platforms will likewise be helpful, if only to picture what you'll need if developing an app and where it might fit within the structure of each platform's app storefront.

Although not strictly necessary, having something tangible to market—a brand, product, or service—and a solid sense of what benefits you can bring to your audience will make your experience of reading this book more practical and less theoretical.

And last, but certainly not least, you'll need patience to get up to speed, and persistence to stay up to speed on what is undeniably a fast-moving subject. Your willingness—and commitment—to devote at least an hour a day to improving your knowledge base will make your business more competitive in our increasingly mobile world.

What's Covered in This Book

Mobile Marketing: An Hour a Day is organized to provide you with a two-month, day-by-day program for understanding and taking advantage of the mobile opportunity for your brand. We've divided up the days into tasks we estimate will take you approximately an hour each. Depending on your circumstances, your familiarity with the subject matter, and your particular goals and strategy, certain tasks may take more or less time to complete.

The book starts off with an in-depth look at the mobile opportunity and a deep dive into the steps you'll need to take to develop a comprehensive mobile strategy for your brand. That means you should start with these first two fundamental chapters to ensure you have a thorough grounding before working your way through the different tactical applications.

Here's what you'll find covered in this book.

Chapter 1: Map the Mobile Opportunity Here we introduce you to the complexities of the mobile landscape, which dictate whom you can reach and how you can do so effectively. In this chapter, we'll walk you through the key market data and insights you'll need to understand in order to successfully capitalize on the mobile opportunity.

Chapter 2: Week 1: Develop Your Mobile Strategy This chapter offers detailed guidance on how to develop a strategic plan that will set you off on your mobile marketing journey. This framework will lay the groundwork for how to use the various mobile tactics we discuss in subsequent chapters.

Chapter 3: Week 2: Start Simple—SMS Starting simple gets you off and running with the mobile channel that enjoys the greatest reach and the largest potential audience. SMS may not be glamorous, but it is efficient and effective, and it continues to engage consumers; for these reasons, it should find a place in your marketing campaigns.

Chapter 4: Week 3: Maximize Reach with Mobile Websites This chapter builds on the basics from Chapter 3 with a focus on your mobile website—what we believe to be most important element of your overall mobile strategy. This is where most of your customers will connect with you and will also be an end destination to which many of your other mobile initiatives will drive customers. We'll walk you through the options for designing and developing your mobile site and provide you with best practices for testing, search optimization, and measuring success.

Chapter 5: Week 4: Maximize Engagement with Mobile Apps Here, we frame apps as a mechanism for forging deeper and repeat engagement with your customers, while also dispelling the notion that apps and mobile websites are an either/or proposition. In this chapter, we detail what you need to know about building and developing your mobile app, and the marketing you'll have to do to get it noticed and keep your audience engaged.

Chapter 6: Week 5: Promote Your Message with Mobile Advertising Now, we'll teach you the basics of mobile search, display, and email; and how you can use these forms of advertising to attract more qualified and engaged consumers to your mobile content. While mobile activity still far outweighs mobile ad spend, we see this point in time as a golden opportunity to test and learn before the demand inevitably begins to exceed the supply.

Chapter 7: Week 6: Leverage the SoLoMo Nexus This chapter reveals how mobile devices enable you to truly deliver on the holy grail of marketing by marrying where your customers are (location) with what they're doing (context), and what they want (intent). In this chapter, we show you how to navigate the fast-evolving geo-social ecosystem without succumbing to the many latent pitfalls.

Chapter 8: Week 7: Check Out M-Commerce Follow your audience as they move toward the end of the customer journey and the bottom of the purchase funnel, building on the SoLoMo nexus as a more refined mechanism for targeting prospective shoppers. From mobile coupons to mobile wallets, we examine your options for monetizing mobile and getting your customers to the virtual checkout counter.

Chapter 9: Week 8: Drive Awareness with Ambient Media This chapter highlights how technologies that trigger a connection between a mobile device and the non-digital world—what we call ambient media—can add a layer of interactivity to traditional media, places, and objects that in the past were completely static. In this chapter, we detail how you can use ambient mobile channels, including 2D barcodes, augmented reality, near-field communications, and mobile broadcasting to render the physical world, digital, and bring your marketing programs to the bleeding edge.

Chapter 10: Chart the Future Forward Map out the road ahead, focusing on what we see as the new four Ps you need to integrate into your marketing—Portability, Preferences, Presence, and Proximity—and the ways in which you can take advantage of them to better engage with your customers.

Appendices Here you'll find a list of vendors, services, and other resources that you might find useful for developing your mobile marketing campaigns.

Glossary Take a look and familiarize yourself with key industry terms.

Companion Websites and Contacting the Authors

As we noted, the one constant with mobile is change: New devices, new ad formats, new ad-tech companies seem to spring up on a near daily basis. If you'd like to keep up with a fast-moving industry, we invite you to check out the following resources:

`www.mobileanhouraday.com` is the companion website to the book. We'll use it to post updates about key developments, interviews with industry luminaries, and other helpful information.

`www.facebook.com/mobileanhouraday` includes information on the book, including promotions spearheaded by the authors, links to posts on the companion website, and a forum for Q&A with the authors and a community of mobile marketers.

`www.twitter.com/TheMobileBook` features links to development in mobile marketing, new stats you may find relevant, and so on.

These resources are also places where you can provide feedback about this book or books you'd like to see from us in the future. In addition, you can reach us by writing to `authors@mobileanhouraday.com` or by following us on Twitter at `@rachelpasqua` (for Rachel) and `@noahelkin` (for Noah). We can't do your job for you, but we'll do our best to answer your questions in a timely fashion.

Sybex strives to keep you supplied with the latest tools and information you need for your work. Please check the book website at `www.sybex.com/go/mobilemarketing`, where we'll post additional content and updates that supplement this book if the need arises.

Mobile Marketing:

An Hour a Day

1

Map the Mobile Opportunity

For many people in the world today, a mobile device will provide their first digital experience. For them, their mobile device is the Web. By eMarketer estimates, 3.9 billion—yes, billion—people will own a mobile phone in 2012, so the mobile opportunity is clearly significant. The best way to get started in mobile marketing is by understanding the current landscape, which dictates whom you can reach now and how to do so effectively. In this chapter, we'll walk you through the key market data and landscape insights you'll need to understand in order to successfully capitalize on this mobile opportunity.

Chapter Contents

Market Size and Growth Potential

When leaving the house, most of us carry a few basic essentials: wallet, keys, and a mobile phone. In time, as the mobile phone becomes more sophisticated and enables you to unlock your home and car and pay for essentials through the magic of *near-field communications (NFC)*, it may end up being the *only* thing you need when you leave the house.

Before long, average consumers will be connected 24/7, sending and receiving a constant stream of data from all the objects that surround them, from sales tags in stores to the refrigerators in their kitchens. The future this heralds is the "internet of things," or as *The Economist* termed it in an article, "the internet of everything" (December 9, 2010). For now, mobile phones are the one connected device most people carry with them at all times, which makes them both highly personal and ubiquitous.

Being more connected has changed the ways consumers use their mobile devices. The fact that mobile phones can make calls is increasingly less relevant. Instead, consumers now expect to network, share experiences, browse, and shop via a wide range of platforms, from *smartphones* to *tablets* to new and increasingly complex-connected devices of all kinds. From home appliances to utility meters to Internet-enabled cars, the growing proliferation—and sophistication—of smart devices that can communicate with each other (commonly referred to as *machine-to-machine* or *M2M communications*) will only accelerate this trend.

As mobile phones have become more universal, their appeal as a marketing vehicle has grown commensurately. Simply put: if your audience is mobile (and we guarantee you that it is), your marketing has to be, too. Yet it is a diverse audience, and we've found that that diversity—often referred to as *fragmentation*—is the number-one reason that most marketers have shied away from using mobile. So, helping you make sense of the mobile user base is our first goal.

In this chapter, we'll share our own expertise as well as what we learned from talking with the following experts:

- Joy Liuzzo, former vice president of mobile at market research and data analytics provider InsightExpress (`www.insightexpress.com`)
- Greg Sterling, founding principal of Sterling Market Intelligence and contributing editor for the online publication *Search Engine Land* (`www.searchengineland.com`)

You'll hear from Joy and Greg throughout this chapter.

The easiest way to make sense of the mobile user base is to illustrate the landscape in relation to ownership of the key device type (smartphones) and the key activity (mobile web usage) as we've done in the pyramid in Figure 1.1. At the base are all mobile users, which includes anyone who owns any kind of mobile phone.

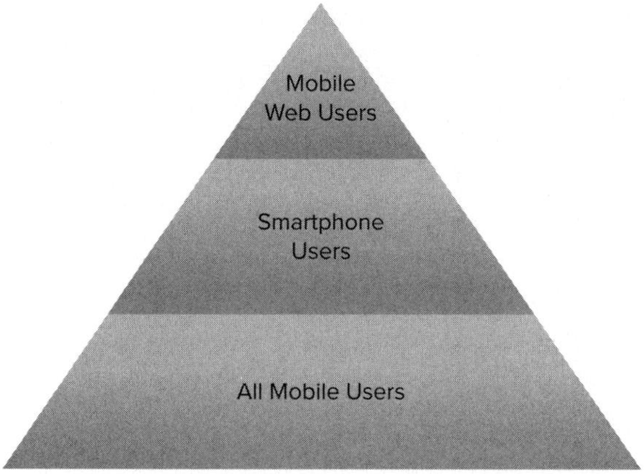

Figure 1.1 Mobile usage can be viewed as a pyramid.

You will often hear older or less-sophisticated mobile devices referred to as *feature phones*, although the definition of a feature phone is somewhat loose. It's generally accepted that the feature phone category includes everything from early devices that were capable of nothing but voice and text all the way up to today's more advanced models that support primitive mobile applications and rudimentary browsers; some, including the so-called quick-messaging phones, even have full QWERTY keyboards and touchscreen displays. The smartphone category is also diverse, including earlier devices with full browsers but no touchscreen or rich-media capabilities, as well as the more recent (and more sophisticated) multitouch handsets on the market, exemplified by the iPhone.

Although some feature phones are equipped with browsers and some feature phone owners do surf the Web, their numbers are dwindling, and with the current rate of handset replacement and the falling cost of smartphones, less-sophisticated devices are fast becoming a thing of the past in developed markets. Feature phones will not disappear overnight, of course, particularly in developing economies. According to eMarketer projections, the share of the U.S. market will be cut in half between 2012 and 2016, falling from 52 percent to 26 percent of the mobile user base.

All smartphones are capable of accessing the mobile web, and most (but not all) smartphone users do so. This makes smartphone users a subset of all mobile users, and mobile web users are a further subset. And while not all mobile web users own smartphones, in the most-developed markets like the United States and Western Europe, where a significant portion of the user population owns a smartphone, most mobile web users own smartphones.

Let's start with the base of the pyramid. As you might expect, the user demographics of mobile are eye-popping: according to eMarketer, 3.9 billion—well over half the world's population—will own a mobile phone in 2012. But it's worth noting that these users are far from evenly distributed. As listed in Table 1.1, over half can be found in the Asia-Pacific region, nearly one-third in EMEA (Europe, Middle East, and Africa) and the remainder in the Americas. The five largest single markets from a mobile-user perspective are, in descending order, China, India, the United States, Brazil, and Russia.

▶ **Table 1.1** Asia-Pacific is home to more than half of the world's mobile users. (2012)

Region	Users (Millions)
Asia-Pacific	2,152.5
Europe	640.3
Middle East and Africa	484.9
Latin America	389.9
North America	265.6
Worldwide	3,933.3

Source: eMarketer, April 2012

Big Numbers: Subscribers versus Users

Any data related to mobile is inevitably going to lead to some big numbers, so when you're looking at mobile population bases, it's important to distinguish in particular between mobile subscribers and mobile users. The two terms are sometimes used interchangeably, but they actually represent different groups.

The number of mobile *subscribers* is the number of active mobile subscriptions, and that tends to be the bigger number simply because a single person can have more than one phone (one for home and one for work, for example), meaning that one person gets counted as two subscribers. This explains why mobile subscriber penetration in many countries can exceed 100 percent, even when it is obvious that not every person has a mobile subscription.

Mobile *users*, on the other hand, signify one user/one phone. As a result, the number of mobile users tends to be significantly smaller—and a generally more accurate measure of mobile penetration—than that of mobile subscribers or subscriptions.

The size of the mobile user population is important, but you need to look past sheer numbers and consider the percentage of the total population that owns a mobile phone. That is a key metric for assessing a market's overall development. See Table 1.2 for a quick reference guide to mobile user penetration rates. They are in the 75 to 85 percent range in North America, across much of Western Europe, and in Japan and South Korea, making these markets the world's most developed.

▶ **Table 1.2** Mobile user penetration varies widely by region and country (2012).

Country or Region	Mobile User Penetration
South Korea	85.0%
Japan	84.0%
United Kingdom	82.8%
Germany	80.7%
Western Europe	79.6%
Australia	79.5%
Italy	79.0%
Argentina	79.0%
Spain	77.9%
United States	76.8%
France	76.5%
North America	75.8%
Russia	74.0%
Eastern Europe	73.2%
Canada	66.6%
China	65.5%
Latin America	65.1%
Indonesia	60.0%
Brazil	58.0%
Worldwide	56.0%
Asia-Pacific	55.1%
Mexico	55.0%
Middle East/Africa	36.5%

Source: eMarketer, April 2012

High penetration rates also indicate that these markets have either reached or are approaching saturation, so growth in new users has slowed to a trickle. The real action in these countries is coming from users upgrading their devices and engaging in higher-value activities. We'll get to that in a bit.

Of course, the sheer scale of China and India's populations make for massive mobile user bases. See Figure 1.2 for details. China's estimated 880.4 million *mobile* users exceed the total populations of the United States and Western Europe combined! India is not far behind, and other populous Asia-Pacific countries like Indonesia, Pakistan, and the Philippines also boast sizable and growing mobile user populations.

In all, eMarketer estimates 75 percent of the world's mobile users reside in the emerging markets of Latin America, Africa and the Middle East, and the Asia-Pacific region.

Mobile Phone Users Worldwide, by Region and Country, 2010-2016
millions

	2010	2011	2012	2013	2014	2015	2016
Asia-Pacific	**1,750.5**	**1,948.2**	**2,152.5**	**2,345.6**	**2,519.6**	**2,690.8**	**2,833.3**
—China*	671.1	780.6	880.4	975.4	1,051.2	1,122.4	1,187.5
—India	387.1	416.2	470.0	524.9	581.1	638.4	684.1
—Indonesia	106.9	130.2	148.9	160.5	169.7	179.0	185.9
—Japan	104.6	105.8	107.0	108.2	109.3	110.4	110.9
—South Korea	40.9	41.2	41.5	41.9	42.2	42.5	42.8
—Australia	15.6	16.6	17.5	18.2	18.9	19.4	19.8
—Other	424.3	457.7	487.2	516.5	547.3	578.6	602.3
Middle East & Africa	**402.7**	**445.1**	**484.9**	**524.8**	**556.6**	**593.8**	**629.6**
Latin America	**347.8**	**369.2**	**389.9**	**409.3**	**427.4**	**444.5**	**461.7**
—Brazil	100.6	109.9	119.3	128.9	137.7	146.5	155.5
—Mexico	55.1	59.1	63.2	67.4	71.7	75.4	79.1
—Argentina	31.0	32.2	33.3	34.5	35.3	36.0	36.8
—Other	161.1	168.1	174.0	178.5	182.8	186.5	190.2
Western Europe	**314.5**	**322.6**	**329.4**	**336.0**	**342.4**	**347.4**	**351.7**
—Germany	62.7	64.3	65.6	66.8	68.0	69.1	69.8
—UK	51.1	51.7	52.2	52.7	53.2	53.4	53.7
—France	47.3	48.8	50.0	51.3	52.4	53.4	54.3
—Italy	45.3	47.0	48.4	49.8	51.2	52.0	52.7
—Spain	34.9	35.8	36.6	37.5	38.3	39.1	39.9
—Other	73.3	75.0	76.6	78.0	79.4	80.4	81.3
Eastern Europe	**293.3**	**302.1**	**310.9**	**319.7**	**328.4**	**337.0**	**345.0**
—Russia	97.6	99.9	102.2	104.4	106.6	108.8	110.9
—Other	195.7	202.2	208.7	215.2	221.7	228.2	234.1
North America	**252.8**	**259.4**	**265.6**	**271.3**	**276.9**	**282.0**	**286.2**
—US	232.2	237.7	242.8	247.5	252.1	256.2	259.6
—Canada	20.6	21.8	22.8	23.8	24.8	25.7	26.5
Worldwide	**3,361.6**	**3,646.8**	**3,933.3**	**4,206.7**	**4,451.4**	**4,695.4**	**4,907.4**

*Note: mobile phone users are individuals of any age who own at least one mobile phone and use the phone(s) at least once per month; *excludes Hong Kong*
Source: eMarketer, April 2012

139093 www.eMarketer.com

Figure 1.2 The scale of emerging market mobile usage is immense.

Emerging markets such as Brazil, China, India, Indonesia, Nigeria, the Philippines, Russia, and South Africa may have large user bases, but overall mobile penetration is lower than in North America and Western Europe, indicating room for growth. In these markets, with their vast geographies and populations, mobile is a more cost-effective means of connecting consumers to communications, media, and commerce than building out and maintaining capital-intensive fixed-line networks.

Not All Emerging Markets Are Created Equal

It's easy to get sidetracked by the massive user numbers in emerging markets, particularly in countries like China and India, because they suggest such a tantalizing opportunity. But they merit a closer look because there is significant variation in terms of spending power and the sophistication of consumers and their devices not only across regions but also within individual markets. So, for example, the mobile opportunity in South Africa will differ from the rest of sub-Saharan Africa, just as the opportunity for reaching urban consumers in Shanghai or São Paulo will differ from the prospects of targeting their rural counterparts. In other words, the global opportunity remains large, but you have to look below the surface to gauge just how large.

Clearly, many factors are working in mobile's favor, but it's about more than the numbers: it's about getting and staying connected, wherever, whenever. That is where the transformative potential of mobile technology lies—in bringing information to people who need it.

One great example is Nokia Life Tools, which distributes vital crop data such as weather forecasts and commodity pricing trends to rural farmers via text messages. The program started in India in 2009 and has since spread to China, Indonesia, and Nigeria. Nokia did extensive anthropological research among rural Indian communities before developing Life Tools, but it's easy to see that the tools effectively met a need of rural farmers, and how connecting them to crucial data for a modest cost could make a big difference in their lives. The bottom line: mobile functions well as a delivery mechanism for media and entertainment, but it serves other purposes with equal effectiveness.

The Global Rise of Smart Devices

Having lots of connected consumers is important, but how they connect and the devices they use are key factors in determining the extent of the mobile opportunity for a particular market. Put simply: The more sophisticated the device, the more sophisticated the activities it enables, and the more occasions and venues marketers will have to engage with consumers. So, let's look at the second level of the pyramid.

Smartphones

Android, BlackBerry, iPhone, Windows Phone … All of these devices may come to mind when you're thinking about smartphones, but for a moment, don't focus on the individual platforms. Instead, look at the shared capabilities they facilitate. Smartphones, when you think about it, are nothing less than sophisticated portable computers with roughly 4-inch screens. In fact, it's often said that the average smartphone sold today has more computing power than the systems NASA used to put the first men on the moon.

Surveys vary on the extent of smartphone adoption, but most agree it is fast approaching the magical 50 percent mark among the U.S. mobile user population. As shown in Figure 1.3, eMarketer estimates it will reach 48 percent in 2012 and then accelerate to 74 percent by 2016.

Us Smartphone Users and Penetration, 2010-2016
millions, % of mobile phone users and % of population

	2010	2011	2012	2013	2014	2015	2016
Smartphone users	62.6	93.1	115.8	137.5	157.7	176.3	192.4
% of mobile phone users	26.9%	39.2%	47.7%	55.5%	62.5%	68.8%	74.1%
% of population	20.2%	29.7%	36.6%	43.1%	48.9%	54.2%	58.5%

■ Smartphone users　■ % of mobile phone users　■ % of population

Note: individuals of any age who own at least one smartphone and use the smartphone(s) at least once per month
Source: eMarketer, April 2012; confirmed and republished, Aug 2012

138189　　　　　　　　　　　　　　　　www.eMarketer.com

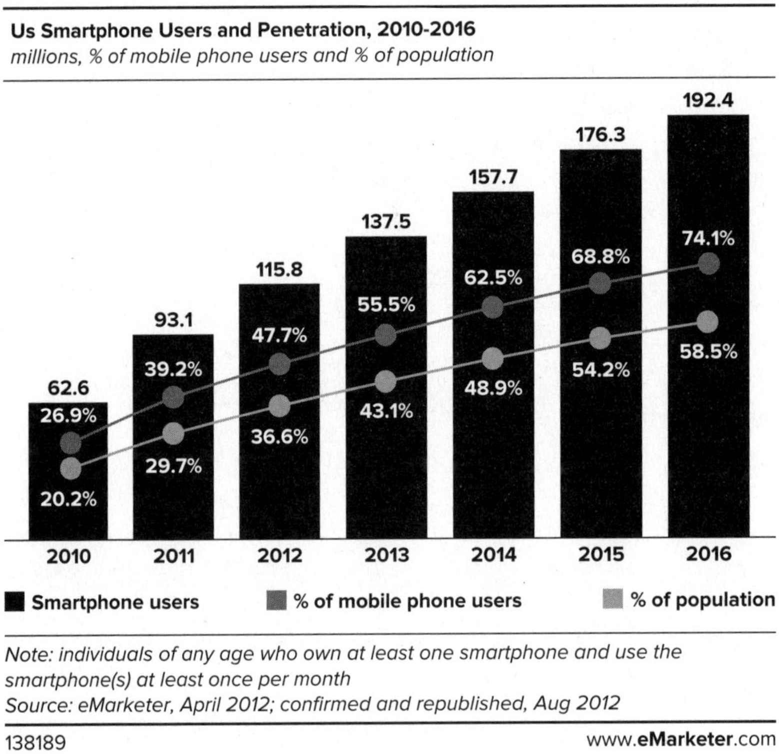

Figure 1.3 Smartphone adoption is rising at a rapid clip in the United States.

What Makes a Smartphone So Smart Anyway?

The range of smartphones available on the market today is dizzyingly vast and expanding with seemingly no end in sight. Specs vary considerably by manufacturer and platform, but common smartphone characteristics include:

- High-density, high-resolution color display measuring two or more inches (four seems to be around the industry average, although hybrid smartphone-tablet devices such as Samsung's Galaxy Note, which has a 5.3-inch screen, are pushing the envelope)
- Touchscreen interface
- Advanced, purpose-built operating system (such as Apple's *iOS*, Google's *Android*, etc.)
- Ability to send and receive email
- Full-featured web browser that can render standard web pages except those elements built with Flash (although Android does support Flash, at least through version 4.0 of the OS)
- Access to and the capacity to run applications (*apps*)
- A camera that can capture still images and high-definition video
- *GPS* capabilities
- Ability to access both Wi-Fi and high-speed mobile broadband networks

While we're approaching the tipping point on a percentage basis, we've arguably blown past it from another perspective. If you're a marketer, chances are you're already focusing some, if not most, of your efforts on reaching the smartphone audience. And if you haven't started thinking about it, stop what you're doing and reconsider the emphasis of your campaigns. The smartphone user represents nothing less than the future of marketing—not just mobile marketing but all of marketing.

That may sound hyperbolic, but consider the anecdotal evidence. Aren't most of the smartphone owners you know glued to their devices—at all times? A Google-sponsored study even asked people whether they look at their smartphones in the bathroom. Guess what? The majority answered yes! Other research has found people consulting their smartphones during sex, or, in the case of a Telenav study, more inclined to forego sex altogether for a week than be without their phone. (Okay, it was only 33 percent of Americans, but you get the idea.)

Now, consider the data in Table 1.3. Look at what it says about smartphone users: market research and data analytics provider InsightExpress (`www.insightexpress.com`) found that smartphone owners were more likely than all mobile users (which includes everyone with a smartphone and a non-smartphone) to perform every activity, sometimes by a factor of two or three. Given that smartphone owners represent less than half of the survey sample (43 percent to be precise), these findings show the significant impact smartphones have on overall usage numbers.

▶ **Table 1.3** Activities of mobile phone owners and smartphone owners, January 2012 (respondents who use the device at least once a week)

Activities	All Mobile Owners	Smartphone Owners
Send/receive text messages	57.2%	74.4%
Use the Internet to visit websites	30.6%	61.6%
Take pictures with the camera in your phone	31.8%	51.8%
Use mobile applications—for example, maps	21.2%	45.8%
Use an app store on your phone	17.0%	38.2%
Play mobile games	25.2%	48.7%
Manage your calendar/schedule on mobile phone	22.9%	40.9%
Listen to streaming music (e.g., Pandora, Spotify)	15.2%	32.7%
Listen to music purchased on phone (e.g., iTunes, Amazon)	12.5%	27.3%
Listen to music burned from a CD	8.7%	17.8%
Watch videos on your mobile phone	15.3%	32.4%
Send/receive email	32.2%	64.9%
Send a picture to someone from your mobile phone	22.5%	39.8%
Check in using something like foursquare, Gowalla, or Loopt	4.5%	10.2%
Update a social networking site such as Facebook or Twitter	23.5%	46.2%
Redeem or download a coupon	4.0%	9.1%
Read an e-book	5.5%	12.7%
Take videos on your phone	12.4%	24.4%
Check the weather	28.5%	57.1%
Scan a 2D or QR code	4.9%	11.3%
Scan a regular barcode (UPC/product barcode)	5.4%	12.4%
Use an Augmented Reality application	2.5%	5.8%
Pay for something at a store using your mobile phone (e.g., waving your phone over a payment system)	3.4%	7.6%
Make a purchase of something that you can have shipped to you or pick up in a store	4.5%	10.2%
Monitor your health (e.g., keep track of your weight/diet, blood sugar, blood pressure, or other health related things)	3.8%	8.4%
Search for information on a product or company in which you're interested	12.0%	25.3%
Search for deals or special offers located near you	9.2%	20.0%
Do a price comparison	7.6%	17.3%
Use a bookmarking/content reader (e.g., Instapaper)	3.7%	8.0%
	N=1046	N=450

Source: InsightExpress, January 2012

Consumers may spend more time overall on a daily basis sitting in front of the TV, but the smartphone captures more of their attention. In fact, most of them are probably using their smartphones (and tablets) while watching television. They're glued to updates and the constant stream of new information coming from the Web or services such as Facebook and Twitter. Sure, you can access that on a connected TV, but people are creatures of habit, and they're already trained in the ease with which they can get that information on their smartphones. When it comes to the amount of time people spend with different media, print is stagnating and TV is flatlining, but mobile is growing at a faster pace than even the desktop, and smartphones are a big reason why (see Figure 1.4). Put it this way, people may spend more time watching TV, but there's no other screen in front of people's faces as many times throughout the day as the mobile phone.

Growth of Average Time Spent per Day with Major Media by US Adults, 2009-2011
% change

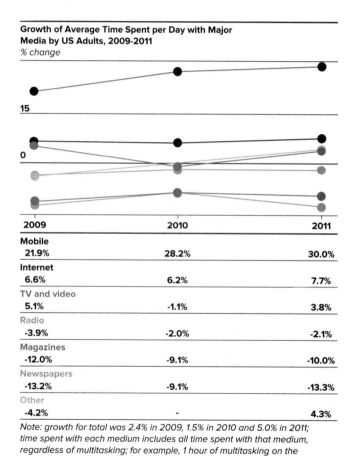

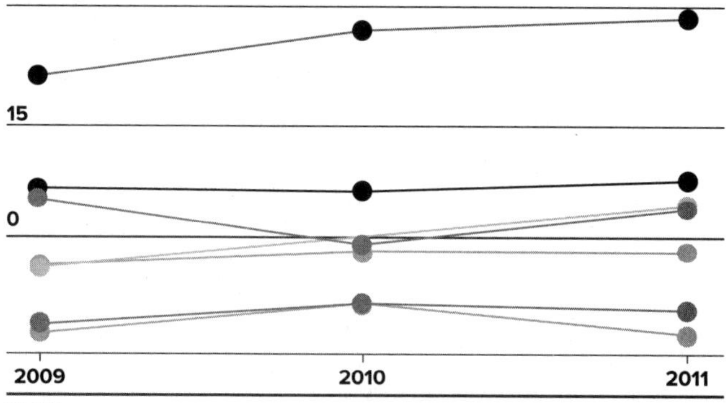

	2009	2010	2011
Mobile	21.9%	28.2%	30.0%
Internet	6.6%	6.2%	7.7%
TV and video	5.1%	-1.1%	3.8%
Radio	-3.9%	-2.0%	-2.1%
Magazines	-12.0%	-9.1%	-10.0%
Newspapers	-13.2%	-9.1%	-13.3%
Other	-4.2%	-	4.3%

Note: growth for total was 2.4% in 2009, 1.5% in 2010 and 5.0% in 2011; time spent with each medium includes all time spent with that medium, regardless of multitasking; for example, 1 hour of multitasking on the internet and watching TV is counted as 1 hour for TV and 1 hour for internet
Source: eMarketer, Dec 2011

134680 www.**eMarketer**.com

Figure 1.4 The amount of time spent with mobile is rising faster than all other media.

Tablets

And then there are tablets, the moribund category Apple almost singlehandedly succeeded in revitalizing with the launch of the iPad in March 2010. Not solely a mobile device nor a computing device, tablets draw on elements of both. Through the end of June 2012, Apple had sold 84.1 million iPads, staking the company to a sizable lead in the tablet market.

No single tablet due out in the next couple of years is likely to outsell the iPad. As with smartphones, the more relevant question is whether, collectively, the growing roster of Android tablets can catch up to the iPad. Most researchers predict that will happen early in the second half of the decade (see Figure 1.5 for an outlook on Apple's gradually eroding market share). That means tablets will see a version of the same two-horse race taking place in the smartphone market.

Tablet Sales Worldwide, by OS, 2011-2016
thousands of units

	2011	2012	2013	2016
iOS	39,998	72,988	99,553	169,652
Android	17,292	37,878	61,684	137,657
Microsoft	0	4,863	14,547	43,648
QNX	807	2,643	6,036	17,836
Other	1,919	510	637	464
Total market	60,017	118,883	182,457	369,258

Note: sales to end users; numbers may not add up to total due to rounding
Source: Gartner, "Forecast: Media Tablets by Operating System, Worldwide, 2010-2016, 1Q12 Update" as cited in press release, April 10, 2012

138972 www.eMarketer.com

Figure 1.5 Global tablet sales seen tripling in next four years.

Tablet: Mobile Device or Computing Device?

The second most frequent question we get after "Is it the year of mobile?" is "Are tablets mobile devices?" When it was first introduced in 2010, many experts derided the iPad as nothing more than a "big iPod touch." Nearly three years later, and after over 84 million units sold, it's clear the iPad is much more than that. But exactly what it is remains in dispute. Is it a mobile device or a computer?

Actually, it's a little of both. The iPad shares an operating system and apps with its smaller screen cousin, the iPhone (Android tablets have a similar relationship to Android-equipped smartphones). At the same time, it has engendered user behaviors such as shopping and buying that are much closer to the desktop than to smartphones. Of course, it is important to distinguish between the iPad (and other large-format tablets), which have found widespread audiences in both the home and the workplace, and smaller so-called "media tablets" such as Amazon's Kindle Fire that are designed primarily for personal media consumption. However, we are still at the early stages of a fast-moving market, so while it is important to be mindful of these distinctions today, you do need to pay attention to the way the category evolves, as these differences may erode over time.

The impact of tablets' success will continue to reverberate across the computing category. Rather than the desktop trickling down to mobile devices, the reverse is taking place, as apps and other user interface features "trickle up" to the desktop. Witness the latest generation of Apple's OS X desktop software, which Apple itself bills as "inspired by iPad," or Microsoft Windows 8, which adapts the tile-based Metro interface from the Windows Phone 7 OS for simultaneous use on both tablets and PCs. Ultimately, the capacity to split the difference between smartphone and PC is possibly the most revolutionary quality of the tablet.

Tablet (and especially iPad) sales have soared since the launch of the first iPad. At the inauguration of the iPad 2 in March 2011, Steve Jobs honed in on the implications, proclaiming the iPad represented the dawn of the "post-PC" era. Depending on how you look at it, Jobs' proclamation was either a bold or precarious position for a computer manufacturer to take because it says the future lies in portable computing and hybrid devices like the tablet—part computer, part mobile—that will effectively change our notion of both categories. Appropriately, Apple is now the leader in the revolution it declared: its mobile devices now outsell its computers. In time, other consumer electronics manufacturers may follow in Apple's path.

Jobs called it post-PC, but we see it as a broader movement toward a post-device world. Here's why: The forces pushing consumers away from PCs to portable computing devices like smartphones and tablets are ushering in a phase in which activities such as accessing the Web and social networking and platforms like Facebook that consumers use to undertake these activities will take precedence over the devices they use to do so.

The ascension of smart devices does not mean the imminent death knell of the PC as we know it, but it is a recognition of the changing nature of communication—not just the devices we use to communicate, but also the ways in which we use them. There is now a growing expectation that we should be able to communicate, message, network, browse, and shop from a range of devices, both portable and stationary, not limited to the phone and not limited to what might be regarded as traditional telephony. The fact that phones can be used to make calls is increasingly irrelevant.

These changing patterns are opening new doors for marketers. Your job is to figure out how to walk through them and reach the engagement that lies on the other side. Just remember: it's about the people using the devices, not the devices themselves.

Beware Platform Fragmentation

Each smart device platform is built on a unique operating system (OS). For example, iPhones and iPads, which are built exclusively by Apple, run the company's proprietary iOS. BlackBerry functions according to a similar model of vertical integration, building its own devices and designing its own software. Android devices, by contrast, are built by multiple manufacturers and run one of the many versions of the Android OS, which is an open source platform controlled by Google. Microsoft splits the difference between Apple and Android, licensing the Windows Phone software to multiple hardware manufacturers but maintaining tight control over the software. Unlike Google, Microsoft does not allow manufacturers or carriers to customize its software interface.

If that sounds like a complex situation, it is. All of these platforms share the same basic browser standards, meaning that you don't need to design your site differently for each one. However, they all have different *app stores* and app platforms, which means to reach the widest possible audience when building an app, you do need to at least consider the top two platforms, which can mean more development time and resources on your part.

Fortunately, the market seems to be consolidating. Increasingly, we believe, smartphone users will be concentrated on two platforms: Google's Android OS and Apple's iOS, with Microsoft and BlackBerry the also-rans in the smartphone race. See the following graphic for a more detailed breakdown of the smartphone market over the next two years. In the tablet segment, Apple enjoys the upper hand for now and for the foreseeable future, although Android will slowly chip away at Apple's dominance.

US Smartphone User Share, by OS, 2010–2014
% of total

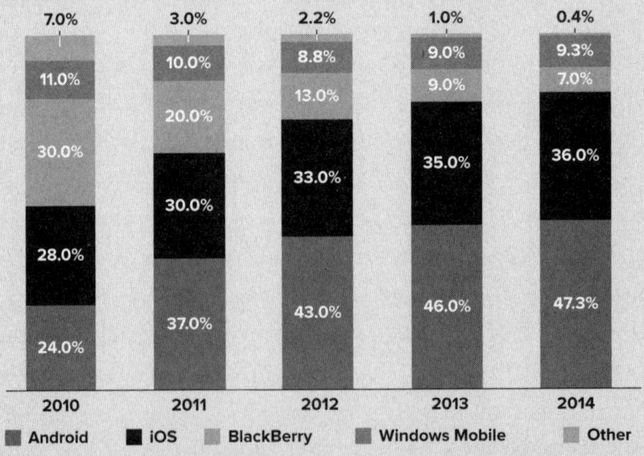

Note: individuals of any age who own at least one smartphone and use the smartphone(s) at least once per month
Source: eMarketer, Aug 2012

143150 www.eMarketer.com

The emergence of a two-horse race, at least in the United States, will ease some of the burden on marketers, but it won't necessarily resolve the problem of intra-platform fragmentation. This isn't really a problem for Apple because of the limited number of iPhone models in circulation, the generally highly structured schedule of software updates, and high upgrade rates. Apple does not disclose data about iOS upgrade patterns, but independent analysis by developers using app download data shows adoption rates of some version of iOS 5 (Apple's last major update prior to the release of iOS 6 in September 2012) in the 75 to 80 percent range.

Android is a different story. There are currently eight versions of Android in existence, in order of origin: Cupcake (1.5), Donut (1.6), Éclair (2.1), Froyo (2.2), Gingerbread (2.3), Honeycomb (3.0), Ice Cream Sandwich (4.0), and Jelly Bean (4.1). Newer devices usually—but not always—get the latest version of the OS, and older models are sometimes upgraded to the newest version, but the decision to do so and the timing for it are determined by the phone manufacturer, not by Google. So, even if Google releases an upgrade, it may take weeks and even months for all the Android smartphones to receive it, if at all. According to the Android Developers website (`developer.android.com`), as of September 2012, 72 percent of Android phones were still running Gingerbread and Froyo, while fewer than 2 percent were running the latest version, Jelly Bean.

What's Driving the Growth in Smart Devices?

A number of factors are contributing to the growth in smartphones and tablets, but the market forces play out a little differently with each.

Price

Lower-cost devices are emerging. Although the newest smartphones come at a premium, even with generous carrier subsidies, older, lower-end smartphones can even be obtained for "free," provided the user signs up for a two-year contract. For example, Apple's iPhone 3GS, introduced in 2009, continues to be a strong seller despite the fact it is three years old. Of course, the fact the phone is "free" to the end user doesn't really make it free. The U.S. carriers that offer the iPhone (which is considered to have the highest subsidies in the business) underwrite an estimated $440 of the phone's approximate $660 average selling price, a figure that is calculated by averaging the costs of all models across the iPhone range, from the low-end 3GS to the highest-end 64GB 4S.

Outside of the United States, where carrier subsidies factor less into the cost of a phone, manufacturers are taking seriously the mandate to produce cheap smartphones that can hook people up to the Web without breaking the bank. Everyone recognizes that data, not voice, is the future of mobile, and that makes it imperative for carriers, device manufacturers, and marketers alike to incentivize easier and cheaper web access from mobile devices.

Subsidies also are less of a factor when it comes to tablet pricing, but here too, lower-cost options are emerging, provided that you don't feel the burning need to own the latest iPad. A number of Android tablets are available at the sub-$300 level, and we expect prices to continue dropping as the market expands and competition heats up.

Faster Mobile Networks and More Ubiquitous Wi-Fi

Smart device owners consume a lot of bandwidth accessing the Web and apps. This puts a heavy load on mobile carriers and often overburdens their networks, particularly in densely populated urban areas with a high concentration of smart device users. Smartphone owners are the primary culprits, because they rely on carrier networks, while the majority of tablets sold depend on Wi-Fi connectivity to access the Web. Wi-Fi networks are becoming progressively more ubiquitous, and even if they're not always free, they're generally available, which can help offload some of the traffic from clogged mobile networks.

Meanwhile, carriers are busy upgrading their networks to *fourth-generation (4G)* specs, which promise far greater speeds and more efficient handling of data. It will take time, likely several years, before all devices are equipped for the faster networks and before the networks reach every point-of-presence covered by current networks. Check out Figure 1.6 for an outlook on global 4G adoption rates.

LTE 4G Mobile Subscriptions Worldwide, by Region, 2011-2016
thousands

	2011	2012	2013	2014	2015	2016
North America	6,039	31,623	60,145	93,836	139,248	197,446
Asia-Pacific	1,815	9,846	32,656	79,140	165,539	309,111
Western Europe	1,368	4,816	15,668	45,547	86,405	140,233
Central & Eastern Europe	46	1,547	3,600	11,592	24,286	35,977
Middle East & Africa	126	883	3,420	12,530	32,266	69,190
Latin America	0	769	3,271	11,517	34,770	69,190
Worldwide	**9,393**	**49,484**	**118,759**	**254,161**	**482,513**	**830,968**

Source: IDATE, "DigiWorld" as cited in press release, Feb 21, 2012

138168 www.eMarketer.com

Figure 1.6 4G subscriber base forecast to grow more than fifteenfold by 2016.

Expect to pay more for more speed when the faster devices and networks do arrive, but in return, you'll be able to do virtually everything you do on a smartphone or tablet that you're accustomed to doing on your home PC and broadband connection.

Note: Marketers seeking scale still need to think beyond a single device class or OS platform.

Part of what is driving the rapid increase in the amount of time people spend on their mobile devices—and arguably the key part—is the ability to access the Web. That capability, either using a browser or a *native mobile app* that retrieves browser-based content, gives you many more options in terms of reaching consumers, and it means more sophistication on the part of your audience. That's why mobile web access constitutes the pinnacle of the user pyramid.

Greater Sophistication Means Higher Receptivity to Advertising

InsightExpress looks at a lot of data around user behavior and receptivity to advertising. We asked Joy Liuzzo, former vice president of mobile, what all of that data said about mobile users. She offered the following thoughts: "The advertising industry has a myth that the more sophisticated users are, the less likely they will be open to advertising. What we've found in the mobile consumer space is that smartphone owners, especially those that are heavy users of their device on a daily basis, are more open to advertising than those that are less frequent users of their devices. In short, the more someone uses their smartphone each day, the more open they are to advertising in general." The bottom line: These findings signal a shift in overall advertising and marketing strategies.

The Web Becomes Truly Mobile

For a long time, we distinguished between the Web and the mobile web, almost as if they were two distinct, albeit distantly related, entities. But that is starting to change—quickly—thanks to the rapid pace of smart device adoption. We're now seeing an acceleration in the unification of mobile and web. Check out the data in Table 1.4. In January 2010, mobile phones and tablets accounted for less than 2 percent of global Internet traffic. By January 2011, it more than doubled; and by January 2012, it more than doubled again. At the current pace, within three years, nearly two-thirds of total global Internet traffic will come from mobile phones and tablets.

▶ **Table 1.4** Mobile's share of total Internet traffic worldwide

January 2010	January 2011	January 2012
1.6%	3.8%	8.8%

Source: Net Marketshare, March 2012

We could write a whole book on the competition between Apple and Android or the disparity between smartphones and feature phones, but ultimately, what matters more than which platform will win is the overall impact of having more connected devices in the hands of consumers.

Simply put, this trend will continue to drive more consumers to access the Internet from their mobile devices. In Figure 1.7, you'll see that nearly 122 million U.S. mobile users, representing nearly 40 percent of the total U.S. population, will access the Internet from their phones in 2012; by 2016, nearly 200 million will do so.

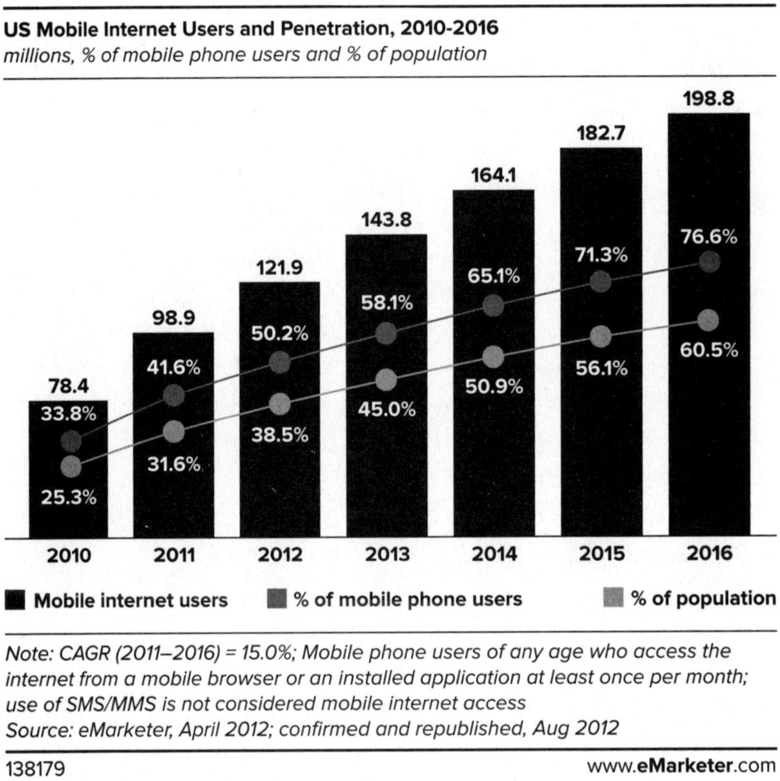

Figure 1.7 Mobile Internet access is moving mainstream.

Those are big numbers, any way you look at it. But again, we'd encourage you to go beyond the totals and focus on who these mobile Internet users are. One figure that leaps out is that 95 percent of them are smartphone owners, and this number is only going to increase. In the United States, where smartphones and the accompanying data plans are relatively affordable (and increasingly seen as a personal necessity), Internet access from feature phones is practically irrelevant. That's not the case in emerging markets, at least not yet; but in advanced economies, figure on most of your mobile Internet users having smartphones.

Also, look at the demographics of these users. By eMarketer's estimates, today, as shown in Figure 1.8, nearly 60 percent of mobile Internet users are between 18 and 44 years old, again corresponding to the bulk of smartphone users. But over time, as Boomers—those between 45 and 64—adopt smartphones in greater numbers, they will become the single biggest group accessing the Web from their mobile devices. It's tempting to ascribe leading-edge behaviors to Millennials, but remember that while a higher percentage of younger mobile users access the Internet, overall, more older folks are going online from their mobile devices.

US Mobile Internet User Share, by Age, 2011-2016
% of total

	2010	2011	2012	2013	2014	2015	2016
0-11	1.0%	1.1%	1.1%	1.2%	1.3%	1.3%	1.4%
12-17	8.4%	8.1%	7.9%	8.0%	8.2%	8.6%	8.9%
18-24	20.6%	18.2%	16.3%	15.2%	14.6%	14.3%	13.9%
25-34	28.4%	25.5%	23.3%	22.3%	21.6%	21.1%	20.7%
35-44	19.2%	19.6%	19.5%	19.6%	19.6%	19.0%	18.7%
45-64	19.0%	22.7%	26.5%	28.3%	29.2%	30.2%	30.7%
65+	3.4%	4.9%	5.3%	5.3%	5.4%	5.5%	5.7%

Note: mobile phone users who access the internet from a mobile browser or an installed application at least once per month; use of SMS/MMS is not considered mobile internet access; numbers may not add up to 100% due to rounding
Source: eMarketer, April 2012; confirmed and republished, Aug 2012

138181 www.**eMarketer**.com

Figure 1.8 Age matters when it comes to mobile Internet usage.

The bottom line: More mobile users accessing the Internet means more opportunities to reach those users by building effective mobile websites, which we'll tackle in Chapter 4, "Week 3: Maximize Reach with Mobile Websites," and by promoting your message with mobile advertising, which we'll examine in Chapter 6, "Week 5: Promote Your Message with Mobile Advertising."

Mobile Users' App-etite Is Growing

Browsers and apps are the two primary mechanisms for mobile users to access the Web. Data from audience measurement firm comScore (`www.comscore.com`), as indicated in Figure 1.9, suggest that browser and app usage are roughly equivalent. Both have increased significantly over the past two years as smartphone adoption has climbed, but they have remained in relative lockstep.

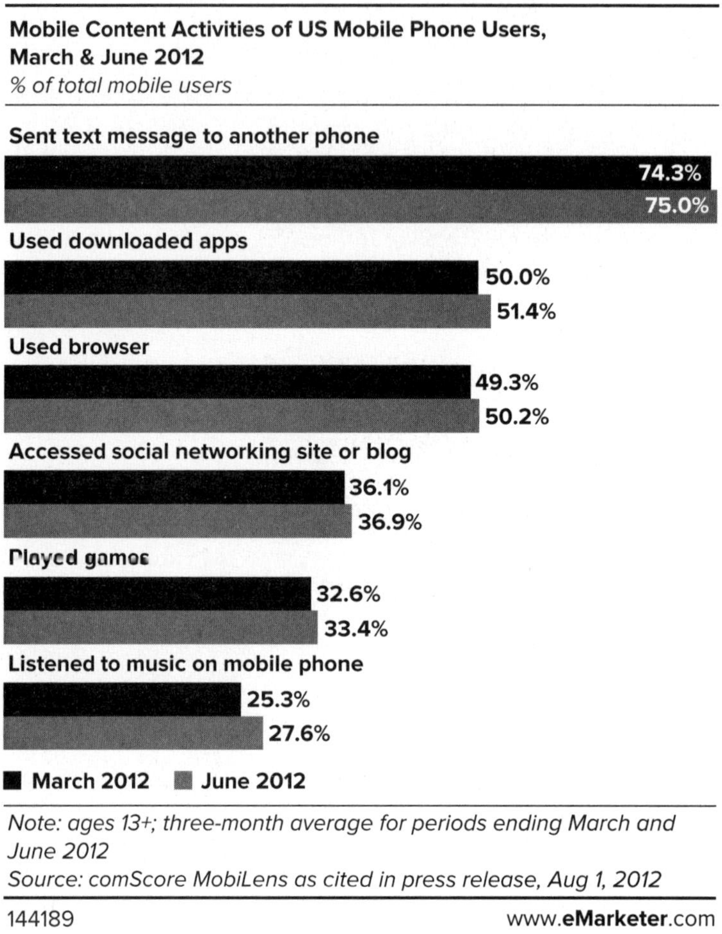

Figure 1.9 Overall mobile browser and app usage are nearly equivalent.

Other research supports this view. Jumptap (`www.jumptap.com`), a mobile ad network, conducted a study of ad requests served over the course of 2011, finding that the mobile web enjoyed a modest lead over apps. However, it also determined that ads served to both the Web and mobile apps are growing at a similar rate. Of course, not everyone agrees. A study by Yahoo! and global market research firm Ipsos (`www.ipsos.com`), for example, found that the preference for browser versus apps depends on activity (see Figure 1.10).

You may be aware that as adoption of smartphones and tablets has increased, a vigorous either/or debate about whether apps or browsers will win has emerged.

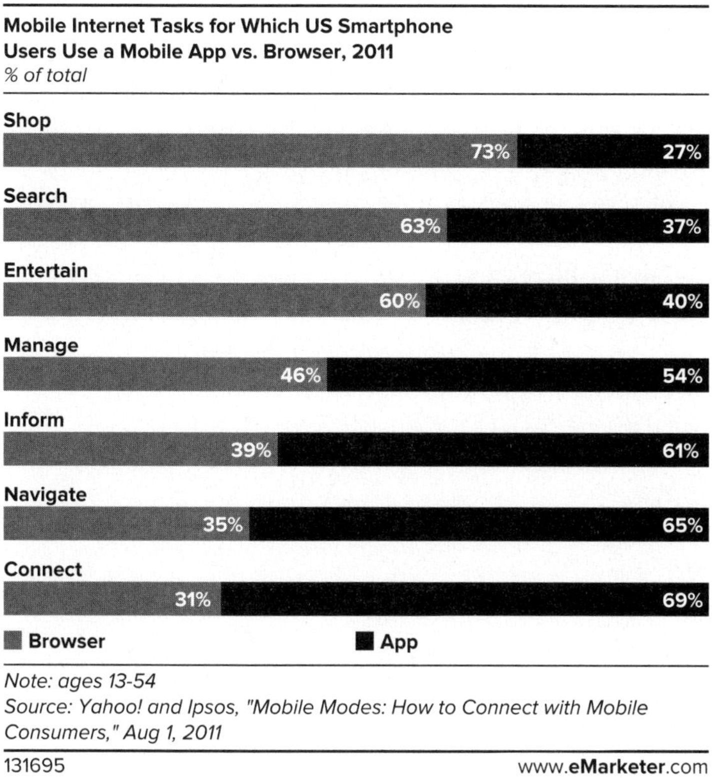

Figure 1.10 Activities determine mobile channel preference.

Understandably, you may be anxious about possible outcomes because you need to know how to most effectively apportion your mobile marketing budget. Rest assured, the outcome is unlikely to be either/or, and here's why: From a user-experience perspective, apps and browsers both bring something to the table. Apps are particularly effective at providing mobile users with an encapsulated experience that filters out the variables of browsing the Web. However, the cross-platform fragmentation we mentioned earlier and the need to ensure a consistent experience across each platform mean apps bring challenges as well as opportunities.

Browsers, on the other hand, are universal; every smartphone and tablet has one. The browsers found on iOS and Android devices are based on the same WebKit open source core, meaning they render web pages in a similar way. In addition, the mobile web allows more control over the user experience in that you are not subject to the guidelines imposed by app stores. So, rather than cancel each other out, apps and browsers will continue to coexist.

Moreover, thanks to the increasingly widespread implementation of *HTML5*, the mobile browsing experience is beginning to more closely resemble that of the desktop. This development may also help browsing the mobile web become more "app-like" in terms of user experience, especially given the noticeable trend toward designing mobile websites to look more like apps. So perhaps the more interesting trend is the effect the rise of apps will have on browsers and the increasing convergence between the two.

Ultimately, most research indicates that smartphone owners are equally active in using the Web and apps. Tablet owners tend to be somewhat more web-intensive, a by-product of the larger screen, which affords a better browsing experience. Correspondingly, they have a reduced need for the type of encapsulated experience that makes apps so vital on smartphones. We'll look at the steps you need to take to maximize engagement with mobile apps in Chapter 5, "Week 4: Maximize Engagement with Mobile Apps."

Future Forward: Ambient Connectivity

As mobile devices become widespread and physical objects become increasingly connected to the Web, marketers need to open themselves up to thinking "outside the browser." NFC chips are expected to become standard in smartphones and tablets in the next several years, enabling not only fast and easy processing of payments via mobile devices, but also enabling consumers to send digital information to and receive it from a wide variety of objects, from sales tags to dressing room mirrors.

But it's not just NFC—numerous mobile technologies that are just catching on now with the general populace will become status quo for marketers over the course of the next two to three years. Image recognition tools such as Google Goggles, mobile barcode readers, *augmented reality* browsers, motion-sensitive, large-format surface technologies, and in-car information systems are just a few of the opportunities that are limited in use now but will become increasingly commonplace in the near future. For marketers, now is the opportune time to become educated about the possibilities and to test and learn. However, given the relative newness of these technologies, understanding how any or all will apply to your business and customers is challenging. In the next chapter, we'll discuss how developing a solid strategic framework can help put these burgeoning opportunities into perspective and match them up to your goals and your customers' needs.

Key Mobile Activities

You've seen how accessing the Web is a key activity among smartphone users. As background for the chapters that lie ahead, we thought it was important to touch on a few other activities that will come into play as you try to market to your mobile audience.

Text Messaging

If there's one activity that nearly universal among mobile users, regardless of the kind of device they use, it is texting. As you can see in Table 1.3, InsightExpress found that 57.2 percent of all U.S. mobile users text at least once a week; among smartphone users, the rate is 74.4 percent (other studies show even higher figures when activity is measured on a monthly basis). For both feature phone and smartphone owners, texting is the number one activity. In fact, according to the semiannual survey by the U.S.-based international trade body CTIA–The Wireless Association (`www.ctia.org`), the number of text messages sent surpassed minutes of use (MOUs), a standard industry metric for talk time, on an annualized basis for the first time in 2011, officially making texting the primary mobile communication mechanism. We can expect the divide between MOUs and text messages sent to grow as talking continues to decline in importance in favor of texting and other post-device communication activities.

SMS Quick Facts

Some of the data around SMS is truly astounding. For example:

- The International Telecommunication Union (ITU) (`www.itu.int`), the United Nations body responsible for information and communication technology, found that worldwide, 192,192 text messages were sent *every second* in 2010, leading to a global total of 6.1 trillion texts (ITU, "The World in 2010").
- CTIA–The Wireless Association, the U.S.-based international trade body for the wireless industry, found that U.S. mobile users sent just over 2.3 trillion messages in 2011 (CTIA, "Semi-Annual Wireless Industry Survey," April 2012).
- Teens are by far the biggest texters, according to global market research firm Nielsen (`www.nielsen.com`). The following graphic shows that 13- to 17-year-olds send and receive well more than 10 times as many texts in a given month than mobile users over the age of 55.

Number of Text Messages Sent/Received Among US Mobile Users, by Age, Q3 2009-Q3 2011

	Q3 2009	Q3 2010	Q3 2011
13-17	3,211	3,729	3,417
18-34	1,848	2,518	2,842
35-55	647	954	1,143
55+	99	173	231

Note: in the past 30 days; per mobile user
Source: Nielsen, "State of the Media: The Mobile Media Report," Dec 15, 2011

135569 www.**eMarketer**.com

Clearly, texting is an integral way that mobile users communicate, both in the United States and around the world. So, whether it's for advertising or customer support and loyalty, SMS should find a place in your marketing campaigns. It's not glamorous, but it is efficient and effective; and it continues to engage consumers. Think of it as a basic support mechanism for your other mobile efforts. We'll delve more into the basics of SMS in Chapter 3, "Week 2: Start Simple—SMS."

Social Networking

When it comes to communication on mobile devices, social networks are fast emerging as a vital platform, not only for peer-to-peer communication but for communication between consumers and brands as well. According to comScore, 36.9 percent of all mobile users (that includes those with feature phones as well as smartphones) accessed social networking sites in the three months culminating in June 2012. That figure has been steadily rising. eMarketer's estimates in Table 1.5 indicate that the number of mobile social network users will more than double in 2012 relative to 2010, and then increase by a further 43 percent by 2014, with the majority of the activity again coming from smartphone owners.

▶ Table 1.5: U.S. mobile social network users, 2010–2014

	2010	2011	2012	2013	2014
Mobile social network users (millions)	39.0	58.4	81.8	99.0	116.8
Smartphone social network users (millions)	32.5	55.9	78.1	94.9	112.6
—% of smartphone users	52.0%	60.0%	67.5%	69.0%	71.4%

Source: eMarketer, August 2012

Among tablet owners, social networking rivals web surfing and email as a leading activity, which suggests that larger-format screens are more conducive to a richer experience in this as in other mobile pursuits. See Figure 1.11.

Mobile Content Activities of Tablet Owners* in the US and Worldwide, Nov 2011
% of respondents

	US	Worldwide
Personal email	93%	87%
Surfing the internet for personal use	90%	90%
Social networking	66%	55%
Watching videos	63%	59%
Reading ebooks and emagazines	62%	58%
Listening to music	54%	54%
Gaming	51%	51%
Work email	43%	41%
Surfing the internet for work use	32%	38%
Create/edit files for personal use	30%	33%
Videoconferencing for personal use	29%	30%
Create/edit files for work use	26%	24%
Use other software for work purposes	15%	16%
Videoconferencing for work use	7%	11%

*Note: *internet users who have purchased electronic or print versions of books, magazines or newspapers in the past month*
Source: Boston Consulting Group (BCG), "Tablet and E-Reader Survey," Jan 23, 2012

136365 www.**eMarketer**.com

Figure 1.11 Tablets offer a richer experience for many activities.

As by far the world's largest social network, Facebook (`www.facebook.com`) absorbs the majority of mobile social networking time. But Twitter (`www.twitter.com`), which was modeled on the 140-character limit of text messaging, also generates a lot of traffic from mobile users. Twitter is heavily integrated into Android, iOS, and Windows Phone, which enables users to easily tweet from a variety of functions on these smartphones. Facebook enjoys a similar integration on these three platforms.

The key takeaway here lies in the changing nature of communication. As mobile users increasingly rely on platforms such as Facebook and Twitter to exchange messages, it has made communication on connected devices both more social and more public. The migration away from closed-loop voice calling to these more visible, web-based platforms gives marketers entrée to consumer interests and preferences in a way that one-to-one conversations could never permit.

Location is often closely tied to social networking because services such as Facebook and foursquare (`www.foursquare.com`) enable users to "check in" to places and share where they are with select contacts or broadcast it to everyone. You may recall that the emergence of foursquare at the beginning of 2010 sparked something of a land rush in the geo-location space. Suddenly, everyone had check-in fever, it seemed. In fact, although basic mobile social networking—messaging, status updates, and the like—and use of location apps such as maps and directions are widespread and growing, use of geo-social services is still a niche activity. The data from the non-profit Pew Research Center's Internet & American Life Project (`www.pewinternet.org`) in Figure 1.12 makes this disparity pretty clear. Witness also the difference in scale between Facebook (955 million monthly active users [MAUs] as of the end of June 2012, including 543 million MAUs on mobile) and foursquare (just 20 million users as of April 2012, although growing at a rapid pace).

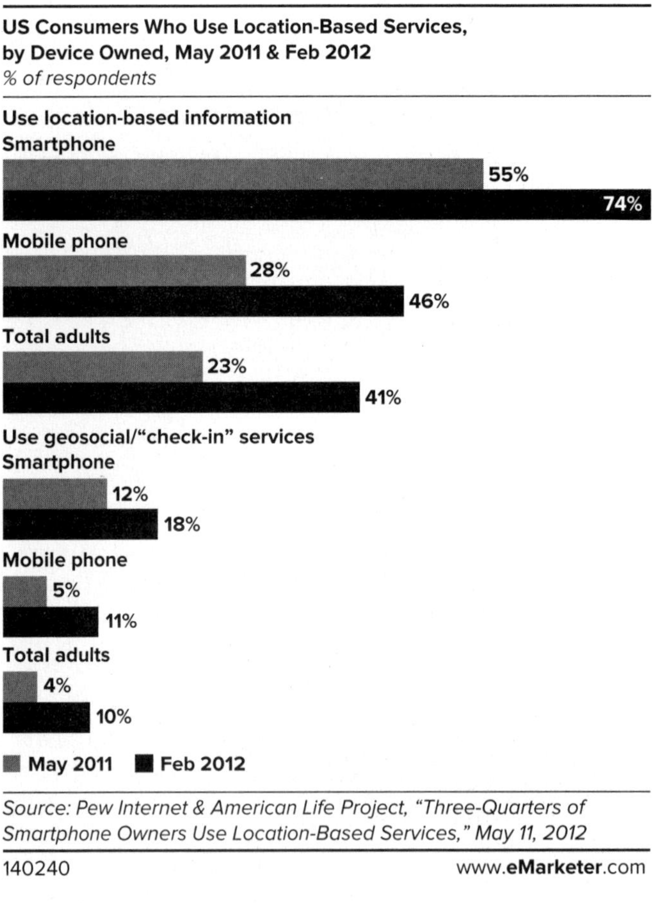

Figure 1.12 Use of geo-social services is still a niche activity.

Even though too many competing check-in services with too little in the way of consumer rewards inevitably resulted in check-in fatigue, marketers and consumers still find some value in services that use location parameters. However, the emphasis here has shifted from gaming dynamics to commerce, and you now see an increasing emphasis on using location to drive actual business. In other words, there is more of a focus on the checkout, rather than the check-in.

Says industry expert Greg Sterling, founding principal of Sterling Market Intelligence: "There are some unique opportunities coalescing around mobile, rewards, loyalty, and payments that are going to be very potent for marketers. It's going to be very interesting to watch." The data derived from location will be an important component in this mix.

Location is undeniably a vital characteristic for ads and promotions targeted at shoppers deep in the purchase funnel. The closer they are to purchase, the more important location becomes. Your best bet is to couple location with timing and context—that's the key to increasing your relevancy. We'll dig deeper into the nexus of social, mobile, and location in Chapter 7, "Week 6: Leverage the SoLoMo Nexus."

Tap into the Power of Location; Tread Carefully Around the Pitfalls of Privacy and Security

Mobile coupons, as we'll talk about in Chapter 8, "Week 7: Check Out M-Commerce," can play a key role in pushing shoppers down the purchase funnel and closer to checkout. Mobile offers allow you to deliver on the promise of timing, content, and location. As you can see in the following graphic, consumer interest in and usage of location-based coupons is high.

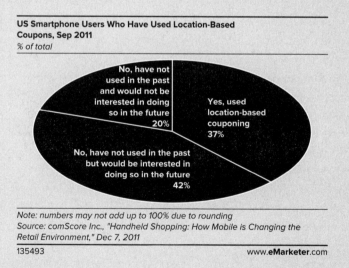

US Smartphone Users Who Have Used Location-Based Coupons, Sep 2011
% of total

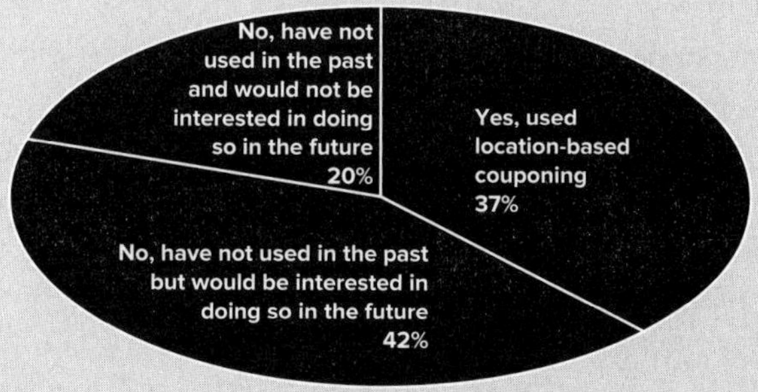

Note: numbers may not add up to 100% due to rounding
Source: comScore Inc., "Handheld Shopping: How Mobile is Changing the Retail Environment," Dec 7, 2011
135493 www.eMarketer.com

But consumers are also conflicted in their attitude toward mobile coupons with a location-based element (see following graphic). Mobile privacy and security are hot-button issues for consumers, who realize they carry a significant amount of sensitive information on their mobile devices.

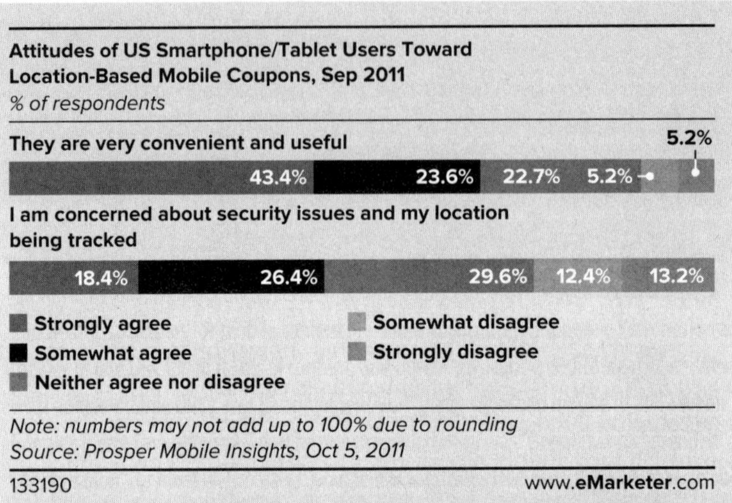

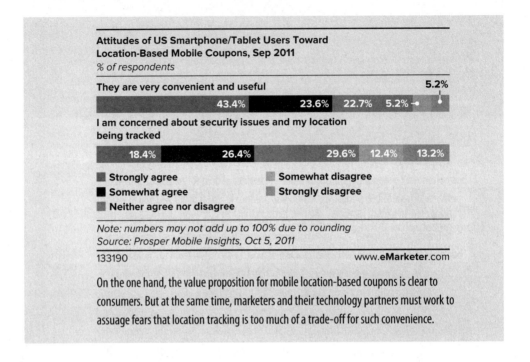

On the one hand, the value proposition for mobile location-based coupons is clear to consumers. But at the same time, marketers and their technology partners must work to assuage fears that location tracking is too much of a trade-off for such convenience.

Search

So much of what we do on our mobile devices starts with a search. As on the desktop, mobile search is a key discovery mechanism for information about brands, products, and commerce opportunities. In Figure 1.10, note that mobile searchers prefer to use browsers rather than apps. That finding is borne out by a comScore survey showing mobile search to rank as the most popular type of site visited by smartphone users (see Figure 1.13). The same study found that 19.2 percent of smartphone users accessed search services using apps, ranking them a distant fifth behind weather, social networking, maps, and news.

Google is the dominant force in mobile search, more dominant even than on the desktop. Since StatCounter (`http://gs.statcounter.com/`) began tracking mobile search referrals, Google has consistently garnered over 90 percent of the total (sometimes as high as 98 percent). According to eMarketer estimates, Google garnered 95.4 percent of a total $1.3 billion in U.S. mobile search ad spending in 2012. Markets do shift, but a longtime near-monopoly is hard to beat, especially when Android's growing dominance in the smartphone space continues to fill Google's coffers.

A new wrinkle in the search field comes from the rise of voice assistants such as Apple's Siri, unveiled with the iPhone 4S in October 2011. Siri allows users to search the Web in addition to searching and activating a limited array of phone apps, such as

Types of Sites/Services Accessed via Mobile Browser Among US Smartphone Users, Dec 2011
% of smartphone users

Search	45.8%
Social networking	36.0%
News	34.3%
Weather	25.9%
Movie information	18.7%
Maps	18.2%
Restaurant information	16.6%
Online retail	15.7%
Shopping guides	11.5%
Credit cards	11.3%
Traffic reports	10.4%
Health information	10.0%
Kids and family entertainment	8.1%
Beauty/fashion/style	7.9%
Travel service	7.1%
Automotive services	5.0%
Insurance services	4.3%

Note: 3-month average
Source: comScore Inc., "The State of Consumer Online Travel," March 5, 2012
137917 www.eMarketer.com

Figure 1.13 As on the desktop, many mobile browsing sessions start with search.

reading and responding to text messages or reading a day's calendar schedule. (Google and Microsoft are said to be readying competing versions for future upgrades to their operating systems.) Siri uses the iPhone's default search engine to assemble results, but in so doing, it often bypasses the search results pages (SERPs), which could have implications for how you optimize for mobile search for maximum visibility. We'll get into the search engine optimization (SEO) and media buying steps you need to take to make your site visible in search results in Chapter 4.

Shopping

Consumers have been using the Web for a long time now to conduct research that leads to in-store, offline sales. In the desktop scenario, these activities typically take place sequentially and can often be separated by days or even weeks (see Figure 1.14).

The major change wrought by the growing ubiquity of smartphones is that research and shopping can now take place simultaneously (see Figure 1.15). Mobile consumers are often in the act of shopping, typically trying to satisfy an urgent product need. Thus, the connection between research and purchase is much closer.

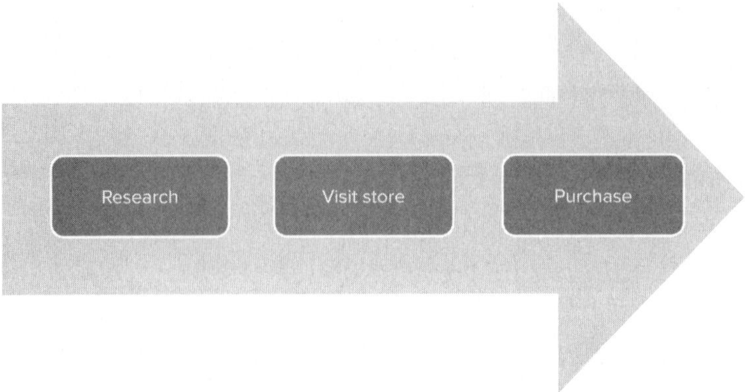

Figure 1.14 Desktop Research-to-Purchase Path

Many smartphone owners preshop on their devices to determine whether a trip to a retail location is worth their time. The calculus changes again once consumers are closer to the point of sale, with mobile in-store shoppers often researching while standing in front of a product they're considering, thereby presenting marketers with the opportunity to influence a person who is ready to buy.

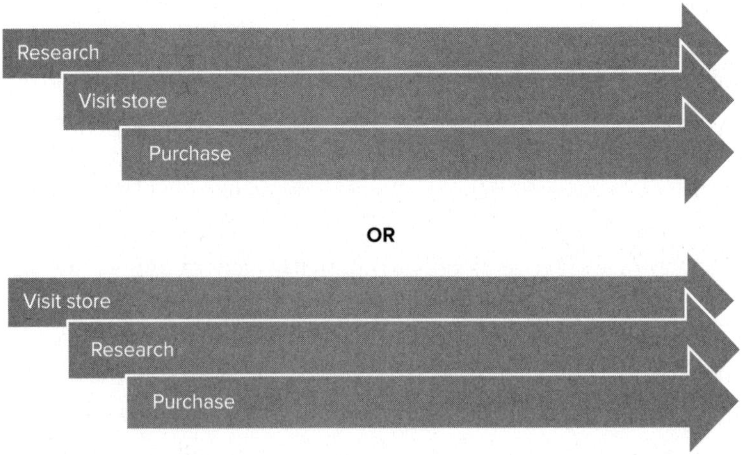

Figure 1.15 Mobile In-Store Research-to-Purchase Path

Gathering information that will help determine a purchase drives much of mobile shoppers' activity. Search engines are the gateway to critical data that can influence purchase decisions, such as store locations, product reviews, in-store product availability, local deals, and, above all, price comparisons. And as you've no doubt gathered, social media plays a supporting role in this process, not only by linking location to commerce but also in obtaining feedback and opinions about a brand or product from one's social graph.

Of course, all this information gathering places new pressure on merchants and brings the term *showrooming* (the practice of researching a product in a store, then buying it elsewhere—online, by phone, or from another brick-and-mortar business) into the retail lexicon. In the face of better-informed, more price-conscious shoppers, retailers are understandably nervous. But some are coming up with creative solutions to incentivize shoppers to stay put. Nordstrom, for example, has tried perks such as free shipping on in-store purchases, while Target has explored offering more items made exclusively for the retailer, which would make comparison shopping more difficult.

"The landscape is a lot more complicated from a marketing and consumer-retention standpoint," observes Greg. Now you have to engage the consumer at multiple touchpoints, including mobile, and that mobile engagement may even take place in the store." He adds, "You also have the real-world problem of how to confront consumers who have all this information and who are disposed to buy from Amazon right in your store."

The bottom line is that we are part of a new generation of data-driven shoppers. So, remember that in-store shoppers have heightened information needs, which gives the data—and service—you provide a higher value and makes it more actionable. A survey of U.S. smartphone owners by digital marketing agency White Horse (`www.whitehorse.com`), for example, asked respondents to rank, on a scale of 1 to 5, the usefulness of different information in helping make them an in-store purchase decision. Price comparison scored the highest, at 4.32, demonstrating that the ability to save money can actually help consumers spend it.

Entertainment

Beyond surfing, searching, socializing, and shopping, media consumption and entertainment rank high among mobile users' preferred activities. Playing games, listening to music, and, increasingly, watching videos occupy a lot of mobile users' time and attention. In fact, data from mobile app analytics platform Flurry (`www.flurry.com`) (see Figure 1.16) suggests that nearly one-half of smartphone users' app time goes to gaming.

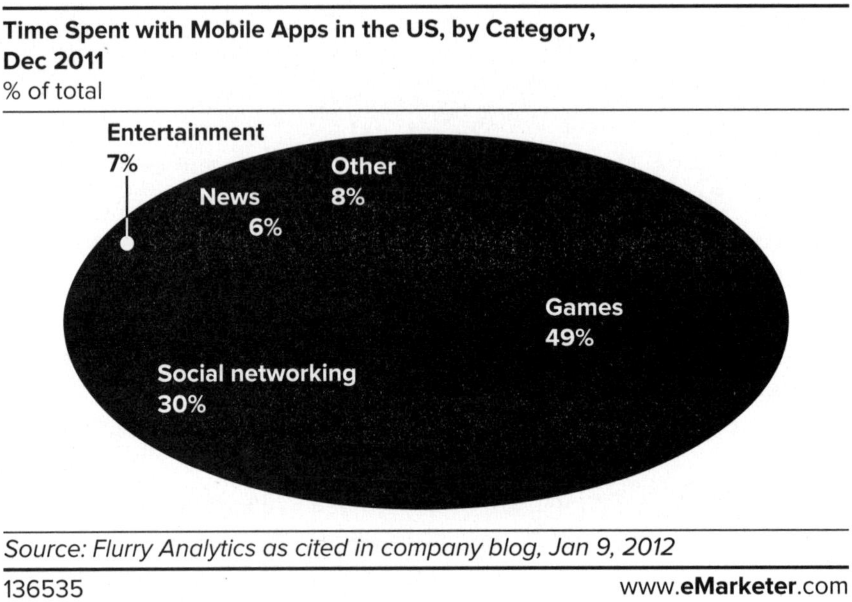

Figure 1.16 Game apps are a big draw for smartphone users.

If you refer back to Table 1.3, you'll see that about one-quarter of all mobile users play games at least weekly, while smartphone owners are more active, consuming games at roughly twice the rate. Listening to music and watching video yield a similar ratio, although neither activity is as popular as gaming. All of these media consumption activities are more prevalent among iPhone owners, according to InsightExpress (see Table 1.6).

▶ **Table 1.6** Activities of smartphone owners, by platform, January 2012 (Respondents who use the device at least once a week)

Device	Android	BlackBerry	iPhone
Send/receive text messages	77.7%	80.3%	80.9%
Use the Internet to visit websites	65.2%	65.6%	71.8%
Take pictures with the camera in your phone	51.3%	55.7%	60.0%
Use mobile applications—for example, maps	46.9%	54.1%	53.6%
Use an app store on your phone	39.3%	42.6%	47.3%
Play mobile games	51.8%	44.3%	57.3%
Manage your calendar/schedule on mobile phone	40.2%	55.7%	44.5%
Listen to streaming music (e.g., Pandora, Spotify)	33.5%	27.9%	43.6%
Listen to music purchased on your phone (e.g., iTunes, Amazon)	20.5%	36.1%	46.4%

Listen to music burned from a CD	15.6%	26.2%	22.7%
Watch videos on your mobile phone	32.1%	31.1%	39.1%
Send/receive email	67.4%	70.5%	71.8%
Send a picture to someone from your mobile phone	38.4%	47.5%	49.1%
Check in using something like foursquare, Gowalla, or Loopt	8.5%	16.4%	13.6%
Update a social networking site like Facebook or Twitter	51.8%	45.9%	50.0%
Redeem or download a coupon	8.9%	14.8%	10.9%
Read an e-book	12.9%	19.7%	10.9%
Take videos on your phone	26.8%	31.1%	22.7%
Check the weather	58.5%	72.1%	64.5%
Scan a 2D or QR code	12.9%	13.1%	10.9%
Scan a regular barcode (UPC/product barcode)	10.7%	9.8%	19.1%
Use an augmented reality application	5.8%	4.9%	7.3%
Pay for something at a store using your mobile phone (e.g., waving your phone over a payment system)	6.7%	13.1%	7.3%
Make a purchase of something that you can have shipped to you or pick up in a store	9.8%	21.3%	7.3%
Monitor your health (e.g., keep track of your weight/diet, blood sugar, blood pressure, or other health-related things)	6.3%	16.4%	11.8%
Search for information on a product or company in which you're interested	24.1%	37.7%	28.2%
Search for deals or special offers located near you	19.6%	21.3%	26.4%
Do a price comparison	17.4%	23.0%	17.3%
Use a bookmarking/content reader (e.g., Instapaper)	8.0%	13.1%	7.3%
	N=224	N=61	N=110

Source: InsightExpress, January 2012

Among tablet owners, media consumption is even more commonplace, which is not surprising given that tablets are purpose-built for these activities (see Figure 1.11). Cisco Systems (`www.cisco.com`), which manufactures much of the infrastructure that routes Internet data, predicts a massive, tenfold explosion in mobile video traffic in the next five years, as shown in Figure 1.17. The combination of smarter devices (especially media tablets), faster mobile networks, and greater content availability will drive this growth.

Monthly Mobile Data Traffic Worldwide, by Application, 2011-2016 *terabytes*						
	2011	**2012**	**2013**	**2014**	**2015**	**2016**
Video	307,869	736,792	1,545,713	2,917,659	4,882,198	7,615,443
Data	174,942	329,841	549,559	864,122	1,349,825	2,165,174
File sharing	76,764	114,503	154,601	204,617	261,235	361,559
M2M	23,009	47,144	92,150	172,719	302,279	508,022
Gaming	6,957	13,831	24,388	40,644	77,568	118,330
VoIP	7,724	10,327	12,491	15,485	22,976	35,792
Total	**597,266**	**1,252,438**	**2,378,903**	**4,215,246**	**6,896,080**	**10,804,321**

Source: Cisco Systems, "Cisco Visual Networking Index (VNI): Global Mobile Data Traffic Forecast Update, 2011-2016," Feb 14, 2012

137452 www.**eMarketer**.com

Figure 1.17 Mobile data consumption is exploding.

By this point, you should be familiar with the implications: More consumers who own more smart devices and consume more media ultimately yield more potential touchpoints. As more content migrates to digital and mobile platforms, marketing opportunities are expanding not only as the audience grows, but also as more publishers diversify their funding from paid to ad-supported content in response. This affects the type of apps you build, as we'll discuss in Chapter 5, as well as where you place your mobile ads, as we'll talk about in Chapter 6.

As Joy put it: "It's back to the age-old issue of breaking through the clutter and niche marketing. With more content, more apps, and more distractions, it will become increasingly difficult to have a simple, flat strategy that works for all executions. You can call it targeting moments or something else, but it won't just be about media plans anymore."

How Mobile Is Changing the Face of ... Everything

Now you have a sense of the mobile landscape. From here, it's easy to envision how radically mobile is changing the way we do business. The implications are significant. Says Greg: "The most apparent change is marketers now must face a multiscreen reality, including tablets, and confront people using and moving between devices. I don't want to call it the Wild West, but there's a lot of uncertainty." Greg is right, but it's also the case that one company's uncertainty is another's opportunity.

Retail and Consumer Packaged Goods

For a look at how mobile is changing retail and consumer packaged goods (CPG), look no farther than Apple itself. The company's phenomenally successful chain of retail stores has done away with the traditional checkout experience by enabling shoppers to buy their products anywhere in the store. Apple associates circulate with specially equipped iPhones that incorporate a credit card reader. More recently, Apple updated its own Apple Store app for the iPhone, giving visitors the ability to scan barcodes on their own and pay using the credit card information stored in their iTunes account. Think about it: No more waiting in line, no unnecessary floor space devoted to expensive cash registers, a totally fluid—well, totally mobile—shopping experience.

As advanced devices become more readily available and marketers and real-life objects become increasingly digitized, the possibilities expand exponentially. Today, you might scan a *quick response (QR) code* to unlock enhanced product information or tap into competitive pricing. Tomorrow, you may simply swipe your NFC-enabled handset over a product on the shelf to see useful data such as customer reviews. Think about the possibilities inherent in scanning a price tag on an item of clothing to see if it's in stock in your size or another color. Imagine standing in front of a digitally connected, floor-to-ceiling fitting room mirror and dressing yourself virtually, swiping to "try on" new outfits and tapping to share a look with your social networks. It may sound like science fiction, but it's all soon going to be part of our reality.

Automotive

Automotive brands were some of the earliest adaptors of mobile technology, including on the marketing side. Many were among the first to develop touch-enabled, smartphone-friendly websites and were early investors in mobile advertising to capture shoppers across the purchase process. Thanks to their future-forward approach, your experience buying, driving, and owning a new car in the years to come will be very different indeed.

The average new car shopper will arrive on the lot well-armed with tools that will help her narrow down her options and customize the vehicle of her choice, before even speaking to a sales representative. Checking availability, adding options, and securing financing will all be easily done via smartphone or tablet, leaving the consumer able to shop at her own pace and freeing up dealership staff to concentrate on finalizing sales.

Rolling off the lot in one's new car will also be a new experience, with owner's manuals delivered via tablet app, and service reminders delivered via SMS. At the end of 2010, Hyundai showed the way by shipping its new flagship sedan, the Equus, with an iPad containing the owner's manual and an app for scheduling service appointments, concierge-style. Hyundai dealers collect the car at the owner's convenience, with no visit to the dealership required.

But *driving* is the experience that will change most of all. The evolution of the connected car is just beginning, with all major automotive brands planning for or already including some form of digital connectivity into their vehicles. Web-enabled dashboards providing GPS and the ability to synch your mobile device to your car's stereo system via *Bluetooth* are just the beginning. Voice-enabled search, contextual advertising/offers, and open developer platforms for in-car apps are just around the corner; and more sophisticated options like augmented reality windows are not far behind.

Expect this vertical to move faster than the rest. In the not-so-distant future, looking at your portable GPS unit or manufacturer-installed navigation system on a family road trip may seem the old-school equivalent of consulting the road atlas today. You'll be more likely to follow visual directions projected transparently onto your windshield while your passengers view facts and stories about passing landmarks.

Financial Services

Financial institutions have long positioned mobile banking as an extension of their online services, emphasizing the anywhere, anytime convenience of checking account balances, paying bills, and transferring funds using the one device customers take with them everywhere. Banks have found mobile customers to be some of their best customers: they tend to use more banking products, keep more money in their accounts, and display deeper loyalty to their institution of choice. Plus, because mobile transactions cost less than those that take place in a branch or via call centers, mobile customers save banks money to boot.

But paying a utility bill or moving money from a savings to a checking account seems rather staid in comparison to what lies on the near-term horizon for the financial services sector. Consider that we're currently able to research products, reach out to friends and family on Facebook or Twitter to get advice on a prospective purchase, retrieve coupons by scanning a barcode in-store, and redeem that coupon at the point of sale—all using our mobile devices. So it seems logical that we should be able to finish the process on our mobile devices as well by using them to pay for our purchases. Instead of trying to pull out your wallet or rummaging through your purse to find it, wouldn't it be cool if your phone *were* your wallet? If a host of technology companies and financial institutions have their way, that's where we're headed. The mobile wallet emerged in 2011 as one of the hottest and most closely contested areas of innovation in the financial services sector, with banks, credit card companies, payment processors, retail chains, and mobile carriers all rushing to bring competing services to market.

And certainly, the potential here is huge. In 2009 in the United States alone, consumers spent over $3 trillion on some 60 billion credit and debit card transactions, according to the Federal Reserve. Even if a small percentage of these transactions moved from plastic to mobile, it would be an unprecedented financial and marketing opportunity for whichever companies facilitate those transactions. Worldwide, the totals would be commensurately larger. In fact, outside of the United States, particularly in less-developed countries with significant mobile penetration but large unbanked populations, mobile payments have already seen significant adoption. In Kenya, for example,

Safaricom's M-PESA mobile money transfer service is widely credited for creating a banking infrastructure for the country's large unbanked population. Other services across the developing world have sprung up in the wake of M-PESA's success.

In other ways, your smartphone is also poised to be become your bank. In 2009, United Services Automobile Association (USAA, an insurance, banking, and investment institution that has one physical branch, in San Antonio, Texas) has long relied on self-service channels. USAA pioneered remote deposit capture (RDC), which allows customers to deposit a check by capturing an image and sending it to the bank. Chase and others soon followed suit. RDC alone may only serve a niche market, but in conjunction with other mobile banking and payment trends, it heralds a future of largely branchless banking. Down the road, we may no longer be asked, "What's in your wallet?" Instead, the question will be: "What *is* your wallet?"

Travel and Hospitality

Consumer reliance on mobile has sparked a profound change in the way brands relate to their customers. Now there's tremendous pressure to quickly adapt to a world where marketing must be far more personal and contextual to achieve success. Nowhere is this more evident than in the travel and hospitality sector. Travelers, and business travelers in particular, are highly dependent on their mobile phones and tablets, and adroit travel and hospitality (T&H) brands are using these devices to provide better service and forge deeper relationships with their customers. A smartphone-enabled website with basic booking functionality and loyalty program management are now table stakes for any hotel, resort, airline, or car rental brand. Being unusable for—or worse, inaccessible to—potential customers on their device of choice is unthinkable in a world where many booking decisions happen on the fly.

Many brands are also upping the ante with additional tools and content that enhance the customer experience. Expect to see the basic look-and-book functionality of the average hotel website expand to accommodate actually managing your stay and enabling you to customize everything from the contents of your minibar to the temperature of your room when you arrive, all via mobile. Similarly, expect the contents of sites and apps to morph on the fly according to where you are at any given time, offering you the best of what your current location has to offer.

Most of all, expect the experience of navigating—e.g., to a hotel or an airport—itself to change drastically, with apps and surface screens designed to help you find your way, plan meetings and activities, network with other guests, pay for incidentals, and even lock and unlock your room or rental car—all via your personal device. By decreasing the need for human interaction, these technical advances will actually enable T&H brands to engage more effectively with guests. Decreased reliance on people for these minutiae will support cost avoidance through self-service and create myriad opportunities for upselling, cross-selling, and building loyalty. Staff will be freed up to provide the elements of customer service that are more personal and pressing, requiring a human touch. The opportunity these mobile technologies present for return on investment (ROI) based on retention may well equal the ROI of acquisition. Brands that learn to utilize them now are making a sound investment in the future.

Pharma and Healthcare

If there's any industry that needs to be on the cutting edge of information delivery, it's the medical establishment. Yet big pharmaceutical companies and hospitals haven't always been the most adventurous adaptors of digital media. Mobile appears to be changing all of that, and rather quickly. It's now common to see your family physician enter the exam room with your medical history neatly recorded on tablet—something that would have been unthinkable until very recently. As fears about the security of digital information have eroded, not only doctors but nurses, administrators, and pharmaceutical reps increasingly rely on mobile devices as they juggle ever-growing amounts of data. Expect big pharma to add mobile devices, apps, and service delivery to their roster of offerings in response to the burgeoning opportunities in the newly dynamic mobile health (often referred to as mhealth) sector.

For consumers, tablets and smartphones now play a key role in managing and improving their own health with apps like charting diet, tracking pregnancy, managing chronic conditions, and improving physical performance. This area is of special interest to watch as mobile connectivity integrates with wearable technology like the Fitbit (`www.fitbit.com`) and Nike+ FuelBand (`http://nikeplus.nike.com/plus/products/fuelband`) and, eventually, migrates from tablets and smartphones altogether into self-contained, digitally enabled clothing and accessories.

Publishing and Entertainment

As we referenced at the beginning of this chapter, in many areas of the world, a mobile device will provide most people with their first—and only—connection to the Web. But the impact of the mobile-first experience goes far deeper. In highly wired societies like the United States and Western Europe, entire generations are growing up thinking the world is a touchscreen surface. Toddlers are learning their ABCs via iPad, and it's not uncommon to see the average three-year-old flummoxed when the family TV doesn't respond when swiped by hand.

In coming years, students' backpacks will be that much lighter as textbooks migrate to e-readers and tablet apps, a trend that is drastically shaking up the way print industry giants look at their business. For the current and future wave of kids growing up mobile—the pinch and zoom generations—a monthly print publication is likely to be as quaint, albeit collectible, as a vinyl record. The rapid experimentation we now see with newspapers, magazines, and books moving to mobile is just the beginning. As with most media revolutions, the publishers are migrating their content to these new platforms as is, but it won't be long before the platform begins to influence the content itself. It's arguable that the idea of what a page is may become something very different when we're no longer confined to a static piece of paper.

Likewise, we're already seeing the drastic waves of change mobile has wrought in the entertainment world. We're surfing and shopping via tablet as we watch TV, not to mention tweeting with other viewers and checking in to our favorite shows. A QR code and/or text opt-in has become a de facto feature of your average coming-attraction poster, and it's a given that TV channels and upcoming film releases have smartphone sites and videos viewable via mobile.

Moreover—and more complicated—is the fact that many of us are turning away from traditional TV and movie screens altogether and getting our entertainment content from the Web via our smart devices. This is especially true in mobile-first developing markets, where services like Vuclip (`www.vuclip.com`) index and optimize web-based video content for efficient replay on mobile devices. Much of that content isn't even coming from studios and big media providers but *from other consumers.* A case in point: YouTube mobile has consistently ranked among the most popular mobile websites since its launch in 2007. However, even YouTube is moving more in the direction of professional content, following the lead of many over-the-top (OTT) players, such as Netflix and Hulu+, which use a home broadband connection to stream video content to the TV but bypass traditional pay-TV subscriptions—and professional content almost always involves a fee.

What's interesting is that, as consumers, we are warming to the notion that content isn't always free and that giving something in exchange, whether money or data, is more acceptable than we thought. Witness the success of Apple's iTunes and subsequently its App Store and the myriad imitators they have wrought. There is value in professionally produced content; the trick is finding the right balance of free and fee.

In Conclusion

What more can we say but that mobile is changing media and it's changing us—how we work, play, shop, bank, and share—in essence, how we live life. The playing field is no longer the same, and it's still changing almost every day. Although we can't see around the corner, we can help you capitalize on what's happening now and prepare you to be as nimble as possible to take advantage of mobile as it evolves.

Woody Allen famously said, "90 percent of life is showing up." We believe that the same holds true for succeeding in mobile—provided you're well prepared. In the next chapter, we'll discuss how to develop a strategic framework and an approach that will enable you to be ready to get the most from the rapidly changing mobile landscape.

2 Week 1: Develop Your Mobile Strategy

The key to survival and success in a fast-evolving digital world is to understand the challenges posed by emerging platforms and adapt to them as they come along. The only surefire way to manage this change is to develop a strategic plan for how you'll handle it—and how you'll incorporate all the mobile tactics available to you. We find that it is easy to mistake tactics for strategy, so we'd like to start out by explaining the difference between the two.

Chapter Contents

Draw the Line Between Strategy and Tactics

People love to say, "Think outside the box!" That's all well and good, but you can't think outside the box until you *define the box*. That's what strategy is, defining the essential elements of your approach to doing business. Here's an analogy we believe nicely illustrates the difference between strategy and tactics.

Say you want to build your dream house. The floorplan you draw to define the house—the layout of the upstairs and downstairs, the location of the kitchen and bathrooms, and the like—is the strategy. The blueprints that define the specific details of the house such as the electrical plan, plumbing, placement of appliances, finishing details, and so forth are the tactics. If you went right to blueprints without drawing a floorplan first, the whole house would never come together in the end the way you envisioned it.

It's no different with mobile marketing. You need to establish a high-level plan for what you are trying to build before you can successfully outline the specific details of how you will build it. Strategy is the framework that defines how you will use various mobile tactics—for example, mobile websites, *short message service (SMS),* and mobile apps—to fulfill your customers' needs and achieve your own marketing goals. Tactics are more tangible and, hence, a lot easier to get your head around than strategy. A smart marketer can pick up a tactic, such as how to set up an SMS campaign, in…well, an hour a day! Strategy takes much longer to master because it needs to be uniquely tailored to your brand and your customers. We can't tell you what the right strategy is for your brand—only you can determine that—but we can teach you how to figure it out.

In our experience, a successful mobile strategy hinges on a harmonious balance between three key spheres:

- Brand
- Customers
- Environment

Often when we see a brand fail with mobile, that failure can be clearly traced to focusing on one of these areas to the detriment of the others. More often than not, mobile is driven by the needs of the brand. This is understandable; it's natural to gravitate toward fulfilling your own needs first. However, you also need to address the needs of your customers if you're going to reach your own goals. Almost as often, we see marketers reacting to the environment and investing in a mobile tactic simply because it's new. This is what we like to call shiny new object syndrome. The mobile marketing industry is still nascent and the next "big" thing excites everyone, but many mobile tactics don't have the user response that they tout. In these situations, we like to remind you that just because something has been labeled the hot new thing does not necessarily mean it is the right thing for you.

Shiny New Object Syndrome

When you experience shiny new object syndrome, you find yourself distracted by the flash and glitz of a hot new technology and rush to use it before determining whether it truly holds value for you.

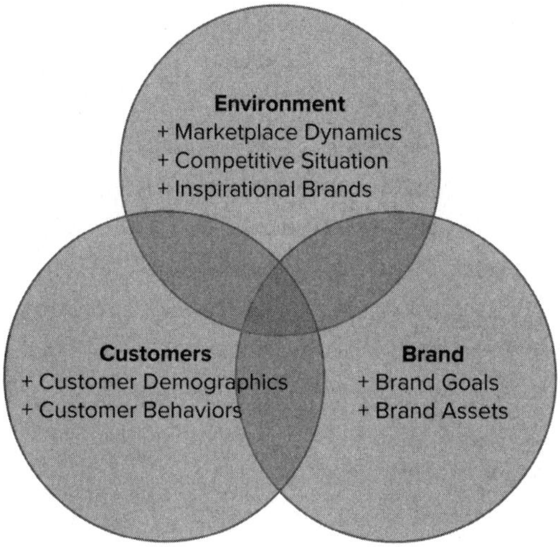

Figure 2.1 A successful mobile strategy will be based on a harmonious balance of your brand's goals, your customers' needs, and what's happening in the marketplace environment.

The reality is that the brand, environment, and customers are of equal importance, and your mobile strategy lies in a harmonious balance of all three (see Figure 2.1). Strategy aligns the factors of each, resulting in a set of tactics and an executional framework for bringing your plans to fruition.

The trick is having the right methodology for figuring all this out. Luckily, it's not an esoteric science. Mobile strategy is no different from any other type of marketing strategy in terms of process, but there's definitely more ground to cover and there are many more tactics to consider. Unlike online advertising, search marketing, or email, mobile touches literally every aspect of your business. It's an activation and access layer to everything you already do, as well as a completely new channel in its own right. In this chapter, we provide you with a framework for developing your own individual mobile strategy and guide you step-by-step through the activities involved.

Monday: Understand What You Can Achieve with Mobile Strategy

For Day 1, let's set the stage with some examples of well-known brands that have taken a successful strategic approach to mobile for a variety of common purposes.

Brand Building and Awareness

One of the most valuable aspects of mobile is the fact it can add interactivity to physical objects and traditional media. This ability to render the offline world interactive has made it unbeatable for real-time brand building and awareness. Few brands have used mobile as successfully for this purpose as Coca-Cola.

Coke's global footprint gave the brand the unique opportunity to experiment with mobile in parts of the world where the third screen comes first and to figure out (earlier than almost anyone else) what actually works.

> **The Third Screen**
>
> The third screen is common marketing industry terminology for mobile devices. The first screen was television; the second, the personal computer; and the third, mobile phones.

Coke's mobile strategy hinges primarily on SMS, the global lingua franca of mobile. This is a very valuable example of a brand balancing the needs of the brand, customers, and environment. While Coke can and does indulge in more sophisticated and future-forward mobile experimentation, it continues to rely on SMS as its core mobile tool everywhere Coke is sold for the simple reason SMS reaches pretty much anyone with a mobile phone anywhere in the world. Using SMS as a call-to-action makes the brand as immediately accessible to someone in rural sub-Saharan Africa as it is to someone in downtown New York City. For all consumers, SMS is a simple, easy-to-use method for engaging with Coke in real-time to rack up rewards points, opt in for alerts (as shown in the My Coke Rewards sign-up process in Figure 2.2), enter sweepstakes, play games, and even (in some countries) pay for a drink. Nearly everyone has it and nearly everyone can use it, which brings Coca-Cola that much closer to putting a Coke in the hands of everyone worldwide.

This is not a flashy use of technology; it's a smart one. Coke understands the environmental sphere like no other brand and chooses to enable the greatest reach rather than reach for the latest shiny object. In Coca-Cola's hands, the simplest of mobile channels has become the number-one tool for connecting with customers at the point of sale and in the actual moment of consumption to strengthen their bond with the Coca-Cola brand.

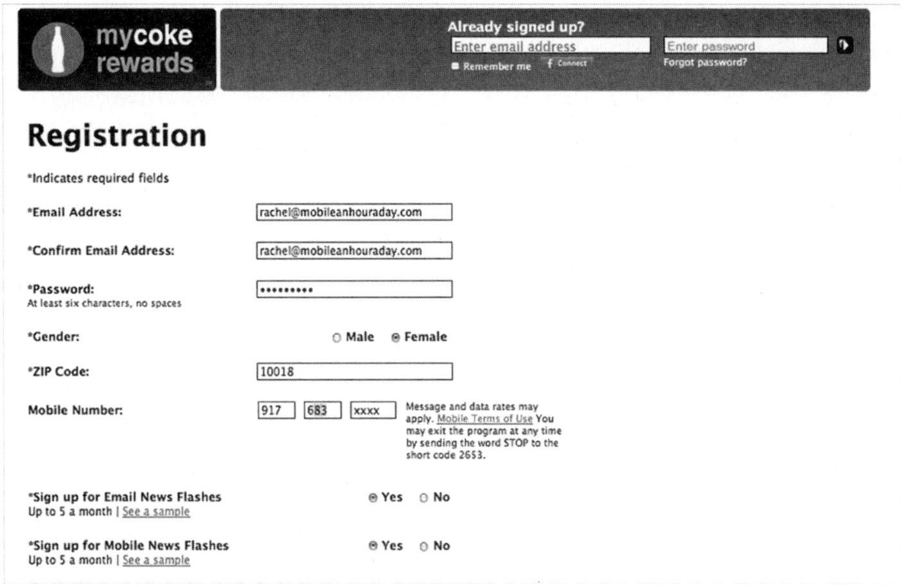

Figure 2.2 My Coke Rewards.com homepage with SMS opt-ins

Tom Daly, Global Group Director, Mobile & Search, Connections Planning, at Coca-Cola, on Coca-Cola's Mobile Strategy

"Coke's mobile strategy was, in some ways, inspired by something The Coca-Cola Company's then-president Robert Woodruff expressed in the 1930s. He described the company's role as 'putting our brands within arm's reach of desire.' Today, at the end of that arm, between it and desire, is a mobile phone. So, our choice is simple: Do we make that phone a barrier to, or enabler of, desire? We have chosen to make mobile an Enabler of Desire. This is a choice that can have a significant impact on our business because while every day, consumers drink 1.7 billion servings of our brands, there are 6 billion mobile subscriptions. Think about it. . .6 billion arms with a phone versus 1.7 billion arms with a Coke. I know 6 billion subscribers isn't 6 billion people, but neither is 1.7 billion servings, 1.7 billion people. The simple point is that while much about the future of mobile may be uncertain, what's clear to me is that for every arm that holds a phone, I want to see the other arm holding a Coke."

Mobile for CRM

It used be that you would never leave the house without your wallet and your keys. Nowadays, it's your wallet, your keys, and your mobile phone. In fact, it's rare for the average person to be separated from their mobile device at all—ever. For many, it has even taken over for the traditional alarm clock, sitting close by on the nightstand while they sleep. And, as we'll discuss in Chapter 10, "Week 9: Chart the Future Forward," it may eventually end up taking the place of your keys and wallet altogether.

It is this always-on, always-with-you aspect of mobile that makes it ideal for building a stronger, more mutually beneficial relationship with customers. There are many mobile solutions that support customer relationship management (CRM), but in our experience, SMS and mobile apps frequently end up being the go-to solutions. As we'll discuss in Chapter 3, "Week 2: Start Simple—SMS," SMS is particularly powerful because it puts control in the user's hand by being opt-in only. Your customers choose what kind of information they get, and how much and how often they want to receive it. It is marketing based on their terms, which makes them that much more open to what you put in front of them.

Mobile apps, on the other hand, provide a level of streamlined anytime, anywhere content and engagement that's unmatched by any other type of marketing. Getting the mobile app formula right is a challenge, but once you do, the level of engagement you can create is unmatched. We'll go deeper into how and why in Chapter 3 and Chapter 5, "Week 4: Maximize Engagement with Mobile Apps," but suffice it to say that if CRM is your goal, these two channels typically play significant roles.

Target is another great example of a brand using mobile strategically to enhance its relationship with customers. The brand's mobile apps are feature-rich and enable customers to shop, find deals and scan barcodes for price checks. Target also uses SMS to alert customers to the availability of new coupons and their impending expiration dates (see Figure 2.3). The strategy behind all these features is quite simple—simplify the task of shopping for life's essentials. If there is a golden rule of CRM, it is "make the customer's life easier" and Target's mobile products do just that.

Figure 2.3 Target provides shopping tools across key mobile platforms.

Mobile for Marketing

When the iTunes App Store first launched, marketers were introduced to a whole new kind of opportunity to get their message in front of consumers. Apps are a different paradigm for content consumption; they are self-contained digital experiences that engage users on a deeper, more personal level than a microsite or email campaign ever could. When they are well planned and well executed, you can stake a claim on the most valuable real estate in the world—your customer's mobile desktop.

Obviously, there are many, many other ways in which you can use mobile to market to your customers, but apps are one of the more exciting options. The interactive experiences they can create often result in users staying engaged for extended periods of time and coming back voluntarily again and again to consume more content. Volkswagen's launch of its halo GTI model is a great example of this kind of app-centric mobile marketing in action. Volkswagen has such confidence in mobile as a marketing medium that it chose to launch the 2010 GTI solely via an iPhone application in late 2009. The free Real Racing GTI game was so popular, it generated 750,000 downloads within the first four days after launch and hit the two million mark within weeks. But the campaign didn't just drive downloads—it drove traffic into the dealership with a Schedule Test Drive function embedded within the application.

The Real Racing GTI campaign is an excellent example of a brand using mobile to meet brand goals (sell cars) while displaying a keen understanding of the latest technology (environment) and its customers. Besides assuring direct, prolonged engagement with the young, predominantly male GTI audience, the app earned VW bonus points by virtue of being the only marketing done for the vehicle. The splash of such a bold move earned the brand as much, if not more, exposure for the new GTI. A screenshot of the latest version for *iPad* is shown in Figure 2.4.)

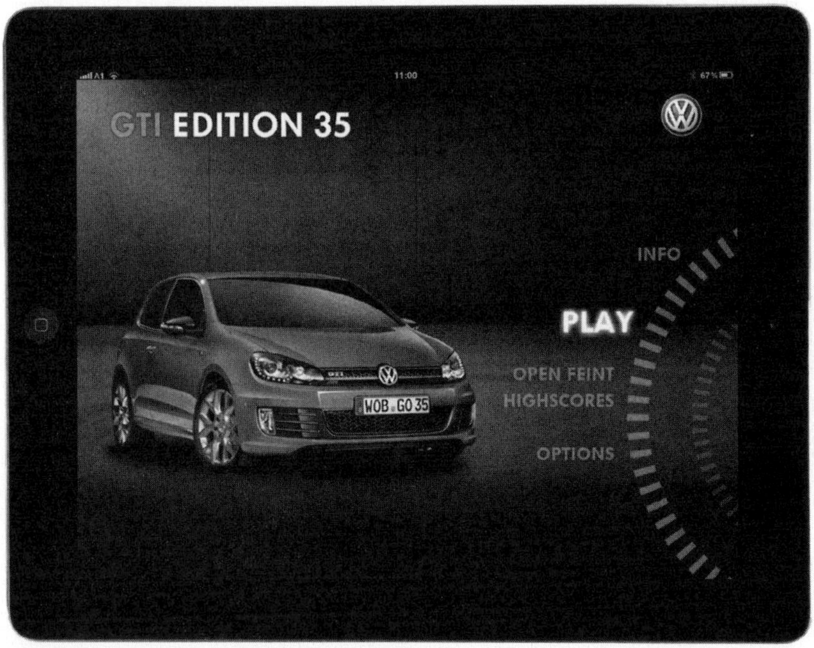

Figure 2.4 Volkswagen's latest Real Racing GTI for iPad in action.

Mobile for Advertising

It is established wisdom among digital marketers that no one cries over a banner ad. Their size and ubiquity often render them effectively unnoticeable and dilute their emotional impact—although banners do retain an important utility role when it comes to online branding. On mobile devices, smaller screen sizes and the relative lack of visual clutter on mobile webpages mean banners get more attention than on the desktop. But, more is also relative: Mobile banners are proportionally smaller, so mobile display ads have their own challenges.

Apple cofounder Steve Jobs once memorably said mobile advertising "sucks" and set out to change that state of affairs by launching iAd, the company's own ad network designed exclusively for iOS devices (iPod touch, iPhone, and iPad). In his vision, mobile ads could be rich, bold, and engaging; and the first iAds broke new creative ground. A reportedly high cost of entry limited access for most brands at first, but those who have used it have enjoyed considerable success. The rich creative pallet of iAds proved just how engaging a mobile ad could and should be. According to a Nielsen study commissioned by Apple and widely reported in the trade press, over a five-week period in 2010, the Campbell's Soup iAd (shown in Figure 2.5), which ran in popular iPhone apps such as that of the *New York Times*, received 53 million impressions and enjoyed approximately a 1 percent click-through rate (CTR). That may not sound high, but it's roughly 10 times the average CTR for desktop rich-media ads. Moreover, Nielsen's research indicated that the 530,000 people who actually clicked on the Campbell's iAd, which highlighted the brand's new packaging and soup varieties, spent close to a minute exploring the ad's interactive features, including the ability to download the Campbell's Kitchen app. The high price tag plus the limitation of reaching an iOS-only audience might have been a roadblock to the mobile ad world domination Steve Jobs envisioned, at least at first, but eMarketer analysis shows Apple still enjoyed an estimated 7 percent of U.S. mobile display ad spending in 2011, behind Google at 23 percent.

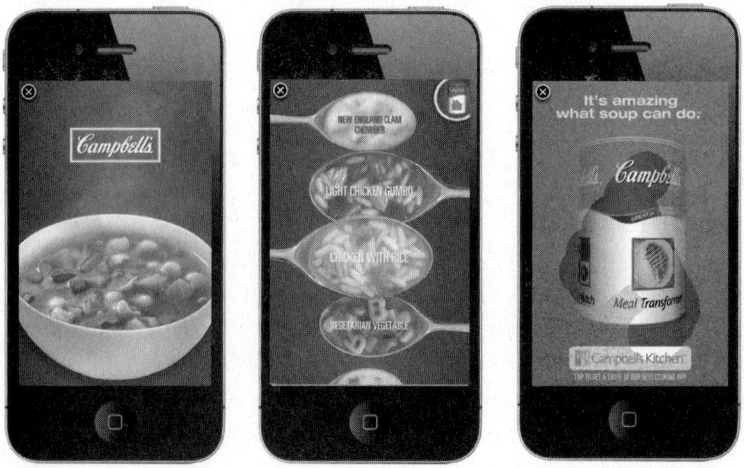

Figure 2.5 Campbell's Soup iAd

The resulting campaign metrics, as reported by Mobile Marketer (www.mobilemarketer.com), a popular website that covers the mobile industry, were extremely favorable, both in absolute terms and also relative to other media:

- **Brand recall:** 79 percent for the iAd versus 20 percent for TV and 17 percent online
- **Message recall:** 38 percent for the iAd versus 14 percent for TV and 11 percent online
- **Ad favorability:** 54 percent for iAd versus 12 percent for TV and 9 percent online

Purchase intent among those who saw the Campbell's iAd banners also rose significantly. Jennifer Gordon, director of global advertising for Campbell's Soups, told Ad Age: "I think the combination of our news and the new platform was great synergy and got people to think differently about Campbell's."

Apple understandably cherry-picked the Campbell's campaign to tout the effectiveness of its platform, but other brands have enjoyed a similar synergy between product and platform. Nissan, for example, used a multilayered, interactive iAd to help launch its LEAF electric vehicle in 2010. It saw customers spend an average of 90 seconds with the ad, around 10 times longer than they spent with comparable online ads, according to figures reported in the *Los Angeles Times.*

Given the amount of time people spend with their mobile devices in their hands, mobile advertising can be a highly effective way to get your brand's message across, especially when used in conjunction with a well-designed mobile website or application.

Mobile for Sales

In the early years of mobile, marketers were skeptical that customers would actually buy anything via a mobile device, but attitudes have evolved considerably. At the annual South by Southwest (SXSW) festival in March 2012, the biggest discussions about mobile were focused on *near-field communication (NFC)* and other forms of real-time payment. The excitement regarding smartphones and tablets as commerce platforms was palpable everywhere you went.

We'll dive into the many different current and emerging mechanisms for *mobile commerce* in greater detail in Chapter 8, "Week 7: Check out M-Commerce," but the best current example we can give comes from Gilt Groupe, the high-end online flash sale website. The brand's decision to invest in a full m-commerce-enabled iPad application (shown in Figure 2.6) in early 2010 is an excellent example of strategy in action.

While most brands developing apps for the first-generation iPad were barely aware of whether they'd be able to reach any of their customers via the medium, Gilt Groupe knew full well its site catered to an affluent, highly digital, urban demographic—the very people who were rushing out to pick up Apple's groundbreaking tablet. Moreover, the app's design displays a keen understanding of how mobile's anytime, anywhere accessibility provides the perfect vehicle for Gilt's time-sensitive sales model. Best of all, the device's large screen provides a visually rich palette that showcases the brand's glamorous content to best advantage.

The elegant application that resulted was generating 3 percent of overall sales within two days of launch and has positioned Gilt ahead of the pack in a very crowded field. In a December 2011 interview with eMarketer Yon Feldman, Gilt's vice president of mobile and global engineering, said that tablets accounted for 5 percent of Gilt's total sales and he expected that number to increase. "We invest a lot in this area because the platform really allows us to highlight our product," Feldman said. "We have beautiful photography and on the tablet screens, you can zoom in and get really close to the fabric or the seams of a dress and inspect it very well. It's the perfect medium to browse our products."

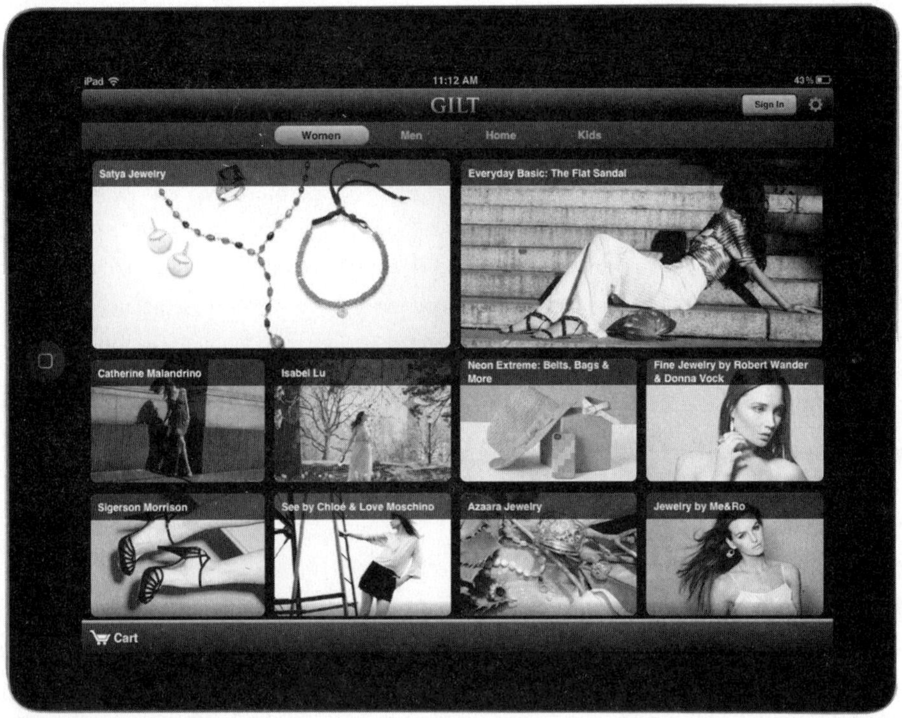

Figure 2.6 Gilt Groupe iPad app

Tuesday: Collect the Right Information to Build Your Business Case

We believe that at least 75 percent of success lies in gathering and synthesizing the right data to inform your strategy. Most of this data is easily accessible. The real challenge is in turning it into actionable insights. We'll get to the process for synthesizing your research by the end of this week, but first, we will explain what you need to collect and how to collect it so that we can build your final business case on Friday.

Internal Insights

Internal insights are information about your business and customers that you can collect from stakeholders and other internal touchpoints within your organization, such as web analytics. They contain the most important data because they define your corporate goals and form the initial composite profiles of your customers. Make no mistake: Gathering this information constitutes table stakes. You can skimp on (or even skip!) certain research recommendations in this chapter, but internal insights are must-haves and they are the starting point for developing your mobile strategy. Our process includes the following activities:

- Stakeholder interviews
- A technical audit
- A content audit
- A desktop website traffic analysis
- An internal audit of market research and audience insights

Stakeholder Interviews

Stakeholders are the people within your organization who should have input into your mobile strategy. These people are the decision makers—the marketing managers, brand managers, customer service leads, key salespeople, and the like. However, the scope of whom to include varies greatly based on the brand involved. For example, when dealing with travel and hospitality (T&H) brands, we often speak with front-desk managers, hosts, and concierges; for automotive brands, we like to include dealers in the mix. In some cases, we've also included external vendors and partners, such as a brand's advertising, branding, public relations (PR), and other agency partners. In other words, whom you speak to in this step of the process will depend on multiple variables. Just keep in mind that your goal is to talk to senior brand decision makers as well a representative sample of people whose jobs will be heavily influenced by mobile. What you want to gain is an understanding of their business objectives and how mobile can help them achieve these objectives.

We recommend that you interview at least four or five stakeholders to get a clear sense of your brand needs. We also recommend you try to keep it under a maximum of 15 interviewees for the sake of time and efficiency; once you reach that number, odds are you will just hear the same things repeated over and over again.

The questions we ask these stakeholders vary according to the brand and the individual's job function, but we've included some high-level examples here to get you started.

Lead-in Questions We recommend starting with some basic lead-in questions that will help you better understand the subject and his or her feedback:

- Tell us about your position within this organization. What does your job entail? What are your individual/group business goals?

- Tell us about any mobile initiatives your team is working on now or has worked on in the past. Were they successful? What did you think about the results?

Qualitative Questions At this point, you'll have warmed the subject up and can progress to more detailed questions that will help you determine the brand aspects of your mobile strategy:

- Tell us any thoughts you have about how mobile can help your team/department achieve its goals.
- Please tell us what you know about your competitor's mobile efforts and what you think about them.
- Tell us about any brands outside your competitive set/vertical that have done mobile work you admire.
- Tell us what you know about your customers and their mobile behavior.
- Have you already established specific mobile tactics (for example, a mobile site, app, or campaign) you would like to execute? Please tell us more about this tactic and your specific goals for it.

Technical Audit

Once you've completed your stakeholder interviews, we recommend moving on to do a technical audit. The *technical audit* is a fundamental step; it helps you understand how much of your current digital content you can extend to mobile. Given the multiple *channels* (mobile advertising, SMS, apps, etc.) and *platforms* (iOS, Android, Windows Phone, BlackBerry, etc.) you have to choose from, it's essential to create a plan for developing and distributing content as efficiently as possible. In later chapters, we'll discuss the importance of *portability* in more detail, but suffice it to say that your technical approach to all things digital should be mindful of the need to distribute content to all the channels and platforms that matter now—and all the channels and platforms that will matter in 12 to 18 months.

Of course, our crystal ball doesn't see that far into the future, so it's hard to say what those channels and platforms will be. The point is to take as nimble an approach as possible to technical execution. Think of it as putting virtual handles on your content so you can pick that content up at will and put it anywhere you want it to go.

The best return on investment (ROI) will be yielded by thinking in terms of portability for the long term, but most digital content environments weren't originally planned that way. The average digital content environment, including web applications, databases, and content management systems (CMS), were designed with the intention of rendering content for desktop web browsers. Of course, now that the digital marketing ecosystem has expanded to include so much more than the traditional computer desktop, your content needs to extend to many more places. The technical audit helps you figure out exactly what you can leverage and how. A qualified digital technologist should perform the audit. He or she should examine your digital infrastructure to answer key questions such as:

- What type of CMS, if any, is in place, and can it support integration/distribution of mobile content?
- What options for device detection and redirection can be best supported if need be?
- How is the front-end site code constructed, and how can it best be extended to various mobile devices?
- How accessible are essential web services and content?

The answers that result from the technical audit will determine what content and web services you will be able to leverage internally and what you may have to build, buy, or outsource to achieve your goals. These insights are instrumental in designing the tactical plans that are your blueprint for mobile marketing.

Content Audit

The technical audit defines what content and services you can access. By contrast, the *content audit* defines what content and services you should use. Based on the technical assessment and your understanding of your internal brand goals, categorize the various segments of content and services according to where and how you think you'll use them. At this point, the assessment is still an educated guess; we haven't fully defined the needs of your customers yet. (We'll do that tomorrow on Day 3.) So keep in mind that the content audit will definitely be refined in some areas and expanded in others as you progress.

Comb through all the content within your digital environment and categorize it according to how accessible it is, where it is located, and how you plan to use it. You can organize your inventory of content in whatever way works best for you—the important thing is to catalog what you've got to work with. We've included an example in Figure 2.7 of a content audit performed for the website we created to support this book (`www.mobileanhouraday.com`).

> **Note:** We find that Excel is the easiest and most convenient tool for collecting and organizing the information in a content audit.

	A	B	C	D
1	Content ID#	Content name	Location	Notes
2	1	About Page	www.mobileanhouraday/about	full about text
3	1.1	Noah's Bio	www.mobileanhouraday/about/nelkinbio	
4	1.2	Rachel's Bio	www.mobileanhouraday/about/rpasquabio	Abbreviated bio text, thumbnail headshot and email link
5	2	Speaking	www.mobileanhouraday/speaking	
6	2.1	May-12	www.mobileanhouraday/speaking/may_dates	Abbreviated event description, dates and link to conference site
7	2.2	Jun-12	www.mobileanhouraday/speaking/june_dates	
8	2.3	Jul-12	www.mobileanhouraday/speaking/july_dates	
9	2.4	Aug-12	www.mobileanhouraday/speaking/august_dates	
10	2.5	Sep-12	www.mobileanhouraday/speaking/september_dates	
11	2.6	Oct-12	www.mobileanhouraday/speaking/october_dates	
12	2.7	Nov-12	www.mobileanhouraday/speaking/november_dates	
13	2.8	Dec-12	www.mobileanhouraday/speaking/december/2012	
14	3	Contact Page	www.mobileanhouraday/contact	
15	3.1	Contact submission form	www.mobileanhouraday/contact_submissionform	Full submission form
16	4	Media	www.mobileanhouraday/media	
17	4.1	Conference presentations	www.mobileanhouraday/media/conference decks	Slideshare
18	4.2	Videos	www.mobileanhouraday/media/videos	Youtube
19	4.3	Audio interviews	www.mobileanhouraday/media/audio interviews	TBD

Figure 2.7 Sample content audit spreadsheet

Desktop Website Traffic Analysis

Along with stakeholder interviews and the technical audit, *desktop traffic analysis* is one of the essential pieces of research that we recommend you do without exception. This step can be easily done in tandem with the technical audit.

You probably have a fairly good understanding of who your customers are, but your desktop website analytics can yield a goldmine of data on their mobile behaviors. Most website analytics packages will segment out traffic for mobile, providing detailed insights into the preferred devices, operating systems, and behavioral patterns of your customers. (An example appears in Figure 2.8.) You will probably find that the majority still use iOS on the iPhone and iPod touch, with Android smartphones a close second, but seeing the mixture of feature phones, tablets, and other smartphone platforms visiting your website will have a significant influence on how you define and prioritize your mobile tactics. As we'll discuss in more detail when we get to segments and personas, the device someone uses tells you a lot about who they are and what they're likely to do and respond to via mobile. This info is a must-have in building your strategy.

At a minimum, your analytics software should be able to give you:

- The percentage of your overall desktop website traffic that can be attributed to mobile devices
- A breakdown of that traffic by device type (iPhone, iPod touch, Android Evo, and so forth), as well as unique visitors, pages per visit, and average duration per visit

Most analytics software will also give you more detailed device data (although getting it may involve some tweaking), such as:

- Traffic by mobile operating system
- Percentage of new visits from mobile devices
- Bounce rate for mobile devices
- Most popular pages including top entry and exit pages for mobile
- Mobile conversions

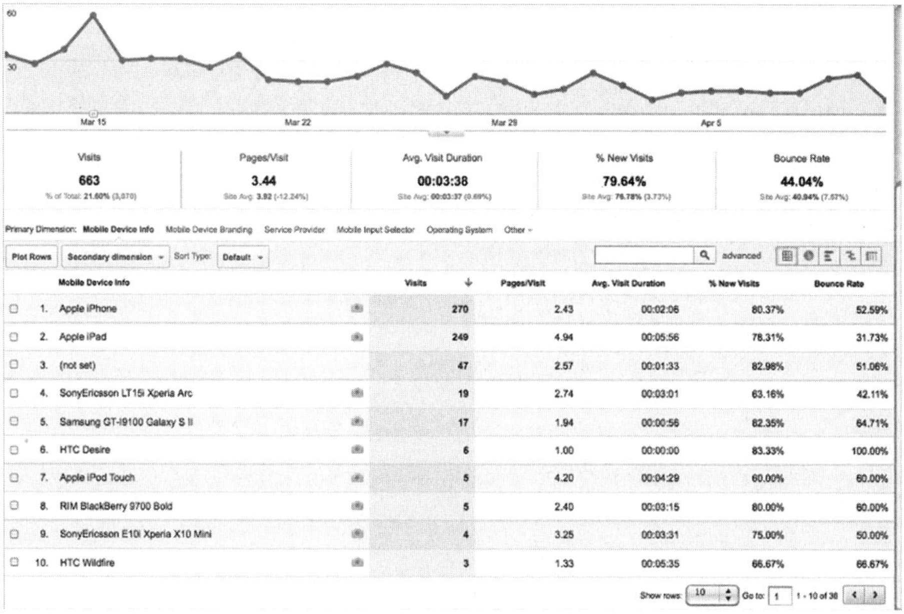

	Mobile Device Info	Visits	Pages/Visit	Avg. Visit Duration	% New Visits	Bounce Rate
1.	Apple iPhone	270	2.43	00:02:06	80.37%	52.59%
2.	Apple iPad	249	4.94	00:05:56	78.31%	31.73%
3.	(not set)	47	2.57	00:01:33	82.98%	51.06%
4.	SonyEricsson LT15i Xperia Arc	19	2.74	00:03:01	63.16%	42.11%
5.	Samsung GT-I9100 Galaxy S II	17	1.94	00:00:56	82.35%	64.71%
6.	HTC Desire	6	1.00	00:00:00	83.33%	100.00%
7.	Apple iPod Touch	5	4.20	00:04:29	60.00%	60.00%
8.	RIM BlackBerry 9700 Bold	5	2.40	00:03:15	80.00%	60.00%
9.	SonyEricsson E10i Xperia X10 Mini	4	3.25	00:03:31	75.00%	50.00%
10.	HTC Wildfire	3	1.33	00:05:35	66.67%	66.67%

Figure 2.8 Mobile device traffic for `www.mobileanhouraday.com`

Internal Market Research and Audience Insights

This step involves taking an internal audit of all the existing data you have that could potentially influence your mobile strategy and the tactics you choose to execute. What can be collected and assessed varies from brand to brand and may include (but is by no means limited to):

Internal Market Research This refers to existing research you may have performed or commissioned from a third party on trends and other marketplace factors influencing your vertical. Internal market research that has been performed in the last 12 months is considered valid here; anything conducted prior to the last 12 months should not be considered, given the rate of change in the mobile world.

Internal Customer Research Internal customer research refers to research on the behaviors of your customers you may have performed or commissioned from a third party. Again, anything conducted within a 12-month window is considered valid for inclusion.

Competitive Insights Any research compiled on your competitors within the last six months should be vetted, but we'll discuss the need for and process involved in doing a current competitive review in more detail later in this chapter.

Marketing Plans Perhaps most important of all, make a careful assessment of your marketing plans for the calendar year. Doing so will help identify areas where mobile can support and enhance your efforts.

Primary Research

Primary research traditionally refers to research based on direct and deliberate interaction with your target demographics. Primary research can be highly valuable, but it can also be very expensive. It's great if you can afford the time and the investment, but internal analysis can also yield insights on who your customers are and what they need. If you factor what you already know about your customers into your strategic process and carefully gauge their reaction to specific tactics, such as bounce rates from your mobile website or their app store comments, you can refine ongoing development of your strategy accordingly. However, if you *can* afford to conduct primary research, you have options to consider. Let's take a look at a few.

Focus Groups

Focus groups are a form of qualitative research in which you gather a group of people matching your target demographics and ask their opinions of and/or feelings toward a product, service, or campaign.

> **Qualitative Research versus Quantitative Research**
>
> Qualitative research focuses on the human aspects of your customers and their behavior, the how and the why; whereas quantitative research focuses on the statistical aspects, the who, the where, the what, and the how much.

Focus groups are invaluable in their ability to give you a better understanding of your target customers and their mobile behavior, which is uncharted territory for most brands. The feedback you get can tell you how they interact with your brand, product, or service on their journey from the earliest stages of awareness to becoming a customer and, hopefully, a loyal advocate.

Focus groups usually consist of 6 to 12 people gathered together in the same space where they can interact with one another and share their experiences and opinions. We find them especially useful in improving the user experience of mobile sites and apps; the group dynamic is often a catalyst to customer-led brainstorming on content and features they'd like to have. Focus groups also are invaluable for beta-testing new mobile products of all kinds. (We will discuss the focus group approach in greater detail in the usability testing sections of each chapter in this book.)

The easiest way to convene a focus group is to delegate execution to a professional focus group company. The process begins with developing a questionnaire that is used to vet potential candidates from the focus group company's pool of resources. While you have the option of developing the questionnaire yourself, most of these companies offer a full-service model in which you simply give them the criteria for your ideal candidates and they'll take it from there, writing the questionnaire, fielding the candidates, and conducting and moderating the sessions on their premises. In these instances, you have the option of being as involved as you choose. You can sit and observe from behind a double-sided mirror, take a direct part in running the group, or you can choose to have the candidates sent to your premises and conduct the focus groups yourself. In this last case, it is best to adhere to a few best practices:

- Have one but no more than two people from your organization involved to moderate and facilitate discussion. You want to guide the conversation, but you never want to outnumber the participants or inhibit their spontaneity.
- Try to keep sessions to one hour; it can be challenging to keep participants on topic for even this long.
- Have some questions and topics ready to seed the discussion, but don't try to too hard to stick to a script; the best insights will come as an organic conversation develops.
- Consider hiring a professional moderator. They are skilled at keeping the conversation balanced, ensuring that unique individuals within the focus group don't dominate the discussion or steer the entire group in the wrong direction.
- There can be good reasons for doing multiple focus groups, for example, getting unique feedback from specific types of customers, or people in specific geo-locations or markets. However, in these cases, try to tailor your questions according to the people with whom you are speaking and the insights you are trying to uncover. Don't get tempted into conducting 10 different focus groups that ask the same identical set of questions.

Customer Interviews

Customer interviews are similar to focus groups, with the same questions and goals, but in a one-on-one format. The same types of demographically appropriate candidates are selected, ideally through a professional focus group company, but instead of a group session, the format changes to intensive, in-person interviews designed to uncover deeper nuances of customer attitudes and behaviors. Customer interviews are ideal for usability testing purposes because they enable you to spend more time with the candidate, assessing his or her feedback on your site, app, or campaign in greater detail. If you choose to go the customer interview route, try to interview a minimum of at least 10 candidates to ensure a sufficient sample and a well-rounded variety of feedback.

Surveys

Think of surveys as the quick-and-dirty version of focus groups, with the same types of questions but conducted virtually and on a broader scale. One of the chief benefits of a survey is that you can reach a much larger number of participants; the average sample size for an online poll is about 1,000 respondents to ensure statistical relevance. You lose the benefit of personal interaction and on-the-fly conversation with your subjects, but surveys are appealing in many cases because they are generally easier to manage and execute than in-person focus groups or customer interviews.

We don't see surveys as an ideal substitute for the more hands-on forms of primary research; you can't achieve the same level of detail and there are some things that they are simply not right for, such as usability testing. But, the larger sample size can be useful in validating user behavior trends, and surveys can be an excellent tool for sourcing additional insights.

While you can move fast with surveys, they aren't necessarily cheap. You can spend a significant amount of money planning and executing a survey with a panel-based research company, such as Harris or comScore. It can be money well spent if you're trying to validate something with feedback from a high number of users. But, skilled marketers who have some experience in conducting primary research can bootstrap a survey quite easily. A SurveyMonkey questionnaire circulated within your own organization or distributed to an opt-in email list of your customers can yield a wealth of information on common user behaviors and attitudes and provide quantitative data that focus groups and customer interviews cannot.

Primary Research Firms

Primary research firms gather data on market trends, customer demographics, and user behaviors on a much larger scale than you can achieve with focus groups, customer interviews, or surveys. Most use a combination of methodologies to collect their data, including surveys, panels of opted-in participants that volunteer their information, and billing data scraped from credit card companies, wireless carriers, and utility providers. Subscribers can then access this data and use it to compile custom reports but most of these firms also publish regular research reports on a variety of topics that are of interest to their customers. Many offer advisory and consulting services in addition to research.

Nielsen (`www.nielsen.com`) and comScore (`www.comscore.com`) are among the most prominent panel-based research firms. Leading research and advisory firms that cover different aspects of the mobile space include Forrester (www.forrester.com), Gartner (www.gartner.com), International Data Corporation (IDC) (www.idc.com), Ovum (www.ovum.com), and Strategy Analytics (`www.strategyanalytics.com`). All offer invaluable data, but individual reports and annual subscriptions tend to be costly and out of range for most small- and medium-sized businesses. If you can spring for a subscription to a primary research firm, we'd say go for it. If not, consider doing primary research yourself on a smaller scale and filling the gaps with secondary research.

Secondary Research

Secondary research is open to everyone. It's the hands-on gathering of data from the Web, print, personal observation and experience, and just about every other first-hand resource you can think of. It takes some skill but can yield much of the insights you need.

Web-Based Resources

In the appendices at the back of this book, we've provided numerous blogs, online publications, and Twitter feeds that we recommend as resources for mobile marketing research. On `www.mobileanhouraday.com` we've also included blogs we find helpful in keeping tabs on mobile trends across key industry verticals, such as Automotive, Travel and Hospitality, and Retail/CPG. However, given the ever-changing nature of the Web in general and mobile in particular, you'll most likely find Google to be your best friend in researching whatever aspect of mobile you are currently focusing on.

Secondary Research Firms

Secondary research firms aggregate massive amounts of publicly available information and analyze relevant trend data in reports and easy-to-digest infographics. They generally sell self-service access to this information on an annual subscription basis, catering mostly to large- and medium-sized businesses. Among the best known secondary research firms are eMarketer (`www.emarketer.com`), eConsultancy (`www.econsultancy.com`), and MarketingCharts (`www.marketingcharts.com`), and we find them very valuable for the breadth of data and insights they provide. When you don't have the resources to engage in primary research of your own or purchase the services of a primary research provider, a subscription to a secondary research firm can be an invaluable option. It can also be an excellent supplement even if you are doing primary research because secondary firms can often provide insights on a scale and from a variety of sources that your primary firm cannot.

Wednesday: Understand Your Audience and Opportunity

If you are reading this book, then you are probably no stranger to the concept of the purchase funnel and the customer journey. For the uninitiated, the *purchase funnel* consists of the phases through which an individual travels on his or her way to becoming a customer. The broadest phase at the top is awareness, and the customer progresses through an ever-narrowing path, from engagement to consideration to purchase and, finally, the narrowest and most refined phase at the very end—loyalty.

Our job as marketers is to get customers through the funnel successfully. To do that, we need to understand the unique paths through it. Each of those paths is a *customer journey*.

Mobile plays into every aspect of that journey, from the earliest stages of awareness to ownership and loyalty (see Figure 2.9). Theoretically, certain aspects of mobile are especially relevant at certain stages. For example, mobile search plays a bigger role when someone is first discovering your brand than it does after they've become a customer. Conversely, a mobile app is more relevant once the relationship is established; someone who's just becoming familiar with you isn't quite as likely to download your app. It's good to understand how individual tactics commonly play out throughout the purchase funnel.

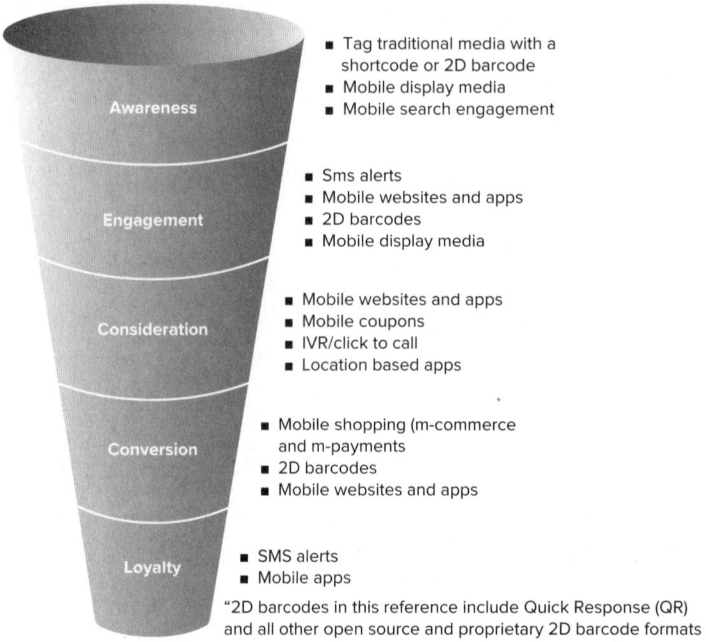

Figure 2.9 Traditional purchase funnel with mobile overlay

2D Barcodes

2D barcodes are two-dimensional graphical images encoded with information that can be read with a specific scanner device or a scanner application on a mobile device.

QR (quick response) is a common term for any kind of 2D barcode, but there are actually many different varieties of 2D barcodes of which the actual QR format is just one kind. Some are available in the public domain and some are still proprietary. The best known are:

DataMatrix: the first 2D code standard, developed in Europe in 1989, allows for 2,335 alphanumeric characters

QR: developed in 1995 by Denso, a Japanese auto brand, allows for 4,296 alphanumeric characters

QR is the de facto standard in the United States due to its ability to include more info than DataMatrix. Hence, QR is the catchphrase for a 2D barcode. However, many other types of open source and proprietary 2D barcodes exist. We'll explore them further in Chapter 9, "Week 8: Drive Awareness with Ambient Media."

This theoretical mapping of mobile tactics to phases of the purchase funnel is just that—a theory. There is undoubtedly some truth to these assumptions, but we know people use mobile in vastly different ways based on who they are and what you have to offer them. There's no set pattern; the trick is to understand exactly how this happens for your particular customers and brand. So, it is essential to understand your customers' unique *mobile technographics.*

Note: Technographics is market segmentation performed according to how your customers' age, gender, ethnicity, household income (HHI), marital status, and many other factors dictate their use of technology. In this case, it defines the types of devices they will use and the types of mobile activities in which they will engage.

The research you performed on Day 1 should have yielded a significant amount of data about your customers: the ratio of males to females, dominant age groups, HHI levels, and so forth. You should also have a good sense of what devices are most popular with your customers based on the analysis of your desktop website traffic. What you don't yet know is how to match your customer demographics to devices and specific mobile actions—and that's what you need to figure out in order to properly refine your strategy and tactical approach.

Some brands will find this very simple because most of their customers fall into a single demographic that's fairly easy to define. The clothing retail chain Forever 21, for example, primarily reaches single women ages roughly 18 to 25. Maybe there are some variations here and there, where women skew older or younger, or married versus single, but for the most part, that's their market. So, their path would be fairly simple:

- Understand how young women in those demographics are using mobile technology.
- Understand the potential paths these women might take on their journey to becoming Forever 21 customers.
- Use what you know about their device preferences and mobile behaviors to determine how you might best connect with them throughout this journey to speed their conversion from shopper to buyer to loyal advocate.

Unfortunately, it won't be this easy for most brands. Most will have a more diverse array of customers that necessitate development of multiple technographic *segments*. So, let's look at a simplified process for doing so based on a hypothetical brand example.

Note: A *segment* is a classification of a group of customers according to specific demographic characteristics and/or behaviors they share.

Assess Your Mobile Technographics

Kiwi Market (a fictional U.S. brand created for illustrative purposes throughout this book that has no connection to the Kiwi Market located at Rruga Deshmoret E Kombit, 1234, Mitrovice, Czech Republic) is a small, upscale supermarket chain looking to develop a strategy for mobile and a method to roll out the tactics it will need to support the strategy. Kiwi Market has a small amount of internal market research and has assessed its desktop website traffic, all of which have yielded information about its customers as shown in Table 2.1.

▶ **Table 2.1** Kiwi Market Internal Market Research Findings

Category	Segment	Percentage
Sex	Female	65%
	Male	35%
Age	18–25	10%
	25–35	20%
	35–45	50%
	45 and up	20%
HHI	$35K or less	12%
	$35K–50K	15%
	$50K–75K	25%
	$75K+	48%
Devices	iOS (iPhone and iPod touch)	51%
	iPad	7%
	Android	20%
	BlackBerry	14%
	Other	8%

Traffic to the Kiwi Market desktop website from mobile devices spikes in the evenings and on weekends.

Based on this data, Kiwi Market has a good sense of who its customers are—mostly female, heavily iOS smartphone users, and somewhat affluent. This is valuable information, but it is still insufficient information on which to actually base a strategy and to determine what tactics will best support it. So, Kiwi Market decides to dig a bit deeper and invest in some additional research.

What Kiwi Market really needs to know is *how* these people use mobile devices in their customer journey. To accomplish this task, the Kiwi Market marketing team purchased subscriptions to comScore and eMarketer and gathered some additional data about the specific behavior of U.S. mobile users:

- Android and iPhone users over-index on use of the mobile web and mobile apps.
- BlackBerry users over-index on mobile email and instant messaging (IM).
- iPhone ownership is fairly well spread out across all ages and income ranges, but is most concentrated with people in the 35 to 45 age bracket and $75K+ HHI range.
- Android users skew slightly more male than iPhone users.
- iPad users are evenly split between men and women but skew heavily higher income—almost exclusively $75K+.

Now, Kiwi Market knows more about how U.S. consumers in general use their mobile devices, but they would still like to know more about how its customers in particular use mobile devices. So, Kiwi Market decides to take its research one step further and conduct a survey of their current customers to learn more about their habits. The marketing team develops a simple SurveyMonkey questionnaire and sends it out to the store's list of opted-in customers via email. The questionnaire asks customers to define themselves with some basic demographic data:

- Are you male or female?
- Please indicate your age range.
- Please indicate your household income.
- Please indicate your marital status.
- Please indicate your education level.
- Are there children under 18 in your home?
- What type of mobile device do you own?
- Do you use your mobile device for activities besides phone calls?

For users who don't use their device for anything beyond voice calls, the survey ends there. For those who use their device for other tasks, the survey goes on to ask a more complex series of questions, such as:

- Do you use your mobile device to access the Kiwi Market website?
- If yes, what types of content/information are you looking for?

The questionnaire goes on to ask customers specific questions about their mobile habits, such as: Do they use apps? What do they think about how the current Kiwi Market website functions on their device? Do they use SMS? Scan QR codes? Access Facebook? Redeem coupons?

Customers who finish the questionnaire are given a coupon for $25 off their next purchase—an incentive that results in 300 responses out of 2,500 emails sent. This low-cost (less than $8,000) research method yields a highly refined set of verified data that Kiwi Market would have been hard pressed to develop any other way.

Develop Customer Segments

At this point, Kiwi Market has collected a significant amount of information about its customers' mobile habits. To truly understand how this data translates into actionable strategy and tactics, Kiwi Market needs to refine this data into a picture of their target customer/s.

The easiest way to do so is to take the data and break it down into *segments*—high-level classifications of customers in groups based on common defining characteristics and behaviors. For Kiwi Market, the segments would be:

Moms 30s to 40s This group includes high-income, well-educated household decision makers who see their smartphones as the remote control for their lives. These women are super-sophisticated mobile users. They send frequent text messages, are loyal app users, familiar with QR codes, and open to receiving and redeeming coupons on their devices.

Moms 50+ These women are also household decision makers and share the same income bracket as the previous segment, but skew differently in their use of mobile. Many own smartphones, but limit their use of mobile primarily to voice calls and text messaging, making their use of mobile primarily utilitarian.

Single Professionals 30s to 40s These customers are high-income, well-educated professionals shopping primarily for themselves. They're also highly sophisticated mobile users, own smartphones and tablets, and engage in the same behaviors as Moms in the same age group.

There is a tiny percentage of customers who don't fit into any of these categories, but the majority can be neatly consigned to one of these three buckets. Based on the synthesized research, Kiwi Market has determined that the ratio of customers among these three key segments looks like this:

- 57 percent Moms 30s to 40s
- 19 percent Single professionals 30s to 40s
- 15 percent Moms 50s+
- 9 percent Other

Because a dominant percentage of customers are high-end device owners who exhibit highly sophisticated mobile behaviors, Kiwi Market now knows that it can safely invest in more sophisticated tactics such as a mobile website, apps, QR codes, and mobile coupons.

Translate Segments into Personas and Journeys

Segments are valuable in that they help you narrow down what you can do in order to reach your key customer groups effectively. *Personas* take this to the next level with an archetypal customer profile that is based on a segment. A persona essentially models a segment into a fictional person, one that you can actually visualize moving through all the actions that a real customer would perform.

To create a persona, you take the segment data and anthropomorphize it, giving the person a name, gender, and life circumstances that match up to the information you've collected. This process enables you to develop an understanding of your customers in human a way that the more abstract segment cannot. The 30s to 40s Mom is still an abstract concept. It's easier to visualize the customer journey of Michelle, as we've done in Figure 2.10, the 43-year-old lawyer and working parent of two who stops by her local Kiwi Market to pick up supper on her way home several times a week and regularly orders groceries to be delivered.

Michelle—The Mobile Mom

Michelle is a 43-year-old corporate lawyer and mother of a ten-year-old boy and an eight-year-old girl.

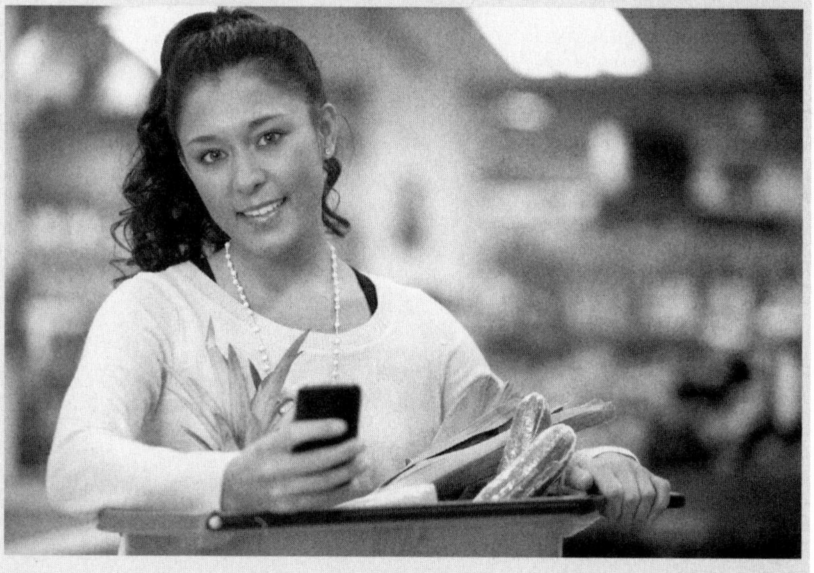

She loves to cook and considers herself an amateur gourmet, but her time in the kitchen is limited to Saturday and Sunday given her busy work schedule. She orders groceries delivered from Kiwi Market on Friday evenings so she can prepare and freeze meals over the weekend for her family to enjoy throughout the coming week. However, she also orders takeout once or twice per week and occasionally stops into Kiwi to pick up prepared meals.

Needs Statement

"I want my family to eat well, but my time to shop and cook for us is very limited."

Demographics

Age: 43

Gender: Female

Family Status: Married

Education: B.A., J.D.

Occupation: Law

HHI: $175K

Location: Urban

Technographics

Apple iPhone 4S

Frequent SMS

Mobile email user

Uses mobile apps for a variety of purposes including shopping, news, banking, games, to-do lists, and fitness tracking

Daily Facebook user

Occasional Twitter user

Does not use local apps like foursquare or Yelp

Goals and Challenges

Indulge her passion for cooking

Feed her family delicious, high quality meals

Eat organic as much as possible

Streamline her weekly grocery shopping process

Plan ahead more efficiently for the nights she'll defrost and serve a home-cooked meal and the nights her family will order out

Keep track of the nutritional value and calorie/fat/sodium value of the takeout and prepared meals they order

Once you've created a persona or, in most cases, multiple personas, you are ready to map out the customer journey. The customer journey takes the stages of the purchase funnel—awareness, engagement, consideration, conversion, and loyalty—and illustrates them on a more detailed level, filling in the possible ways in which these phases might occur and the actions the customer and brand might take to connect with one another. We've visualized a sample journey in the map in Figure 2.10.

Your initial goal is to understand the phases and the various ways in which mobile might help the customer progress from one phase to the next, so keep your options open and brainstorm as many possibilities as you can. The rest of this book will lead you through an explanation of these tactics that will enable you to determine those that are workable and those that are not.

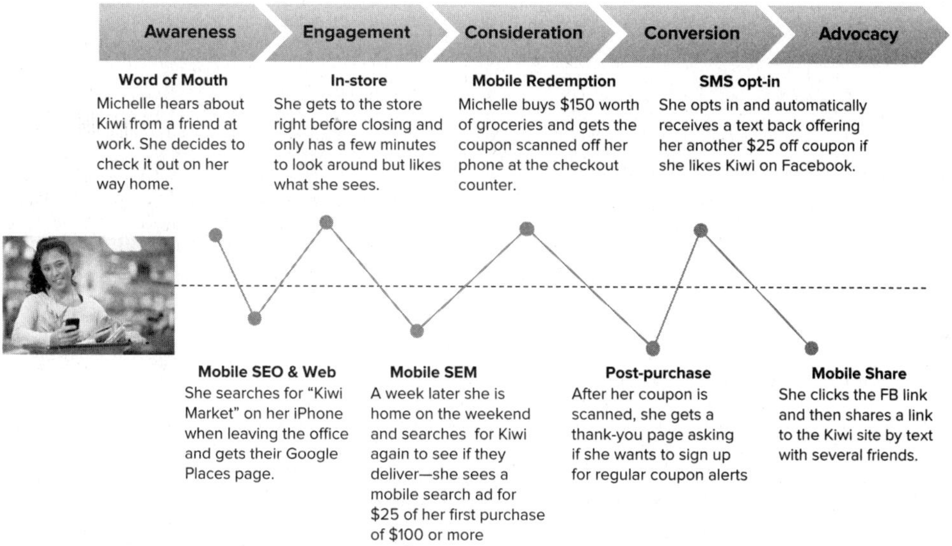

Figure 2.10 Sample customer journey map

If all of that activity sounds time-consuming, then you're on target. The upfront work involved in developing your mobile strategy requires a lot of heavy lifting, but the more conscientious you are about collecting the right data, the better off you'll be once you begin formulating your strategy.

Thursday: Evaluate Your Mobile Presence and Benchmark Your Mobile Readiness

By this point, you've done a tremendous amount of the heavy lifting involved in developing your mobile strategy, but there are still a few key activities left to address. It's very important to have an internal benchmark of your current perceived level of usefulness to, usability for, and overall engagement with mobile consumers. Even if you haven't yet executed a single mobile tactic, *do not skip this step*. It will reveal opportunities you might not otherwise uncover. If you do focus groups and customer interviews, you'll get lots of valuable feedback on how your brand is performing in the mobile space, but you can't rely entirely on this. Customers might not be able to fully articulate areas in which your brand may be weak. For example, a customer interview could tell you a lot about how findable your website is in *natural* mobile search results, but the customer is unlikely to notice your visibility or lack thereof in *paid* mobile search results. Point being, customer insights are invaluable, yet there are some things the customer just won't clearly see—but you will.

It's equally important to look at your entire marketing mix from a holistic viewpoint and think hard about where you can use mobile to improve your efforts. Examining your own internal plans for online and offline marketing, branding, advertising, and other types of promotions may unearth opportunities to enhance them with mobile integration. Likewise, you must understand what your competitors are doing. Assessing their performance in the mobile space will tell you the table stakes: the essential tactics, content, and features that customers like yours have come to expect. It can also reveal opportunities to innovate. For example, if your research has told you that your customers are asking for a certain product or feature and none of your competitors has implemented something similar, that could be your opportunity to gain a first-mover advantage. Both these steps are essential homework for your mobile strategy and will probably be the easiest and most enjoyable part of the whole process, so don't skip them!

Benchmark Your Current Mobile Readiness

If you've engaged in any form of primary research, you should have a fairly good sense of how easy it is for your customers to engage with you on their platforms of choice, but there's still some additional assessment you need to do to determine your current level of *mobile readiness*—how useful, usable, findable, and engaging you are to mobile users. At this point, you've developed your customer journey (or journeys) so you should now have the opportunity to look at your brand through this lens.

We recommend that you break down the journeys by phase and conduct a first-hand assessment that answers a few key questions for each phase. Think like a customer and answers questions such as:

Awareness

Can you find your website via mobile search?

Have you included appropriate mobile awareness elements on your desktop website? For example, a page dedicated to showcasing your mobile site, applications, and any other mobile programs?

Are there opportunities to insert mobile calls to action in your traditional (TV, print, direct) and digital media campaigns?

Engagement

Can you access your website on key mobile device platforms such as iOS, Android, and BlackBerry?

Can you engage with your print, out-of-home, digital-out-of-home, TV, and other offline media via mobile?

Consideration

Can you access vital content via your website on the aforementioned key mobile device platforms?

Can you perform important information-gathering functions on your website using a mobile device: get pricing, view photos, compare products, or contact customer service for information?

Can you utilize your mobile device to act on calls to action in your digital and traditional campaigns?

Conversion

Can you use your mobile device to purchase, become a member, sign up for more information, or convert in some other way?

Loyalty

Can you easily share information about your brand via key channels such as mobile email or SMS?

When viewed on a mobile device, does your site allow you to like your brand or products on Facebook? Post them to Twitter or Google+?

Assessing your strengths and weaknesses in these key areas will ensure you cover all of your bases from your customers' perspective and from your internal perspective of what you have planned for your brand.

Develop and Assess Competitive Insights

Once you have assessed your level of mobile-readiness, your next step is to assess the mobile readiness of your closest competitors. This analysis enables you to finalize the table stakes of your mobile strategy, the must-have tactics, content, and features customers will expect. It also will enable you to find opportunities to do things your competitors aren't doing, creating a powerful first-mover advantage for your brand.

In the example in Figure 2.11, we've illustrated a high-level *competitive analysis* in which Kiwi Market vets the basic mobile tactics available to them against the efforts of their three closest competitors.

Note: Include at least three to five competitors in your analysis, if possible.

Feature	Importance	Spuntina Organic	Simonetti's Market	Greenblatt's Gourmet Foods	Kiwi Market
Mobile website	High	●	○	○	○
Smartphone touch site	High	●	○	○	○
Tablet site	Low	○	○	○	○
Mobile search visibility	High	●	○	○	◢
Mobile SEM	High	○	○	○	○
Mobile advertising	Low	●	○	○	○
Native mobile apps	Medium	●	●	N/A	○
SMS	High	○	○	○	○
Location-based marketing	Medium	○	○	○	○
Mobile/Social marketing	High	○	○	○	○

● Tactic executed with a high level of detail and sophistication
◓ Tactic executed with a moderate level of detail and sophistication
◢ Tactic executed with a minimal level of detail and sophistication
○ Tactic not in use at this time

Figure 2.11 Sample high-level competitive analysis

Once the initial competitive analysis of high-level tactics is complete, we recommend drilling down and analyzing the mobile site efforts of your competitors who have web-based mobile content. We've provided a sample analysis in Figure 2.12. It's a given 99.9 percent of the time that the mobile web will be the foremost element of your strategy and assessing your competitors' mobile site according to features and content will help greatly in building and/or improving your own.

Feature	Importance	Spuntina Organic	Simonetti's Market	Greenblatt's Gourmet Foods	Kiwi Market
Product inventory	High	●	●	●	○
Product images	Moderate	●	●	●	○
Rich UI/HTML5	High	○	●	○	○
Automatic location detection	High	●	●	●	○
Product pricing	Moderate	○	○	●	○
Weekly specials	High	●	●	●	○
Coupons	High	●	●	○	○
Store finder	High	○	●	●	○
Store hours	High	●	●	●	○
Customer assistance	High	●	●	○	○
Social sharing	High	○	●	○	○

● Feature executed with a high level of detail and sophistication
◓ Feature executed with a moderate level of detail and sophistication
◢ Feature executed with a minimal level of detail and sophistication
○ Feature not in place at this time

Figure 2.12 Sample site-specific competitive analysis

Identify the Unique Mobile Opportunities for Your Brand

Finally, you are ready to refine your strategy and select the right combination of tactics to connect successfully with your customers. In this last section, we'll guide you through the process of mapping tactics to your personas and corresponding customer journeys. We'll also provide recommendations as to how to build your business case for mobile within your organization, based on what you learned this week.

Define Your Strategic Imperative

As we discussed in the introduction to this chapter, the strategic imperative lies squarely in the overlap between your business goals, your customers' needs, and what the marketplace and competitive environment dictate. In the case of Kiwi Market, the brand goals are pretty clear: to bring more customers into the store and keep them coming back, whether they buy groceries or prepared gourmet meals. For customers like Michelle, who represents Kiwi Market's largest demographic, there are many goals, but they all boil down to the same essential overarching need—make the shopping experience easier.

- **Business Goals:** increase sales and loyalty
- **Customer Goals:** easier shopping experience

From here, we're able to synthesize a high-level strategic direction:
Mobile as a shopping companion and mealtime planning tool

Map Out Your Mobile Tactics

Now that your strategic imperative is in place, you are finally ready to define your tactical plan. While this was probably an intensely intimidating thought at the beginning of this process, by this point you know:

- What your goals for mobile are
- Whom you are trying to reach
- What they want and need
- What your competitors are doing
- What tactics are available
- What content and resources you can leverage

With these resources at hand, we recommend that you gather together all of the tactics you've identified as being important and put them through a process of weighted prioritization. For each tactic, you'll assess how it stacks up in priority against several key criteria. What these criteria are exactly will be unique to your brand, but some common examples are:

- How valuable is this feature to your customers?
- How instrumental will it be to achieving your brand goals?

- How cost effective will it be to implement?
- How much of a competitive edge (or parity) will it give you?

...and so forth. Each tactic should receive a score of 1-5 for each question, with 1 being the least favorable score and 5 being the most favorable. When the total scores for each tactic are tallied up, the highest scoring tactics will have the greatest priority, as shown in Figure 2.13.

Tactic	Importance to customers	Ability to drive in-store sales	Ability to drive online sales	Ease of execution (5 easiest- 1 hardest)	Final weighted score
Mobile website	5	5	3	2	15
Mobile search engine optimization	5	5	3	2	15
Mobile search engine marketing	3	3	2	3	11
Opt-in SMS alerts	3	3	2	3	11
Mobile Application	3	2	3	1	9
QR codes in-store	2	2	1	2	7

- 15-20 primary priority tactic
- 10-15 secondary tactic
- 5-10 tertiary tactic

Figure 2.13 Weighted prioritization of mobile tactics

Once you've gone through this final prioritization process, your tactical goals will be well validated and crystal clear. In Figure 2.14, we show a visual segmentation of mobile tactics based on *weighted prioritization* and mapped to Kiwi Market's top three demographics.

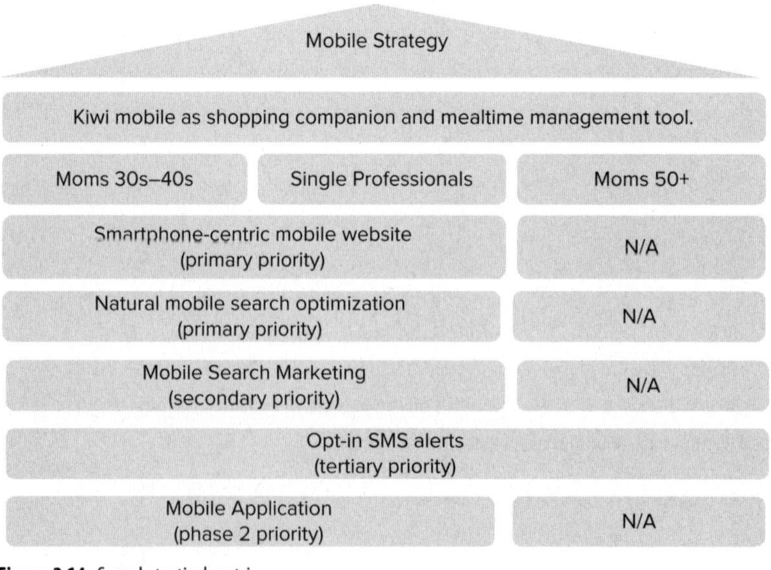

Figure 2.14 Sample tactical matrix

Friday: Create a Business Case for Mobile within Your Organization

At long last, you have a strategy and tactics based on an understanding of your brand goals, what your customers want and need, and what the environment dictates. That's a lot of heavy lifting in a week, but you're not done yet! In many (if not most) cases, you will have to take all of this information and convince others within your organization that you've done your homework and have a solid strategic and executional direction. In all honesty, to really tell you how to do this, we'd have to write another book. Because there are so many variables that could factor into your success (or lack thereof), we can't promise you a blueprint that will work, but we can make a few suggestions that will help.

Plot Your Mobile Plan

At this point, you know what you want to do and why you want to do it, but you still have to determine what's possible logistically. This is where you start to estimate budget and cost, and a lot of that will depend on what you are able to execute internally and what you need to outsource. We have included lengthy lists of well-known vendors for various mobile tactics, such as SMS, mobile testing, and so forth, in the appendix for this book; we'll keep them up-to-date on the website companion to this book, `www.mobileanhouraday.com`. These lists will be helpful to you as you begin selecting partners to help you execute your strategy.

Figuring out what you'll do internally and what you will partner for will take some time, but it will help you with your final prioritization of tactics. Ideally, you'll want to move forward with the highest priority tactics on your list first. However, the costs involved in outsourcing and the availability of internal content and technical resources may influence how certain tactics are emphasized or deemphasized.

We find that a visual calendar of desired tactics and their interdependencies is an excellent tool for formalizing a blueprint. Figure 2.15 illustrates Kiwi Market's initial roadmap for mobile.

What Is a Roadmap?

A roadmap is a set of planned tactics arranged according to the timeframe for execution. A roadmap is often represented visually in a calendar format showing the planned start and end dates of each task and where it overlaps and/or affects other tasks on the list. This kind of visual often includes brief notes on the particulars of each task and is very helpful in showing the bigger picture of your mobile blueprint.

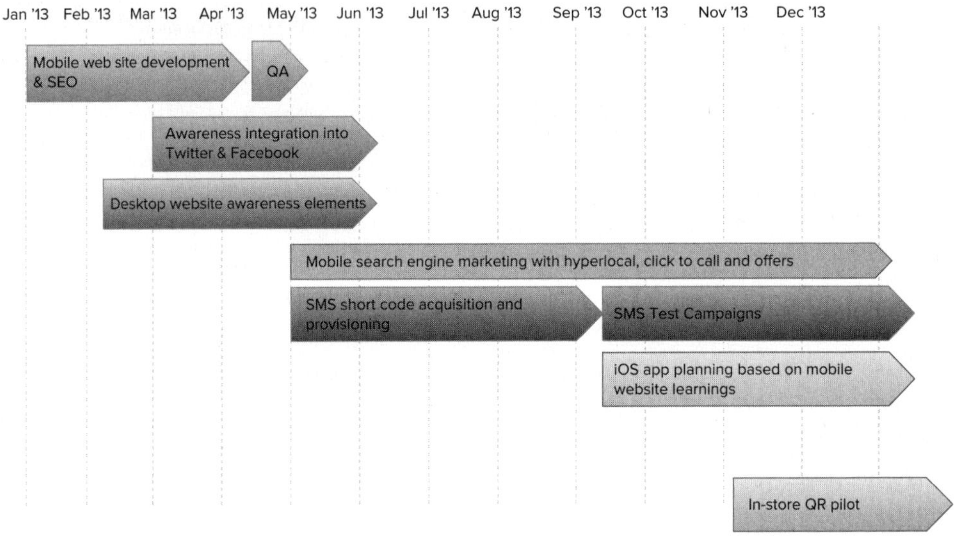

Figure 2.15 Sample mobile roadmap

Build Your Mobile Business Case

In most situations, unless you are the final decision maker or a sole proprietor, you will have to petition higher-ups within your organization (such as your CEO, CMO, CFO, or other senior company officer) to sign off on your plans and allocate the budget you need. Here are a few guiding principles that will help in the process.

Emphasize the percentage of mobile traffic to your site. Most of the brands we spoke to while writing this book have seen the mobile traffic to their websites increase to account for roughly 15 to 20 percent of all visits in 2012. If you can prove to the decision makers within your organization that 15 to 20 percent of your customers are actively engaged with your website on mobile devices, that is going to make them sit up and take notice.

Emphasize the competitive landscape. While we discourage you from making decisions on what to do with mobile based on what you see your competitors doing, the competitive landscape can be very useful in making your mobile business case internally. If your closest competitors are doing great things in mobile, the final decision makers will be more likely to green light your efforts if they feel it's going to help them maintain parity in the marketplace. If your competitors aren't doing anything, all the better, since you can then position your mobile plans as a chance to get a first-mover advantage.

Approach mobile as an ROI exercise. We think it's smart to approach your mobile tactics with return on investment (ROI) in mind. If you clearly establish the benefits you expect a particular tactic to yield, it will be that much easier to justify investment in your efforts from those who control the cash flow. The formulas you use to calculate ROI for your mobile plans will vary greatly and depend on the tactic in question (and in some cases may get pretty complex), but there will always be a way to figure it out. We'll discuss ways in which you can calculate ROI for a tactic, when possible, in subsequent chapters. For now, just remember, if you can't assign a positive ROI of some kind to something you want to do, you probably shouldn't be doing it.

In Conclusion

According to Heraclitus, the Greek philosopher, the only constant is change, and that's as true in today's digital marketing landscape as it was when he said it over two thousand years ago. We don't know what new opportunities will come our way courtesy of Apple, Google, or some as-yet-unknown startup. What we can do is understand our customers and prepare a strategic plan for interacting with them in real time. As we expressed in the introduction to this book, mobile is not about devices but about creating and fostering real-time relationships with your customers. The devices will change, and change rapidly, so it is the concept of enabling real-time relationships that should remain at the core of everything you do.

In the next chapter, we'll look at how to take the first steps toward executing your mobile strategy with building mobile websites.

Week 2: Start Simple—SMS

Getting started with SMS makes sense for the simple reason that regardless of phone type, demographic, or geography, nearly everyone texts. Remember the ITU statistic from Chapter 1, "Map the Mobile Opportunity?" Almost 200,000 texts are sent every second *around the world. Because texting is an integral way that mobile users communicate, it should find a place in your marketing campaigns. It may not be glamorous, but it is efficient and effective, and it continues to engage consumers. As a basic marketing support mechanism, SMS has many use cases, from advertising to customer support to loyalty.*

3

Chapter Contents

Learn where, how, when, and why to use SMS
Determine business considerations
Define your partners
Integrate SMS into your overall marketing strategy
Manage and measure your mobile messaging campaigns

Monday: Learn Where, How, When, and Why to Use SMS

It's Monday and that means it's time to begin focusing on where, when, how, and why to implement *short message service (SMS)*, the mobile channel with the broadest reach. As we discussed in the last chapter, it's vital to first have a strategic framework so you'll know where SMS fits within your overall marketing plan. We'll share our own expertise, as well as what we learned by talking with the following experts:

- Greg Sterling, founding principal of Sterling Market Intelligence and contributing editor for the online publication *Search Engine Land* (`www.searchengineland.com`)
- Jeff Hasen, chief marketing officer (CMO) of Hipcricket
- Tom Daly, global group director, mobile and search, connections planning at Coca-Cola

You'll hear from Greg, Jeff, and Tom throughout this chapter.

Remember the fictional Kiwi Market in the last chapter? We spent a good portion of that week determining which mobile channels and tactics applied to our "client" and how to use them to maximize our strategic goal of making Kiwi a better shopping companion and mealtime management tool. SMS, we concluded, was a central mechanism for reaching all three of our target segments and was important at every stage of the purchase funnel, from engagement to advocacy. (Flip back to Figure 2.10 for a refresher on the sample customer journey.)

So, let's start to look in more detail at the SMS implementation process. It's worth reviewing a bit of history on the evolution of SMS before we jump into the context you'll need to get started.

Evolution of SMS as a Marketing Medium

The first commercial deployments of SMS date to 1993, but SMS didn't achieve popularity in the United States until a decade later. As both a personal communication medium and a marketing channel, SMS owes its ascent to the second season of television talent show *American Idol*, in 2003. By this point, texting was already widespread outside of the United States, in countries where pay-as-you-go calling predominated, and consumers latched onto SMS as a more cost-effective way to communicate than voice. In the United States, by contrast, monthly subscription plans with large buckets of voice minutes were (and still are) the norm, which gave consumers little incentive to pay for additional communications services such as SMS.

That all changed when AT&T came aboard as an *American Idol* sponsor, and the show incorporated texting into the voting process. Bear in mind that the show was already a ratings juggernaut by its second season. According to Nielsen, it reached an average of 21.7 million viewers per episode and consistently ranked in the top ten most-viewed programs each week. Moreover, and perhaps most crucially for its impact on SMS, that season, *American Idol* ranked second among the 18 to 49 demographic, which, as we saw in Chapter 1, now comprises the population of heaviest texters. The 2003 *American Idol* campaign generated 7.5 million text messages according to AT&T. Overall, messaging volumes have grown exponentially since then and rose 2,744 percent between 2005 (the first year CTIA—The Wireless Association began tracking SMS volumes on an annualized basis) and 2011.

As adoption climbed, marketer opportunities emerged. Prior to the days of widespread smartphone penetration, SMS enjoyed a lot of currency as an advertising delivery method. Remember industry expert Greg Sterling, founding principal of Sterling Market Intelligence? You first encountered him in Chapter 1. Greg offers this perspective on SMS advertising: "Once upon a time, that was the broad reach mechanism."

Here's how it worked: Mobile users subscribed to alerts for time-sensitive information such as sports scores and breaking news. Some of these alert services were paid subscriptions and others were free and ad-supported. In the free alert messages, advertisers purchased media space and thus were able to capitalize on both users' interests and their desire for up-to-the-minute information.

The rise of smartphones and the availability of apps, either paid or free (often supported by in-app display ads), has helped shift the norm of information consumption from *push* to *pull*. This shift toward an on-demand model has put a major dent in SMS as an advertising medium. Yes, feature phone users may still subscribe to such services; and yes, they may add value for specific audiences, such as commodity prices delivered to farmers, for example. Overall, however, with the user population trending decisively toward smartphones, as you saw in Chapter 1, the market for SMS-based ads is destined to wane. "Now, there are so many other, richer ways to present brand messages," Greg adds.

As an advertising channel, the importance of SMS may be ebbing, but as a marketing medium, the opposite is true. In truth, a number of related factors have actually enhanced SMS's appeal to marketers. Notes Greg: "For the same reason agencies were initially hesitant about paid search—the limit to 160 characters, no images, just text—there was similar resistance to using SMS. There were also stringent carrier rules [for setting up and managing campaigns] and, in the past, before consumers had unlimited texting plans, there was also the notion that consumers might be paying to receive an ad, so there were a number of built-in inhibitors."

Carrier rules remain in effect, as we'll discuss later in the chapter on Wednesday. But with texting by now a nearly universal mobile communication mechanism and most consumers enjoying large bundles of or unlimited messages, many of the other inhibitors have dropped away.

This means SMS not only can but also should retain a place within your marketing mix—and a consistent one at that. Jeff Hasen, chief marketing officer of mobile marketing services firm Hipcricket and author of *Mobilized Marketing: How to Drive Sales, Engagement, and Loyalty Through Mobile Devices* (John Wiley & Sons, Inc., 2012), charts the evolution as follows: "The biggest change we've seen since the mid-2000s is that the idea of the 'one-off' campaign is loudly discouraged. I tie it back to the difference between doing SMS for SMS's sake and looking for a bigger goal, which is to drive people into a loyalty club, into a database, into an opportunity to remarket to them." Jeff should know: As of July 2012, Hipcricket had developed over 200,000 mobile marketing campaigns for brands such as Macy's, Miller, Coors, Nestlé, and Clear Channel.

Getting Started with the Basics

The common thread that ties the fictional Kiwi Market experience with these real-world examples is the emphasis on solutions that attract and engage audiences, and then enable marketers to retarget them. Success comes from identifying hand-raisers, determining their interests, enticing them to opt into your database, and keeping them satisfied with the right offers or information delivered with the right frequency.

Remember the space you have available is at a premium—SMS is limited to 160 characters—so your focus on your objectives needs to be razor-sharp. To hone in on what you want to achieve, think about not only the current opportunity before you but also future opportunities—how you can engage your audience today, then grow and reengage that same audience a month or year from now. It's a question of integrating your near-term and long-term goals.

Ask yourself: What about the time-sensitive offer I want to distribute will make it possible, even likely, that I will attract an interested customer? What do I have to do as a follow-up to maintain his or her loyalty? How can I delight that customer to the point he or she will become an advocate for my brand and help me market my products?

One part of the answer to these questions lies in the basics of marketing, like having a compelling offer and a clear call-to-action. Another part of it lies in the unique qualities of digital and, specifically, mobile marketing—the ability to target and segment by geography, demographics, and behavioral preferences.

That said; don't think about using SMS in a vacuum. The trick is to consider it as one of a number of coordinated mobile tactics. Jeff cites the example of Hipcricket client Macy's, which started out with an SMS-focused strategy designed to build its database. Since the advent of its in-store Backstage Pass marketing program in early 2011, Macy's has broadened its efforts to include *multimedia messaging service (MMS)*, which we'll discuss in more detail later on Monday; *quick response (QR) codes*, which we'll talk about in Chapter 9, "Week 8: Drive Awareness with Ambient Media"; and the mobile web, which we'll cover in Chapter 4, "Week 3: Maximize Reach with mobile websites." Jeff observes, "We're past the point where brands can issue a call-to-action and give consumers just one way to engage. We have to provide every consumer the option to engage on his or her terms."

Providing multiple options is a consideration that goes beyond simply your mobile marketing. SMS, for example, can also work wonders both for and with your traditional and static media. We've all experienced the emotional rush from a well-crafted TV spot or a beautifully shot print ad in a favorite publication. At the same time, we also know the call-to-action associated with ads in traditional and static media is often diluted by the lag time between seeing the ad and being in a position to act on it (not to mention our ability to recall the message at that later point).

Because most mobile-enabled consumers keep their device at hand at all times, take advantage of that ubiquity. Think about activating your existing media or product packaging by including a short code.

What Is a Short Code?

A *short code* (also known as a *common short code*) is a five- or six-digit number to which text messages can be sent. Short codes are the basis of mobile marketing campaigns—they are the conduit for consumers to interact with your brand via SMS. In the United States, short codes can be leased from the *Common Short Code Administration (CSCA)* www.usshortcodes.com/. Note that the CSCA is administered by Neustar (www.neustar.biz).

Short codes can be randomly assigned, or you can request a vanity number that ties into your brand to make it easier to remember. For example, for SMS-based search queries, Google has locked up the short code 46645, which spells "GOOGL" on a traditional telephone keypad. In something of an exception to industry convention, Coca-Cola uses 2653, which spells "COKE" (Coca-Cola got its short code very early on). We'll talk more about the ins and outs of short codes and working with the CSCA and wireless carriers on Wednesday.

Adding a short code to, for example, a print ad you've already paid for doesn't cost you anything and voilà, you've given a reader a mechanism to respond to the ad—to get more information about your product, sign up for your club, or whatever action you'd like to promote. All of a sudden, it's gone from being a static message to one that's actionable. It's all about starting the conversation in as friction-free a way possible and then building on that engagement so your customers become your advocates. We'll talk more about integrating SMS into your broader marketing strategy on Thursday.

As you learned in Chapter 2, "Week 1: Develop Your Mobile Strategy," no one uses SMS more effectively or with greater consistency than Coca-Cola. The world's largest soft drink manufacturer understands implicitly the benefits of utilizing the most basic mobile channel to achieve the broadest possible reach. Tom Daly (Coca-Cola's global group director, mobile and search, connections planning) often cites SMS as a cornerstone of his company's mobile strategy. He explains it this way: "The value of SMS lies in its ubiquity. It's the one technology, other than voice, that can be used by every mobile subscriber." He adds: "For a brand like Coke, with a clear global perspective about what it stands for and a legacy of using global platforms to tell our stories (everything from the Olympics to FIFA World Cup and more), the uniform reach and experience of SMS is unmatched."

But like Jeff's Macy's example, Coca-Cola offers its customers multiple channels through which to experience the brand. For example, Coke tags its product packaging—under individual caps and inside tear-offs on multipacks—with codes that consumers can text to get rewards points, enter sweepstakes, play games, and even pay for a beverage in some countries. Texting a code from a bottle cap requires minimal effort, and the opportunity to rack up points ties into the gamification trend—injecting an element of competition into everyday activities. The MyCokeRewards website (pictured in Figure 2.2) is the central point for registering and managing your points, but Coke offers a mobile-optimized website, as well, thereby effectively covering all of its bases and ensuring a seamless interaction between offline, online, and mobile.

For the 2012 Summer Olympics in London, for which Coke is a worldwide sponsor, the company aimed even higher. "We've integrated SMS as a way to move people through an experience that is real-world and digital, mobile and desktop, and localized by country," Tom says.

The takeaway is that SMS is a proven engagement mechanism—it's just not the only one. Think of it more as a team effort, where each tactic plays a unique and important role. Skim back to the sample customer journey map depicted in Figure 2.10 to see what we're talking about. Ignore SMS at your own peril, but also assess how you can use it to connect your audience to richer experiences.

What About Multimedia Messaging Service (MMS)?

MMS, created in 2001 as a more sophisticated cousin to SMS, enables consumers—and marketers—to send and receive embedded audio, pictures, and video clips in a messaging format not subject to the same 160-character limit as SMS.

Yet despite the proliferation of MMS-capable, camera-equipped mobile phones (virtually all new phones come equipped with a camera, even if the sophistication varies widely), MMS has not caught on to nearly the same degree as SMS. Part of the reason is carriers were slow in offering full MMS capabilities to their subscribers.

According to CTIA—The Wireless Association (`www.ctia.org`), U.S. mobile users sent 53 billion MMS messages in 2011, compared to just over 2.3 trillion SMS messages. In fact, after several years of steep increases, MMS volume saw its first decline in 2011, as listed next.

▶ U.S. MMS Message Volume, 2005–2011

Year	MMS Messages (billions)
2005	1
2006	3
2007	6
2008	15
2009	35
2010	57
2011	53

Source: CTIA—The Wireless Association, "Semi-Annual Wireless Industry Survey," April 2012

Even if MMS is not a mobile activity for the masses, one of its benefits is the ability to deliver a rich experience to feature phones and smartphones alike. In other words, it is not another case where the good stuff is reserved solely for those with smartphones.

You may be limited, however, by the fact not all *SMS aggregators* (we'll discuss them in more detail tomorrow) support MMS on every carrier. If you are considering MMS as part of a campaign, make the level of aggregator support one of your evaluation criteria. For your campaign planning, you may also want to look to firms such as Iris Mobile and Mogreet that specialize in rich-media messaging. Whatever your choice, be sure to temper your expectations. "We include MMS as part of a portfolio of services," explains Jeff, "but not as a standalone because you can't rely on enough people to participate that way."

Tuesday: Determine Business Considerations

Now, you have a good sense of where and how you might use SMS. The next step is learning the rules of the road, and this is one road that actually has a lot of rules.

Get Permission

Because mobile devices are so personal for most consumers, receiving marketing messages on them is akin to inviting your brand into their home. With that metaphor in mind, it's pretty obvious you won't be able to build a relationship with customers if you start things off by barging in the door. For the relationship to work—and grow—you have to be invited in and continuously prove your worth. As Jeff Hasen, Hipcricket's CMO, says, "The first thing you want to do is make sure you follow the *opt-in* guidelines. Invite people to opt in and provide clear language for how they can *opt out*."

That's step 1 in building a lasting relationship. Get permission, demonstrate reciprocal value, and loyalty will follow over time. Adds Jeff, "The number-one thing a marketer needs to know is consumers will participate if they believe they are in control." This advice resonates. It's almost axiomatic that people tend to be more open to marketing messages when they've made the choice to receive those messages in the first place.

These guidelines probably sound reminiscent of basic email marketing best practices. There's a simple explanation for that: No one wants to repeat the early excesses of email, which saw a flourishing spam trade and subsequent damage to email's reputation as a marketing medium. Regulations such as CAN-SPAM have since helped curb—but by no means eliminate—the spam problem. In mandating stringent double *opt-in* guidelines for SMS campaigns, the Mobile Marketing Association (MMA) (`www.mmaglobal.com`), the global trade body that oversees mobile marketing and its related technologies, hoped to prevent spam from the start.

Opt-In and Double Opt-In Guidelines

The MMA put stringent opt-in guidelines in place early on to prevent fraud and abuse, specifically to ensure mobile subscribers understood when and how much they would be charged to participate in an SMS or MMS campaign. These guidelines are the hallmark of message-based marketing and advertising campaigns.

Here are short summaries of single and double opt-in recommendations, but you should study and follow to the letter the numerous cross-carrier standards and individual Tier 1 carrier (AT&T, Sprint, T-Mobile, and Verizon) policies the MMA provides in *U.S. Consumer Best Practices* (available for download from `www.mmaglobal.com/uploads/Consumer-Best-Practices.pdf`). This lengthy (over 160 pages in its most recent iteration) tome is updated annually.

Single Opt-In

When a mobile subscriber sends a message to your short code indicating interest in opting into your campaign or program, per MMA guidelines, you must send a reply containing the following information: "Service description; additional carrier costs (e.g., Msg&Data Rates May Apply); frequency of messaging; customer support information (HELP); and opt-out information (STOP)." Single opt-in guidelines apply to most standard-rate campaigns, meaning the regular rate a subscriber pays on a per-message basis or when a message is deducted from a monthly bundle.

Double Opt-In

The guidelines are stricter if you provide a fee-based service. For example, imagine you're offering a sports scores alert service that costs subscribers $4.99 per month in addition to *standard messaging costs* (known as a *premium-rate campaign*). When a subscriber opts into your service, your first message back should clearly delineate the costs (both standard and premium) for participation and prompt the subscriber to reply in the affirmative ("YES" or some variant such as "OK" [the MMA provides guidelines on acceptable responses]). This is the double opt-in, designed to protect subscribers (and, by extension, the carriers) from paying for something they don't really want.

In the mobile environment, the stakes are arguably higher. Because consumers view their mobile devices as extensions of themselves, sending any message that might be perceived as spam could generate serious backlash for your brand, especially in an age when your audience has so many mechanisms at its disposal to call you out for your business practices. The last thing you want to see is your brand's name and spam in the same sentence together.

The good news is that consumers are interested in engaging with brands. Hipcricket has done an annual survey for several years among U.S. consumers in which over one-third of respondents have consistently indicated their interest in joining a loyalty club (see the results from the latest findings in Figure 3.1). Says Jeff: "That's over a 100 million people who are saying, in effect, 'if you provide value to me, and do it on my terms, I will be open to having an opted-in, permission-based interaction with you.'"

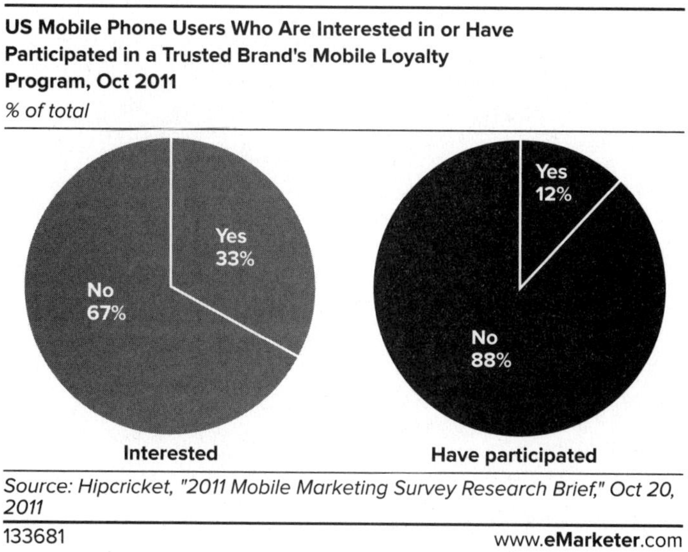

Figure 3.1 Try to capitalize on consumers' interest in participating in loyalty programs.

Of course, more people are interested than have yet to participate. That translates into unrealized opportunities for your brand. To take advantage of these, you need to abide by some basic best practices. When it comes to driving opt-ins and building your mobile database, consider the following:

Leverage your other media. As we said, by including short codes on your other advertising, you can make it work harder for you and help you build your opt-in database.

Incentivize your audience. Offering consumers something tangible, such as a free sample or money-back coupon, can be an effective relationship-starter. Showing them the money, so to speak, indicates their business is important to you.

Clearly delineate the terms and conditions of your marketing program. Make sure you communicate—without any ambiguity—what consumers are getting themselves into when they sign up for your program, including messaging frequency, any costs they might incur, and how often they can expect to be billed. Above all, MMA mandates that you make clear whether consumers are opting into a one-time campaign or an ongoing subscription.

Make it easy to opt out. The process for opting out should be as simple and streamlined as that for opting in. Be sure to include the opt-out steps in all of your advertising and promotional material, as well as any HELP messages you send out as part of the campaign. Once someone texts to sign up for your campaign, the MMA also mandates that your first message should state any other requirements, such as age, for participation in the program, as well as clearly stating that texting STOP will cancel participation in the program and terminate any further messages (see Figure 3.2).

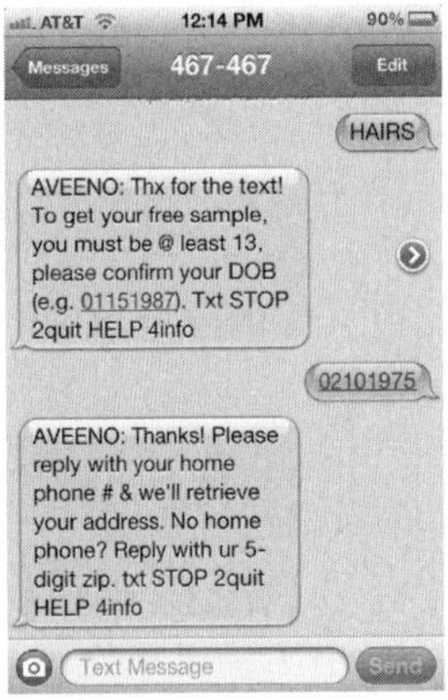

Figure 3.2 This SMS campaign signup clearly states the campaign participation requirements and opt-out steps.

You'll notice that the signup shown in Figure 3.2 takes care to state the requirements for participation (you must be at least 13). In addition, each message clearly states how participants can opt out or get help. The screen capture in Figure 3.3 depicts the messages you'll receive when choosing either the HELP or STOP options.

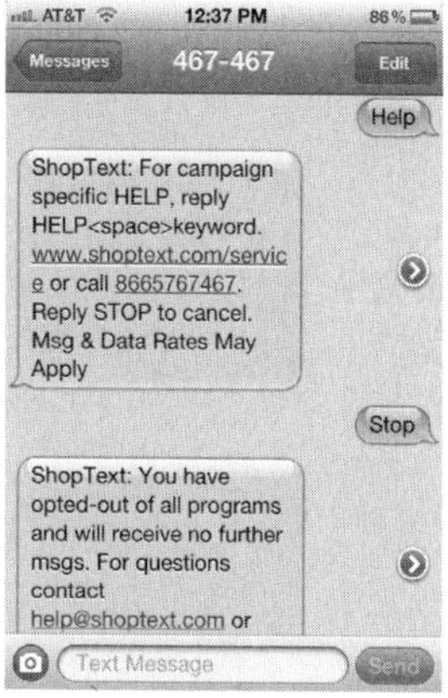

Figure 3.3 SMS campaign help and opt-out messages.

Consider this: The SMS signup process, similar to search, is a pull mechanism, with consumers indicating an interest in your brand, product, or offer. The subsequent messaging process, by contrast, functions on a push basis, making SMS, like email, somewhat unique among marketing tactics in the way it combines pull and push.

"In the case where consumers have opted in to receive alerts or offers, SMS can be tremendously effective," says industry expert Greg Sterling. The opt-in nature of permission-based marketing is part of what makes it work for consumers and marketers alike. Done right, consumers get what they expected when they signed up for your campaign, and you get engagement and their attention in return.

Find the Right Balance Between Message Quantity and Quality

After you've covered all of the previously listed bases and begin building your campaign database, other considerations come into play—the most important of which is to avoid overstaying your welcome. Lesson number one is to moderate the frequency of your communication. "There needs to be a cadence," Jeff explains, "and not every brand has the same one, because it depends on what you're providing." Overall, he continues, "We advise brands do less rather than more. What you don't want is to have someone say 'this is intrusive to me, this isn't what I signed up for, I need out.'"

Take Coca-Cola again as an example. When you sign up for MyCokeRewards, the website clearly indicates that the number of mobile news flashes (SMS alerts promoting offers and rewards) will not exceed five per month. The signup page from the site's mobile version appears in Figure 3.4.

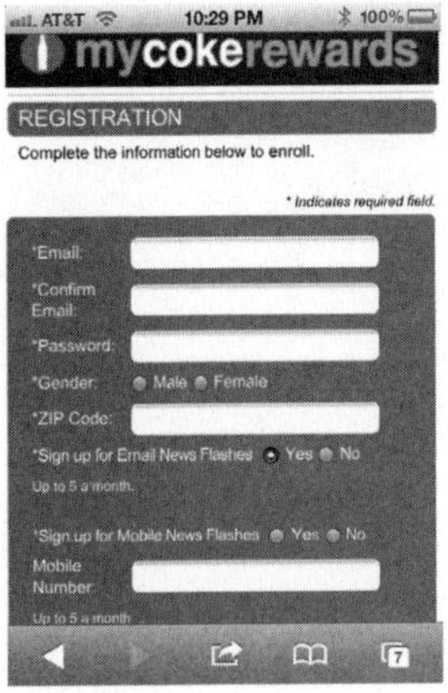

Figure 3.4 The MyCokeRewards mobile registration page clearly indicates message frequency.

Other brand marketers offer similar advice. Referring to K&G Fashion Superstore's customers who sign up for the company's SMS marketing program, Matt Stringer (senior vice president of marketing for Men's Wearhouse, K&G's parent company) told eMarketer in August 2011: "When they receive that first message, we give an indication of the frequency with which they will receive messages. We say four messages a month just to lay the groundwork. We think that kind of communication is important in order to set expectations for how often we're going to be speaking to them via text. This has helped us with low opt-out rates."

OfficeMax's vice president of direct and loyalty marketing, Chris Duncan, imparts a complementary perspective. "The one thing I've tried to tell my team is 'Let's not think of mobile, especially when it comes to couponing, as the new email,'" he explained in an August 2011 interview with eMarketer. "A lot of brands have really gotten carried away with how they use promotions in email." The bottom line, he said, is that mobile promotions are great, but "make sure they're relevant and timely, and don't let them become annoying." These are words to live by.

Get Personal

We've made a point of stating on several occasions the importance of respecting the personal nature of mobile phones. But don't let that quality scare you. To the contrary, use the fact that phones are highly personal to your advantage. It can help you target your audience more effectively.

In indicating interest and by signing up for your program in the anticipation of receiving something of value, consumers give you personal information—that's the value they provide. In turn, once consumers have granted permission, you can use that data to improve the accuracy of your marketing.

As Jeff puts it: "Personalization and the ability to remarket to consumers is where SMS has evolved." For example, he says, "In a typical winter, you wouldn't give someone in Boston an ice tea offer; you'd want to give that to someone in San Diego."

In building your database, you learn vital information about your customers, which enables you to segment and market to them more effectively.

Wednesday: Define Your Partners and Develop Your Campaign

There are a lot of moving parts to an SMS campaign, and you have two principal options for managing them. One approach is to work with an agency or service provider that will take responsibility for most of the day-to-day tasks. The other is to go it alone (or mostly alone). The first option will cost you more money, while the second will require more time and effort on your part.

Beyond a certain scale, cautions Hipcricket CMO Jeff Hasen, you need to consider the benefits of working with an agency or third-party vendor (companies that specialize in doing all of the little things that make an SMS campaign possible) so you can concentrate your efforts on marketing, not minutiae.

If you're planning on a running a campaign on your own, without third-party assistance, "the best thing you can do," Jeff advises, "is spend some time learning the rules and familiarizing yourself with what's been done in the past. Follow the rules and follow precedent. That's the easiest way to get a program fielded without third-party help."

Both the managed and do-it-yourself approaches require a degree of familiarity with a common set of partners: CSCA, wireless carriers, and SMS messaging aggregators. The depth of familiarity will vary depending on whether you opt for a managed solution or go it alone, but understanding the right criteria to consider will be important in either case. So, let's get you acquainted with the roster of partners you'll need to work with to get your campaign off the ground. Bear in mind that you can begin to address a number of these tasks concurrently rather than sequentially.

Get Short Code-y

As we stated at the beginning of this chapter, if you're going to use SMS, you'll need to invest in a short code. In the United States, that means setting up an account with and working through the CSCA. If you're working with an agency or mobile services provider, that partner should be able to take care of the account set-up process. If you're managing your campaign yourself, rest assured that the set-up process is fairly simple.

In either scenario, be aware that the CSCA leases two basic types of codes:

Random Short Codes: A *random short code* is a five- to six-digit number that is automatically generated when you apply for a code using the automated application form on the CSCA website.

Vanity Short Codes: A *vanity short code* actually spells something out on the phone keypad, so-called "vanity" because they tie into your brand, making them easier to remember. Some examples, as we noted earlier: Google uses 46645, which spells "GOOGL," and Coca-Cola uses 2653, which spells "COKE."

The major difference between random and vanity codes (besides the branding factor) is cost—a vanity short code costs twice as much as a random one. Much like URLs, short codes are leased for certain time periods; only with short codes, the time periods can be much shorter. You have the option of leasing a code for a three-month minimum and then extending the lease for additional three-month increments.

There is a third option: You can, in some cases, work with a vendor that owns short codes approved for general use by multiple brands. This is usually referred to as a *shared short code*. These codes are often a great option for brands just getting started with SMS because they offer a faster time to market than obtaining your own code. Keep in mind, however, that what you gain in speed to market, you sacrifice in terms of branding.

If you're just wading into SMS and planning some limited tests, then a shared code should suit you just fine. On the other hand, if you're planning on investing heavily in SMS and including it as a call-to-action in public-facing marketing campaigns or as a customer relationship management (CRM) mechanism, your best bet is to obtain your own code right from the start. Using a shared short code in customer-facing messages now and migrating to a branded code down the road has the potential to cause confusion among your subscribers and will require them to go through the opt-in process all over again. That's a disruption you simply don't want to risk.

Consider also that if one of the other campaigns using the shared code is, for whatever reason, barred by the carriers, all of the campaigns using that code will get shut down, including yours. You don't want to risk losing all of your hard work simply because someone else failed to follow the rules as carefully as you did.

"Finally, whether opting for a managed solution or running your own campaign, think of short codes as akin to URLs," says Jeff. Once you develop consumer awareness around a short code, it will become part of your brand equity, so you'll want to maintain it even beyond the life of a campaign.

Possible (but Not Generally Recommended) Short Code Workarounds

Technically, there are three ways you can send a text message without leasing a short code. For brands and business owners marketing at scale, none of these are great ideas but we'd be remiss if we didn't at least explain these options.

Email to SMS

Most U.S. wireless carriers support delivery of text messages via email through a special domain convention, for example:

AT&T: `number@txt.att.net`

Qwest: `number@qwestmp.com`

T-Mobile: `number@tmomail.net`

Verizon: `number@vtext.com`

However, you should know that although the carriers support these special email-to-SMS conventions, they're designed primarily for person-to-person messaging. The carriers do not support the idea of brands using them as marketing conduits. At best, doing so can and probably will result in a slap on the wrist from the carriers, and at worst, can result in problems doing business with them down the road. So, we advise you not to risk it!

GSM Modem

You can also distribute text messages through the use of a special device called a GSM modem, a piece of hardware that essentially acts like a mobile phone, sending SMS messages from one wireless number to another, but in bulk. There's nothing wrong with this in theory, particularly if your use of SMS is limited to internal communications with your employees or opted-in customers. However, if you plan to use SMS in publicly visible marketing campaigns, and especially if you foresee sending and receiving SMS in bulk, then you need to obtain an official short code.

Long Numbers

A third workaround for receiving text messages is to use 10-digit (or 12 in the case of international, which include the country code) "long numbers" (also known as virtual mobile numbers), such as (212) 123-4567. The benefits of this approach include international number availability and proprietary number leasing. The downside is that both the carriers and the MMA frown on this approach.

Choose an Aggregator

Just as you need a short code to run an SMS campaign, you also need to work with an aggregator. Your agency can oversee the aggregator selection process and manage that relationship on your behalf, but you alone cannot run a campaign without some level of aggregator support. The reason? SMS aggregators are specialty businesses that have built technical integration and business relationships with the wireless carriers. These relationships enable aggregators to do two key tasks:

- Buy SMS messages from the carriers in cost-effective bulk (which they then resell to customers—like you!
- Send SMS messages quickly and efficiently across the wireless carriers' networks. These are tasks you cannot do yourself, not as an individual nor as a major corporation.

When you work with an aggregator, says Jeff, "What you're buying is a combination of reach, relationships, and reliability." All three of these characteristics are important, but reach perhaps most of all. "One of the main reasons you'd choose to do SMS," notes Jeff, "is to be inclusive. And one of the biggest reasons why SMS gets sold into brands is because everyone within reach of the call-to-action has the ability to participate. You need to work with an aggregator that can connect you to all mobile subscribers within your target."

In other words, don't put yourself in a situation where you can reach only three-quarters of your audience. If you're forced to include a disclaimer in your messaging that your program excludes subscribers on Verizon, for example, when you actually want to reach those subscribers, you know you've made the wrong choice. So here's what you need to know about SMS aggregators in the United States: Per the CSCA website (`www.usshortcodes.com/`), they are categorized into tiers based on their capabilities and relationships with the carriers, as described in Table 3.1.

Table 3.1 U.S. SMS aggregator tiers

Tier	Description
Tier 1	Tier 1 SMS aggregators maintain direct short-message peer-to-peer (SMPP—an industry protocol for exchanging SMS messages) connections and premium settlement agreements with at least four of the five major U.S. wireless carriers (AT&T, Sprint, T-Mobile, US Cellular, and Verizon). They support carrier-grade SMS and MMS capabilities and provide a high-level 24/7 service agreement. They publish content only where the rights to that content are clearly owned by the customer (e.g., they won't knowingly plagiarize or spam). Examples include Air2Web, Ericsson, mBlox, Mobile Messenger, Motricity, OpenMarket, Sybase 365, and Vibes Media.
Tier 2	Tier 2 SMS aggregators maintain direct SMPP connections agreements with at least three of the five major U.S. wireless carriers, and settlement agreements with two of the five. Unlike Tier 1 firms, they support carrier-grade SMS capabilities only, but still provide the same type of high-level 24/7 service agreement. Similarly, they publish content only where the rights to that content are clearly owned by the customer (e.g., they won't knowingly plagiarize or spam). Examples include ClearSky, 3Cinteractive, and Syniverse.
Tier 3	Tier 3 SMS aggregators are not officially aggregators in the truest sense of the word, but rather mobile marketing companies that specialize in SMS and run their campaigns on the backbone of a Tier 1 or Tier 2 provider. They tend to mark up the costs of their services beyond what a Tier 1 or Tier 2 provider would charge. On the other hand, they also offer a full-service model that the larger Tier 1 and Tier 2 aggregators often do not, including managing your campaigns for you from short code acquisition to analytics. Examples include Aerialink, 4INFO, i2SMS, Mobile Accord, Netpace, and TeleMessage.

The criteria for selecting an aggregator boil down to two very basic questions:

- Do you have a limited ability to manage SMS in-house from a personnel perspective?
- Do you have the infrastructure and budget to manage SMS content in-house?

The decision really comes down to this: Can you do most of the work yourself, or do you need a more full-service approach? From there, your decisions will be further influenced by:

Cost The costs for basic services (i.e., code and campaign provisioning, bulk-rate SMS, and message delivery via API) from Tier 1 and Tier 2 aggregators are pretty much apples-to-apples comparisons. But when you look at more advanced services from either category or turn to Tier 3 aggregators, the costs can vary greatly.

Reach In most cases, you'll want to work with a Tier 1 aggregator or with a Tier 3 company that has strong ties to a Tier 1. In some cases, a Tier 2 aggregator might make the most sense if you are primarily trying to reach the subscribers of a specific carrier. It all depends on your needs and your target audience.

Service The level of service and/or quality of tools—campaign management dashboards, reporting processes, service level agreements—often factor into the decision-making process.

If you opt for the managed solution route, there is very little you truly need to know beyond how to select a good partner. The selection criteria we've included in this section can help you understand what goes into the process and ensure that you or your agency partners make the best possible choice.

Work with the Wireless Carriers

At some point along the way, the wireless carriers will become essential partners in any SMS campaign you undertake. Simply put: the airwaves belong to them and they set the rules you must follow in order to reach their subscribers. Here's the catch: each carrier imposes a similar but unique set of rules, meaning as a marketer, you have to make sure you tailor your messaging accordingly to meet each guideline. This is part of why you need an aggregator, to navigate the complexities of the carrier requirements.

Still, if you're new to SMS, beyond the *U.S. Consumer Best Practices* (available for download from `www.mmaglobal.com/uploads/Consumer-Best-Practices.pdf`) we referenced on Tuesday, the MMA has a few other publications you may also want to peruse to familiarize yourself with some of the basics of permission-based mobile marketing:

- *Mobile Messaging in North America: A Fresh Look at Current Options for Marketers* available for download from `http://mmaglobal.com/whitepaper?filename=Current-State-of-Messaging-in-NA-March2012-FINAL.pdf` (March 2012)
- *Permission-Based Mobile Marketing Whitepaper* available for download from `www.mmaglobal.com/PermissionBasedMarketingOct2011.pdf` (October 2011)
- *Global Code of Conduct* available for download at `http://mmaglobal.com/codeofconduct.pdf` (July 2008)

These resources can save you time and effort when working with the carriers. Most of what we've listed here pertains to the U.S. market, but as a global organization, the MMA has other resources for non-U.S markets as well.

Hurry Up and Wait: Getting Your Code and/or Campaign Approved

Following all of the guidelines takes time, especially when you're starting an SMS campaign for the first time. This holds true whether you have a team of partners behind you or you're undertaking a largely solo effort. Observes Jeff: "One of the things people have said for years that's held SMS back is the time it takes from the moment a brand says 'I want to run this campaign' to when that program gets approved by all the carriers."

Worse yet, there's a lack of consistency in the amount of time it takes to get a program approved by the Tier 1 carriers. We've seen a campaign take as little as a few weeks to get approved and we've also seen the process drag on for months at a time. Multiple factors can complicate the process. Consider these:

Time of Year As a rule, it takes longer to get a new short code provisioned or a new campaign approved around holidays, especially the period between Thanksgiving to New Year's. Brands often rush to get started with SMS around the busiest shopping time of the year, resulting in a backlog of applications.

Campaign Complexity The more campaigns you want to run on your code and the greater the complexity of those campaigns, the more touchpoints and messages flows you will need to evaluate. To make a long story short: The more you want to do with your code, the more effort you will have to expend in explaining it to the carriers.

Track Record Starting from scratch is kind of like applying for your first job, where you often find yourself in a "you need to have experience to get experience" situation. The more history you have with the carriers (provided, of course, that you've followed the rules), the easier it should be to get a campaign up and running.

The process itself varies little regardless of whether you are working with a Tier 1 aggregator or a smaller Tier 3 vendor. All vendors will assist you in the process of putting together the brief, and most will do the majority of the heavy lifting, asking you just for the basic input required to complete the process. This includes the following:

Code Acquisition In some cases you will have already obtained your code, but any vendor will be willing to do this for you for a nominal additional fee or, in some cases, as a value-add.

Campaign Brief Development The campaign brief is based on the information supplied in your common short code application. It outlines who you are and what you plan to do with the code at a more granular level of detail. Most carriers will want to see examples of message flows—the process by which the users opt in and out and the types of messages they will receive along the way. The aggregator will work with you to create a master brief and then send different iterations of the brief to each carrier with various amendments and formatting designed to meet each carrier's specific requirements.

Provisioning The aggregator will then follow the process of provisioning with the carriers—working with them to get the brief approved and the short code recognized and registered with each one. The process includes testing the proposed campaigns and, often, making revisions to the campaign content and message flow. Provisioning costs vary from vendor to vendor but generally run just a few thousand dollars.

This drawn-out process can be trying if you're looking to get a campaign in-market quickly, but consider the upside: The hurdles put in place protect not only the carriers but also their subscribers and, by extension, your brand from spam-related backlash. We said it before and we'll say it again: The last thing you want to see is your brand's name and spam in the same sentence.

Thursday: Integrate SMS into Your Overall Marketing Strategy

When you stop and think that it took a traditional medium—television—to help make an emerging medium like SMS popular, you start to see how the different moving parts can and should work together. You need only chart the trajectory of SMS responses to American Idol to get a sense of the potential synergy. In the show's second season in 2003, when SMS was first introduced as a voting mechanism, viewers sent 7.5 million messages. By the seventh season, in 2008, AT&T reported that viewers had sent more than 78 million messages. That tally more than doubled in season eight and climbed past 178 million messages. Nearly 2,300 percent growth in seven years (2003–2009) isn't too shabby!

Advertising on TV, in print, on the radio, or on outdoor billboards can be very effective from a branding perspective. There's really no substitute for a big, bold, beautiful image, especially if it's moving and accompanied by a persuasive voice. Plus, TV and radio, although suffering under the weight of continued audience fragmentation and ever-increasing media multitasking, still succeed in bringing together large audiences for particular programs or at specific times of day. Depending on the programming, you might get a large audience (say with a major sporting event) or a highly segmented one (with a radio talk show or a station dedicated to a specific musical genre). Either way, TV and radio provide broad reach and a lot of repeat exposure. Still, beautiful images, no matter how moving at the time we see them, are transitory, and our memories of them can easily fade with time. That's where mobile comes in. It helps bridge your different media and the physical world. Mobile devices are, in effect, an always-at-hand direct response tool.

Ford Directs Referrals to Dealerships

There are many examples of this dynamic at work. Starting in the first half of 2011, FordDirect, a Ford Motor Company joint venture with its dealers, began working with

Hipcricket to coordinate a direct response mechanism to Ford's television and print advertising. Ads in both venues featured a short code to which interested consumers could text the name of a model to receive local offers. Those who texted were then prompted to send their zip code in order to get the relevant incentives. A further step gave consumers the option to submit their name if they were interested in being contacted by a local dealer. Those who did had their information routed to the dealer for follow-up within a matter of minutes.

Capitalizing on consumers' in-the-moment interest proved valuable to both prospective car buyers and dealers alike. In September 2011, FordDirect reported a 14 percent rise in lead conversions as a result. Thanks to the information about model preference provided in the SMS exchange, the program also gave dealers a leg up with customers, making interaction more personalized.

Jeff Hasen, Hipcricket's CMO, offers a useful perspective here: "You can't count on one aspect of your campaign to do everything. You undertake certain tactics for branding purposes, but when you want to actually get customers in the door (or whatever your objective happens to be), you have to turn to a mechanism like SMS that's going to convert interested consumers into paying customers."

SMS Is a Slam Dunk for Sprite

Beyond the SMS-based interactions with consumers we cited earlier in the chapter, Coca-Cola is a major sponsor of high-profile events. One such partnership is the Sprite brand's ongoing promotion of the annual National Basketball Association (NBA) Slam Dunk competition, which is held during the NBA's All-Star Weekend. (The Sprite Slam Dunk Contest is broadcast in a Saturday evening primetime slot in conjunction with other sponsored events. All-Star Saturday Night brought in 8.1 million viewers in 2011, and 6.2 million in 2012, according to Nielsen.) Since 2008, fans have been able to vote for their favorite dunker. From the start, SMS has been a primary voting mechanism. (Votes can also be cast at the NBA.com website, and in 2012, the contest incorporated Twitter as a voting platform.) Sprite leverages the television audience as well as the in-venue audience to promote voting through a call-to-action on the bottom of the screen and digital signage, respectively. The voting window is short—no more than five minutes—so to minimize keypad entries, each contestant is assigned a one-letter keyword, which fans can text to the short code 38657 (DUNKS). The results are tallied in real time, are announced as soon as the dunking contest is completed, and help to maintain the event's kinetic pace.

"We've been running the same basic mechanics for five years," says Coca-Cola's Tom Daly, "with SMS as a component part. The really valuable lesson is the 'stick-to-itiveness,' if you will: the ability, even though it's a really short-duration deal, to refine it, perfect it, keep SMS at the core. The real story here is that the brand teams in the U.S.A. have stuck with it, driven it, and continued to make it better every year. And every year the numbers get bigger and bigger."

By integrating a short code into your existing advertising, you're effectively asking the media you've already purchased to work harder for your brand. At the same time, adding a short code makes that same media more measurable; you've now added a direct response mechanism to a branding vehicle. If you want to test the effectiveness of a TV or radio spot on different programs or at different times of day, you could use different short codes. The same goes for testing how well an ad performs in various print publications.

Friday: Manage and Measure Your Mobile Messaging Campaigns

SMS campaigns vary in duration depending on what you're promoting. If you're launching a product, for example, you might run a short-term program that lasts a couple of weeks. But you can also use SMS more episodically as part of an ongoing campaign. Hipcricket CMO Jeff Hasen cites Macy's Backstage Pass as a case in point. He notes that it is characterized by active phases interspersed with quiet periods of little or no activity. Assuming that most active campaigns will be of short duration—ranging from the five or so minutes in the Sprite example to as long as a few weeks—the ability to look at results and make adjustments in real time is crucial. Says Jeff, "We've had customers view a campaign and make adjustments while it's still live. Mobile gives you the ability to look at a live campaign and say 'my call-to-action isn't working hard enough.'"

As a marketer, this is where working with a third-party firm with direct ties to the carriers comes in particularly handy because their business model isn't set up to work directly with a brand. Rather, the carriers rely on intermediaries to package campaign data and push it out to marketers. Assuming you've established a relationship with such an intermediary, as we talked about on Wednesday, you will be able to obtain metrics and make adjustments on the fly.

In terms of measuring how effectively an SMS program is working, any key performance indicators (KPIs) are going to be specific to your brand and the objectives of a particular campaign. The degree of integration and how well the campaign is working in conjunction with your traditional and digital media efforts are important considerations to track. However, doing that is not without hurdles. "One of our biggest challenges," observes Jeff, "is the closed loop. A lot of times we don't have access to what ultimately happens at the point of sale. That has to do with the brand's interest in sharing that data and the ability to report back data based on the campaign. There's no consistency when it comes to track ability."

In Conclusion

We started off the tactical portion of the book with SMS for two key reasons:

- It reaches the broadest possible mobile audience.
- It plays a vital role through the purchase funnel.

There's no denying SMS is a low-wattage marketing tactic. But what it lacks in flash, it compensates for in effectiveness. If mobile marketing were a baseball team, SMS would be the utility player—solid but unspectacular, able to fill in at multiple positions, a reliable performer year in and year out.

So don't get caught up in the perceived limitations of SMS; focus instead on its strengths. "The challenge," says Coca-Cola's Tom Daly, "is getting outside the box of character limits and perceptions of the limited depth of experiences you can offer." He goes on to wax philosophical about what motivates him: "The night sky is big and vast and the stars in the sky inspire big thinking. SMS...160 characters...not so much." But, he adds, "Have you ever seen the Milky Way? It has maybe as many as 400 billion stars, formed since the beginning of time. And SMS? Seven trillion messages sent in 2011. Surely, one can find inspiration in those kinds of numbers."

Greg Sterling, founding principal of Sterling Market Intelligence, offers a more earthbound perspective: "There's definitely a place for SMS; the best analogy might be email, which is similarly effective but often similarly maligned." "That said," he adds, "I don't see it as an all-purpose mobile marketing tool; it's more like something you'd use for follow-up messaging or offers from online, traditional, or even mobile advertising."

Therein lies the enduring appeal of SMS. It serves as the glue that can bind together your overall marketing campaign, keep your customers on the hook, and push them into richer experiences on the mobile web and in applications. We'll begin to tackle these more immersive channels next week, so get ready to delve into maximizing the Web for your mobilized audience.

Week 3: Maximize Reach with Mobile Websites

4

You now have a framework for developing your strategic approach to mobile and a firm grasp on the most basic mobile marketing channel, SMS. At this point, it's time to focus on your mobile website, which we believe is the most important element of your overall mobile strategy. This is where most of your customers will connect with you. It will also be an end destination to which many of your other initiatives will drive customers, including SMS, mobile ad campaigns, QR codes, and mobile email. In this chapter, we walk you through the options for designing and developing your mobile site and provide you with best practices for testing, search optimization, and measuring success.

Chapter Contents

Monday: Establish a Development Approach for Your Mobile Site

In late 2010, famed then-Morgan Stanley analyst Mary Meeker predicted that mobile Internet traffic would exceed that of desktop Internet traffic by 2014. So far, her prediction seems to be tracking according to schedule. We want to remind you that Ms. Meeker was speaking from a global perspective—in certain areas of the world where mobile is more accessible to the general populace than the fixed Internet, we're likely to reach this tipping point much sooner than she predicted. There's no doubt this shift is coming on a global level, and now is the time to rethink your overall website strategy with mobile in mind.

Consider the current status quo: According to comScore (`www.comscore.com`), a leading Internet research firm, roughly 10 percent of U.S. Internet traffic comes from mobile devices as of June 2012, but the numbers we are seeing firsthand among our clients actually skew even higher. Across multiple industry verticals, from automotive to consumer packaged goods (CPG), we see mobile accounting for 10 to 20 percent of total traffic to desktop websites. Yet only a year ago, the average range was just 5 to 10 percent.

At first glance, an increase of 50 percent seems astonishing, but when you consider the marketplace factors, it's actually not that surprising. High-end smartphones and tablets that support a superior browsing experience are more available and more affordable than ever before, spurring regular usage among consumers. In the United States, eMarketer reports that smartphone penetration reached 48 percent by the end of 2012 and according to research released by Google and Ipsos in October 2011, 69 percent of U.S. smartphone users access the mobile web daily. Older devices without a browser are destined for the dustbin of history. Analysts predict that 85 percent of mobile devices will be web-enabled by 2013. Meanwhile, the 4G mobile networks currently being developed and slowly rolled out by U.S. wireless carriers promise data speeds 10 times faster than the 3G and 3.5G standards offered to most consumers now.

All About 4G

You've no doubt heard a lot about 4G, but like most of us you aren't completely clear as to what it is. 4G is a blanket term for the fourth generation of wireless technology standards, promising the high data speeds that will take mobile usage to the next level. There are currently two different standards competing for the official 4G title: Long Term Evolution (LTE) and WiMax. The projected speeds of 4G networks promise an average of 1 Gbps (gigabits per second), but the current iterations of each standard deliver much less. So when you hear about 4G being available somewhere, keep in mind that it isn't 4G in the truest sense—not yet. Yet it is still considerably faster than the current 3G networks in place.

This rapid growth is alerting marketers to the growing importance of mobile consumers, yet a quick review of the top 20 Fortune 500 companies in the United

States shows that as of June 2012, *less than half* of them have a mobile-optimized site. There's no doubt this will change and change fast. We believe 2012 and early 2013 will be a watershed time in which brands evolve their website strategy to embrace the mobile consumer. However, there's no one standard starting point—multiple options abound and the right choice varies according to your brand, your current web technology, your goals, and your customers. So let's take a look at your options for mobilization.

In this chapter, we'll share our own insights on mobile web development as well as commentary from experts Shiva Vannavada (head of the Technology Center of Excellence) and Nicholas Roshon (senior analyst, Natural Search) of the digital marketing agency iCrossing. You'll hear from Shiva and Nicholas throughout this chapter.

Mobile Development Options

You have a number of options for developing your mobile site, all of which differ in approach. We'll do a high-level overview of each and then walk you through a side-by-side comparison and decision process for selecting the right approach for your brand.

The Fully Hosted Mobile Site

A *fully hosted* site is completely or mostly separate from your desktop site and hosted on the servers of a vendor. The simplest form of fully hosted site is one in which you deliver content, usually copy and images, to the vendor and the vendor then builds a simple, template-based site and hosts it on its servers. A more complicated version may integrate content or services from your desktop site via an *application programming interface (API)*, but for the most part it functions as a completely separate entity. Mobile devices visiting your desktop website, whether via direct URL input or search, are then detected by a script and redirected to the hosted mobile site. We'll refer to this process from here on as *device detection and redirection.*

> **Device Detection and Redirection**
>
> When a browser sends a request to your website for a page, it also sends along an identifier known as a *user agent*. A script on the website then detects that user agent and returns the right content for the particular device.

The fully hosted approach was one of the first options available for creating a mobile site and is still popular for a couple of reasons:

- Fully hosted sites can be built quickly and cost effectively.
- Fully hosted sites require little or no technical involvement.

As a rule, fully hosted sites are built with prefabricated templates and code so you can usually get a site launched in a matter of weeks for a moderate upfront cost and a reasonable monthly hosting fee. In most cases, there will be little or no interaction between the vendor and the technical team that runs your website. You hand off assets and the vendor does the rest, building a new site with the content you've provided and their library of reusable assets.

If you're looking for a fast time to market for a reasonable upfront cost, the fully hosted option can make a lot of sense. In some cases, it's the *only* sensible option if you have a site (one built entirely in Flash, for example) that would be difficult to mobilize any other way. It's also an ideal solution if you're looking to create simple, standalone mobile websites (also known as microsites) that aren't based on a preexisting desktop site—to support a mobile ad campaign, for example.

However, there can be a few drawbacks:

- Reduced long-term return on investment (ROI)
- Design limitations
- Maintenance challenges
- SEO limitations—a hosted site is often the worst choice from an SEO perspective because it usually utilizes cookie cutter page templates and third-party domains

With the fully hosted approach, you aren't buying a website, you're buying a service. If you eventually decide to work with a different vendor or take a more sophisticated approach, you'll have few or no tangible assets to leverage. Most fully hosted vendors use prefab templates to get sites up quickly and inexpensively. As a result, they are often limited in the amount of customization they can offer in design and functionality. You may end up with a site that looks very similar to others the vendor hosts and that offers a lower level of functionality than you had envisioned. The vendor hosts your content and, therefore, the vendor is 100 percent in control of it. If you want changes made to your site, you'll need to deliver your request to the vendor and wait for the vendor to implement those changes. The fully hosted approach can get you up and running quickly, but you're not investing in something you can repurpose later and you will most likely sacrifice a certain degree of design and functionality. What's more, your content is not in your control—changes or updates depend on the vendor's schedule, not yours.

The Reverse Proxy Site

A reverse proxy site is a variation on the fully hosted site model. In this case, the vendor uses a reverse proxy to repurpose your existing desktop site on the fly for mobile devices. Think of it as an interpreter of sorts. The vendor detects mobile page requests coming to your site and reformats the page on the fly, assembling a mobile-friendly version. Your desktop website then redirects the mobile device to the mobile-friendly version of your site hosted on the vendor's server. So while the resulting site is hosted elsewhere, it isn't exactly separate in the strictest sense. A reverse proxy site will always depend on your desktop site as its source, and it will stay in sync (within reason) with the content and functions that exist there.

The benefits of a reverse proxy mobile site include:

- Low-to-moderate upfront costs
- Minimal effort
- Fast time to market

The cost structure of a reverse proxy hosted site is similar to a fully hosted site with an upfront development fee and monthly hosting and maintenance costs. However, because reverse proxy solutions tend to offer higher levels of customization and functionality, the costs skew a bit higher. The reverse proxy site is very hassle-free in that it basically transforms your existing site on the fly. There's minimal need to involve the technical team that maintains your site because the vendor isn't really touching your code. This low level of technical dependency is very appealing to marketing managers who are often at odds with their technical colleagues when they want to do something new with their website. Very little will be required of your technical team because little or no custom coding is involved—at most, they will have to do some tagging on your website pages—so the time to market is often as fast as four to six weeks.

There are, however, potential drawbacks to bear in mind:

- Reduced long-term ROI
- User experience limitations
- Maintenance challenges
- SEO limitations—the proxy approach is an improvement over the hosted approach, but still not ideal

As with the fully hosted approach, when you purchase a reverse proxy solution, you are not buying a mobile website—you are paying for a service. If you aren't happy with the vendor and decide to go elsewhere or if you eventually decide to build a more sophisticated site, you have no tangible assets to repurpose for those efforts. Reverse proxy vendors tend to be more capable of creating a rich, mobile web experience than fully hosted vendors, but the way they function creates limits. Although some can create custom content and functions within reason, most of these vendors can usually repurpose only what is there on your desktop site. They're also unable to easily repurpose Flash content and may have trouble transforming sites that are visually complex and/or contain lots of imagery. Theoretically, because the reverse proxy is translating your desktop site in real time, the mobile site will always be in synch with your .com content. However, making complex changes to the user interface or functionality can and often does interfere with the translation process. So in the interest of keeping your site up and running, you often need to give the vendor weeks of advance notice before you make any changes to your desktop site. We like to think of the reverse proxy approach as the next step up from the fully hosted approach. If you're in the market for a slightly more sophisticated mobile design that's in sync with your desktop site, but aren't ready for a more advanced approach, then it's a great option. Ultimately, your content is still in someone else's control, but you can get to market fast and learn a lot before investing in something more complex.

Domain Concerns Posed by Hosted Mobile Sites

When you use a hosted (fully hosted or proxy) vendor for your mobile site, the site resides on the vendor's server, so the actual URL will reflect the vendor's domain. For example, www.kiwi-market.com might become mobilevendor.kiwi-market.com. Most vendors will alias the domain so consumers and search engines will see it as one of your own URLs, but an extra fee is often charged to do so.

The Cloud Platform Mobile Site

Although it still involves utilizing a third-party vendor, the *cloud platform* is a more advanced approach to mobile websites than the previous two options were. You create the actual site content, usually with HyperText Markup Language (HTML5), JavaScript, and Cascading Style Sheets (CSS3), integrating additional proprietary markup and web services from the cloud platform vendor. You host the final site within your own `.com` environment, calling the services from the vendor as needed to detect mobile users and modify elements of your site to work properly on users' specific devices.

Most cloud platform services have evolved from the fully hosted model. These vendors realized that many brands want and need to host and manage their own site and have developed their original suite of services to be exportable via API. As such, they are a relatively new option on the market, but they are already showing terrific promise for a number of reasons.

The benefits of a cloud platform mobile site include:

- Expansive reach
- Custom content and user experience
- Control over URL structures for SEO

The tools and services that cloud platform vendors offer enable you to translate your site to meet the needs of low- and high-end users alike. In many cases, you can easily create multiple tiers of user experience and morph your site on the fly based on the capabilities of the device. The overall site layout—as well as images, video, and downloadable file formats—can be automatically repurposed in real time for almost any device. This enables a rich media experience for the broadest possible number of users. If you have the technical resources to build your own site content and have a little more time to invest in building your site, the cloud platform approach is a great option to consider. You have control of your own content and you can create a fairly rich user experience that reaches many different devices. However, as with the other solutions, a cloud platform mobile site does have drawbacks, including:

- Increased cost of ownership
- Reduced flexibility in changing your approach
- Advanced level of effort vs. proxy or hosted solutions
- Increase level of effort in maintenance

With a cloud platform, you build and host your mobile site (necessitating a certain amount of investment), but you also are purchasing a monthly or yearly service from the vendor, which entails added cost. As with the fully hosted and reverse proxy models, you are purchasing a service, and without that service, your site won't work. If you later decide to change vendors or go with a more sophisticated approach, you may be able to repurpose some elements of the site, but probably not much. The key benefits of the cloud platform approach are the ability to own your content and service multiple levels of devices. However, to make the most of this opportunity, you need to have the internal design and technical resources to achieve this and commit the time and effort required to make it happen. The cloud platform approach requires that you maintain your own mobile content, which necessitates delegating ongoing technical resources to keeping the site updated and running smoothly.

Cloud platforms are ideal—we would even go so far as to say a necessity—in two very specific cases:

- You want to reach a very broad expanse of users from feature phones to tablets.
- Your site is very complex visually and/or includes images and video that need to be rendered on the fly for every type of user.

Given the variations among device platforms, the cloud platform might be the easiest and only way to reach everyone you want to reach unless you build your own infrastructure for rendering mobile content on the fly. If you are a brand with a global footprint, offering the best possible user experience to a diverse array of devices may be very important to you. In this case, adopting the cloud platform approach might be your only practical option. As we mentioned earlier, most cloud platform vendors started life as fully hosted vendors, so many will be willing to host your mobile site as well as build it. However, their true value is in their ability to reach a broad expanse of users with rich mobile content while enabling you to maintain control of your mobile website.

The Content Management System (CMS)-Driven Mobile Site

If you have a CMS-driven desktop website, your path to mobilization may be far easier than you think. Most of the top CMS platforms now have full support for mobile baked in. If your site is CMS-driven by one of the top commercial platforms, you can develop mobile page templates and integrate them into your holistic .com environment. From there, you simply need to integrate device detection to route mobile visitors to your .com domain to the appropriate content for your device.

The CMS-driven approach has numerous benefits:

- Total control over URL structure and SEO
- Centralized content management
- Easier maintenance
- Improved long-term ROI

With the fully hosted and proxy approaches, you can alias your URLs, but the CMS-driven approach gives you total control over your content and URLs. Mobile content can share the same URL as a desktop page, enabling you to capitalize on the natural search equity of your .com URL. However, some CMSs will automatically assign different URL structures to mobile and desktop content, which can cause SEO problems down the road as we'll soon explain. Because your .com and mobile sites are hosted within the same CMS, you are able to seamlessly update both, keeping your content in sync. Hosted vendors put you at the mercy of their deployment schedules, but the CMS-driven approach enables you to exert complete control over when and how your site is maintained and updated. Utilizing the same database, services, and content for your site across multiple platforms enables you to maximize the investment in your business over time. If you already have a CMS-driven .com website, the CMS-driven approach can be an effective and efficient path to mobilization. However, you'll need to have access to the technical resources, whether internally or through an agency partner, to make it happen and that can be the real challenge.

There can be other potential challenges as well. Keep in mind the following drawbacks to a CMS-driven mobile site:

- Cost
- Time to market
- Support for multiple form factors

In the case of a CMS-driven site, you are creating real, tangible assets and integrating them with your .com environment. This will almost always cost more money up front in terms of time spent, whether you are using your own internal resources or paying an agency partner. Vendor-based solutions offer you a fast time to market because they rely on prefab page templates and code libraries. In this case, however, you are designing, developing, and testing unique pages, which will necessitate a more intensive level of time and effort—usually months instead of weeks in time to market. The single biggest hurdle in developing for the mobile web is device fragmentation. From device to device, JavaScript support, multimedia formats, and screen sizes can differ radically. Creating a single experience that adequately serves the needs of your entire audience can be a challenge with the CMS-driven approach and, in many cases, can prove to be impossible without a very significant investment in design and technical efforts. Multiple iterations of your mobile site may be required and, in some cases, additional services from a cloud platform vendor may still be needed. More often than not, with the CMS-driven approach, you'll be faced with focusing only on your most sophisticated users with a high-end site or creating a very basic site that will be accessible to everyone. Neither situation is ideal. We'll discuss the decisions to be made in serving the high-end user compared to the low-end user tomorrow.

The CMS-driven approach has a lot going for it: You have total control of your content and you're creating tangible assets that you can build on for the future. On the other hand, you need to be willing to invest more time, money, and effort up front and you need to have the design and technical resources to create and maintain the content. You'll have a longer time to market and costs can spiral out of control if you are trying to support multiple tiers of high- and low-end devices. If you're catering almost exclusively to users on iOS and Android, you can probably get away with creating a single, high-end site. In this case, the CMS-driven approach is ideal if you have the resources to do it. If you have many high- and low-end devices visiting your site, you might want to consider a fully hosted, proxy, or cloud vendor solution, at least in the near term. But keep in mind that these low-end devices are steadily dwindling in number.

Responsive Design

Responsive design is currently one of the hottest topics in digital and rightly so. It offers brands the opportunity to create web content that will flow fluidly across multiple devices—an ability that will continue to escalate in importance as new device types flood the market. We'll discuss the actual design aspects of the responsive approach tomorrow, but for now we'll look at it from a high level as one of your options for developing a mobile site.

First and foremost, you have to understand what responsive design is. It entails creating a single website that uses *HTML5* and *CSS3 media queries* to modify its layout on the fly according to the device width being used to access the site. Unless you are in the position to redevelop your entire .com site from scratch, responsive design probably won't be an option for you.

Most of the brands we work with aren't in the position to make a radical redesign and re-architecture of their .com site and are simply looking to mobilize a select portion of their existing content. It is possible to take a responsive approach to an existing desktop site that was not responsively designed. However, you can only do so successfully with a site that was very spare and well designed to begin with—and let's face it, most websites are not. But if you are in the process of developing an entirely new site or doing a complete overhaul of an existing one, the responsive approach deserves your consideration. Naturally, there are several pros and cons of which you should be aware.

The benefits of the responsive design approach include:

- Economy of design
- Reduced long-term cost of ownership
- Optimal SEO

The informational and creative design phases for your site will be fairly extensive as you consider various consumer need-states across multiple platforms. You'll spend more time planning content and more time creating it. However, doing all this planning upfront for an entire ecosystem of desktop and mobile devices means less time spent later trying to play catch-up and figuring out how to serve mobile users after the fact. In this case, you aren't paying for outside services to host and maintain additional content. Responsive design is the only approach to mobile that allows you to truly serve all users with device-appropriate content from a single URL—no subdomains, subdirectories, or unique mobile URLs required. A single URL allows your mobile site to piggyback on the desktop search equity you've built up over time, ensuring optimal, cross-platform desktop and mobile search visibility. For this reason, responsive design is the number-one mobile web approach promoted by Google.

That said, responsive design is not a panacea for your mobile woes. In addition to the fact that you need to be able to start from scratch, there are still potential drawbacks to keep in mind:

- Reach
- Load times
- Design limitations

Reach is where the device fragmentation we've talked about gets really challenging because not every mobile device supports the technologies that responsive design utilizes. If your target audience includes anything but high-end smartphones and tablets with optimal support for HTML5 and CSS3, the responsive approach alone won't suffice. With the responsive approach, you aren't creating a mobile site; you are creating a single website that works on desktop and mobile devices. CSS3 media queries will enable you to make the desktop and mobile versions look different if you choose, but it's still one single site. Therefore, even if you aren't showing certain images or page elements to the user, the mobile browser still loads the full page—and that can be very taxing for mobile devices because the data speeds provided by the wireless carrier networks are much slower than those provided by the ISPs serving desktop sites. Users may end up waiting a long time for the content they want, and we know that mobile users have minimal patience for extended load times. You can change your site's appearance for different devices to a certain degree, but you can't achieve the same level of customization you'd get with a distinct mobile site using responsive design alone. In many cases, you'll still want to create additional mobile-specific content and functionality on top of your base responsive page design in order to adequately serve your mobile users.

Tuesday: Determine Your Design Approach

The importance of having a mobile website seems fairly obvious at first glance; your website is your brand's calling card, and it should be findable, useful, usable, and engaging on any device a customer uses to access it. Yet, we still hear one question over and over: "Should I build a mobile site first or a mobile app?"

Mobile Web versus Mobile App

We'd like to answer this question by framing it in the context of the customer journey that we explored in Chapter 2, "Week 1: Develop Your Mobile Strategy." When developing a mobile strategy for our clients, we always ask several key questions designed to help us understand the circumstances in which customers might find an app or a mobile site more desirable. For example, when talking to customers of the fictional Kiwi Market, we might ask the following:

> If you were looking for information on Kiwi Market on your mobile device, how would you start?
>
> Would you search the mobile web first and expect to find a mobile site?
>
> Would you look in an app store first, hoping to find a Kiwi Market mobile app?
>
> Would you download a Kiwi Market mobile app if they had one? If yes, how would you use it? Would you use it *instead* of the website? Would you use it differently?

Invariably, customers give us the same answers, whether they are shopping for groceries, a car, or a hotel room, or looking for any other type of information from a brand. In the early, getting-to-know-you stages of building awareness and consideration and even during a purchase, they prefer to use the mobile web. However, after they have converted and become a loyal customer, they often prefer an app if one is available.

When we ask them to explain these preferences, we hear:

"When I'm first looking for a product or service, I'm almost always using Google, Yahoo!, or Bing. Whether I use the site or app versions of these search engines, the results I get are website results—my mobile search habits lead me to a mobile website 99.9 percent of the time."

"If I'm only going to connect with this brand a few times or if my interaction with it will be intermittent, say one to two times per month, I'll probably stick with using the mobile site."

"If my interaction is going to be more frequent, whether short- or long-term, I'd prefer an app if possible, but I'll use the mobile site if there is no app."

"I like apps better once I've become connected to a brand because the user experience is better. There's less content I don't want/need and it seems to be more tailored to my specific needs as an existing customer as opposed to the website, which tends to be more geared toward getting me to become a customer in the first place. Plus, the app often lets me save info and access it even when I don't have a data connection."

A mobile app does play an important role in the relationship between brand and consumer *after that relationship has been established.* As a rule, consumers see app usage as a sign of commitment, and they need to get to know you a little before they're willing to download your app. That's not to say apps never play a role in earlier stages of acquisition or awareness (in some cases, they clearly do), but it's important to understand their position in the overall ecosystem in relationship to mobile websites. We'll explore that more in Chapter 5, "Week 4: Maximize Engagement with Mobile Apps."

The increasingly common accepted wisdom is that your .com site should be your first concern when getting started with mobile and should almost always come before developing an app. There are a few key reasons for this.

Reach Technically, SMS reaches the most consumers overall; however, at a limit of 160 text-only characters, it's not exactly an info-rich channel. Roughly 39 percent of the U.S. population (122 million people) use the mobile web regularly. Estimates suggest roughly the same number of people use apps; but remember, the app market is fragmented between multiple platforms. You'd need to develop applications for iOS and multiple versions of Android to even come close to reaching the same 122 million people you'd reach with a single mobile site.

Visibility Google is the single most popular mobile search channel and the most popular mobile website in the United States. According to comScore, 97 percent of smartphone users visited a Google site on their device in March 2012. Interestingly enough, the majority of these consumers used an app to access these Google sites. This supports our contention that, once users are deeply engaged with a brand, they tend to prefer an app. Bear in mind, however, that, Google Maps aside, the majority of the results these Google sites returned to consumers were websites. A mobile site that is well search-optimized will consistently reach the highest possible volume of mobile consumers.

Effort and Maintenance While it takes a fair amount of planning and expense to design, develop, and maintain a mobile website, the effort of creating a mobile app is far greater. At present, you'd need to develop your app for iPhone with possible variations required for the iPod Touch and iPad as well as for multiple versions of Android. You may also have to consider BlackBerry and Windows Phone, depending on your audience's technographics. Designing, developing, and maintaining for these multiple platforms as well as maintaining optimal visibility for your apps in the various app stores is a level of effort that eclipses development of a single, solid mobile website.

The bottom line is that it's smart to make your mobile website your first priority. It enables you to best support the needs of as many new and current customers as possible, at a lower level of effort relative to apps. An added benefit of mobile websites is they will also be accessible to consumers who still own feature phones.

Of course, there are exceptions to the "mobile web first" line of thinking. You might find yourself in a situation where you're dealing with a market or demographic that uses SMS more than the mobile web, which makes text messaging your ideal starting point. Or, you might have content (a game, for example) that's simply better suited to an app-first approach. But for most consumer facing brands, particularly here in the United States, the mobile web will be your primary starting point. So with that in mind, where do you go from there?

In the early days of mobile, users had a lot more patience. Most of us were glad if a site worked on our phones at all! Long load times were expected; broken links and images, and missing plug-ins were a fact of life. However, our expectations have evolved along with technology, and we're now a lot harder to please.

Google has some keen insight into our expectations. Given how search-oriented mobile web usage is, the world's leading search engine should know! In a June 2011 study, Google found:

- Sixty-one percent of users are unlikely to return to a mobile site they had trouble accessing from their phone.
- Forty percent said they would visit a competitor's site instead.
- Nineteen percent would have a negative overall perception of a brand if they were dissatisfied with the performance of its website on a mobile device.
- Fifty-seven percent of users say they won't recommend a business with a poorly designed mobile site.

Simply put, design matters. Fortunately, we have more options than we used to, even since Google conducted that study. The original mobile websites that first began to surface around 2005 were virtual skeletons with minimal text, tiny thumbnail images, and little or no functionality beyond click-to-call or click-to-email. But the growing sophistication of mobile devices and increasing standardization of cross-platform web technologies such as HTML5 and CSS3 now offer us a much richer design palette. The question you'll need to ask as you determine your design approach is, "How rich an experience can you realistically create for your particular users?"

It's become generally accepted that your mobile site can and should be different from the desktop version. After all, people aren't visiting your site on a smartphone to read your annual report. The, odds are they are looking for quick, action-oriented content. Your goal should be to address the context you can infer from the fact they are visiting your site on a mobile device, one that usually involves information-gathering, social sharing, way-finding, and making direct contact with you.

The point is that the mobile user, whether on a smartphone or tablet, is in a different place both physically and metaphorically than the same user viewing your site on the desktop. Your job is to make the mobile user's journey faster, easier, more enjoyable, and ultimately, successful.

The development approach you chose yesterday will no doubt have been influenced by what you hope to achieve with design. However, odds are that factors like cost, internal resources, the state of your .com environment, and desired time to market all carried equal or greater weight than the look and feel you desired. Your primary concern was probably getting a decent mobile site in place as quickly as possible for a reasonable cost. That doesn't necessarily mean you have to sacrifice in terms of design, but the development path you've chosen will have an effect on the design you are able to create.

To best explain your options, we'll categorize your choices as three different types of user interfaces (UIs):

Universal UI A simple, often template-based layout that will be accessible to as many users as possible.

Smartphone UI This is a more sophisticated, touch-centric layout that will be fully usable only by high-end smartphone users.

Tablet UI This is a hybrid approach in which you serve content that is almost identical to your desktop UI. It removes certain usability barriers unique to touch interfaces and makes slight modifications to your homepage and navigation to cater to the heavy content consumption habits of tablet users.

The Universal UI

The universal UI has come a long way from the extremely basic sites of 2005, but they're still very simple. Navigation tends to be presented in the form of menu lists, images are kept to a minimum, and functionality remains limited (see Figure 4.1 for an example). Originally, this type of approach was by necessity because it was what most devices could handle. Now it is by design, in an effort to support the needs of as many users as possible with a single UI.

Figure 4.1 Nissan's mobile website exemplifies an effective universal mobile UI.

You will most often see the universal UI approach taken with sites built using a fully hosted or proxy platform. These sites rarely, if ever, present a highly attractive or useful user experience; they are usually designed to be accessible to the lowest common denominator in the device ecosystem. That's not to say that these vendors cannot support more sophisticated approaches; they often can. However, doing so does take a high level of effort to design, develop, and support multiple iterations of a site for high-end and low-end devices. Most brands that have chosen to work with a hosted vendor have done so to take advantage of their speedy time to market and low cost, which rely on using a template-based, one-size-fits-all approach—hence, the tendency toward a very simple and template-based look and feel.

The universal approach is great in that you can serve pretty much every user from a single, simple site. It's also low effort and low cost, but you do make certain sacrifices in terms of design and functionality. In an effort to make a site that's accessible to everyone, you run the risk of short-changing your more sophisticated users.

The Smartphone UI

The smartphone UI approach targets a more sophisticated group of touchscreen devices that feature intuitive, app-like navigation schemes, complex functionality and, often rich imagery and media (see Figure 4.2 for an example).

This approach has drawbacks, of course. Most users with relatively modern devices will be able to view your site but, depending on how complex it is, may not be able to actually use it well. Users of older devices might not be able to view it at all.

Figure 4.2 Toyota's mobile website exemplifies an effective smartphone UI.

So with the smartphone approach, you have a catch-22. You can create a great experience for the high-end users who probably make up the dominant percentage of your customers, which is an important consideration. In our experience, most of the brands we work with see more than 90 percent of their smartphone and tablet traffic coming from iOS and Android devices. However, especially if you cater to a broad, international audience, you still might be alienating a certain percentage of users with older feature phone devices if you go with a smartphone-centric design.

Please note that the numbers we've provided are averages—some clients find their smartphone traffic from iOS and Android devices is much higher, some much lower. So, there's no standard rule of thumb; you have to assess what's right for your unique set of users. We do encourage you to keep in mind that almost 50 percent of U.S. mobile users own smartphones in 2012 (an estimated 116 million smartphone owners). Given the rate of new handset adoption, that number is expected to continue growing briskly. Meanwhile, the number of low-end devices will continue to dwindle in coming years.

The Tablet UI

"Won't my desktop website work on an iPad?"

This is another question we now hear on an almost-daily basis. The answer is yes—and no. The simple answer is the most dominant tablet, the iPad, doesn't support Flash. If your site depends on Flash to deliver content, you'll have to consider whether you can live with tablet users seeing big blank spaces and missing plug-in error messages. If not, you'll have to think about how you can remove that content for tablets or replace it in some way.

It's a more serious problem if your site is built entirely on Flash. In this case, you'll need to consider directing tablet users to your mobile site. In most cases, the mobile site will fall short of a tablet user's expectations. Tablet users tend to stay engaged for longer periods of time than smartphone users and consume larger amounts of content, so it's likely that your smartphone site will fail to meet their needs. If you do choose to route tablets to your smartphone site, it's wise to provide a link to the full desktop site experience, provided your desktop site isn't entirely built on Flash. This at least gives your tablet users the option of getting more content if your smartphone site doesn't suit their needs

Flash aside, desktop sites pose other challenges for tablets. Navigation elements designed for the desktop can throw a monkey wrench into the way a website functions on a tablet. While the iPad still dominates the tablet landscape, the reality is that many other form factors are on the horizon and their browsers handle common navigation elements differently, so while your desktop site may work on one tablet, it may prove to be extremely hard to navigate on another. For example, when some tablets are turned to portrait orientation, navigation elements designed with fixed positioning for a desktop site might bunch up and overlap, leading to frequent mis-clicks. On others, mouse-over navigation might trigger the copy-paste function making the navigation unusable.

The bottom lines that you'll have to carefully assess the performance of your desktop site on the iPad and a selection of other tablet devices to determine just how well—or poorly—it performs. You might be able to use your desktop site as is, or you might simply have to make some tweaks to your navigational structure. On the other hand, you may also have to invest in a unique approach. The only way to effectively do so is to weigh the importance of tablet users (usually based on their overall percentage of traffic to your desktop site) against the performance of your site on a tablet. As illustrated in Figure 4.3, *The Guardian UK* is an example of an effective tablet UI.

Figure 4.3 The Guardian UK website exemplifies an effective tablet UI.

And, what if you choose to create a unique mobile site? It's too early in the game to determine what exactly makes an ideal tablet experience. We know tablet users are more likely to stay on-site longer, more prone to consuming long-form content, and more prone to making purchases than desktop users. Making sure that you address usability barriers and create UIs that support content consumption are a great first step, but our understanding of what a web experience should be on a tablet will be evolving for some time to come.

Wednesday: Make Key Development Decisions

Some people still refer to a mobile site as a WAP site, but this is archaic terminology. WAP stands for Wireless Access Protocol, a technology that hasn't been in active widespread use for many years. The fact is, most smartphones and tablets can now support most modern front-end technologies, with the exception of Flash. This is great news because it frees you up to do pretty much anything with your mobile site that you'd do with your desktop site—within reason, of course. A lot of things you'd want users to do on the desktop might not make a lot of sense in the mobile context, but the point is that you can actually do them *if you choose*. The question then becomes: How do you pull it off technically?

HTML5 and CSS3: Catering to High-End Users

When you're developing the front-end of your mobile website, the safest bet is to use *progressive enhancement*, an approach to web design that focuses on creating a core level of content that will be accessible to all users and then adding subsequent layers of enhanced content that can then be accessed by devices according to their specific capabilities. The experience is then delivered on a device-by-device basis using tools that detect the specific features of the device—their screen size, for example, or support for JavaScript—and rendering content accordingly. However, if you want to get truly innovative with your mobile layout, the right choice is to use HTML5 in tandem with CSS3. These next-generation web technologies are still being standardized, but they've been fine-tuned to the point where they are widely available and many of the features they enable are accepted by mobile and desktop browsers. The key word here is "many"—not all. HTML5 and CSS3 enable features that are highly valuable to mobile users such as geo-location, offline data caching, and video and audio streaming support, to name but a few. When fully standardized and supported by all browsers, HTML5 and CSS3 will enable you to create mobile sites that are just like apps in their ability to create rich, engaging experiences. But for now, the way these features are supported is fragmented across the various browsers that populate the mobile ecosystem. If you're going to go with the HTML5/CSS3 approach, you can create an impressive site, but you need to have a firm understanding of the features that are supported on the devices you want to reach. If we were to include specifics on what is supported now, that information would definitely be outdated by the time this book is published because the supported standards are changing quickly across all devices. Therefore, we've included resources in the appendix of this book that will help you understand, at the time of publication, the state of support for HTML5 within the mobile browsers you want to target.

Responsive Design versus Tiered Development

The most common approach to mobile web right now is to develop separate, distinct experiences for smartphone, desktop users, and, in some cases, tablet users. Traditionally, this involves creating separate code for your mobile webpages. Conversely, responsive design creates mobile, tablets, and desktop experiences using the same code. The sites you create using a tiered approach are valuable in that they are always designed with mobile specifically in mind. Unique tools and content can be designed specifically to take advantage of the device's capabilities and to make the most of the mobile context. The layouts that result can be very unique, as illustrated in Figure 4.4.

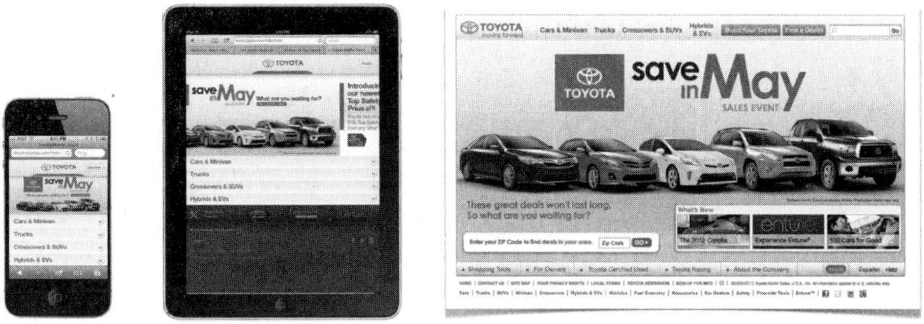

Figure 4.4 Toyota.com's tiered development across smartphone, tablet, and desktop

We think it's important to point out that tiered development evolved as a stopgap measure. As mobile users became a significant percentage of desktop site traffic, brands realized that they had to find a way to make their existing sites work on mobile devices.

Responsive design is a new approach to holistic web design that stemmed from the growth of mobile devices and other nontraditional web platforms. In the strictest definition, it uses HTML5 and CSS3 to create a single code base that renders in slightly different ways depending on the device at hand. Essentially, desktop and mobile devices load the same site—the content is simply laid out differently according to the device making the request.

Because of this, mobile user experiences that are created using the responsive approach are a bit more similar to the desktop than a distinct mobile site would normally be. See the example in Figure 4.5, which shows how *The Boston Globe* renders content differently across multiple devices using the responsive approach.

Figure 4.5 *The Boston Globe's* responsive design across smartphone, tablet, and desktop

There are benefits to the responsive approach, the most obvious of which is a write-once-run-anywhere site that delivers multiple efficiencies in cost and maintenance. There are also SEO benefits because all of your content resides on a single URL, and you can enjoy the peace of mind that comes from knowing your site works equally well on desktop and mobile devices.

However, there are drawbacks as well, including:

- Page weight
- Design and content prioritization

When the same content is loaded by all devices—regardless of whether they will actually use that code or not—the load for mobile can be considerable. A load time that's acceptable to a desktop user will probably be completely unacceptable to the same user on a mobile device. The more complex the experience, the harder it will be for a mobile device to load. However, it will be harder to create a layout for mobile devices that's aesthetically pleasing, functional, and tailored to the abilities and form factors of unique devices. So, while responsive design is extremely promising, there are certain limitations in its strictest definition. However, there's already a movement within the digital design and technology communities to address these limitations. To best illustrate the pros and cons of responsive design, we turned to Shiva Vannavada, head of the Technology Center of Excellence at the digital marketing agency iCrossing. You'll see what we learned in the following section.

Shiva Vannavada on Responsive+

Responsive design is a smart and efficient solution for an ever-changing, ever-multiplying device landscape. However, the traditional responsive design approach with front-end-only optimizations based on CSS3 media queries has potential challenges:

- Larger file sizes, especially for mobile connection speeds
- The need to add device specific features/enhancements
- The need for content prioritization based on device usage scenarios

Addressing all the needs of responsive design quickly adds a significant amount of code to the HTML, JavaScript, and CSS files, which has a direct relation to increased code maintenance, up-front build times, and QA time for regression testing all devices. In order to overcome these challenges, iCrossing came up with a design approach using known techniques, frameworks, and best practices that, when applied appropriately, improves the maintainability and performance of traditional responsive design. Share this information with your tech team and you might just become a hero!

- In a Responsive+ design solution, server-side device detection is used to tailor the base HTML page to a defined class of devices. This tailoring includes customizing images, JavaScript, and CSS files for each device class, as well as providing optimized assets for the target device type where appropriate.

The base solution for a Responsive+ approach consists of the following elements:

Device Classification Rather than targeting all devices uniquely, the idea is to start by defining device classifications and assign devices so that you can deal with them at a broader level. Classification can be handled through the use of device detection tools, such as ScientiaMobile's WURFL (Wireless Universal Resource FiLe) APIs or DeviceAtlas. For example, you can group by devices and their functionalities or by their form factor:

- Desktop (traditional PC, laptop, or desktop)
- Mobile (smartphone, iOS, Android, and the like)
- Tablet (iPads, Android tablets, and Kindles)
- Touch (devices that support touch events)

By applying these logical groupings to targeted devices, you can modularize much of the CSS, JavaScript, and even content including images. As new capabilities make their way online, such as speech and gestural control, the list can grow as the APIs emerge.

Responsive Modules The JavaScript and CSS files should be developed in a modular fashion to support your device classification. So, the CSS structure for a Responsive+ design based on the form factor groups previously listed would include:

- a `base.css` (normalizer, link colors, font faces)
- a `phone.css` (layout)
- a `tablet.css` (layout)
- a `desktop.css` (layout)

Each file, with the exception of the `base.css`, contains media queries for that device classification, including portrait/landscape. As new devices demand new layouts, you would add other files for those devices. In essence, you modularize the CSS based on device (or device classification).

The JavaScript structure for this Responsive+ design would include:

- `core.js`
- `module.js`
- `module.capability.js` (for each targeted capability)

The JavaScript is modularized through asynchronous module definition (your tech team will know it as AMD); but rather than being broken down by device classification, it's broken down by device capabilities. As new capabilities are needed, you simply add another file that represents only that change.

Continues

Shiva Vannavada on Responsive+ *Continued*

UI Build Framework Here, iCrossing developed a neat way to combine (concatenate) CSS and JavaScript files based on device classification. Creating an optimized and targeted user interface (UI) is a critical piece of the Responsive+ approach. For each device classification, only the necessary files are sent down to the client. Server-side build tools such as Apache Ant and RequireJS scripts, when automated from a build-time event, will reduce the file size (minify) and combine the needed files and their dependencies. For example, when your tech team creates the UI, they will bundle the CSS files for the target device classification as follows:

`tablet.min.css` = `base.css` + `tablet.css`

`phone.min.css` = `base.css` + `phone.css`

`desktop.min.css` = `base.css` + `desktop.css`

`full.min.css` = a bundled version with all queries intact for a device-agnostic build

Devices receive only the CSS that is required.

For JavaScript, the build script will go so far as to remove the need for `Require.js` (or similar AMD management scripts) and AMD ceremony for the devices that receive the module dependences as a single concatenated file. This has the advantage of removing a layer of complexity for browsers with anemic caches and wireless carrier connections with high-latency issues.

Server-Side Template Framework The final piece of the high-level solution is to leverage a server-side template library that supports basic display logic and formats the UI based on the device classification. The details of this last component really depend on the type of site you are building. If you are building a small, quick-and-dirty site, you can probably get away with just coding straight PHP, ASP.NET, or JavaServer Pages (JSP), but for larger scale projects, it's best to set up a Model-View-Controller (MVC) and force a more strict separation between the business logic (the information you want the end user to see) and the view logic (the code that determines how the information is displayed). To keep the back-end code cleaner and easier to maintain, select a templating engine based on the technology stack you use.

For Java: Freemarker (`http://freemarker.sourceforge.net/docs/dgui_quickstart_template.html`)

For .NET: Razor (`http://weblogs.asp.net/scottgu/archive/2010/07/02/introducing-razor.aspx`)

For PHP: Smarty (`www.smarty.net/crash_course`)

By following the Responsive+ approach, your tech team will be able to streamline the overall page size and performance concerns while taking full advantage of responsive design methodology that works on all kinds of devices. Note that we at iCrossing don't claim to have invented the wheel here—Anders M. Anderson first talked about Responsive Design + Server Side Components (`http://prezi.com/tgh0nmubj0xs/ress-responsive-design-serverside-components/`), an approach to combine responsive web design with server side components to make advanced responsive web solutions that work for all kinds of devices. What we have done is to streamline this methodology and create an architectural representation that we feel makes the solution scalable, maintainable, and easy to implement utilizing any server-side technology.

QA and Usability Testing

Testing your mobile content, both for bugs and for general quality, is definitely a point of frustration. You want to be certain your content works as it should on all of your target devices, yet actually testing on all of those devices is nearly impossible. In theory, creating an in-house test lab is a nice idea, but actually buying the tablets and handsets that show up in your analytics would be a tremendous investment and, with new devices continually making their debut, an inevitable money pit. Fortunately, we have some sound advice on how to tackle your mobile QA hurdles.

Hardware Purchases

We recommend that you purchase a limited amount of actual hardware for hands-on testing. Acquire the devices most popular with your users. In most cases, they will be iPod Touch, iPhones 3 (although these are decreasing in circulation) 4, 4S and 5, and several newer Android devices running 2.3, 3.0, 3.1, 3.2, 4.0, and 4.1 versions of the operating system. You may also want to acquire several iPads (one example of each iteration) as well as a Kindle Fire and Samsung Galaxy Tab. Unless your brand is a radical departure from the norm, these devices should leave you well set to test hands-on with the hardware used by the majority of your visitors.

Remote Testing Tools

Many developers rely on web-based simulators to test their mobile content across all the devices they want to cover. However, we find that simulators often fail to provide an accurate picture of how real devices perform on a live carrier network. Fortunately, there are models for remote device testing that will enable you to test efficiently across multiple devices and carriers.

Self-Service Test Vendors These vendors offer web-based simulator tools that enable you to remote-control real devices running on live wireless carrier networks. Most have an extensive library of devices and enable you to develop and run custom test scripts. If you have the internal resources to write and execute test plans, this is an option that enables you to test quickly and efficiently across all devices and carriers.

Full-Service Test Vendors These vendors design and develop a test plan according to your goals and specifications. Most also go a step beyond QA testing and do usability testing with focus groups of users who match your specific demographics and technographics. Full-service vendors are an excellent solution when you need to ensure that your content is bug free and resonates with the people you are trying to reach.

Thursday: Make Your Site Findable with Mobile SEO

Search is a fundamental mobile activity. Mobile consumers search via the browser, apps, SMS, and even visual interfaces such as Google Goggles and augmented reality. However, it's widely acknowledged that the majority of mobile search traffic, at least for now, flows through mobile browsers, so making sure that your mobile site content is properly indexed is of the utmost concern.

The good news is, in these nascent days of the mobile web, with so little mobile-specific content in circulation, if your desktop website is well optimized, your chance of ranking well on mobile is quite good. Much of your earned search equity will carry over from the desktop and most of the same basic best practices for SEO will apply. However, there are some unique differences to note.

Mobile Search Engines and Indexing

Google, Yahoo!, and Bing rule the mobile search ecosystem. Odds are, however, that most of your mobile search traffic will come from Google. Various industry reports over the last several years have claimed that Google, in its many iterations, owns upward of 95 percent of mobile search traffic, so the biggest engine will remain your primary concern for mobile.

Most content owners realized early on that Google, as well as Yahoo! and Bing, don't serve exclusively mobile content in mobile search results for smartphones. Realistically, they *can't* just serve mobile results; there isn't enough mobile content in circulation. What's more, content owners quickly observed that their desktop sites, with their superior search ranking and history, were outranking the mobile sites they created using separate mobile URLs. So it quickly became a best practice for content owners to redirect mobile clicks to their desktop domain to the mobile version of their website. This was highly beneficial to content owners because they could piggyback on the earned search equity of their desktop URL. All you had to do was worry about creating the mobile content and putting redirects in place. If your site ranked well on the desktop, that high rank would carry over to mobile.

Over time, however, Google increased efforts to modify search results for mobile users. There's now a higher prioritization of locally oriented content and natural results for the same terms will often appear slightly different, even across multiple different smartphone devices. So it's important to understand how Google serves search results according to device. Older, non-smartphone devices are served content almost exclusively from a mobile-specific index. Smartphones, like the iPhone and Android devices, are served results from both the mobile index *and* the desktop index. Historically, Google's advice to content owners on how to get their mobile content appropriately indexed has been confusing. For some time, it was suggested that because smartphones can (at least theoretically) display desktop websites, Google would display both mobile and desktop results to smartphone users and a separate smartphone experience was not necessary. This caused no small amount of confusion as to whether the search crawler for Google's mobile index, Googlebot-Mobile, should be allowed to crawl mobile websites that were designed with smartphones such as the iPhone in mind. In light of this confusion, there are now three separate web crawlers that Google uses to understand your web presence:

- **Googlebot:** Emulates a desktop user and indexes content meant specifically for desktop and laptop computers.
- **Googlebot Mobile:** Emulates older, feature phone devices and indexes lo-fi mobile content meant specifically for consumption on devices that do not have fully capable HTML browsers.
- **Googlebot Mobile for Smartphones:** Launched in December 2011, this crawler was specifically designed to emulate smartphone devices and index the unique content developed to cater to them—content that is less complex than a desktop site, but considerably more sophisticated than the "mobile" content created for feature phones.

These crawlers work together to understand the full extent of a brand's web content and ensure that each page is properly indexed and that users are served device-appropriate content when and where possible. Now the recommendation is not to block any of the three crawlers and to trust that Google will index appropriately. This is a huge step forward for mobile SEO, and we expect to see more mobile search innovation from Google in the near term. In the meantime, we've included some tips on how to develop your mobile site content to be SEO-friendly and make certain it indexes properly.

Define a URL Structure

Unless you've chosen to go the responsive design or CMS-driven route, your mobile content will, by necessity, have a different URL structure. Whether you are using a fully hosted, proxy, or cloud platform, the desktop and mobile versions of single page cannot share a single URL. You have a few options in this regard.

`.mobi` Domain You can choose to host your mobile content at a distinct domain that uses the `.mobi` extensions. For example, `www.kiwi-market.com` would become `www.kiwi-market.mobi`. We don't see intrinsic value in this approach. There's no clear indication that the `.mobi` domain convention is highly recognized among consumers nor do search engines appear to have any clear preference for it. At best, it has no clear benefit; at worst, it might confuse your users to promote a whole new domain.

Subdomain With this approach, your mobile content is structured as a *subdomain* of your desktop site—for example, `http://m.kiwi-market.com`.

Subdirectory Here, the mobile content is relegated to a *subdirectory* of the main desktop URL—for example, `www.kiwi-market.com/mobile`. Some SEO experts believe this approach enables mobile content to borrow equity from the authority of the full domain, but there's much debate about this and we can't say so with authority.

Overall, our recommendation is to go with a subdomain or subdirectory.

iCrossing's Nicholas Roshon on Responsive Design and SEO

There was a longstanding disagreement among many noteworthy SEOs on how best to handle URL structures for mobile content — some advocating Responsive Web Design and the use of one URL for all forms of content, and others advocating dedicated mobile sites with unique mobile URLs. This disagreement was finally squashed in June of 2012 when Google's Pierre Far announced that responsive web design was "Google's recommended configuration" for most webmasters. Google still lists "Sites that have separate mobile and desktop sites" as an option for webmasters to consider, but the message is clear: from a strictly SEO sense, Responsive Web Design is a no brainer. Using one URL for both desktop and mobile versions of the content means that all of the links, social media shares, and other ranking signals are consolidated to that one URL, rather than fractured across several versions of the URL. This makes both the desktop and mobile content even stronger and increases your likelihood of ranking for either user. While Responsive Web Design may be harder to implement, and there may be user experience reasons to go with alternative mobile web design standards, the SEO benefits of going Responsive are undeniable.

Device Detection

Redirects remain the number one golden rule of mobile SEO, and there are several ways to implement them.

Client-Side Redirect These are on-page redirects that use JavaScript to route mobile browsers or devices to appropriate mobile content. The content in question might be separate pages but may just as easily be a modified layout of the same page with a different style sheet. This type of redirect is most appropriate if you're trying to reach a small subset of primarily high-end, JavaScript devices. However, client-side redirects aren't ideal from an SEO perspective because (or as) search engines won't respect this type of redirect command and run the risk of missing your mobile content altogether.

Server-Side Redirect These redirects happen server-side, which enables you to redirect on a much more granular device-specific level if you choose. According to Google, a redirect should always be implemented as a 301, which is a permanent redirect.

Develop a Mobile Keyword Strategy

Google's Mobile Keyword tool (shown in Figure 4.6), provided for free in the Webmaster toolkit, will be invaluable in helping you develop a keyword strategy for your mobile content. Bear in mind that many of your keywords from the desktop will be equally important on mobile, but you may discover new ones and/or see an emphasis on certain specific keywords in the mobile context.

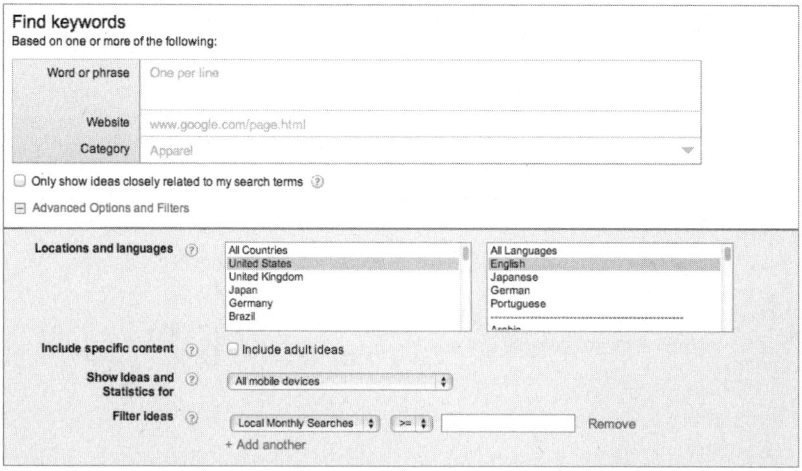

Figure 4.6 The Google Mobile Keyword tool

Mobile SEO Best Practices

Most of the traditional SEO best practices with which you are familiar from the desktop carry over to mobile, albeit some in slightly different ways.

Crawlability

301 redirects: As indicated in the section on redirects, all mobile redirects should always be implemented as 301s.

Avoid duplicate content issues: Scrupulously avoid creating multiple URLs for identical or very similar content where possible. Examples of duplicate content/URLs for mobile users include adding parameters (such as ?user=android, ?user=ios, ?user=tablet, and so on), Session IDs, timestamped URLs, mirroring the site on multiple domains, and other versions of URL/content duplication. Ideally, you want to try to use the "one URL" approach mentioned earlier, as responsive design and CMS design options use.

Robots.txt: Ensure that your `Robots.txt` file allows for all versions of Googlebot to crawl your site and find the content—do not block Googlebot-Mobile from your desktop content or Googlebot from your mobile content. Each bot will automatically be redirected to the appropriate content based on its user agent, much like a human user would.

Avoid using crawlability barriers: These include Flash, frames, pop-ups, and other potential hurdles for mobile crawlers.

Continues

Mobile SEO Best Practices *(Continued)*

Sitemaps: Create and submit sitemaps for your mobile content.

Avoid malicious cloaking: Ensure the content seen by Googlebot, Googlebot Mobile and the Google Smartphone crawler are identical or very similar to the content seen by the devices they serve.

Avoid third-party domains: If you have chosen to use a fully hosted or proxy service to develop your site, insist that URLs are aliased to reflect your domain, not the vendor's.

Use as little JavaScript as possible: When you do use it, make sure that it is nonobtrusive and that there is a clear separation of markup, look, and behavior.

Page speed: Measure the amount of time it takes for a page to load, as this is a ranking factor for both desktop and mobile search results. Google offers a plug-in called "Page Speed" for Chrome that will grade your webpages on a scale of 1-100. We recommend you shoot for a minimum of score of 90 on each page. This is especially important for mobile and tablet users who may have slower connections, and, as such, may be a stronger ranking factor for searchers on these devices.

On-Page Relevance

Keywords: Shoot for two to three keywords per page that target high-volume search phrases relevant to the page's content and tailor these keywords toward mobile users where feasible.

Page titles: Limit the title to 35 to 44 characters, including target phrases first.

Body content: Use descriptive navigational links and action-oriented copy.

Internal linking: Use static, crawlable links; optimize anchor text; add static navigation to all pages; and link static sitemap from all consumer facing pages.

On-page markup: Use rich text markup to make your location, phone number, and email addresses clickable.

Images: Include alt-text for all images, and make sure alt-text is brief but descriptive.

Off-Page Relevance

Links: Acquire links from appropriate on-topic mobile and desktop sites. Make sure they point to the most relevant page within your site to develop a good deep linking ratio.

Cross-link from the desktop: Create awareness content and navigational links to your mobile content from your desktop site.

Claim your Google Places and Bing Local Pages: Claim and verify these listings if your business has brick-and-mortar locations because local search results often receive additional prominence for feature phone and smartphone users.

Friday: Define Your Mobile Analytics

Mobile analytics—or more to the point, a lack thereof—have historically been one of the biggest deterrents to developing mobile content. In fact, according to webtrends (`www.webtrends.com`), a leading web analytics platform, 63 percent of global brands don't understand how their customers engage with their content via mobile. It's hard to justify investing in content you can't successfully measure. Poor to nonexistent support for JavaScript on mobile devices has made it an historical challenge to consistently track user behavior.

Thankfully, support for JavaScript is on the rise as mobile devices become more sophisticated. You can now collect much, if not all, of the same data you would expect to track from a desktop site. For devices with poor or no JavaScript support, Google and other analytics providers have implemented numerous workarounds and use image pixels and server-side scripting to collect data.

At this point, the state of mobile analytics still isn't as straightforward as it is on the desktop, but it's nowhere near as difficult and inconsistent as it was even a year ago. There's no reason for it to impede your mobile web development efforts. We'll close this chapter with some advice on how to get started.

Assess Mobile Visitors to Your Desktop Site

Most commercial and open source analytics solutions now support tracking for mobile devices as a standard feature, including

- Google Analytics
- Adobe SiteCatalyst
- webtrends
- IBM Coremetrics
- Yahoo! Analytics

Odds are you are already using one or more of these solutions and, as we discussed in Chapter 2, they provide valuable data that will shape your mobile site. The data you can segment out for your current mobile visitors should include:

Percent of Mobile Visitors This is a valuable metric; it tells you how much of your overall traffic is coming from mobile devices. Industry stats tell us that the average is now around 10 percent, but we know that for many brands that serve more mobile-savvy consumers, it skews even higher. This is the most powerful number in getting internal buy-in within your organization for building a mobile site.

Device Types This data tells you how sophisticated your mobile users are and what devices you should have in mind when designing the look, feel, and functionality of your mobile website.

Bounce Rate This is an excellent indicator of just how satisfactory (or not) your desktop site is on mobile devices and, hence, how accelerated your timeline should be for creating a mobile-specific version.

Most Visited Pages This gives you an idea of what mobile users have come to your site to accomplish. However, this data can be misleading. Often, in cases of a desktop site that performs very poorly on mobile, users may click on things out of desperation or because there is no other available option. You should always cross-reference these metrics with usability testing, as discussed earlier in this chapter, and, if possible, with personas and customer journeys developed in the strategy phase.

Integrating Analytics into Your Mobile Site

You actually have a much richer range of options available to you for tracking your mobile sites than you do for the desktop. In most cases, you can opt to use your current desktop solution to tag your mobile site, but numerous mobile-specific analytics solutions are also on the market.

The value of investing in a separate, mobile-specific analytics solution for your mobile site is debatable. A solution tailored specifically for mobile will usually offer you more granular data on the types of devices visiting your site, the carriers they come from, and the specific behaviors of visitors from handset to handset. All of this is nice data to have, but if you are just starting out with mobile, you can probably do without it. Our philosophy is that if you are targeting an international audience or one that is very diverse in terms of devices and/or you are delivering very complex multimedia content (such as videos, ringtones, games, and the like), then a mobile-specific analytics solution is essential. Otherwise, you can safely get away with Google or Yahoo! analytics or a commercial desktop solution that supports mobile. Of course, in a perfect world, you'd have both and compare the results of each. In the real world, the cost this incurs is often a deal breaker.

Tag CMS or Responsive Design Sites

If you have gone the CMS-driven or responsive design route for building your mobile site, integrating Google Analytics, Omniture (`www.omniture.com`, now known as Adobe SiteCatalyst), webtrends, or some other commercial package that supports mobile into your mobile site should be a relatively simple process. You'll tag your content just as you would any other website, following the specific instructions of the vendor, but with one difference: if you have a significant number of lower-end smartphones and feature phone devices, include image tag scripting as a workaround for poor or no JavaScript support.

Tag Cloud Service or Proxy Sites

If you've gone the cloud route, you can use a web analytics package to track visitors to your mobile site and you might also have the option of receiving some additional data from your provider. If you've chosen a hosted or proxy solution, you'll be solely dependent on your provider for gathering data. Some are able and/or willing to add third-party tags (Google, webtrends, et al.) for an additional fee.

Obtainable Data

Whether you are using a desktop analytics solution that supports mobile, a mobile-specific analytics package, or a proprietary service provided by your mobile web vendor, you can expect to collect a standard set of data. All analytics packages that support mobile should provide the usual expected data, including:

- Total visits
- Unique visitors
- Total page views
- Page views per visit
- Visit duration
- Bounce rate
- New visitors
- Return visits
- Organic search traffic
- Paid search traffic
- Direct Traffic
- Referral traffic
- Visits with conversions
- Visits with transactions
- Landing pages
- Keywords
- Device make and model
- Mobile browser
- Mobile operating system
- Screen resolution

Wireless carrier data is not obtainable with every analytics solution, but it can be extremely useful. Look for it as you consider various solutions. Also, not every analytics solution will provide the same level of support, but most are able to provide fairly granular mobile metrics on an overall basis, as well as by unique device (such as the iPhone 4S and iPhone 5) and/or device family (for example, Android smartphones running the Cupcake version of the operating system).

Establish Mobile Web KPIs and Measure Success

Your end goal is always going to be to build your business, whether that's through awareness, advocacy, or direct sales. How those goals are measured via your mobile website will probably be somewhat different from the desktop. We encourage you to start with your desktop key performance indicators (KPIs) as a baseline when developing your metric plans for mobile, but be prepared to modify them according to the expected behavior of your mobile users. For example, in the case of the fictional client, Kiwi Market, the company's desktop site is designed primarily to help customers compile grocery orders for delivery or design and order catering for events.

Kiwi Market's main desktop web KPIs include:

- Unique monthly visitors
- Repeat monthly visitors
- Bounce rate
- New customer registration
- Registered customer logins
- Completed orders
- Abandoned orders
- Email newsletter sign-ups

The understanding here that is the desktop site is a virtual version of the Kiwi Market in-store experience, and the key goal is to get users to become registered customers, save their credit card and other personal info, and come back to shop regularly online—all of which are reasonable and expected behaviors for a desktop user.

The behavior of a smartphone user might look quite different. Our persona customer, Michelle, might log in to her Kiwi Market account to place an order on her smartphone, but given what we know about shopping behaviors and smartphone users (courtesy of the research performed in Chapter 2), she might be far more likely to perform a very different set of more action-oriented behaviors. Hence, KPIs for the Kiwi Market mobile website might look more like this:

- Unique monthly visitors
- Repeat monthly visitors
- Bounce rate
- Phone calls for customer service or orders
- Store locator views

Kiwi Market's primary goal is the same in either case—to increase the size and frequency of Michelle's purchases. Both sites help to achieve this objective in different ways. The desktop site makes it easier for her to shop remotely; the mobile site makes it easier for her to shop in-store and on-the-go, curate her purchases both online and in person, and manage her overall experience as a customer. Both have separate but equal roles in the ecosystem that call for tracking of the same basic KPIs, such as unique/repeat visitors and bounce rate, but also necessitate unique metrics tailored to the context.

Mobile Measurement Roadblocks

That said, mobile devices still present some unique measurement hurdles that we need to address.

Inconsistent Support for JavaScript

While iOS and Android devices support JavaScript, many mobile devices only support it partially, and many feature phone devices do not support it at all. Therefore, if you rely solely on a JavaScript-based analytics solution, you face inaccuracies in reporting. The image tag workaround that we discussed earlier in this section is efficient for this issue. You will most likely find that devices with full JavaScript support will make up the bulk of your mobile traffic, but including the image pixel as a failsafe is recommended as a precaution. It's true that there are older devices that are unable to render images of any kind, but they represent such an infinitesimal portion of U.S. mobile web users that we believe they are no longer of any concern.

The Third-Party Cookie Conundrum

High-end smartphones and tablets now support cookies, but it's *how* they support them and how users manage them that are the problem. Some devices will periodically clear cookies as storage space fills and, of course, users can and often do choose to disable cookies due to privacy concerns. All of these are additional justification for including the image tag workaround as a failsafe.

The most pressing issue, however, has to do with the iPhone and third-party cookies. The default setting for all iOS devices, as depicted in Figure 4.7, is to accept cookies from "visited sites only," also known as first-party cookies. This means that the cookie placed on the device must be identified as belonging to the site the user is visiting. However, many commercial analytics solutions use third-party cookies as defaults—cookies that identify the analytics vendor as the entity placing the cookie. No doubt you can see the problem here—iOS devices will factor significantly in your mobile web traffic, yet all are set to reject third-party cookies by default. No statistics are available as to how many iOS device owners proactively change their cookie settings, but you should simply assume none do and approach mobile analytics accordingly. Google Analytics always uses first-party cookies by default, but if you are using another solution or vendor, it's important that you specify the necessity of using first-party cookies to track your mobile users.

We should note that there are multiple workarounds using redirects to fool the iOS into allowing you to place a third-party cookie on a mobile site, and many are very effective. However, we believe the best course of action is to use first-party cookies. Doing so will require a bit of resource investment because a developer will need to go in and change the tags embedded in your website—but it will be time well spent.

Figure 4.7 The iPhone's iOS default Cookie setting

First-Party versus Third-Party Cookies

First-party cookies are cookies set by the site you are visiting—that is, the URL you can see in the browser address window. The information they contain identifies that cookie, whether it is for analytics, advertising, or some other purpose, as belonging to the site you are currently viewing. A third-party cookie is set by a site that is *different* from the one you are currently viewing. The information in a third-party cookie identifies it as belonging to that third party—for example, an ad server or analytics vendor. These cookies can cause privacy concerns because users are usually not aware that they are being set.

Persistent Cookies Converted to Session Cookies

Some devices automatically convert *persistent cookies*, which are stored in the device's memory, into *session cookies*, which are wiped after the user session ends. Although there is no clear workaround around for this issue, it usually pertains to older, non-smartphone devices. Although you need to be aware of this issue, it probably won't be a pressing concern unless a high proportion of feature phones and older smartphones (pre-iPhone and Android era) visit your site.

Broken Requests Caused by Interrupted Connections

Another issue of concern is broken requests that occur when a user's data connection is interrupted. There is no clear workaround for this issue—it remains a fact of life in the world of mobile analytics.

> **Device Identification Numbers**
>
> You will hear about unique identification numbers for mobile phones. There are many different types of unique identifiers, and they vary in form from carrier to carrier and device to device. Although they appear valuable at first glance, being unique to the device, we don't recommend them as one of your desired metrics—and not just because they are hard to retrieve. Attempting to collect them has serious privacy implications as well.

Apply Lessons Learned/Iterative Refinement

We're willing to argue that applying what you learn from your mobile analytics is even *more* important than it is on the desktop. We're still in the early days of figuring out what causes mobile users to respond; keeping tabs on how your mobile site is performing will help your refine your content and overall user experience. Some metrics will be essential to helping you understand who your mobile users are, what they've come to your site to do, and how well your content meets their needs. Keep a close eye on the following:

- Bounce rate (overall and by device)
- Most visited pages
- Top smartphone and tablet devices
- Conversions

That's not to say that your other metrics don't matter! But metrics are meaningless without analysis, and certain metrics, like those listed here, will give you deeper insights into how your mobile website can be improved. It is what you do with the data that you collect that matters.

In Conclusion

Even in our increasingly mobilized world, your website remains a vital hub. Given the vast array of mobile devices currently on the market and in the hands of consumers, mobile site development efforts are almost equally varied. That's why we spent a lot of time discussing the pros and cons of a number of approaches. But bear in mind, this space is evolving with nearly the same speed as the devices themselves. You'll want to make ongoing education a priority so you can keep up with your audience.

We also tried to dispel the notion that mobile websites and apps are an either/or proposition. We do recommend focusing first on the mobile web, simply because browsers are more universal and you'll be able to maximize your development efforts with a well-tuned mobile website. But depending on your brand, audience, and objectives, you might want or need an app as well, particularly when focusing on repeat engagement. That's where we'll pick up next week, so get ready to dive into the expanding app universe.

5 Week 4: Maximize Engagement with Mobile Apps

When Apple launched the App Store in June 2008, it ignited a new emphasis on marketing beyond the browser. App stores now exist for every major smartphone platform, and the total number of available apps has mushroomed well past one million. Apps are appealing to marketers on a number of levels. In-app advertising and commerce plus paid downloads present an obvious monetary benefit, but it's not just about revenue. Apps also provide an opportunity to get closer to your customers by staking a claim to the mobile desktop—arguably the most valuable real estate in the world. In this chapter, we detail what you need to know about building and developing your mobile app, and the marketing you'll have to do to get it noticed and keep your audience engaged.

Chapter Contents

Monday: Understand Native App Considerations

It's hard to imagine our world without apps. They enable us to quickly access the information we need, listen to the music we love, buy the products we desire, read bedtime stories to our children, and plan almost every element of our work and home lives. In a very short time, we've come to rely on them. According to research firm TNS (www.tnsglobal.com), a member company of the Kantar (www.kantar.com) global insight, information, and consultancy group, 45 percent of U.S. mobile phone owners (comprising those with both feature phones and smartphones) use apps, and an additional 24 percent who don't are interested in doing so (see Figure 5.1). Globally, research and advisory firm Yankee Group (www.yankeegroup.com), an established longtime tracker of mobile marketplace trends, estimates the number of active mobile app users at 969 million in 2012, rising to 2.1 billion in 2016.

Usage/Interest in Select Mobile Features Among US Mobile Phone Users, Jan 2012
% of respondents

Web browsing
51% | 25% | 24%

Personal emails
48% | 25% | 27%

Applications
45% | 24% | 31%

Social networking
43% | 19% | 38%

Location-based services
40% | 29% | 31%

Wi-Fi
40% | 27% | 33%

QR codes
24% | 30% | 46%

Mobile wallet
14% | 26% | 60%

■ Currently use ■ Are interested ■ Are not interested

Source: TNS, "Mobile Life," April 24, 2012

139587 www.**eMarketer**.com

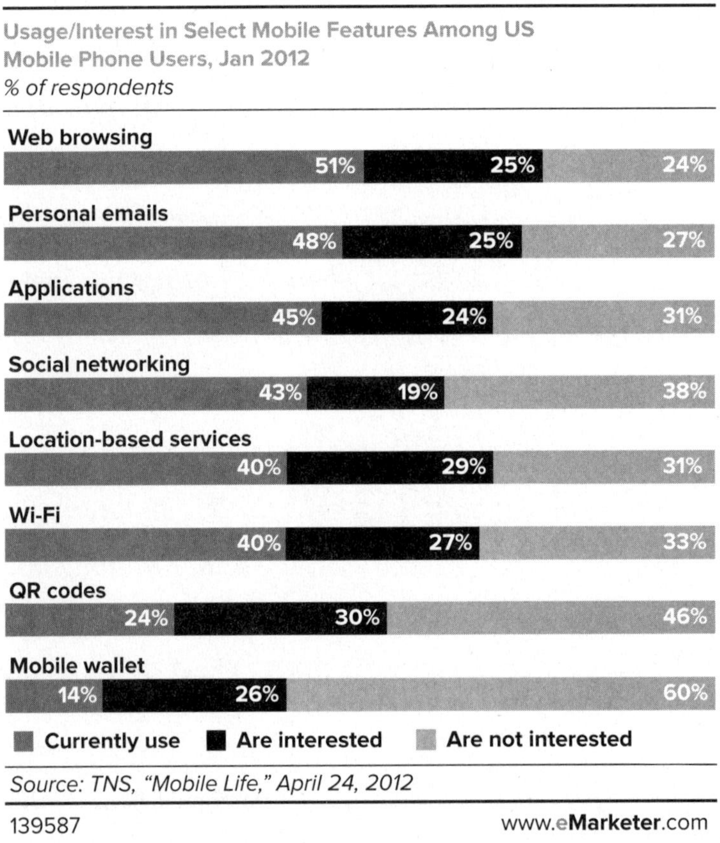

Figure 5.1 Apps have become indispensable.

Smartphone Apps versus Feature Phone Apps

Most branded apps target smartphone owners, but there are apps for feature phones as well. These apps tend to be distributed directly by the mobile carriers and/or come preinstalled on phones by the original equipment manufacturer (OEM). For the purposes of this chapter, we'll focus on smartphone apps, specifically for the two leading platforms—iOS and Android—as these will be the focus for most readers.

Apple's signature tagline—"There's an app for that"—rings true, not only because we've heard it a million times on Apple's TV commercials, but because it seems like there actually is an app for everything. As consumers, we expect we will be able to get an app for just about any purpose, just as the Apple ad says. And all signs indicate we've been getting a lot of apps—billions of them in fact. As shown in Figure 5.2, Strategy Analytics (`www.strategyanalytics.com`), a reliable forecaster of digital technology adoption, estimates the total number of apps downloaded reached 23 billion worldwide in 2011 and grew nearly 50 percent to 32 billion in 2012.

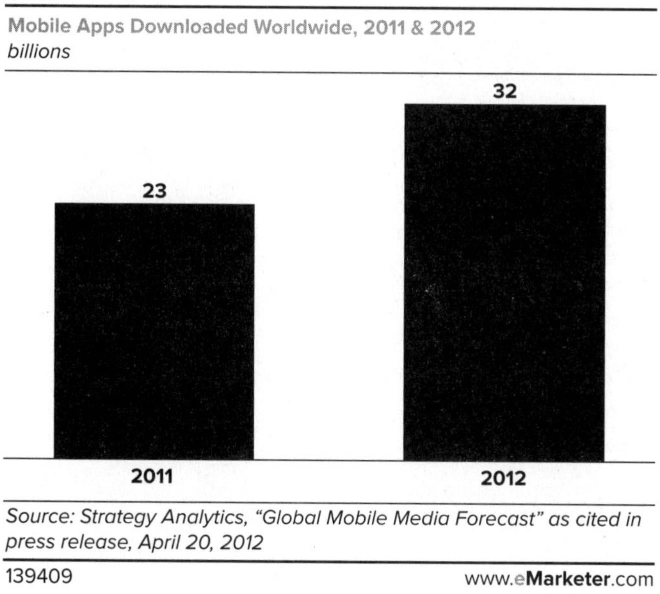

Figure 5.2 Mobile users have a healthy "app-etite."

To recap an important point from Chapter 4, "Week 3: Maximize Reach with Mobile Websites," the ascent of smart devices has given rise to a vigorous debate (in which prioritization is often posited as an either/or binary) about mobile websites versus mobile apps. But as we discussed, from both a user experience and marketing perspective, each brings something valuable to the table. As you may recall, our customer research indicated that mobile consumers like apps better once they've become connected to a brand because the user experience is better. They find there's less content they don't want or require, and the experience seems more tailored to their specific needs as an existing customer. Mobile sites, by contrast, leave the impression of being designed to get people to *become* a customer. Remember, that's *generally*; there obviously are exceptions in both cases.

If we were to use a metaphor to sum up the mainstream consumer sentiment, we'd say mobile sites are about dating, while apps are about commitment. Part of that commitment derives from the fact that apps are particularly effective at providing mobile users with an encapsulated experience that filters out the variables of browsing the Web.

There's no doubt that app usage is on the rise. The question is, Are your customers open to using *your* branded app? If so, what kind of app do you build? And how can you make it successful? These are the key questions we'll answer in this chapter. Our goal is to help you determine whether an app is right for your brand and how to proceed if it is. We also want you to understand that while building an app can do many wonderful things for your brand or your product, you cannot live on apps alone.

Validate Your Customers' Receptivity to Apps

Apps are not the end-all, be-all of mobile, but they do enjoy one very specific benefit that no other mobile channel or tactic has: prominence. By that, we mean a combination of constant visibility, accessibility, and connectivity. According to a study conducted by the Helsinki Institute for Information Technology (`www.hiit.fi`), a Finnish research body, and published in May 2011 by the technology journal *Personal and Ubiquitous Computing* (`www.springer.com/computer/hci/journal/779`), smartphone users look at their devices up to 34 times a day on average to check email and text messages, surf the Web, and use apps.

Given this common behavior, the value of having your logo clearly visible on the first few screens of a user's smartphone or tablet is quite clear—it's not unlike the importance of ranking in the top 10 results on Google or other search engines. The mobile desktop is fast becoming the most valuable real estate in the world; and if you can stake a claim to it, you'll go a long way to establishing a truly connected relationship with your customers.

Unfortunately, getting your app onto one of those first few screens—and keeping it there—isn't that simple. The first order of business is to determine whether your customers are actually going to use your branded app and whether building one will help you meet your business goals. That's the easy part. The major hurdle you're going to face is the newest form of ADD: "app-tention" deficit disorder. Simply put, with all those apps from which to choose, both in *app stores* and on your audience's devices, the days of building an app and watching the users roll in are long past. Getting found and keeping users engaged are tremendous challenges.

The May 2012 *State of the Appnation* report from Nielsen `http://blog.nielsen.com/nielsenwire/online_mobile/state-of-the-appnation` highlights this challenge. It revealed that U.S. smartphone owners were downloading more apps in 2012 (an average of 41) than in 2011 (an average of 32), but spending roughly the same amount of time with them (39 minutes per day in 2012 versus 37 in 2011). In this respect, apps are no different than other media: the options keep proliferating, but the amount of time available in a given day remains the same. Consumers' attentions are by necessity further divided.

Peter Farago, Vice President of Marketing at Flurry, on the Growing but Ultimately Finite Amount of Time Spent with Apps

"We're clocking users spending 94 minutes on average inside of apps per day, versus 72 minutes on average on the Web [mobile and desktop]. We know that app number is growing, but we also know it's finite. When I was in the foods business, we used to talk about 'stomach share'—you can only eat so much in a day. It's the same concept here; users can only spend so much time using apps."

Adding to the challenge is that most users spend the majority of their time with a very limited set of perennially popular apps. Nielsen's research indicates that the top five apps across Android and iOS remained consistent year-over-year: Facebook, YouTube, Android Market (now Google Play), Google Search, and Gmail. Overall, the top 50 apps ate up 58 percent of users' app time (a highly useful fact if mobile advertising is on your agenda). If nearly 60 percent seems like a lot, keep in mind that figure was down from 74 percent in 2011.

The good news is you have at least *some* opportunities to capture consumers' divided attention. You just have to do your homework to figure out exactly what will capture and keep it.

If you've gone through the strategic process we outlined in Chapter 2, "Week 1: Develop Your Mobile Strategy," you should have a good sense of who your customers are and where apps fit into their journey. As you weigh your app options, reassess certain aspects of your strategy by posing the following questions. Use them as a checklist each and every time you weigh app options.

Do I have a high percentage of smartphone and/or tablet users on the top app platforms? If you have a high percentage of iOS and Android users (and most likely you will), you can feel confident your customers are fairly app-friendly and will be favorably disposed to at least consider a mobile app from your brand. Take as an example the fictional Kiwi Market. Remember that in our sample audience research, we determined a dominant percentage of Kiwi Market's customers are high-end device owners who exhibit highly sophisticated mobile behaviors. Consequently, Kiwi Market knows it can safely invest in more sophisticated mobile tactics, including developing an app. Even if your mobile users include a higher percentage on platforms such as Windows, BlackBerry, and OEM-specific operating systems, an app may still be an appropriate option. However, remember that the total universe of users you will be able to reach will be proportional to these platforms' smaller market share relative to iOS and Android.

Does an app fit within my customers' journey and, if so, where? Will your app be relegated to the loyalty phase of the customer journey or are there ways in which it can improve (and be relevant to) earlier phases as well? Understanding an app's value proposition for your customers will help you determine just how much usage you can expect, which, in turn, will help justify your expenditure. In the case of Kiwi Market, the supermarket chain determined that an app could be relevant across the customer journey.

Do I have the ability to design and build app content and functionality (or access to specialists who do)? To keep users engaged, you'll need to have a firm understanding of the factors that will get them to download your app and keep them coming back, as well as the design and technical resources to actually create the app. The skills required to design an effective app *user interface (UI)* and to actually code the UI and functionality are highly specialized. Moreover, the process of managing the design and development of an app constitutes an expertise in itself. We couldn't begin to teach you everything you need to know to design and develop a native app—that's a book in its own right. Suffice it to say that you most likely will have to invest significant time and resources in hiring the right people and/or building the right skills in-house.

Is there potential for return on investment (ROI)? This won't always be an easy question to answer, but in many ways it's the most important. Building and marketing an app are often pricey endeavors, so you'll want to make certain you're investing wisely. Will you drive revenue by selling it as a premium app? Engage in-app sales? Utilize in-app advertising to subsidize costs? Drive customer acquisition? Manage customer relationships? Kiwi Market, for example, expects to compensate for making its app free by driving increased sales and using it to build a community of loyal customers who will use the app to make shopping lists, set up recurring orders, and share photos of the fabulous dishes they've created with the food purchased at the store. Like Kiwi Market, you want to be sure you have a strong value proposition for your brand—and your audience—before you move forward.

When you've answered these questions, then and only then you can truly understand whether or not it's a good idea to move forward with your app. As you review your answers, keep in mind a point we've emphasized throughout the book: with an app as with any mobile tactic, proceed based on how it can meet your goals and your customers' needs. If you're moving ahead with an app because your CMO wants one or your closest competitor has one, stop and then go back through the checklist before you proceed.

> **Johnny Vulkan, Founding Partner at Anomaly, on the Importance of Providing Utility and Not Succumbing to Shiny New Object Syndrome with Mobile Apps**
>
> "Many companies feel compelled to create ideas that use the latest technology and thinking purely for the technology's sake. We've seen it with augmented reality, apps, and QR [quick response] codes. All these technologies have high function when used correctly but can be irrelevant distractions when not.
>
> "However there are occasions when the technology itself can also be important for what it symbolizes beyond its actual usage. The old version of this is customer care numbers that appear on packaging. Few people will ever call that number but the fact that it exists on the packaging suggests that the company cares and will seek to resolve problems.
>
> "The modern version comes to life in ideas like the app we helped build for Budweiser, Track Your Buds. You can check a code on any bottle to see when and where it was made, the brewmaster responsible, and learn about the brewery. There is not an expectation that people will be checking every bottle or do the check more than once if they did, but the capability speaks volumes about the company's belief in its product. Budweiser is delivering beer fresh and brewed locally and can prove it. In this case, the idea of a code is akin to a quality seal; it's Budweiser standing by its quality and using technology as an enabler to prove it should you wish to check."

Choose Native or Web (HTML5) Apps

The debate over *native mobile apps* versus *mobile web apps* has grown very heated in recent years. In order to understand the argument, you need to appreciate the similarities and differences between the two. You can create a native app and web app that look the same and function in very much the same way, but how you go about creating them and the way they *actually* function are quite different:

- Native mobile apps are, in effect, mini-programs that you download from an app store and install on your mobile device.
- Mobile web apps run in your mobile device's browser.

Because *HTML5* will eventually be able to accomplish much of what you can do with a native app, many argue native apps will eventually disappear in favor of web apps. The argument has some validity: with a mobile web app, you can develop one application that is accessible to any mobile device with an HTML5 browser and achieve maximum reach with minimum effort. With native apps, you'll probably need to develop several separate iterations for the dominant app platforms and deal with the ongoing hassle of app store approvals and update processes. However, there are significant pros to the native approach. For one thing, you can tap into unique features of the device hardware that are, at least for now, inaccessible to a web app—the camera, for example, or *near-field communications (NFC)*. There is also the benefit of enabling users to store data offline in a more consistent way than HTML5 can currently achieve.

Both native apps and web apps can add value; what, where, and how much depends on your specific mobile strategy. In Table 5.1, we examine more decision-making criteria side-by-side to help you better assess which route to take.

▶ **Table 5.1** Native mobile apps versus mobile web apps

	Native Mobile Apps	Mobile Web Apps
Audience	45% of U.S. mobile user population (approximately 109 million)	50% of U.S. mobile user population (approx. 122 million): Biggest reach
Development	Need to develop for multiple platforms results in complex and expensive development cycles	HTML5: Standard open source platform; one easy, fast development cycle
Design	Rich, complex user experiences that can tap into device hardware functions such as camera, accelerometer, and contact list	Rich, touch-centric user interfaces, but some limitations in terms of interaction with hardware
Accessibility	Offline caching enables users to save personal info and access key content and functions with no data connection	Limited offline data caching: Data connection required for optimal performance
Relevance	Usually most relevant for the loyalty/advocacy phases of the customer journey, but can be relevant throughout in some cases	Play a key role in initial phases of the customer journey, but are accessible, useful, and usable every step of the way
Maintenance	Code and design updates are contingent on app store approval processes; potential for red tape	Streamlined desktop and mobile content updates

The comparisons in Table 5.1 may suggest that a mobile web app would be the easier or more rewarding path, but don't overlook the importance of expectations. Consumers increasingly *expect* a brand to have a native app, and that constitutes possibly the most compelling argument for having one. With the consumer imperative in mind, we'll focus the remainder of this chapter on native mobile apps and what you need to do to satisfy your audience's growing "app-etite."

Fully Native Mobile Apps versus Hybrid Mobile Apps

We should clarify one thing in our discussion of native versus web apps: very few apps are *fully native*. This means that there are very few apps that do not rely on an external data source to provide some aspect of content and functionality. Don't believe us? Try turning off your smartphone's data connection and using some of your favorite apps. Odds are most of them won't work to a certain extent, and many won't work at all. The fact is most native mobile apps are actually *hybrid mobile apps*: They integrate web-based content and services into the native app interface. This approach isn't just valid—it's highly strategic. If you bundle all of your content and services into a hermetically sealed native app interface, any time you want to make a change to your app, you'll need to develop a new version and go through the headache of app store submission. Keeping certain elements of your app dynamic makes it easier to keep your content fresh and makes for an easier maintenance and update cycle.

Determine the Appropriate Platforms

We've talked already about the fragmentation that plagues the app universe. Smartphone users are divided among a number of competing platforms. Android is the current leader both in the United States and worldwide, with Apple's iOS a distant second and BlackBerry and Windows Phone the also-rans in this increasingly two-horse race. The tablet market is currently dominated by Apple, but Android is expected to gain ground over the next few years. Fragmentation extends to the individual platforms as well, especially Android, as we discussed in Chapter 1: "Map the Mobile Opportunity." Ultimately, your audience and your audience's technographics should determine the platforms for which you develop. This is one instance, above all, where you should avoid the lure of the shiny object: If your customers are predominately BlackBerry users, don't go out and spend half a million dollars building an iPhone app! That will generate buzz, all right, but it will only be negative and ultimately reflect poorly on your brand.

You'll need to do more than just determine which platforms to develop for; there are multiple branches within each platform to consider. Here's a high-level look at what you'll have to think about when you develop native mobile apps.

iOS Android may be the biggest platform in terms of total users (smartphones and tablets), but iOS represents the largest audience of consistent app users. If you're planning to develop iOS apps, you'll want to consider those devices within the iOS family for which you will design *and* develop.

> **Design** The iPad, iPhone, and iPod touch are all very different devices with different capabilities, and consumers use them in different ways. Two main factors will help determine which of these you choose to develop for: the technographics of your users and what you hope to achieve with your app.

Development You'll also need to decide which versions of iOS you'll be willing to support. Most iOS devices in circulation now run one of the following: iOS 4.0.1, 4.1, 4.2, 4.3, 5.0.1, 5.1, or 5.1.1. As of this writing, iOS 6 had just become publicly available; based on previous iOS version updates, we expect it to see widespread adoption on supported devices (iPhone 3GS and above; second- and third-generation iPad; and fourth- and fifth-generation iPod touch) soon after its release. Which versions you choose to support with your app will depend once again on the technographics of your users and the type of user experience you want to create. As a developer, you have the option of creating a Universal App for iOS—one app that fluidly adapts to the capabilities of the iOS device on which it is running. Once you understand which iOS devices and OS versions prevail with your users, you can code your universal application to specifically support them.

Android Google Play (formerly known as Android Market) boasted more than 600,000 apps as of June 2012. It's still a less lively ecosystem than Apple in terms of consumption, but it is growing fast and will no doubt be an important platform for you in the near future, if it's not already. When developing for Android, you'll have a slightly bigger challenge, however, because the *operating system (OS)* is open source, and many carriers and OEMs have made modifications to the original code. Moreover, there are an estimated 250-plus devices running Android globally versus four running iOS—iPhone, iPod touch, iPad, and Apple TV. There's simply no guarantee that one app developed for Android smartphones and tablets will function uniformly across multiple devices and multiple versions of the Android OS. In fact, we can almost guarantee it won't. Unfortunately, there's no easy workaround here. The only thing you can do is look at the Android device traffic among your users, hone your development toward those specific devices, and hope that your device will function as expected on all the others.

Windows Phone Windows Phone devices are still relatively new to the market. Odds are they will comprise a small percentage of your customer technographics for now, so it's unlikely you'll be developing Windows Phone apps in the near term. But, we do think the devices are promising, and you may see them inching upward in your overall site traffic over the coming year. For now, if you do choose to develop for Windows Phone, it's a less daunting proposition than developing for iOS and Android (at least for now) thanks to Microsoft's tight control over software updates. The current device landscape is limited to a series of HTC and Nokia devices that are very similar in screen size and other hardware elements, making your life much easier in terms of your development process. You can develop a single Windows Phone app and be confident you are reaching and adequately serving the needs of all current users. This will carry over to Windows Phone 8, which shares core technology with the Windows 8 platform that powers both desktop and tablet PCs, thereby easing the burden of multiplatform development.

BlackBerry BlackBerry remains the most complicated app development platform for many reasons. The current Blackberry App World supports the Playbook tablet and the latest versions of the Bold, Pearl, Curve, Style, Storm, Touch, and Tour smartphone devices, as well as the 8800 series. All support OS 4.5.0 or higher. However, many developers report that minute variations between devices and operating systems can make it very challenging to develop an app that works uniformly across all the aforementioned. Given the challenges BlackBerry is facing in the marketplace, it's possible you will see the number of BlackBerry devices that visit your site dwindling. Still if you see a significant percentage of BlackBerry users among your audience technographics, this is an instance where you may want to strongly consider opting for a web app over a native app to ensure uniform performance and timely development cycles.

This is by no means an exhaustive list of app platforms, but it is representative of the most important device families that are of concern to most brands today. Regardless, the lessons we outline in this chapter are equally applicable to less dominant platforms.

White-Labeling Mobile Apps

Many brands consider buying or licensing an existing app and reskinning it with their brand instead of building their own app, a practice known as *white-labeling*. There are advantages to this approach, most obviously in terms of cost and time to market. White-labeling an existing app can be a lot faster and cheaper than creating your own.

However, we've rarely seen it work to a brand's advantage for the simple reason that the most popular and successful nonbranded mobile apps usually aren't interested in diluting their brand. Fruit Ninja is doing just fine on its own, thanks, and its developers probably don't need your money! Consequently, most apps available for white-labeling tend to be the less successful ones in their particular category. We've seen cases where a white-labeled app can work; a good example is a casual game white-labeled and distributed as a prize or incentive. All things considered, we're big believers in developing your own app that specifically meets your goals and your customers' needs. Go big or go home!

Tuesday: Build Your App Content Strategy

The end goal for all brands that develop an app is engagement—an always-on connection with consumers and a permanent spot on their mobile desktop. The not-so dark secret of native mobile apps is that most brands fail in this regard. Using a sample of 25 apps downloaded a total of 550 million times, app analytics platform Flurry (`www.flurry.com`) determined that after three months, less than one-quarter of iOS and Android smartphone owners continue using an app; after a year, the percentage drops to 4 percent (Figure 5.3).

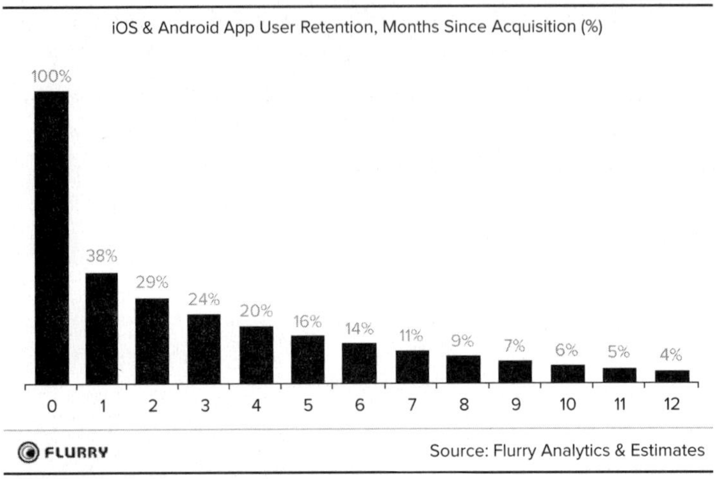

Figure 5.3 App retention is a big challenge.

This insight underlines something that we feel is a serious disconnect among brands that have developed mobile apps. Most brands focus on downloads as the key success metric for their app, but downloads are meaningless without engagement. It doesn't matter if your app generated 10 million downloads if only 100 people use it. Engagement is what we're all after and engagement starts with content strategy. To help you develop your app content strategy and understand that content strategy is key to driving engagement, we'd like to introduce you to the concept of the mobile app lifecycle.

The Mobile App Lifecycle: A Holistic Overview from Start to Finish

A successful mobile app starts with a good idea. Sounds simple enough, but developing that idea is actually a complex process. To succeed in this competitive space, content owners must understand the full extent of the mobile app lifecycle, outlined in Figure 5.4, which stretches from content strategy to post-launch marketing.

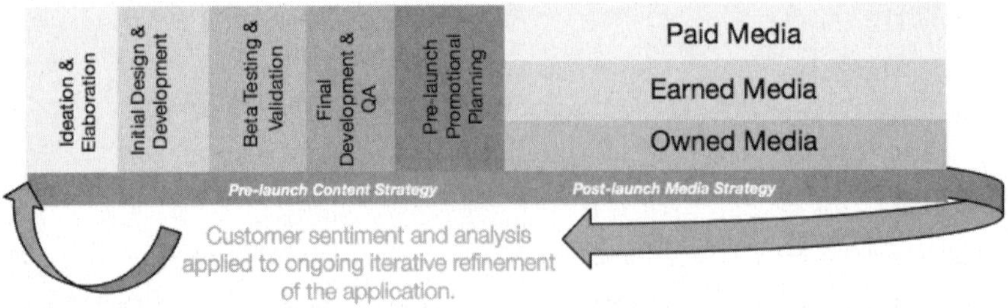

Figure 5.4 The mobile app lifecycle

Ideation and Elaboration: Develop and Validate an App Concept

Ideation is the starting point—this is where you develop your concept. Ideally, your core idea will have stemmed from defining who your target customers are and mapping out their unique customer journey or journeys. Following this process should net out with an app concept that's based on whom you're trying to reach and what you're both trying to accomplish.

Of course, this won't always be the case. Your initial concept might come from a burst of out-of-the-box creative inspiration from a team member, or you might get your initial ideas from looking at a competitor's app. In either case, you'll want to vet your concept against your overall strategy and technographics. Just because an app concept sounds brilliant doesn't mean it will be useful and engaging for your customers. Likewise, just because your competitors have an app that looks great doesn't necessarily mean it's getting the job done. Don't get us wrong, looks are important, they're just not everything.

So, do your homework. Look at your app concept in the context of your consumer technographics and ask yourself the following questions:

Does it offer your audience some unique benefit that your site does not or cannot?

Does it meet your audience's key needs in one or more of the specific journey phases?

Does it give your audience a reason to keep the app prominently displayed on their desktop and to come back to it consistently?

In this phase, you would commonly write a brief document called an application definition statement that defines what you want to create and why.

What Is an App Definition Statement?

The *app definition statement* is something Apple recommends in its *Human Interface Guidelines* for iOS, but by no means is it something you can or should do only for an iOS app. The app definition statement is extremely useful no matter what platform you are targeting. It helps you establish clear goals for your application and create a general consensus among your team members about what you are trying to create. Your app definition statement should include:

- The overall purpose of your app—what it should achieve for you and what it should do for your customers
- The features and content you want to include (to help define the initial level of effort for design and development)
- Your target audience (to help determine the overall level of effort for design and development and define which device families, specific device types, and operating systems you will include)

The process of developing the app definition statement will help you further refine your concept and truly determine whether you're on the right track.

Initial Design and Development

This is the phase in which you map out the content and user experience. It generally includes:

- Determining what existing content you have that can be repurposed for the app and how, if at all, it must be edited or otherwise modified

- Developing any new content that your app definition statement calls for
- Designing the app user flow beginning with a high-level *app map* (similar to a site map) and elaborating into a series of wireframes for each screen and user flows that show how users will progress through using the key functions of the app

Once you've pulled together the content for your app and organized it into a holistic framework, it's time to *validate* your content. We'll discuss some of the particulars of development tomorrow, but we'd like to point out that at this juncture what you are shooting for is a working beta—the full and final phases of development will take place later.

What you want to have by now is something tangible that you can put in front of a target group of users, so they can get a sense of what the experience will be, and you can get feedback on what they think of it. You can go one of two routes here, depending on the development path you choose. One is the quick-and-dirty option where you create a click-through demo of the app using HTML5. Another is to actually do your initial coding and pull together a working beta of the final app. Several different factors will influence your decision here, and we will discuss those tomorrow. For now, let's discuss *beta testing* and validation.

Beta Testing and Validation

In our opinion, this is where the app development process really gets exciting. We recommend you collect a group of four to five beta testers that roughly match up to your target demographics and sit them down in front of your beta app or app demo. Let them play around and get a feel for it, and then ask them some key questions. The scripts we create for this process vary greatly depending on the app and the audience, but at a high level, they boil down to this:

- Do you like this app? Why or why not?
- What would you add?
- What would you take away?
- What would you change?
- Would you pay for it? If not, would you pay for it if it cost less? Would you download it if it were free?
- How would you feel about ads within the app?
- Would you tell a friend about it?
- Would you use it more than once? How often?
- Where would you place it on your device? First screen? Second? In a subfolder?

There are many variations on these themes; you might ask about specific content or features, whether they'd share the app itself or share content from the app to their social networks, and to which ones, and so forth. But these are the core questions we almost always include.

Premium versus Freemium

Determining whether to charge for an app and if so, how much, is always a tough call. Generally, branded apps are free. Typically, the only brands that succeed in charging for their apps are those selling *premium content*—magazine publishers, for example, or game developers. Opinions from reputable research firms vary widely on the size and shape of revenues associated with apps, in large part because their forecasts focus on different facets of the "app-conomy."

ABI Research ABI Research's (`www.abiresearch.com`) February 2012 "Mobile Application Business Model" study predicts that global revenues from mobile applications, including in-app purchases, pay-per-downloads, in-app advertising, and subscriptions will reach $46 billion by 2016, up from $8.5 billion in 2011. Notably, ABI believes 2012 will be the first year revenues from in-app purchases will surpass those from pay-per-downloads, as in-app purchases become more widely available in apps other than mobile games.

IHS Screen Digest IHS Screen Digest (`www.screendigest.com`) has a similar outlook on the importance of in-app purchases, reporting they generated $970 million worldwide in 2011, or 39 percent of total smartphone app revenues. IHS expects in-app purchases to grow to $5.6 billion, or 64 percent, of smartphone app revenues by 2015. Note that the IHS forecast is lower overall than ABI's because it only includes in-app purchases and pay-per-downloads.

Berg Insight Berg Insight's (`www.berginsight.com`) October 2011 "The Mobile Application Market" study, which looks at revenues from paid app downloads, in-app purchases, and subscription services, estimated the global market at €1.6 billion ($2.2 billion) in 2010, increasing to €8.8 billion ($12.2 billion) in 2015.

There is more agreement about which platforms benefit most from paid app downloads. Strategy Analytics found Apple's iOS reaped 54 percent of paid app downloads worldwide in 2011, double Android's share. The research firm further predicts that same ratio will remain in effect in 2012. Given that the majority of Android apps are free (68 percent as of September 2012, according to AndroLib), while the balance of iOS apps favors paid, this outlook is not altogether surprising.

If you are reading this book, chances are you'll be going the *freemium* route. That means you'll be hoping your app will make back its cost through in-app sales, increased traffic to your brick-and-mortar stores, elevated brand awareness, or improved customer relationship management (CRM) metrics. As we noted earlier, that's certainly the approach the fictional Kiwi Market expects to take.

You may also find yourself interested in supplementing this revenue with in-app advertising. We'll explore the pros and cons of in-app advertising on a more granular level next week in Chapter 6, "Week 5: Promote Your Message with Mobile Advertising." However, we'd like to caution you that your chances of generating revenue are directly dependent

Continues

Premium versus Freemium *(Continued)*

on a few primary factors: the quality of content and user experience and your commitment to driving ongoing engagement. Bear in mind that downloads don't equal page views—to generate ad revenue, you'll need to build a strong community of consistently engaged app users.

Wednesday: Consider Development Options

Once you've sourced feedback from your beta testers, it's time to finalize development of your app, run quality assurance (QA) tests, and get it submitted to the app store(s). Today we'll discuss your development options, overall best practices for design and development, and how to get through the app store approvals process as quickly and painlessly as possible.

Development Decisions

Traditionally, native mobile apps have been developed like desktop software using programming languages like Java, Visual Basic, or some version of C (C++, C#, Objective C). Nowadays, with demand for apps on the rise and no end in sight, there are myriad alternatives for creating a native app. So let's look at a few.

Software Development Kit (SDK) An *SDK* is a toolkit for developing software, in this case, a mobile application. It generally includes sample code, documentation, application programming interfaces (APIs), and other tools that enable a developer to create an application that will run on a particular mobile device and use the device's hardware and software. Apple, Android, Windows Phone, and BlackBerry all offer SDKs that facilitate development of native mobile apps for their platforms. Apple has a stated preference that developers only use its SDK when creating iOS apps, although there are workarounds. SDKs have pros and cons. The cons are generally the learning curve and level of effort involved. Creating an app as a true piece of software using compiled computer code can be time-consuming, and the process almost always requires greater skill than front-end web development, so your development cycles can be lengthy and costly. Another potential drawback is the fact that the code you create is specific to one platform only and can rarely, if ever, be repurposed for another. On the plus side, apps developed using the native SDK are often faster and superior in terms of overall performance than apps developed using less rigid methods.

Cross-Platform Mobile App Toolkits SDKs set a high bar for app development, too high for many developers who wanted to create apps. *Cross-platform toolkits* for mobile app development subsequently sprouted up to help these developers realize their app ambitions. One of the first and best known is Phone Gap, but many others have evolved since the launch of Apple's App Store in 2008. These frameworks all operate on the same basic premise; they allow developers to develop native apps using HTML and CSS (most commonly HTML5 and CSS3), JavaScript, and/or other scripting languages and markup code. The frameworks also allow a developer to integrate native APIs that enable the app code to communicate with target device platforms. The developer can then package the app in a number of ways. Some frameworks actually allow developers to compile their scripted app into native code, while others create a native code "wrapper" for the scripted content. In either case, the final product can be submitted to app stores as a native application.

Hosted Mobile App Frameworks Remember the mobile-web cloud platforms we discussed in Chapter 4? This is a similar situation. Hosted mobile app framework platforms enable developers to create native apps using a framework and/or native SDKs and then connect that app to a cloud that hosts content and provides services including, but not limited to, feeds, media streaming, real-time image and media format optimization, and, of course, analytics.

Which route you choose for developing your app will depend on various criteria including your budget, technical resources, desired time to market, and most importantly, what you want the app to do.

Native SDKs versus Toolkits and Frameworks

We've seen great apps developed with toolkits and frameworks. In many ways, they are great options and can help you get to market faster and more cost effectively than using a native SDK. But, there are certain ways in which starting with SDKs is advantageous. Games and other complex touch-oriented user interfaces (where you'll want users to be able to manipulate an object on the screen, zoom in and out, or spin to see details) can be created using HTML5. However, when this code is integrated into a native app, performance can slow considerably and lead to a less-fluid user experience than desired. So, if you are developing a game or an app with a game-like, heavily touch-oriented design, we strongly encourage you to consider the native SDK approach.

Design and Development Dos and Don'ts

Suffice it to say, there are things that work within apps and things that don't. The app ecosystem is so vast that it's impossible to give you a set formula for success. For example, elements that work for a utility will be very different than what works for a game. We won't focus on true design or development best practices here—there are countless excellent books on both subjects, many of which we list in the appendix. But there *are* specific tactics we've seen lead to success—and to failure. In this section, we provide you with some high-level insights into each category.

The Dos

Let's start with what you *should* do.

Keep it lean and mean. Avoid extraneous content—users prefer apps because they contain the key elements they want and none of the ones they don't. Only add a function or piece of content if you can attach a specific, contextually relevant purpose to it.

Support sharing. Enable your users to tell others about your app, explicitly via SMS and email, but also consider adding implicit sharing elements. Allowing your users to share elements of content via Facebook, Twitter, Google+, and other social networks creates an endorsement of your application within your users' peer networks.

Solicit feedback. Don't wait for the app store comments. Allow your users to share feedback about your app from within the app itself. This has two key benefits—it filters comments to you quickly and, ideally, keeps negative comments out of the app store where potential users might see them. One of our favorite examples of this tactic is an iOS app that includes two small feedback buttons on its About page: "Send Feedback" and "Send Love." Send Feedback leads to a form in which users can type a short comment whereas Send Love automatically triggers the process of leaving a review. These clever developers found a way to solicit feedback, keep negative commentary off their app store landing page, and garner only positive reviews. Learn from their example! In addition, don't be afraid to ask openly for reviews. If users love your app, many will undoubtedly write a positive review for you, which will help lead to higher rankings.

Create an eye-catching icon. Your icon is the first thing users will see when they search the app store—make it as visually appealing as possible, but also make sure it is relevant and conforms to your brand guidelines.

Develop compelling landing page copy and visuals. Your landing page is where you sell the user on downloading your application, so put maximum effort into making it look and sound good. Develop body copy that describes the key benefits of your app and don't be afraid to include any positive media mentions and/or comparisons to similar, successful apps. Also, include screenshots that illustrate the most compelling and visually appealing elements of the application.

The Don'ts

Be sure to pay close attention to the don'ts as well.

Don't ignore customer feedback. There's often a lot of truth to negative feedback, especially when the comments you get are predominantly negative, so ignore it at your peril! You cannot respond to app store feedback directly in the comments on your page, but you can take negative feedback to heart. You can also use alternative channels, such as Facebook and Twitter, to respond to app store commentary, acknowledge bugs and other issues, and share your plans to address them. However, not every user of your app will also be a follower, hence the value of directing your users to provide their feedback within your app. If you encourage them to contact you directly with their input, you'll have a direct means for responding to their issues—and a better chance of turning a critic into an advocate.

Don't crowd the UI. Avoid trying to pack too much text or too many images into a single screen—the stripped down look and feel of apps is the main reason users prefer them over mobile websites in the first place. In fact, if you are observant, you'll notice the streamlined design model of apps is starting to carry over to mobile websites with bigger buttons, briefer text, and more sparing use of logos and other brand imagery. Of course, this applies more with smartphone apps where space is limited than it does with tablet apps, but as a rule, apps are a proposition where less is more.

Don't skew too small with the navigation elements. There are few things more frustrating than mistakenly clicking on something because the navigation buttons on an app are too small and too closely crowded together.

Don't be 100 percent data dependent. Even if many or most elements in your app will be dependent on a live data connection, your users should be able to access some content and features even when a data connection is not available. This is one of the main value propositions for an app, so take advantage of it!

Don't just recreate your website. When the Apple App Store first debuted, we saw many apps that were just mobile websites inserted into a native app wrapper. Thankfully, this trend seems to be waning as brands realize their mobile app can and should be different from their mobile site. Some elements will be the same of course—a hotel app, for example, would have the same booking engine as the mobile site. However, the way that information is presented might be quite different. The point being, think contextually when you design your app and sculpt your content and the overall user experience to complement the parts of the customer journey in which the app plays a key role.

Don't engage in gratuitous use of device attributes. We often hear people say, "Do something cool with device attributes" (accelerometer, camera, GPS, and the like), but we think this can often be a mistake. Making the app do something when you shake—just for sake of it—is gratuitous and can end up complicating a feature or, worse yet, creating one that has no clear purpose. Consumers sour quickly on frivolity, so don't create useless features!

Submission Guidelines and Best Practices

A common misconception is that submission happens once you've designed, developed, and tested your app. The truth is, the submission process needs to start in tandem with the initial design and development phases. You won't actually submit until you have a final build, but there are many steps to go through and many assets to gather prior to uploading your app for approval.

In this section, we give you the lowdown on what you need to prepare. For the sake of brevity, we'll focus on the iOS process simply because it's the most demanding and complex. If you succeed in pulling together the information Apple requires, you'll be well prepared for any other app store. The process can be summarized in two general steps:

1. Get a developer license.
2. Collect your App Store metadata.

Get a Developer License

This step sounds relatively simple in theory, but it can get rather complex. Consider that your completed app will appear in the App Store under the name of the *developer license* used to create it. Say, for example, that Kiwi Market hires Mobile Agency X to create a mobile application. If Mobile Agency X then uses its own iOS developer license to create and submit the application, the app will appear in iTunes as being owned and distributed by Mobile Agency X instead of Kiwi Market! That's not so great from a brand equity perspective.

If you are contracting an individual or agency to develop your native app, here's what to do: Make certain a developer license is purchased and registered in your name—as you want it to appear in the App Store. Conversely, if you are a developer or agency creating an app on your client's behalf, make them aware at the very start of the process that you will need to acquire a licenses in their name.

That said, there are also several types of licenses to consider.

iOS Developer Program, Individual Consider this option if you are a sole proprietor or hobbyist developer. You'll need to provide Apple with your Apple ID, your legal name (which will appear in the App Store as your seller name), street address, and a credit card for processing of the enrollment fee. If you choose to sell premium apps, Apple will also require your personal taxpayer identification, as well as direct deposit information for distribution of your payment from app sales.

iOS Developer Program, Company Select this option if you are an agency or company that has official status as such—that is, if you do business as an LLC or corporation. You'll need to provide Apple with your Apple ID, the legal name of your business (which will appear in the App Store as your seller name), the legal street address of your business, and a credit card for processing the enrollment fee. Apple will also require legal documentation post-submission to prove existence of your business, which may include but is not limited to: your Federal Tax ID number, Dun & Bradstreet (D&B) number, articles of incorporation, or business license. Note that, as per the current iOS developer program website, Apple does not accept "DBAs, fictitious businesses, or trade names at this time." So, if you want to register for a company developer license, you need to be ready to prove you're legitimate. Also, the person who submits your application must have legal authority to represent your company. If you are a developer or agency submitting on behalf of your client, you will need to have a client representative create the initial application with your assistance.

iOS Developer License, Enterprise This program enables you to develop applications known as *in-house apps* for distribution within your organization. Please note that you will not be able to distribute these apps within the App Store—they will only be for direct use by your employees. You will be required to provide the same information as you would for a Company license, but some details, including your (D&B) number, will be required earlier in the application process.

iOS Developer License, University Program This unique license is provided free to accredited educational institutions that want to integrate iOS app development into their curriculum. This type of license basically grants teachers and students the right to create development teams in which they can collaborate on app projects—developing and sharing apps within the group, but not distributing them to the App Store.

> **Note:** If you submit for a Company or Enterprise license, the email you use in the submission process must match the corporate domain and identity of the company for which you are submitting the request. For example, the person submitting an application for a Company developer license on behalf of Kiwi Market must do so using a Kiwi Market email address—for example, `marketing@kiwi-market.com`.

Once you've submitted your online developer license request, you'll get an email acknowledging receipt of your request. If you've applied for an individual license, you may get approval right away—as soon as 5 to 10 business days, although approval times can vary greatly. If you've submitted a request for a Company or Enterprise license, you will most likely get an email within the same 5 to 10 business day timeframe asking you for the legal documentation of your company's existence. Once you've submitted all the requested documentation, you may wait several weeks or more for final approval.

All things considered, to be on the safe side, assume you will need at least a full month to acquire the appropriate developer license prior to submitting your app.

Collect Your App Store Metadata

When you upload your app, you'll be required to submit a lengthy list of metadata that describes it. This data is vital to your appearance, visibility, and findability in the App Store, so it's not something that you want to just throw together a few days before submission. Carefully vet the criteria required per the descriptions in Table 5.2. We'll use the Kiwi Market app as an example and provide some sample copy.

Table 5.2 An iOS app store metadata submission worksheet

Required metadata for Apple App Store Submission: iPhone, iPad, and iPod touch		
Category	Please Fill In	Explanation
Apple Account	Use the brand app owner's iTunes Connect account here. This is the ID that will show up as the app owner in the App Store.	The user name/password for an account in Apple iTunes Connect with full admin rights.
App Name	The full name of the app as it appears in the App Store. Sample copy: The Kiwi Market Meal Planner	Apple allows up to 255 characters for the full app name—this is an opportunity to add important searchable keywords. Many blogs say that only 11 characters can appear on the actual desktop icon, but we've seen as many as 16 appear. It seems more reasonable that the number of characters that will appear depends on how many pixels each individual letter takes up. In any case, it's best to keep your app name as short and sweet as you can while maintaining its descriptive qualities so that users can get a good sense of what it is about at first glance. Some developers believe it's best to start your app name with one of the first few letters of the alphabet to take advantage of the alphabetical "sort by name" option in iTunes. We think this makes sense to a certain extent, but it shouldn't dictate what you name your app—choose a name because it fits your brand and content, not because of the letter it begins with.
App Description	Sample copy: With more than 50 locations in the U.S.A., Kiwi Market offers the finest in domestic and imported gourmet foods. With the free Kiwi Market app, you can: • Browse and shop by category • Search for items • Order grocery delivery and catering • Set up recurring deliveries • Create shopping lists and menus • Read product reviews • See recipes • Share your own recipes and photos of your masterpiece menus with the Kiwi community Download the app today!	Apple allows up to 4,000 characters for the app description. Be sure to describe functionality, features, benefits, accolades, and links to web content. References to competitive apps are also permissible, but should be carefully considered on a case-by-case basis.

Category	Please Fill In	Explanation
What's New in this Version	Details on updates to content functionality, for example: • New "upload a photo of your masterpiece meal" feature • New product reviews feature • New opt-in feature for geo-fenced alerts	The details of what's new in this version of the app: new features, UI improvements, or bug fixes. Not applicable if the app is launching for the first time.
Device Requirements	Information about the devices for which your app is optimized. Sample copy: Compatible with iPad; requires iOS 3.2 or later.	If the app requires a specific device capability (for example, telephony, GPS, or accelerometer) to function properly, users must be made aware of this. The individual or individuals who executed technical development of the app will be able to provide this information.
Primary Category	The primary category for listing. For the Kiwi Market example: Lifestyle.	List the category or categories that best describe the app in question: Select from Books, Business, Catalogs, Education, Entertainment, Finance, Games, Healthcare & Fitness, Lifestyle, Medical, Music, Navigation, News, Newsstand, Photo & Video, Productivity, Reference, Social Networking, Sports, Travel, Utilities, and Weather.
Secondary Category	The secondary category provides an opportunity to stand out in a category in which there may be less competition for the app. For the Kiwi Market example: Utilities.	Any additional category or categories that could describe the app; select from the previous list.
Copyright	Must be provided by the brand app owner. Sample copy: 2011 Kiwi Market, Inc.	The name of the person or entity that owns the exclusive rights to the app, preceded by the year the rights were received, for example: "2008 Acme, Inc."
Version Number	Must be provided by the brand app owner. Sample copy: Version 1.0.	The version number of the app. Please note that if the app was developed by a third party, that person or business may have their own distinct form of version control. However, a distinct number may be developed for the content owner to use in iTunes.
SKU Number	Must be provided by client.	A unique numerical identifier for the app. This is defined by the content owner and may be random or tied to an internal tracking system.
App URL	Must be provided the brand app owner. For our Kiwi Market example: `www.kiwi-market.com/mobile`.	A distinct URL for a web page that provides information on the app. It must be visible to customers in iTunes.

Continues

▶ Table 5.2 An iOS app store metadata submission worksheet (Continued)

Support URL	Must be provided by the brand app owner. For our Kiwi Market example: www`.kiwi-market.com/mobile_support`.	A distinct URL for a web page with contact details for app support. It must be visible to customers in iTunes. Note this URL may be the same as the app URL, assuming support info is provided.
Support Email Address	This domain must be identifiable as belonging to the brand app owner's domain. For the Kiwi Market example: `customerservice@kiwi-market.com`.	This email address will be used by Apple to contact the content provider about any problems with the app. This email address will not be seen by customers.
Demo Account—Full Access	A login/password from Kiwi Market to test app capabilities that require a user login, such as checking the status of an order, placing an order, and adding a recipe or other user-generated content.	For apps that restrict certain content and functionality to users with login credentials, you must provide Apple with a means to test these areas of the app.
App Icon	This is the icon that will appear in the App Store and on the user's mobile desktop. It must be delivered in PNG format.	For iPhone/iPod touch, the binary must contain an icon that is 57 × 57 pixels. If the app is for the iPad, the binary must contain an icon that is 72 × 72 pixels. If the app is for both, the binary must contain one of each size. These icons will display on the iPhone, iPod touch, or iPad home screen.
Large 512x512 Icon	The larger format of the icon that will appear on other featured areas of the App Store. It also must be delivered in PNG format.	A large version of the app icon. This will appear in the App Store. It must be flat artwork, without rounded corners, that has not been scaled up, and is at least 512 × 512 pixels and at least 72 DPI.
iPhone and iPod touch Screenshots	These screenshots are the art that appears in the App Store on your app landing page. These visuals will help tempt users to download your app, so try to choose the most exciting and eye-catching elements.	iPhone and iPod touch screenshots must be a `.jpeg`, `.jpg`, `.tif`, `.tiff`, or `.png` file that is 320 × 480, 480 × 320, 320 × 460, or 480 × 300 pixels, at least 72 DPI, and in the RGB color space. Up to five images are allowed.
iPad Screenshots	These screenshots are the art that appears in the App Store on your app landing page. These visuals will help tempt users to download your app, so try to choose the most exciting and eye-catching elements.	iPad screenshots must be a `.jpeg`, `.jpg`, `.tif`, `.tiff`, or `.png` file that is 768 × 1024, 1024 × 768, 748 × 1024, or 1004 × 768 pixels, at least 72 DPI, and in the RGB color space. Up to five images are allowed.

QA Best Practices

App quality assurance is, thankfully, less labor intensive than testing a mobile website since you are just focusing on one or, at most, a handful of devices. If you're testing an iOS device, your process will probably be fairly smooth. You may face more challenges with Android, due to platform fragmentation, but if you've followed our advice from earlier in this chapter and identified the devices most important to your customers, that should make your life somewhat easier. In this section, we'll concentrate on the benefit of a dual approach to QA that includes hands-on and automated testing.

Test Service QA Tips

Let's face it; there's a lot to test even in the simplest app. The iOS developer program offers a variety of tools, including a graphical debugger that enables you to identify and troubleshoot issues in real time, as well as a limited amount of technical support. With these, you can test throughout the development process. But if you want to thoroughly test multiple devices and platforms, you will definitely benefit from enlisting the services of a test vendor.

There are multiple vendors on the market that will write and run customized test plans for you or offer you a software-as-a-service (SasS) platform that will enable you to do so yourself. We've provided a list of test tools and services in the appendix—you'll have to vet more than one to find the right fit for your needs and budget. However, we do have a few recommendations:

Create an initial test inventory. Even if you are outsourcing your QA process 100 percent, you should have an initial sense of what you want to test.

Make sure the service or vendor tests on real devices. Simulators simply aren't enough—your app should always be tested live, on real devices running on both Wi-Fi networks and carrier data networks.

Test for functionality; test for usability. It's important to ensure that your app is bug-free, but being bug-free doesn't necessarily equate to a good experience. Include testing of the experience itself. Ask questions like, "Does this feature make sense?" and "Is this function is easy to use?"

The usability aspects are, of course, subjective and require a human perspective. The technical aspects, however, can often be automated, saving you considerable time and money. Things such as memory and battery usage, load times, and validity of specific functions can be scripted and executed far more efficiently as automated processes.

Hands-On Content Validation

Testing with a service enables you to access myriad devices running live on all the carrier networks. In our opinion, that ability is indispensable. However valuable, it's still no substitute for hands-on testing with real, physical devices. If you're only developing for iOS, it should be no problem. With Android, you may face more of a challenge, given the 250-plus devices (including smartphones and tablets) on the market globally as of August 2012 (Google maintains a full, up-to-date list at `www.android.com/devices`). However, if you follow our recommendations from earlier in this chapter, you should be able to narrow your Android target to a manageable list of devices for the purposes of hands-on content validation.

This aspect of testing is much more about determining what works and what doesn't in terms of the user experience. Your hands-on test team might catch a bug here or there that your automated test team did not, but the most important thing they will bring to the table is the human element. Pull together a team of 5 to 10 team members and have them do the following:

- Record the load time of the device overall and of specific content elements.
- Check text content for grammatical errors and misspellings.
- Check visual elements—logos, fonts, photos, and other images.
- Check navigation and the flow of content for overall intuitiveness.
- Check the specifics for each function:
  - Does the email form submit successfully and return a response?
  - Does the shopping cart allow you to check out?
  - Does the click-to-call button connect to a valid, working number (and is that number the right one)?
  - Test any and all functions to make sure they work and work well.

You can have your human test subjects deliver their feedback in any number of ways. We find that it's simplest to create a test plan in Word or Excel and have them simply fill in their feedback, but if you have an automated bug repository set up online, that works too!

Whether you invest in an enterprise test service or just QA your app on a few iPhones among a handful of friends, the important thing is to test, test, and test again. Users are less forgiving of bugs in an app than they are in a website. If they are unhappy, they won't just tell you about it, they'll tell the whole world courtesy of negative app store comments. If that's not enough to convince you, then consider the fact that to fix a bug after submission, you may well have to create a new build and submit all over again. That's a headache you definitely don't want.

The App Store Approval Process

So, just how long does it take to get an app approved? Apple won't say for sure. In our experience, it can happen in as little as week—or as long as a month. It helps, of course, if your app is bug free, but keep in mind that App Store approvals are a human process. There's an actual person reviewing and approving your app, and what one person might approve right away, another might take more time to review. Long story short, it's the luck of the draw. We've seen no noticeable difference in the process when submitting an update to an app: The process and average duration seems to be roughly the same. However, when you submit an update, your current version remains live in the app store while you await approval, so it's less nerve racking than waiting for an approval the first time around.

Thursday: Develop an App Marketing Plan

On Tuesday, we discussed the importance of content strategy and its role in generating engagement. We'd like to take a moment to elaborate a bit further on this subject because content strategy isn't something that you just do once—it's an ongoing cycle.

Analysts estimate that roughly one-quarter of your app users are potentially loyal customers—the ones that will use your app consistently and become, and stay, connected with your brand. Content strategy focuses on identifying, understanding, and communicating with these customers and using their insight to inform ongoing app development and marketing.

In essence, content strategy equals engagement. Research, user testing, and user feedback are instrumental in defining and refining your original app concept. As detailed in Figure 5.5, they are also essential to continually shape and validate your app concept over time, keeping it fresh and engaging so that your users *keep coming back*. And that's what you want, because continual use *is the name of the game*. As we said earlier, downloads without engagement are meaningless.

Figure 5.5 Mobile app content strategy leads to ongoing engagement.

Of course, you can't create engagement unless you get the app into a user's hands in the first place. That's where your media strategy comes into play. Whereas your content strategy leads to engagement, you'll rely on your *media strategy* to create awareness and drive downloads. A well-planned and carefully curated combination of paid, earned, and owned media, which we've laid out in Figure 5.6, will produce the downloads required for natural visibility and create a consistent level of awareness that will help capture new users.

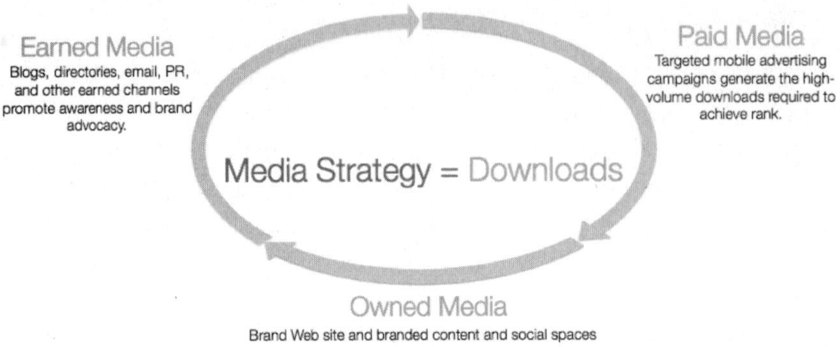
Earned Media
Blogs, directories, email, PR, and other earned channels promote awareness and brand advocacy.
Paid Media
Targeted mobile advertising campaigns generate the high-volume downloads required to achieve rank.
Media Strategy = Downloads
Owned Media
Brand Web site and branded content and social spaces

Figure 5.6 Mobile app media strategy leads to awareness and downloads.

Paid Media Strategy and Execution

Paid media is instrumental in driving downloads at launch. This is essential for one key reason: Downloads are primarily what define your rank within the app store.

The higher your downloads in a given category, the higher your rank in that category. The higher your rank for a particular keyword, the higher your rank in search results for that keyword. Mind you, neither Apple, nor Google, nor any of the other app store platforms have ever come out and admitted that this is the case, but it's pretty much the general consensus in the developer community. If you observe the rank of your app on a daily basis and then map it against your downloads, we have no doubt you'll see a clear correlation between how many apps you've moved and how high or low your rank has gone for that day.

The truth is, no one knows for sure what Apple's, Google's, or BlackBerry's algorithms are for app store rank. But, we do know that achieving a high rank is instrumental to being found by your existing customers and discovered by new ones. So for the sake of argument, let's assume that if downloads do indeed have a lot do with it, as we suspect, the equation for app store rank is most likely a factor of your last four to five days' worth of downloads, with the most recent day's numbers carrying the most weight, as some, including Baptiste Benezet, product development director at global innovation agency faberNovel (`www.fabernovel.com`), have proposed. The bottom line: rank matters. Paid media can create a high volume of downloads at launch, which leads in turn to an elevated rank and higher natural app store visibility.

What About App Store Reviews?

Many brands ask us, "But what about app store reviews? Don't they count toward my app's rank?" Our answer is yes, but indirectly. To the best of our knowledge, your app store reviews, whether positive or negative, don't factor directly into how Apple or any of the other app stores calculate your rank. They do, however, influence whether someone downloads your app. Since every download helps buoy your rank, positive reviews will help you in this regard and negative ones will hurt. But as far as we can tell, reviews do not factor into the ranking algorithms.

There are also rumors that engagement is now a ranking factor—that is, the number of times your app is used in a certain time period and the amount of time the app is used in an average session. However, this would be very difficult for Apple to measure fairly and accurately, so we believe this to be conjecture, at least at this point.

The paid media elements of your app marketing plan will break down into prelaunch and post-launch components:

Prelaunch Paid Media Planning

The prelaunch activities include reviewing your ad options and planning your ad messaging.

Review your ad options. We'll elaborate more on ad options in Chapter 6, but suffice it to say, you have a lot of options. Most mobile ad networks now offer some kind of pay-per-click or pay-per-download option at a reasonable cost, and Google now offers an "ads for apps" and "app extensions" option as well. Aside from these well-known networks, there are also opportunities to place advertising on some of the many blogs and YouTube channels devoted to app reviews—we've seen many brands have success with this model! In addition to all these, there are many niche startups that promise to help you drive downloads for a price. We'll review these in more detail next week when we dive into advertising.

Plan your ad messaging. Keep in mind that your goal isn't just to drive downloads; it's to drive downloads to the most engaged users possible. Ad copy and imagery that clearly illustrate the benefits of your app will help ensure your apps find their intended audience. We'll include examples of some successful ads for app in the next chapter.

Post-Launch Paid Media Execution and Management

The post-launch efforts boil down to all the tasks involved in managing your campaign, starting with paid media and layering in earned and *owned media*.

Manage your campaign. Post-launch, it's simply about managing your campaign. Display media will be handled for you almost entirely by the mobile ad network. As the client, you should simply be aware of what, if anything, your ad network account managers are changing as they manage your campaign, including but not limited to modifications to your creative and placement of your ad in different apps and on different sites. Again, we'll review this in greater detail in the coming chapter. Paid media can be indispensable in getting the word out about your app. But, the important thing for you to keep in mind about paid media is it *only works as long as you pay for it*. The goal should never be to keep paying for downloads, but rather to use paid media to create an initial lift that makes your app highly visible and easily discoverable within the app store ecosystem and in key areas around the Web. Your earned and owned plans should start in tandem with the paid component so that your paid efforts can scale down over time as earned and owned take over. The basic concept here, outlined in Figure 5.7, is that earned and owned media create an organic framework that continues to support the initial high rank you've achieved with paid media.

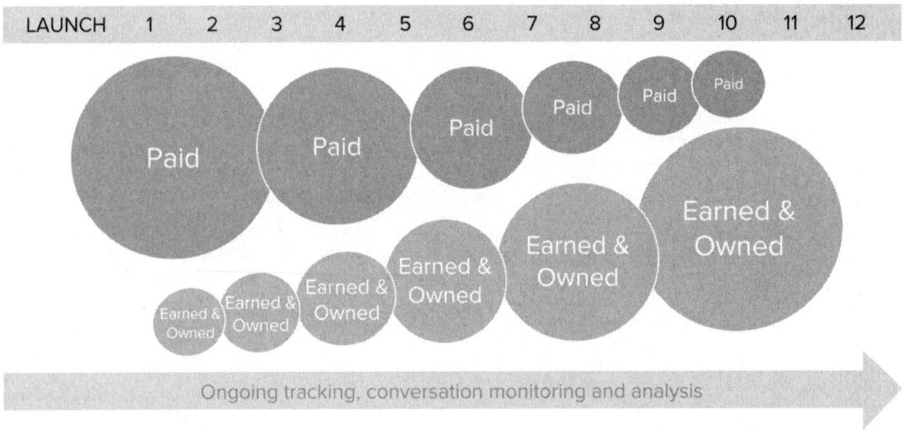

Figure 5.7 The symbiotic relationship between paid, earned, and owned media in the mobile app ecosystem.

Owned Media Strategy

In app marketing, owned media focuses on optimizing your owned spaces to maximize awareness for your app. Owned spaces include:

Desktop Website Awareness Elements Desktop elements can take many forms, from a simple banner on your homepage that links to your app store landing page to a full dedicated area of the site for mobile. We highly recommend creating a unique page on your site to showcase your mobile products and services and a unique link to this page in your site navigation. Your app can be included on this page or, in many cases, command a subpage of its own with screenshots, an overview of the app's features, excerpts from positive reviews and comments, and a link to the app's landing page in all relevant app stores.

Redirects Server-side detection can route users trying to access your website on a tablet or smartphone to a splash page that encourages them to download your native app instead. This method can be effective, but proceed with caution and always allow your users the option to go ahead and click-through to the site instead. Not every user wants to download you mobile app, so don't force the issue.

Email Your email marketing list is an ideal place to start, as these customers probably represent your most loyal user base. A preview email a week or two before your anticipated launch and then an email sent the day you are approved and in the app stores will work wonders in fueling your initial downloads.

Facebook Your Facebook followers are also among those most likely to download your app, especially when you consider that many of them view your Facebook page on a mobile device; they are only a click away from downloading. Regular posts about your app immediately prior to and after launch will jumpstart your downloads. Regular posts thereafter will keep your app top of mind, especially if you have new content and features to announce. A dedicated Facebook tab for your mobile efforts is also highly recommended, but that's going the extra mile. Simply ensuring that your app is represented in your owned social spaces is the important thing.

Twitter Like Facebook, your Twitter followers will be among your most loyal—and mobile—users. Preview tweets about your upcoming app and promotional tweets thereafter are great tools for keeping it top of mind with your users and driving downloads.

Your owned efforts in social spaces have particular value because they can potentially spread the word about your app outside your immediate circle of current customers and brand loyalists. Every Facebook share and retweet introduces your app to a given user's circle of friends, creating a wider net of awareness than you could ever accomplish through more traditional methods.

Prelaunch Owned Media Planning

Prelaunch planning activities focus on preparing content for your desktop website, email campaigns, and your pages on leading social networks.

Desktop Website Awareness Elements Work with the design and technical teams managing your desktop website (and, if applicable, mobile website) to determine what is feasible. Design and develop additional elements including promotional copy, page layout, app imagery, and other elements. Plan to fully QA and integrate them into your site by the date of your anticipated launch.

Email Design and write your full series of prelaunch and post-launch emails. Keep in mind that most of the recipients will be reading the email on their mobile device, so designing your message to be mobile-friendly is essential! In Chapter 6, we'll provide detailed guidelines for mobilizing your email campaigns.

Facebook Plan and write copy for your initial prelaunch and post-launch posts; design and develop your unique Facebook tab, if applicable.

Twitter Develop a content calendar of promotional tweets, including copy and a plan for timing your posts. Also, plan to allot time for scanning Twitter post-launch for positive and negative mentions of your app.

Post-Launch Owned Media Execution and Management

Post-launch efforts should emphasize distribution and delivery of the messaging you've prepared about your app.

Desktop Website Awareness Elements Ideally, your site awareness elements will be in place well before launch with "coming soon" messages. Post-launch your copy should be modified to reflect the fact that your app is now live and should include links to the landing pages in all relevant app stores. Plan to keep the dedicated awareness elements on your desktop (and mobile) sites up to date with positive reviews, press mentions, and info on updates to content and features.

Email Your initial email should go out one week prior to your anticipated launch and a follow-up "It's Live!" email should be queued up to be sent the minute your app appears in the app stores. Thereafter, plan to send additional emails only when you have something to announce, such as new content and features, or the release of a new and improved version.

Facebook Much like your desktop website, your Facebook-awareness elements should go live prior to launch to get your followers excited about your app. Post-launch, copy should change from "coming soon" messaging to "it's live" messaging, and content should be curated from thereon to reflect what's happening with your app. Posting about your app daily might be a bit over the top unless you have overwhelmingly good reviews and downloads to share or negative comments to address. Weekly posts reminding your users about your app should be sufficient. You'll also want to post about changes to the app, such as new versions or problems that have been fixed.

Twitter Twitter will be one of your best conduits post-launch, not only for spreading the word about your app but also for keeping tabs on its success or lack thereof. Regular tweets about your new app are de rigueur. Also, spend time daily scanning the Twitterverse for your brand keywords, especially the name of your app. Positive mentions warrant a retweet and a thank you. Negative mentions warrant a publicly tweeted reply that constructively acknowledges the negative feedback (whether you agree with it or not) and a direct message to the individual thanking him or her for the feedback.

We can't recommend this last piece of advice enough—listen to your users! Sure, some people will slam your app for no good reason but these will be in the minority. Apps are such a new medium and we're all in the learning phases—no one has a formula exactly right. Hence, most negative comments you receive will be constructive, if you're willing to see them as such.

Here's a perfect case in point: There have been many instances in which a brand has been in too much of a rush to release an app to address the issues we've uncovered in usability testing with focus groups. And, in each of these cases, the app store commentary clearly reflected all the issues we discovered in the usability testing process. *Listen to your customers* and let them help you; their feedback will make your app better every time.

Earned Media Strategy

Earned media strategy completes the cycle by spreading the word about your app and capitalizing on the positive responses you are able to generate. For earned media, we concentrate on two specific areas of effort:

Influencer Outreach Influencer outreach in app marketing focuses specifically on reaching out to bloggers and requesting a review of your application. We recommend contacting bloggers in the app review space as well as niche bloggers that covers your specific vertical or type of app. For example, Kiwi Market would reach out to bloggers covering iOS and Android apps as well as to bloggers that target working moms and food bloggers. If your app is attached to a major household name, we also encourage you to reach out to the top gadget and technology blogs such as Engadget and Mashable. They're not in the habit of reviewing every app that comes along, but if you are a major household name, they may make an exception.

PR We've seen many apps get a big bump in downloads from a good old-fashioned press release. Remember that these go out to journalists and many of them will go out and download your app to review it, so that will add downloads right there. You also then have the added possibility of them writing about the app and generating downloads among their readers.

Let's look at some prelaunch and post-launch activities.

Prelaunch Earned Media Planning

Concentrate your prelaunch earned media efforts on reaching out to key influencers and maximizing the mileage you can get from press releases.

Influencer Outreach First, assess the blogosphere and determine which sites you will target. In the appendix to this book, we've included a list of app reviews, blogs, and directories that will help you formulate your plan. For industry specific blogs, we recommend using a site like `www.alltop.com` to determine the key influencers in your specific vertical.

PR Assemble a standard press release that clearly describes the purpose and benefits of your app and assess the various wire services at your disposal. Apple-specific wire services such as PR Mac can be especially effective at garnering coverage.

Post-Launch Earned Media Execution and Management

The focus of your prelaunch activity should carry over post-launch as well.

Influencer Outreach Your outreach campaign starts the minute your app appears in the app store. Your requests should go out in the form of a politely worded introduction to your brand and the features of your new app. Ask bloggers nicely (it doesn't hurt to flatter them a bit!) to review your app on their site and link back to your app store landing page(s) as well as your desktop site. If your app is premium, *always* offer a complimentary download code (Apple gives you 40 with each release) that will enable them to download the app for free if they are willing to review it. Be prepared for reviewers to be honest—no reputable blogger will promise you a great review. Some will request a fee for reviewing your app and other will review for free but request a fee to "expedite" your review. Whether or not these fees are worth it depends on the blog and we can't really blame app review bloggers for making this request; most of the more highly trafficked blogs have a considerable backlog of requests. So, if a blogger asks for a fee, weigh the amount of publicity you are likely to get from appearing on their site versus what they've asked you to pay. If you can project the number of downloads you think you might get and break the fee down into a cost-per-download you think you can live with, then it may be worth the investment. Last but not least, *always* send a thank-you email for a positive review.

Embedded Social Sharing This is an element that really comes into play in the process of developing your content strategy, but it also reaps great benefits for your app post-launch. Enabling your users to share content from within the app to their social networks will expose your app to that user's social sphere, broadcasting your app to an ever-broadening circle of users. Whether it's enabling them to share an image, a photo, a game score, or a piece of content, the value of empowering your users to promote your app to their social spaces from within your app's interface is tremendous.

PR Your press releases should also go out the minute your app is live. As with blogger outreach, keep tabs on the journalists who review your app favorably and *thank them*—a little gratitude goes a long way, and they will be more disposed to reviewing future versions and new apps you release.

Keeping Tabs on Your App in the Blogosphere

We recommend you scan the Web daily for mentions of your app, positive or negative. Simply setting up Google Alerts for your app name will provide you with reasonable coverage of the blogosphere. A daily search of Twitter is recommended, as well.

Friday: Outline Unique Measurement Considerations and Optimization Tactics for Native Apps

Getting metrics on your app is relatively straightforward when compared to the challenges you'll encounter with mobile web analytics. In this section, we'll share not only our expertise, but also what we learned through talking with Peter Farago, the vice president of marketing for the prominent app analytics vendor Flurry.

Analytics Options

We've said over and over again in this chapter that when it comes to apps, usage and engagement are far more important than downloads. That remains true, but there is one specific case where downloads become important—within the app stores themselves. App popularity is based on downloads because that is primarily what the app stores are set up to measure. As we discussed on Thursday, this *can* have a direct bearing on your larger objectives because awareness, popularity, and the often positive reviews and ratings that accompany popularity can spur engagement. After all, the larger your app's user base, the more chances you'll have at resonating with a portion of those users.

But that doesn't mean you should dedicate your efforts solely at maximizing downloads. Rather, you're better off aiming for quality, not quantity, when it comes to users. And there are now dedicated platforms, such as Fiksu (`www.fiksu.com`), that are designed to help maximize loyalty. In fact, Fiksu analysis of app usage data indicates that focusing on a smaller number of loyal app users—those that register their information, come back repeatedly, and make in-app purchases—can end up being twice as profitable as emphasizing a high volume of app downloads.

Peter uses an evocative metaphor: "I always imagine a bucket filled with water that has a leak in the bottom, but you're also filling it at the top. The water I'm adding is my new customer acquisition, the water level inside the bucket is my retention, and the water I'm losing represents churn."

The bottom line here: keep your eyes on the prize. Repeat engagement from active users is what you're after, because that's what ultimately ties back to your ROI. As Peter says, "The battle for the consumer begins after the download." But, he adds an important caveat about the inter-relationship of acquisition and retention: "I don't push on one until the other one is ready."

All-Purpose versus App-Specific

With that context in mind, you have a few choices when it comes to gaining access to app analytics. Most of the big players in desktop web analytics—Adobe SiteCatalyst, Google Analytics, webtrends—and other off-the-shelf analytics suites offer extensions for tracking native mobile apps. Bear in mind, however, that these software packages were originally designed with the desktop in mind and have been reverse-engineered to support mobile. They all work well at tracking the basics, but run into challenges with more granular interactions that are specific to native mobile apps. So, if you're really investing in apps and want to track down to that granular level, you will probably want to consider an analytics solution tailor-made for mobile, such as Localytics (`www.localytics.com`), Mobilytics (`www.mobilytics.com`), or Flurry (`www.flurry.com`).

Obtainable Data

You will be able to get some data on app downloads from the app stores themselves. Along with total numbers, you might, depending on the platform, get less or more information about users' device type, OS version, and the carrier they're on. Data on new user acquisitions and the rate of acquisitions is important; you'll want to understand the factors behind user growth. For example, if you're running an acquisition campaign, you'll want to be able to gauge how effective it is. Similarly, if your app has the good fortune of being a featured app or an editor's choice, you'll want to track the impact of that free exposure on your user acquisition rate.

App stores will also be able to give you information on app deletions. Hopefully, however, the steps we've outlined in this chapter will minimize how many times your app gets removed from users' devices!

From there, you'll need to turn to a dedicated app analytics platform to get the truly meaningful data about usage and retention. Peter points out that app analytics providers start tracking on a user's first launch of an app, but they typically can't give you visibility into the initial download action.

Whether you are using a homegrown analytics solution or a free or fee-based third-party service, there is a standard set of post-download data you can expect to collect. All analytics packages should provide the following data:

- Frequency of use
- Average session length
- Total time spent

You should also be able to get custom cuts of the data that factor in audience segmentation and composition (demographics and geographic distribution) and provide benchmarks against both the universe of apps and others in your category or categories.

If you integrate the analytics platform into the coding of your app, you can also track any number of specific metrics that will be determined by what your app is and does. For example, you could set up a funnel analysis that tracks whether users complete certain tasks and the conversion rate for each task. Bear in mind, however, that even if you define engagement as a combination of frequency plus duration, that measure will vary across app categories. For instance, you might open your Citibank app twice a month to check your account balance or pay a bill and play your Angry Birds app twice a day. That doesn't mean you value Angry Birds more than Citibank. Rather, your usage patterns for each app are simply different by virtue of the type of app.

Here's one additional consideration: If you're charging for your app, the revenues you generate from downloads will be an important metric to track as well. However, if the app market continues to develop in the way the various analyst firms we cited on Tuesday have forecast, paid app downloads may cease to be an important metric. Says Peter: "Consumers have a lot of compelling free choices, so the perceived value of an app is lower. At the same time, the reason the freemium model works so well is if you develop a compelling enough experience, you'll find that some users are willing to pay $500 over time, some are even willing to pay $1,000."

As we discussed on Monday in the app development checklist, determining the potential for ROI is something you should do very early in your strategic evaluations. And as we was noted on Tuesday, you should do so with an eye to building a sufficiently engaging experience that users will feel compelled to come back repeatedly and pay for additional content or functionality. Done right, you may recoup your app development costs through recurring micro-transactions that, over time, will add up to the kind of substantial spending Peter describes. The takeaway here is, don't focus on the short-term gain. Instead, consider the long-term value that the micro-transaction model can add for your app and your brand.

Measurement Roadblocks and Workarounds

Remember that one of the benefits of native apps is that they do not require a data connection for users to enjoy at least some of their functionality. For example, someone going onto a plane or into the subway could refresh the *New York Times* app on a smartphone or tablet and then read the latest articles while in the air or underground. Any links within the articles or multimedia features in the app would not be available while that user was offline, but the app will cache the articles and enable the user to read them.

This leads to what Peter calls "the on-off problem." The user may be reading an article in the *New York Times* app or playing a session (or 10!) of Angry Birds while offline. Consequently, there will be some latency involved in recording the data. If you opt to go with a third-party analytics provider, you'll have the option to code the tracking software into the app's SDK, which will enable the app to record offline sessions and upload the data from those sessions the next time the user opens the app with a live data connection.

But as a result, any average usage data (such as time spent) associated with a given app regularly needs to be recalculated, and that, in turn, will affect category averages. This is especially true when you're talking about a category-dominating app whose popularity tends to be fleeting. As Peter explained to us, somewhat hyperbolically, "Anyone who says analytics are real-time on mobile is lying." He added this more toned-down thought: "Real-time is really more of a theoretical concept."

Iterative Refinement

No matter how good your app is and how well it satisfies your brand's and your audience's needs, you'll still have work to do. Building an app, whether as an appendage to an existing business or as a standalone, opens the door to an ongoing process of improvement. Provided you want to increase audience engagement, setting out a roadmap for upgrades and enhancements is not an option—it's an absolute must.

As Peter puts it, "It just depends on how serious you are about your app business. Most developers who are seriously in the game of building apps update every three weeks on average, because for them, apps are not a launch-and-forget service—they're a live service and they have to work on the apps all the time and constantly improve them."

Pay close attention to the download and usage data, take in the comments users post in app stores, send to you directly, or submit on app recommendation platforms like AppsFire, Appolicious, AppTap, and even Facebook, which launched its own App Center in June 2012. Factor all of this information into your development roadmap and make sure you're addressing key user concerns or functionality requests as you move forward.

Peter Flurry, Vice President of Marketing at Flurry, on the Evolution of App Analytics

"When I was in mobile gaming before the iPhone, we couldn't see anything. It was like driving at night on a windy road along a cliff with no headlights. Now, you get all kinds of information. It's almost the opposite—you have to pick and choose what's relevant from the data deluge."

In Conclusion

Peter summed it up nicely: "Building apps is really like running a business." In some cases, it will be your only business. What we've outlined in this chapter is a way to get that business up and running—and keep it running and flourishing.

Whether you work for a brand and your app is designed to support your business or your app is your business or service, it will need care and attention in order to ensure that your users stay with you and deepen their relationship with you. The longer they stay and the more they use your app, the more valuable they will be to you.

Given that you'll most likely be traveling along the freemium route with your app, a good portion of that value will come from mobile advertising. So sooner or later, and probably sooner, you'll need to know about how to use ads to turn loyalty into dollars. We'll turn to that magical equation in the next chapter.

Week 5: Promote Your Message with Mobile Advertising

6

"If you build, it they will come" isn't a guaranteed scenario in any kind of marketing, let alone mobile. More and more users are searching for and engaging with brands on their smartphones and tablets. Active outreach in the form of search, display, and other types of mobile advertising plays a big role in facilitating this interaction. In this chapter, we'll teach you the basics of mobile advertising and how you can use it to attract more qualified and engaged consumers to your mobile content.

Chapter Contents

Develop a mobile ad campaign strategy
Define your mobile SEM plan
Define your mobile display plan
Decide where mobile email fits into the mix
Outline your approach to mobile advertising campaign management, tracking, and analysis

Monday: Develop a Mobile Ad Campaign Strategy

In this chapter, we'll again share our own expertise, as well as what we learned from talking with the following experts:

- Nikao Yang, senior vice president of New Business Development and Marketing at AdColony
- Jim Lecinski, vice president, U.S. Sales & Service, Google, Inc., and author of *Winning the Zero Moment of Truth* (`www.zeromomentoftruth.com`)
- Jason Spero, head of Global Mobile Sales & Strategy at Google

You'll hear from Nikao, Jim, and Jason throughout this chapter.

In her May 2012 *Internet Trends* report, Mary Meeker, partner at venture capital firm Kleiner Perkins Caufield & Byers `www.kpcb.com`) and widely acknowledged mobile industry oracle, declared that mobile advertising has a long way to go before meeting its much-vaunted potential. She cited research from eMarketer showing that although mobile now accounts for 10 percent of online activity, it is currently allotted a scant 1 percent of overall ad spend, as depicted in Figure 6.1.

Share of Average Time Spent per Day with Select Media by US Adults vs. US Ad Spending Share, 2008-2011
% of total

	2008		2009	
	Time spent share	Ad spending share	Time spent share	Ad spending share
TV	43.2%	38.5%	44.1%	41.0%
Internet*	23.3%	14.9%	24.1%	17.3%
Radio	17.3%	11.2%	16.2%	10.9%
Mobile	5.4%	0.2%	6.4%	0.3%
Newspapers	6.5%	22.1%	5.5%	18.9%
Magazines	4.3%	13.2%	3.6%	11.8%
	2010		2011	
	Time spent share	Ad spending share	Time spent share	Ad spending share
TV	42.9%	42.6%	42.5%	42.0%
Internet*	25.2%	18.8%	25.9%	22.2%
Radio	15.6%	11.0%	14.6%	10.7%
Mobile	8.1%	0.6%	10.1%	1.0%
Newspapers	4.9%	16.4%	4.0%	14.3%
Magazines	3.3%	11.0%	2.8%	10.6%

*Note: *time spent with the internet excludes internet access via mobile, but online ad spending includes mobile internet ad spending; due to this, the total of the ad spending shares for all the media adds up to more than 100%*
Source: eMarketer, Dec 2011 & Jan 2012

137753 www.eMarketer.com

Figure 6.1 Mobile ad spending trails behind mobile usage.

Meeker is bullish on mobile. According to her, it is just a matter of time before ad spend on mobile catches up with the amount of time we spend on it. Yet, most brands remain in the test-and-learn phase with mobile ads. It's hard to gauge what the average annual spend is without mobile ad networks giving up their numbers in aggregate, but let's just say that $25,000 test budgets are not out of the ordinary—a pittance compared to online ad budgets that regularly range in the $100,000-plus range.

The reality is that mobile advertising is growing very fast—faster than other media or channels; it's just that the total spend across the industry is lower than desktop digital advertising. The reasons for the slower growth of investment are nebulous. Perhaps some marketers believe that because mobile ads are smaller, they have less impact and, therefore, aren't worth a significant investment. Others might be hesitant because mobile ads are more challenging to track. And, of course, while click-through rates on smartphones often surpass the desktop, the conversions they lead to often happen offline, leading to a highly challenging attribution model—and it's difficult to justify investing in an ad model when conversions are much harder to prove. These are all real challenges, and no doubt, all have an impact on how quickly brands are moving to invest. However, we believe that it's just a matter of time until we move past them.

AdMob's Jason Spero on the Growth of Mobile Advertising

As we researched this chapter, we spoke to several mobile advertising industry leaders about what will drive the inevitable uptake of mobile ads—AdMob executive Jason Spero had this to say:

"Two factors will drive brands' mobilization and the growth of mobile advertising: scale and a mature advertising infrastructure. Together, these will produce value for the entire mobile ecosystem—advertisers, publishers, app developers, and mobile users. On the scale-front, mobile usage continues to skyrocket as a result of the continued adoption of smartphones and tablets. According to a recent Google survey, eight countries around the world already have more than 40 percent smartphone penetration. Today, usage of mobile devices is very much mainstream. The scale is there, right now.

"Likewise, the infrastructure of advertising on mobile is evolving extremely fast. This is being driven by improvement in systems that, increasingly, are designed for the mobile device and mobile context, specifically. From ad formats, to ad serving, to analytics, and more, we're seeing the mobile ads ecosystem mature on a speedy timeline."

So, why do we believe that we'll be investing more in mobile advertising in the future? There are several reasons. For one, mobile ads might be small (at least in the case of smartphones), but they're also more discreet, generally limited to one at the top of the page and one at the bottom in the case of mobile display (a maximum of two at the top and two at the bottom of a search engine results page for search ads). Ads tend to stand out a bit more when there is less ad clutter. They're also considerably more focused, with mobile ad networks offering advertisers the option of targeting criteria that far surpass the options available for desktop ads. Location is the most obvious, but others abound and vary from network to network and device to device. Options are available via mobile devices that have the potential to target messages far more precisely than the average display ad does—for example, gender, age, household income, education level, and content consumption habits to name a few. And, of course, there's the opportunity to drive immediate action that the desktop can't support, such as click-to-call or immediate in-store offer redemption.

Overall, we'd say that the lower spend is due more to the fact that mobile is still in its early days than to anything else. That said, success starts with understanding your options and being as prepared as possible, so let's look at the landscape.

Selecting the Correct Media/Ad Type

As with any other aspect of mobile, your mobile ad strategy will be defined by your customer's mobile technographics, your brand goals, and, of course, the customer journey, which we outlined in Chapter 2, "Week 1: Develop Your Mobile Strategy." The mobile ad landscape is very diverse; as mobile devices become more sophisticated, your options will become more diverse as well. For the sake of clarity in this chapter, we'll separate mobile ads into two basic categories: Search Engine Marketing (SEM) *and* Display Advertising including banners, rich media, in-app, and video). We'll explore some of the more complex aspects of mobile advertising beyond these two core categories, such as mobile social advertising, in subsequent chapters.

Search Engine Marketing

Most mobile search is conducted through mobile versions (both the browser and apps) of the major search engines (Google, Yahoo!, and Bing in the United States). At present, Google owns the vast majority of global mobile search traffic, commanding 96.6 percent as of September 2012, according to web analytics service StatCounter (`www.statcounter.com`)—so for most brands, the mobile search landscape will be very familiar territory. Mobile SEM targeting smartphones will be most appealing to you if:

- You have a brick-and-mortar business.
- You drive leads, subscriptions, or direct sales over the phone.
- You are marketing mobile content, such as apps.
- You have time-sensitive offers or content to distribute.
- You are doing local marketing of any kind.

Basically, you'll often (though not exclusively) find yourself gravitating toward mobile SEM for smartphones when your goal is to support in-store decision-making, offline conversions, and app downloads or other types of downloadable digital content such as books, magazines, games, and music. Mobile SEM for tablets, on the other hand, will look much more like the traditional desktop with a few unique, mobile-centric twists. We'll discuss specific tactics tomorrow, but for today, let's look at a few high-level details.

Search Engines Your main options for placing mobile search ads are Google, Yahoo!, MSN, and Bing (the last three managed collectively through Microsoft AdCenter). You're most likely to concentrate your efforts on Google, because it commands the largest audience. Of course, that's not to say the other engines don't matter. Bing, for example, is the default search engine on BlackBerry devices, which might be very important to you, depending on your technographics. However, Google will give you the most bang for your buck at this point, so we're going to concentrate largely on Google in this chapter. Don't worry, though; many of the lessons you learn about mobile SEM on Google will be applicable as you start to run campaigns on other engines.

Search Apps and Carrier Portals The SEM campaigns you set up on Google, Bing, and the other big engines will also run in their native apps, so you're covered there. You might, however, decide you want to run SEM campaigns in niche search applications, such as Yelp (`www.yelp.com`) or on the mobile web portals of wireless carriers. Niche search apps are more likely to offer a display model of advertising though some offer keyword-based search ads as well; you will have to assess these opportunities on a case-by-case basis. To run campaigns on carrier portals (proprietary mobile websites that are embedded in the browsers of a particular carrier's devices), your best bet will be to work with an ad network. Many of the larger networks aggregate inventory for both search and display advertising with the wireless carriers.

Carrier Portals

Wireless carriers have their own proprietary mobile websites, also called *portals* or decks, that aggregate mobile content of interest to their customers—for example, sports scores, horoscopes, news, and current events. These portals are accessible only to subscribers of the wireless carrier and are often programmed to be the default homepage on the browsers of the phones they sell. Placing ads on a carrier's mobile web portal can be a very appealing proposition because the carriers can often target these ads according to very granular billing data.

Targeting You can target mobile search ads by keyword, of course, but Google offers a multitude of additional options such as device platform, operating system (OS), language, dayparting, geography, and wireless carrier and/or users on Wi-Fi networks. Other engines offer similar options.

Ad Types You'll find the Google mobile ad format very familiar. There are a few small differences; but for the most part, it's the same old search ad we're used to from the desktop, which is probably why it ends up being the first step in mobile for so many of us. Figure 6.2 shows an example.

Figure 6.2 Prototypical Google mobile search ad

Tomorrow, we'll dig deeper and examine all your mobile search advertising options in detail. For now, just be aware that search is the most common and fundamental form of mobile advertising. For most of you, it will be indispensable and likely your first step into the medium.

Learning More About SEM

Search engine marketing is a highly detailed area of the digital marketing ecosystem. As much as we'd like to guide you through all its complexities, we would need a few hundred more pages to even begin to do so! Our goal here is to help you understand the nuances of SEM in regard to mobile, and we hope we've been able to do so. If you want to learn more about search engine marketing, both mobile and desktop, you have an excellent resource at your fingertips in Google Webmaster Tools (`www.google.com/webmasters/tools`). Create a free account and you will gain access to the Adwords Help Center and Community, a rich repository of tools, FAQs, and forums that will teach you anything and everything you ever wanted to know about search engine marketing.

Display Advertising

With display advertising, the landscape gets a bit more complex, ranging from standard banner ads to rich media to video and highly complex in-app advertising. Unlike mobile search, which is largely intent-driven, mobile display reaches users in a more ambient state as they browse and consume web or app content. Mobile display ads are often less likely than search to generate a monetary conversion (although they see higher click-through rates than their desktop counterparts). However, the richer visual experience they provide can have a far more powerful branding effect than a basic search ad. Hence, mobile display ads are highly effective for marketing purposes that are less direct, such as:

- Marketing a new product or service
- Introducing your brand to a wider audience
- Driving traffic to a website or app store download page

Consequently, mobile display media will be a common go-to choice for branding and marketing purposes. Of course, there will be crossover: Just as mobile SEM can be used to support brand experiences, mobile display ads *can* drive conversions, depending on your goals and customers. But the real power here tends to be in the experience they create. Mobile display, especially video and rich media ads, are capable of driving a much higher engagement factor than search ads can and the results can be as impressive—in some cases more so—than the desktop. Whether to invest in mobile SEM, mobile display, or both is something you'll have to evaluate on a case-by-case basis.

Ad Opportunities There are myriad mobile ad networks, and choosing the right one(s) will probably be your biggest headache. Numerous small, niche mobile networks offer very unique opportunities, but we've found the larger networks are often apples to apples in terms of their services, rates, and inventory. The differences tend to lie in targeting and tracking capabilities, customer service, and the willingness to include the occasional value-add in the form of landing pages or ad production.

Ad Targeting Ad targeting is where mobile advertising gets interesting. Your targeting options for mobile display vary from network to network, publisher to publisher, and platform to platform. Wireless carriers, for example, can offer extremely detailed targeting criteria based on customer billing data—anything from marital status to types of credit card to presence of children in the household. Networks providing in-app advertising can often target based on content consumption habits. The variety is endless—in addition to the aforementioned, some of the options you might have at your disposal include, but are by no means limited to: device type, device settings, gender, age, ethnicity, education level, household income, content preferences, education, marital status, spoken language, and exact geolocation.

Ad Types A few years ago, your mobile display ad options were limited to basic banners, but you now have many more choices. Rich media expandable banners, *interstitials* (a web page displayed before the expected content page), video ads, and in-app ads that function as an app-within-an-app are now the norm. In our experience, if you are using mobile display ads to fulfill an intent-driven function—for example, driving traffic to a hotel booking engine—you can comfortably veer toward the more basic formats. However, if you're going for more of a brand awareness angle or developing an extension to a creative online campaign, you'll probably find the richer, the better.

Tuesday: Define Your SEM Plan

We've long said that mobile isn't so much a *surf* medium as it is a *search* medium. When you are in the mobile context, particularly when you're using a smartphone or even a feature phone (as opposed to a tablet), you're almost always surfing with specific intent. Sure, sometimes you're killing time with Angry Birds or Words with Friends, but for the most part, you're looking for something: an address, a fact, a product, a phone number. Mobile (smartphone) behavior, in short, focuses most often on *finding* rather than casual browsing. Hence, our ever-increasing need to search. Google, for example, stated in October 2011 that 40 percent of mobile searches on its network carried local intent, suggesting that there is a significant amount of intent—and imminent action—in a smartphone search. Google and Ipsos OTX released more interesting insights in a 2011 study entitled *The Mobile Movement* (`www.thinkwithgoogle.com/insights/library/studies/the-mobile-movement`), regarding mobile search behavior, including:

- Seventy-nine percent of smartphone users use their smartphones to help with shopping.
- Ninety-five percent of smartphone users have looked for local information.
- After looking up a local business on their smartphone, 61 percent of users called the business, 59 percent visited, and 58 percent looked the business up on a map or got directions.
- Thirty-six percent take action immediately, 39 percent within a few hours, and 14 percent within a day.

So how do you get started with mobile SEM and use it to best advantage? As we've established, mobile search marketing is at its most effective when used to reach consumers in an intent-driven state—what Google's Jim Lecinski has christened, the *Zero Moment of Truth*. When we spoke to Jim while writing this chapter, he noted the importance of "being there" with the right information when consumers are looking for it. Clearly, a big part of "being there" is having mobile-specific content, as we discussed in Chapter 4: "Week 3: Maximize Reach with Mobile Websites." But directing customers to this content in the Zero Moment of Truth, when it is most relevant to their needs, is equally important as well. As Jim pointed out when we spoke, "mobile search is a broad and growing definition and can encompass not just the browser but SMS, voice, and myriad other ambient and visual search channels." We'll address the potential of these emerging search channels in upcoming chapters. For now, though, let's take a look at how traditional SEM extends to mobile.

Mobile SEM Use Cases

A person using mobile search is in an action-oriented state of mind. When speaking at SES San Francisco in 2011, Andy Chu, director of Bing for Mobile, said that 70 percent of mobile searches result in a completed action *within one hour*. Meaning that, if you're searching for "flower delivery" on Bing Mobile (or Google, or Yahoo!, or any search engine), within an hour or less, you will probably buy a nice floral arrangement. The value of this kind of intent is huge, especially for e-commerce sites and brick-and-mortar or service brands. There is a probability of conversion that you'd never be able to match on the desktop. To see how they might leverage this advantage in mobile SEM, let's look at a few hypothetical case scenarios starring our fictional Kiwi Market.

The Need to Find a Service A client services director at a large ad agency just got word after close of business for the day that an important client wants to visit her office for a breakfast meeting at 7~ AM the next morning. Frantic, she searches Google for "gourmet catering" plus her zip code. On the first search engine results page, she sees an ad for Kiwi Market's catering service in the first position. She clicks the phone number link in the ad, gets connected, and after a brief chat with the customer service rep, places her order.

The Need to Find a Product An Italian expat in NYC is craving his favorite sweet from home—a delicious, coffee-flavored hard candy called Pocket Coffee. He hasn't seen it anywhere in the city and decides to see if he can order it online. To his surprise and delight, a smartphone search for "Pocket Coffee" results in a Google SEM ad for Kiwi Market, whose local branch (only a block away) has the treat in stock.

The Need to Locate a Place A businesswoman who is a regular Kiwi Market customer at home in New York is in San Francisco on business. After a long day of meetings, she wants to grab a meal to enjoy on the flight home and she knows Kiwi Market has a few locations in the Bay area but doesn't know exactly where. A mobile search for "Kiwi Market SF" yields a Google SEM ad at the top of the page that includes a direct link to a location page.

Mobile Search Ad Formats

Google's commitment to mobile is stronger than ever, and the search giant is continually workshopping new mobile search ad formats. Let's look at the most popular ones and their benefits.

Click-to-Call Phone Extensions

Enabling a customer to call you directly from an ad viewed on their phone is a no-brainer. We might use our phones for actual voice calls less often than we used to, but it's still a natural inclination to dial when you have the opportunity. And it is an opportunity that consumers take—according to the Google Mobile Ads Blog (`http://googlemobileads.blogspot.com/`), click-through rate (CTR) increases 6 to 8 percent when you add a phone number to a mobile search ad.

The *click-to-call* ad model offers few interesting options; on a basic level, the number appears within the body of your ad and can be set to show on all devices but only be clickable on mobile. You can also choose to:

- Create a call-only ad—that is, a click-to-call is the only kind of click the ad can generate.
- Set your ads to dynamically display the number of a local location or to route directly to a national call center.
- Opt for a vanity phone number—for example, 1-800-KWI-MRKT.

This ad model provides a basic set of data in call analytics, including:

- Area code
- Duration of call
- Missed calls
- Phone-through-rate (percentage of users exposed to the ad who clicked to call)

If you have a brick-and-mortar business, conduct e-commerce or offer real-time customer support of some kind, this ad model will be invaluable to you. Figure 6.3 illustrates how click-to-call might work for Kiwi Market.

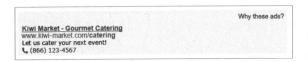

Figure 6.3 Kiwi Market mobile search ad with click-to-call link

Click-to-Download

Click-to-download ads are designed specifically to drive consumption of mobile apps. The ads appear only on the devices for which your app is designed. For example, an ad for an iPhone app will appear only on iOS devices. Clicking the download link takes the user directly to the app's download page in the app store (iTunes or Google Play), as shown in Figure 6.4.

Click-to-download ads are actually available as image ads (running on the Google Display Network) as well as text ads. Google's ad group policy requires that you create separate ad groups for your Android and iOS campaigns for this ad model—please note that these are the only two app platforms currently supported! Also, if you plan to include the keywords iPhone, iTouch, Apple, or iTunes in your ad creative, you will need to get permission to do so from Apple by filing a trademark approval form.

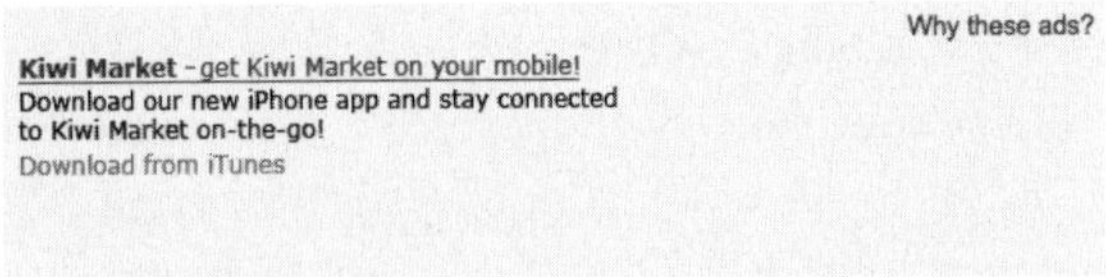

Figure 6.4 Kiwi Market mobile search ad with click-to-download link

When click-to-download ads first came out, we were skeptical. Based on observation, we felt that most people begin their app discovery journey directly in the app stores. However, over time, we've seen click-to-download work very well for many different types of apps, supplying a steady stream of downloads.

Mobile App Extensions

Mobile app extensions enable advertisers to add a link to their mobile app within a regular mobile ad. The ad will have two clickable links, as shown in Figure 6.5—one to the site's URL, for example, and one to the app's download page in the iTunes App Store or Google Play. You can also choose to deep link to a specific page within your app; consumers without the app will be directed to the download page; for those who already have it installed, the app will automatically open to the specified page within the app. For example, the Shop link would take a user with the Kiwi app installed directly to that page within the app. In the beta phase of testing this ad model, Google saw a 6 percent increase in CTR for ads that included mobile app extensions compared to those that did not. So if you have a mobile app, it's worth testing out!

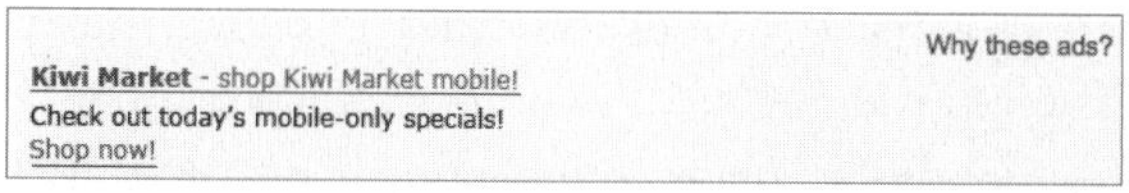

Figure 6.5 Kiwi Market mobile search ad with app extension link

Click-to-Offer

Click-to-offer enables you to insert a special deal into the body of your ads, as shown in Figure 6.6. Users can then redeem the deal online, offline, or send themselves the ad via text message or email for future redemption. Click-to-offer is especially appealing because it can drive sales online *and* in-store. Ads can be set up to display your phone number and other location info, thereby enabling a user to easily map your location and redeem the offer in person if they choose (and if your retail location is set up to redeem the offer at point of sale).

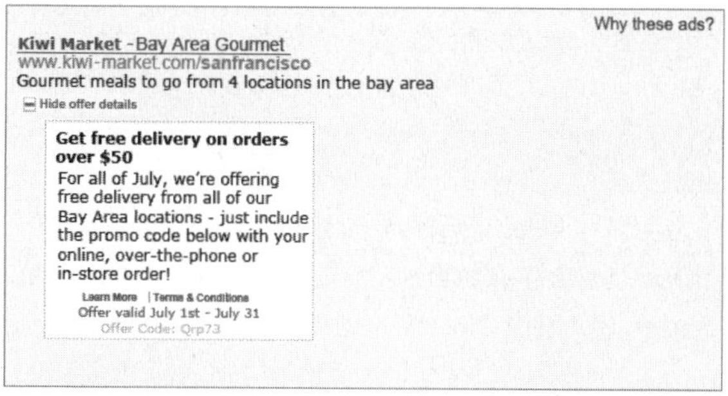

Figure 6.6 Kiwi Market mobile search ad with click-to-offer link

Mobile Site Links

Site links create more useful ads in that they include additional text and links that can catch the user's attention, driving them to additional pages within your mobile website and creating a faster, more efficient path to conversion, as shown in Figure 6.7. Site links are available globally and will appear in ads both above and below the fold on a mobile search engine results page (SERP). However, unlike desktop ads, mobile site links are limited to two links (in addition to the main clickable URL at the top of the ad). Note that site links will appear only on high-end devices with full Internet browsers. Google claims that ads with site links see as much as a 30 percent increase in CTR, so this is another ad format we believe is worth testing out on mobile.

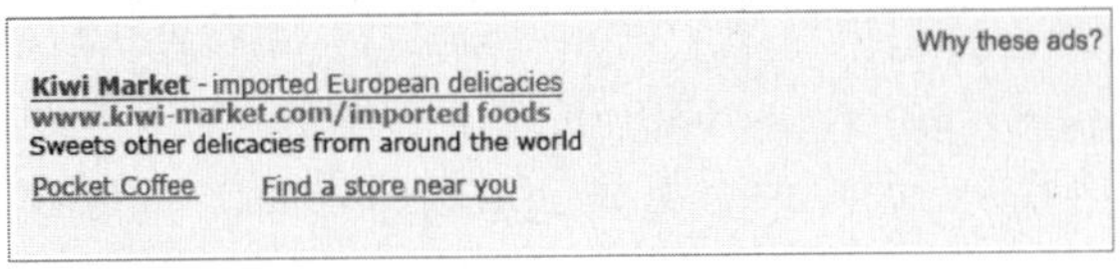

Figure 6.7 Kiwi Market mobile search ad with site links

Local and Hyperlocal Extensions

As we referenced earlier in this chapter, 40 percent of mobile searches have local intent. Location is quite possibly the most effective targeting you can do in a mobile search ad. Local and hyperlocal extensions for mobile enable users to find local locations faster and easier and speed the path to in-store purchase. Local extensions can be fairly simple—a phone number and/or a link to a maps application, as seen in Figure 6.8. Hyperlocal takes it one step further by including a map within the body of the ad itself, providing block-level data that drives more customers to your location.

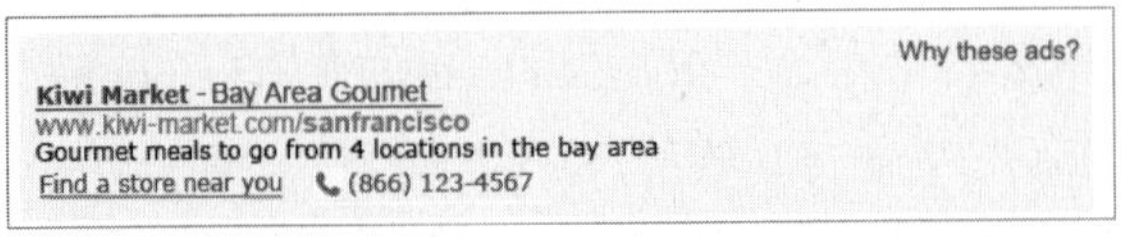

Figure 6.8 Kiwi Market mobile search ad with local extensions

Mobile Search Ad Strategy by Device Platform

Although smartphones and tablets are both mobile devices, the way we use them is quite different. As we discussed in the beginning of this chapter, smartphones tend to be about way-finding and other purpose-driven activities. Based on our observation of hundreds of mobile search marketing campaigns, the most successful mobile ads are ones that keep this action-oriented context in mind. Smartphone ads are consistently efficient in driving users to brick-and-mortar locations, connecting them with customer service reps by phone, and getting them to purchase items that are immediate needs—for example, a hotel room or movie tickets.

Tablets, however, are quite different. Tablet users tend to be heavy content consumers and, generally, in more of a browse and experience frame of mind. They are far more likely to engage in complex activities after clicking an SEM ad and far more likely to spend. According to a January 2012 study from Adobe:

- Tablet users spend 50 percent more than PC users.
- Tablets generate higher average order values, lower cost per click (CPC), and more time on site

Structure your mobile ad strategy with these fundamental differences in mind!

Tools, Tips, and Tricks: Campaign Best Practices

So now that you know the basic mobile search ad types, assuming you know how to use Google AdWords, setting up your mobile campaigns should be a piece of cake. But we have a few tips to help you through the process.

- Separate campaigns are a must.
- Use Google's mobile Keyword Tool.
- Bid to the first two positions on a mobile SERP.
- Daypart effectively.
- Send mobile users to mobile content.

Separate Campaigns

According to Google, advertisers experience, on average, an 11.5 percent increase in mobile click-through rates when they run a mobile-specific campaign as opposed to a hybrid (running simultaneously on both mobile *and* desktop) campaign. In short, campaigns that are specifically optimized for smartphones and tablets perform better than those that are not. Table 6.1 outlines the pros and cons of running separate, mirrored mobile campaigns versus hybrids or small mobile tests.

Table 6.1 Common Mobile Campaign Setup Options

Campaign Type	Pros	Cons
Separate	More control over bidding, budgeting and optimization. Ability to create more relevant messaging in ad copy. Superior targeting. Ability to build history and quality score.	Added time and effort required to manage additional campaigns.
Hybrid, desktop/mobile	Simple to opt-in—advertiser only has to select High-End Device (HED) targeting in campaign settings. Advertisers are able to run separate reports that separate out mobile and desktop activity.	Cannot create separate bids for mobile. Unable to have mobile specific creative. No separate budgets. No ability to build history and Quality Score (QS).
Small mobile test	Option to slowly test High End Device campaigns at limited budgets.	Inability to fully capitalize on the mobile opportunity. Risk of losing ground to competitors who might be building history while you are not.

To make a long story short, separate campaigns give you more control, allow you to create more relevant messaging, and enable you to take advantage of the increasingly granular, mobile-specific targeting that Google now offers.

Google's Mobile Keyword Tool

Mobile keywords don't always differ radically from desktop keywords, but they do differ. Google's free keyword research toolbox (`http://www.googlekeywordtool.com`) has a number of mobile options baked in that will help you construct your mobile campaign keyword strategy, as shown in Figure 6.9.

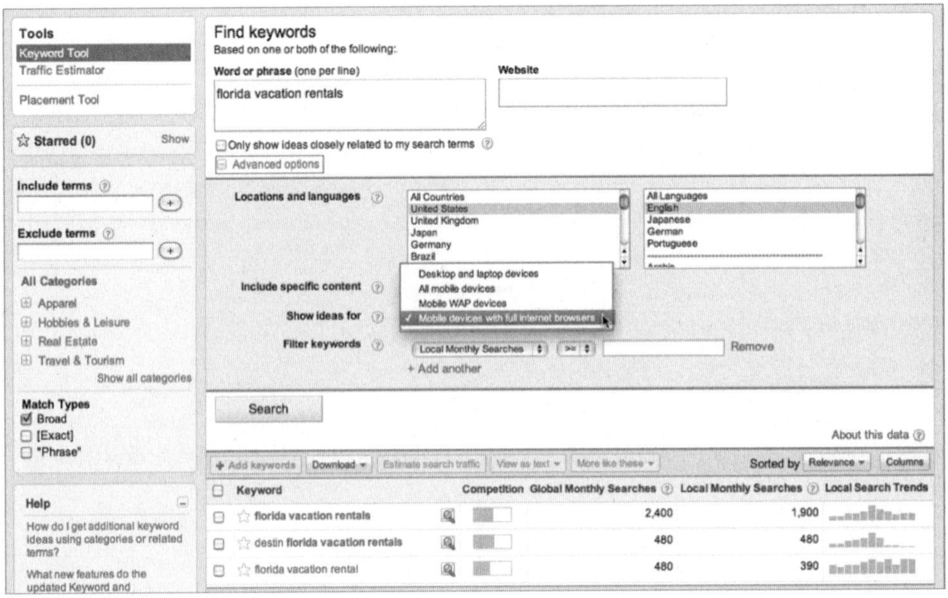

Figure 6.9 Google Keyword Tool displaying mobile options

Bid to the First Two SERP Positions

According to iCrossing, a digital marketing agency with deep roots in search, mobile ads consistently see a drop of roughly 90 percent in click-through rate between the first and fourth positions on a mobile *search engine results page* (*SERP*). Given that the average smartphone SERP can be as much as eight screens long (Figure 6.10), it's easy to see why this is. Scrolling is tedious even on the most sophisticated mobile devices, and many users will simply rely on the initial handful of results that appear above the fold. With this in mind, you should set your initial bids high in order to reach the first position, and manage to maintain that position from there.

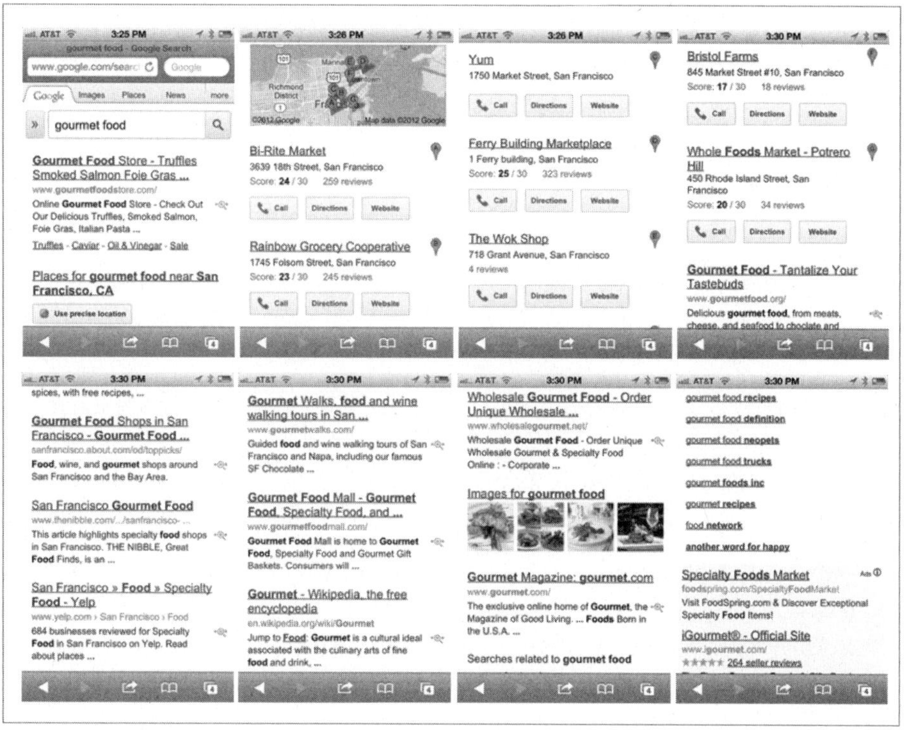

Figure 6.10 A mobile search engine results page

Daypart Effectively

Dayparting is a traditional ad planning strategy in which you run your campaigns during specific times of day that you believe will be most effective. According to iCrossing, mobile device traffic traditionally peaks in the evenings and on weekends, when users are away from their regular desktop environment. Smartphones tend to own the mornings and lunchtime; in the evenings, many users shift toward tablets (Figure 6.11). These are general trends that we find to be consistent across most verticals but, of course, there are always unique patterns from brand to brand. Examining your site's .com analytics will clearly illustrate these types of patterns and enable to you to efficiently apply dayparting to your mobile search (and display) ads.

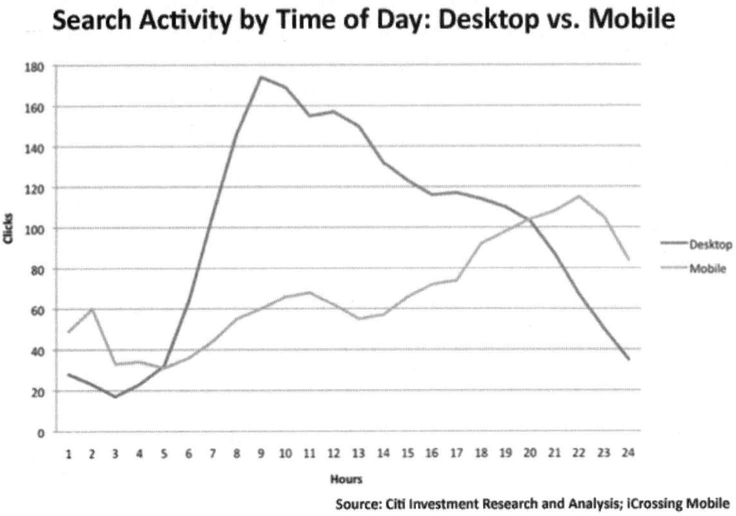

Figure 6.11 Search activity by time of day, desktop versus mobile

Send Mobile Users to Mobile Content

At this point, it almost goes without saying that you should send mobile users to mobile content! A well-constructed, highly targeted search ad will be wasted if the user is routed to a website that is unusable on his or her mobile device. According to Google's *The Mobile Movement* study, referenced earlier in this chapter, 71 percent of smartphone users who see a TV, press, or online ad, do a mobile search for more information, but 79 percent of large online advertisers still do not have a mobile optimized site.

Google's Jason Spero on Why Mobile Content Is a Must for Mobile Advertising

"Today, businesses have recognized the skyrocketing growth of mobile and the now mainstream usage of smartphones and tablets. However, many still don't know where and how to start when they're developing a mobile strategy. In other words, the why of mobile has been answered for brands, but the *how* remains a difficult question.

"Brands' most common and problematic assumption is that investing in mobile is akin to just another digital investment and does not require a unique strategy unto itself. This is a critical mistake and will limit businesses' success on the platform. The technical capabilities of a smartphone or tablet, and the usage trends on these devices, are distinct from the desktop. As a result, a website or an advertising campaign that was originally designed for desktop may not translate well (or at all) on mobile. Brands need to understand mobile's unique characteristics before investing in a mobile strategy.

"We've seen time and again, the businesses creating experiences based on the specific characteristics of a mobile device are seeing very strong results. And yet, despite this insight, most still are not properly equipped to connect with their customers in a mobile context. Looking at websites alone, we found that 62 percent of our largest advertisers do not have websites that are optimized to be viewed on a mobile device. Indeed, there is still a lot of work still to be done.

"Businesses need to take a step back and ask themselves: How are our customers likely to engage with us on mobile—and how is it different from the desktop? Are our customers walking down the street looking for a nearby store location? Do they want to make a phone call? Are they browsing my inventory on a tablet while they watch TV? Understanding mobile usage is the critical prerequisite to developing an effective mobile strategy. Before investing anywhere else, invest in this data first."

Wednesday: Define Your Mobile Display Plan

Mobile display is a diverse and growing ecosystem of networks, publishers, ad formats, and tools. In the next sections, we'll describe some of the key elements in each area of mobile display and the various ways in which you might find yourself working with them.

Work with the Mobile Ad Networks

You will hear the phrase *mobile ad network* used liberally to describe very different types of vendors. We've categorized the various segments of the mobile display advertising business to give you a better understanding of what they offer.

Mobile Ad Networks

Mobile ad networks are vendors that purchase inventory from publishers, usually mobile websites and mobile apps, and resell this inventory to advertisers. Often, this inventory is what we would label "remnant," because many publishers choose to sell their premium inventory ad space—their homepage, for example—directly to advertisers. However, most of the well-known mobile ad networks now offer of mixture of premium and remnant inventory. Let's do a quick overview of the various mobile ad network models—we've categorized examples of some of the networks themselves in the appendix of this book.

Premium Mobile Ad Networks Premium mobile ad networks limit their inventory to a select number of premium publishers, which tend to be the mobile websites and apps that are household names and command a huge number of eyeballs—the Angry Birds and ESPNs of the world. These networks typically command the highest cost per thousand (CPM) and *cost per click* (CPC) prices in mobile advertising. They generally allow you to cherry pick inventory and select only the apps and mobile websites on which you want your campaign to run. For example, Kiwi Market with its target audience of professional moms might choose to work with a premium network in order to target websites and applications popular with the working mom demographic, such as Oprah Magazine for iPad or iVillage's iPhone app.

Blind Networks *Blind networks* aggregate a vast quantity of inventory among less trafficked mobile sites and apps. Their costs are often much lower than a premium mobile ad network, but this comes with a catch because you have very little control over where your ad will run. The networks usually bundle their publishers into virtual segments that fit certain demographic targets—for example, sports fans or business travelers. Your ads will run within mobile websites and apps in segments that match your budget and targeting criteria, but you'll never know exactly where your ad is appearing.

Premium Blind Networks These are premium networks that utilize a blind segmentation model. They offer the same top-notch inventory as a regular premium network but don't allow you to choose where your ad will appear. You provide specific targeting criteria and desired CPM, CPC, or cost per installation (CPI), an ad pricing model designed for marketing mobile apps. The network then runs your ads within segments of its network that match up to those specifics—for example, soccer moms or business travelers. Kiwi Market's specifications might include college-educated women in the 30-to-45 age range with children in the home. However, some of them will let you include or exclude certain apps or sites from your buy.

Incentivized Networks Incentivized networks are a relatively new model but have evolved quickly with the introduction of mobile applications. These networks actually aggregate *users* as opposed to inventory. Users in the network are offered an incentive to download and, in some cases, review an application. The invitation usually comes via opt-in email, and the incentives are in the form of a small monetary sum. Advertisers (app owners) usually pay a small fee for each user exposed to their ad who actually downloads and installs their app.

The Skinny on Using Incentivized Networks to Promote Mobile Apps

Incentivized networks are a gray area in the world of marketing mobile apps. Apple is not keen on app owners buying installations and definitely frowns on any networks that promise positive reviews for a price. In mid-2011, Apple started cracking down on incentivized networks in earnest, forcing a number of applications that utilized an incentivized in-app advertising model to change their ways. These apps encouraged users to download another app advertised within the app the user was currently engaged with, for which he or she would receive some compensation, usually in form of points or credits. Many apps were forced to withdraw their content and resubmit under new app store guidelines that strictly prohibit this type of in-app advertising.

Of course, these apps were very obvious about their incentivized advertising model. Most incentivized networks operate far more discreetly, contacting users directly via email, which makes it nearly impossible for Apple to figure out which downloads they are generating.

We're of two minds on the incentivized model. Yes, it can generate large numbers of downloads very quickly, but as we discussed in Chapter 5, "Week 4: Maximize Engagement with Mobile Apps," downloads aren't really the main point. If you're considering an incentivized network, look very closely at what they promise. Consider only those that allow you to target your buy to users that fit your criteria and stay far, far away from any that promise you a positive review. Most will promise you a review in general but won't guarantee whether it's positive or negative. That model is acceptable, and it's up to you whether you want to take the risk of paying for a download that results in a bad review. But, buying a guaranteed positive review is gaming the system—something Apple takes very seriously and something that will inevitably come back to haunt you.

Given the large and growing number of mobile ad networks, describing the pros and cons of each individual network would be futile. However, to give you a representative overview of the current landscape, we've included a list of the most prominent, as well as a few interesting niche players, in the appendix.

Ad Exchanges

Mobile ad exchanges are virtual mobile ad marketplaces where advertising publishers can engage directly with advertisers to buy, place, and optimize mobile ad campaigns. Once you have some mobile advertising experience under your belt from working with a network, ad exchanges are a very valuable option because you have more transparency into where your campaign will run. You can gain much more efficiency with ad exchanges, but be aware that it's not a beginner's option. You need to understand a lot about display advertising in general, and mobile in particular, before you can really succeed using an ad exchange.

Demand-Side Platforms

Demand-side platforms (DSPs) are vendors that enable you to buy—and sell—your ad campaigns across multiple ad networks *and* ad exchanges. DSPs are considered to be especially efficient because most of them utilize a process called real-time bidding that enables you to maximize the efficiency of your ad spend. DSPs are a great option to consider for your mobile advertising needs if you have the resources to do hands-on campaign management. Your bidding, targeting, optimization options, and reporting are centralized, making it easy for you to get a firsthand view of how your campaign performs.

What Is Real-Time Bidding?

Real-time bidding (RTB) is a process of allocating and reallocating mobile ad spend, impression by impression. A DSP collects a variety of targeting data from its ad network and ad exchange partners that enables it to assign a specific, real-time value to a unique impression. The DSP's customers are then able to bid on the specific impression in real time and can target very specific types of users for a specific price. In reality, the process is automated—it's very much like Google's AdWords model, where you specify whom you want to reach with your ad and set the maximum price you want to pay. The system then bids on your behalf, based on the targeting and pricing criteria you have set.

Mobile Ad Types

Mobile ad formats were once relegated to static banners, but as devices have evolved, so too have the ad formats. Here, we break them down into a series of high-level categories. Be aware that many networks have their own unique standards and ad types. You may find yourself modifying and remastering your creative many times based on where you want to run your campaigns!

The Mobile Marketing Association (MMA, the global trade body that oversees mobile marketing and its related technologies) refined its official mobile ad guidelines in February 2012 in hopes of establishing industry-wide standards for smartphones and tablets. Table 6.2 lists the MMA dimensional standards by ad and device/application type. The Interactive Advertising Bureau (IAB, the global trade body that oversees online advertising standards and related technologies) has also released its own set of standards for successful mobile ad types (`http://www.iab.net/guidelines/508676/mobile_guidance`).

▶ **Table 6.2** MMA Ad Format Guidelines

Standard	Dimensions in Pixels	Ad Type (Formats)
MMA Standards	300 × 50	X large image banner (GIF, PNG, JPEG)
	320 × 50	XX large image banner (GIF, PNG, JPEG)
	300 × 75	X large high image banner (GIF, PNG, JPEG)
	216 × 36	Large image banner (GIF, PNG, JPEG)
	216 × 54	Large high image banner (GIF, PNG, JPEG)
	168 × 28	Medium image banner (GIF, PNG, JPEG)
	168 × 42	Medium high image banner (GIF, PNG, JPEG)
	120 × 20	Small image banner (GIF, PNG, JPEG)
	120 × 30	Small high image banner (GIF, PNG, JPEG)

IAB Mobile Rising Stars Ad Units	320 × 250 – 320 × 480 (maximum extended pixel dimensions)	Smartphone filmstrip
	300 × 600	Tablet filmstrip
	320 × 50 – 320 × 480	Mobile pull
	3320 × 50 – 480 × 50	Smartphone adhesion banner
	768 × 90 – 1024 × 90	Tablet adhesion banner
	320 × 50 – 320 × 480	Full page flex
	320 × 50 – 320 × 480	Mobile slider

So, which set of standards should you follow? Well, much of this will be dictated by the ad network with which you choose to work. During the process of evaluating them, keep in mind that the MMA is a trade organization specifically devoted to mobile with the goal of advancing the growth of the medium and helping advertisers and publishers understand the opportunity. The IAB is devoted to advertising from a higher, more holistic level. Their standards are still being codified and don't have the same defined parameters as the MMA guidelines. You should view the MMA standards as your starting point, but allow yourself some creative deviation in testing elements of the IAB formats—the best of both worlds!

The formats in which your ads must be delivered will vary from network to network and device to device. The publishers and networks you work with will provide you with the specific criteria for your campaign creative. Many will be willing to produce your final ads for you from raw creative as a value-add or for a small additional fee. However, you might also want to enlist the services of a rich media ad platform. These vendors will create, host, and track your ads in all the required formats for your particular campaign, and their services are especially valuable if you are making a sizable investment in mobile advertising and running campaigns across multiple networks and/or targeting a diverse array of devices. They enable you to support very complex campaigns with a low level of effort, albeit at an added cost. The third-party pixel-tracking service that many provide is also a very valuable counterbalance to that provided by the ad network and allows you to refine your campaign to a higher degree of efficiency.

Nikao Yang on Mobile Video

With all this talk about mobile rich media, where does mobile video fit in? We spoke to Nikao Yang, senior vice president of new business development and marketing at in-app mobile ad network AdColony, to gain his perspective.

"For advertisers, the ability to target engaged consumers on mobile devices with high-impact visuals and engagement makes mobile video ads particularly compelling. Mobile video ads can deliver an unparalleled experience that emotionally engages with the consumer and allows the consumer to instantly interact with the brand or product on their devices through a clear call-to-action. For consumers, mobile video ads deliver a superior experience in explaining the value proposition of a brand or product versus other mobile ad units, which lack the sight, sound, and motion to tell a story or effectively educate the consumer about a product.

"Ultimately, mobile video inventory running on both smartphones and tablets is extremely valuable to advertisers—it doesn't have to be a zero-sum game. The savvy advertiser will know to target and segment between the two device types based on their advertising needs to drive maximum ROI on their mobile video advertising campaigns."

Thursday: Decide Where Mobile Email Fits into the Mix

The majority of emails are opened via either a webmail client or a desktop email client. According to a study conducted by digital messaging solutions provider Knotice (`www.knotice.com`), mobile accounted for only 27 percent of all email opens in late 2011. Peanuts, right? But then consider a few additional facts you might find eye-opening.

- According to email vendor Return Path (`www.returnpath.net`), email open rates grew 82.4 percent year over year between March 2011 and March 2012 and, in all likelihood, will surpass desktop open rates before this book is published.
- In a December 2011 study conducted by Spring Creek Group (`www.springcreekgroup.com`), a digital agency specializing in social media, 38 percent of respondents admitted to checking their email on their mobile device before even getting out of bed in the morning.
- eDialog (`www.e-dialog.com`), an email marketing agency, states that 63 percent of Americans, 67 percent of APAC consumers, and 41 percent of Europeans would, upon receiving an email poorly formatted for mobile, close it immediately and/or delete it altogether.
- More than one half (56 percent) of U.S. consumers who have made at least one purchase with a smartphone bought in response to a marketing message delivered via mobile email, according to email marketing provider, ExactTarget (`www.exacttarget.com`).
- Of all recipients who have opened an email on their mobile device, only 2.39 percent also opened that email via a desktop interface (again, according to Knotice). In fact, over 95 percent of emails are opened on one device and one device only and 97 percent of mobile recipients never see the desktop version at all.

To make a long story short, your email campaigns need mobilization just as urgently as the rest of your business. Today, we'll look at some best practices and examples for taking this most fundamental aspect of your marketing mix mobile.

Mobile Email Delivery Options

According to Knotice's *Mobile Email Opens Report* for the first half of 2012, (`www.knotice.com/reports/Knotice_Mobile_Email_Opens_Report_FirstHalf2012.pdf`), iOS and Android accounted for 98.9 percent of all mobile email opens in the United States. We'd say that's a fair assessment. A quick look at your own site analytics will no doubt prove these two device platforms dominate. But the reality is with the hockey-stick growth in smartphones and tablets, you can't bank on the iPhone and Android being your only targets. As you develop your mobile email strategy, you'll want to strategize an approach that works for multiple mobile devices. With this in mind, let's explore a few options.

Text-Only Mobile Email

This is the lean-and-mean route. If you know your device audience is diverse, extending across the desktop and various smartphone and tablet platforms, you can play it safe with a text-only approach. A few basic best practices to keep in mind include:

- Use capitalization for the headline to help visually separate it from the body text.
- Use ***asterisks*** at the beginning and end of words or phrases that you want to set in **bold type.**
- Use line breaks to separate headlines, body text, and calls-to-action.
- Remember that plain text emails can't support hyperlinks—spell out URLs!

Rich Media Mobile Email

This is your preferred option if you know your mobile device users are fairly high-end and if your message truly depends on including visual design elements to get its point across. All high-end smartphones and tablets have email clients that support full HTML and CSS, so you can create a fairly sophisticated design if you choose. However, even if you choose to do a very basic HTML email, it is more complex than a simple text email version. Again, there are several different technical approaches and a number of design considerations to keep in mind. First, let's look at the technical options for actually getting the right email content to the user.

The View on Mobile Approach This is the simplest option—not so much a technical approach as it is a workaround. Here, you create different versions of your email, one for mobile and one for desktop. Then, you simply place a view on mobile link in the email *preheader* (the descriptive text that follows the subject line when the email is viewed in the reader's inbox) to deliver the user to a web page version of the email formatted specifically for mobile. It's not the most sophisticated approach because it involves an extra step in opening the user's browser, but it works.

The Media Query Approach With this approach, you take a slightly different angle by creating different style sheets for your email, one for desktop and one (or more) for mobile.

However, instead of asking the user to choose which version of the email they want to view, you make the delivery seamless by including the CSS media query @Media in the email's HTTP header to swap out a different style sheet according to the width and/or height of the device's *viewport* (the addressable area of the device's screen on which content will appear). This way you create one email but use media queries and CSS to create a layout customized to the device.

Note: So, what's a viewport, you ask? The strict definition is the rectangular area (in pixels) that is viewable on the device screen. Isn't this the same as the device's screen size? Well, yes. . .and no. For desktop and laptop computers, the viewport and screen size are one and the same, but for many mobile devices this is not the case. Many mobile devices actually have a much wider viewport that enables users to scale pages up and down to view details. The iPhone, for example, has a screen size of 320 pixels but a viewport of 980 pixels. Viewport meta tags placed in the HTTP header of your mobile email allow you to specify that the email should be viewed using a specific viewport—for example, one that matches the device's screen size.

The Responsive Approach Many high-end device platforms (iOS, for example) support media queries, the CSS3 elements we discussed in Chapter 4. As we just discussed, media queries can be used to detect the viewport of the device making an HTTP request. However, with a responsive approach, instead of implementing a separate style sheet, the media queries implement specific styles within the same style sheet to modify the way the content is presented.

The responsive approach to email design is gaining traction, and we believe it will become the de facto standard for email design in due time. As with designing a responsive website, this approach requires most heavy lifting upfront in terms of design and coding but delivers higher value post launch by enabling you to create truly fluid experience in which a single email is perfectly usable on a wide variety of popular devices.

Note: Gmail systematically removes all style sheet info from the header, and that's where media queries must be placed for the responsive approach to work. In order to accommodate Gmail and other email browsers that behave similarly (and we don't have to tell you there are a lot of them), you'll need to use inline styles to ensure that Gmail users can read your messages. The responsive approach also forces the mobile email browser to load the entire set of images intended for the desktop, which can quickly eat into the user's data plan. So, if you go for the responsive approach, you may want to go lighter on the images.

Mobile Email Design Best Practices

Now that you know your options for delivery, let's look at some design best practices:

Less is more. If you can keep your emails to 20K or less, that is ideal; but it is clearly unrealistic if you are following a responsive approach. Just keep in mind that less is more and try to keep it light.

Design for the most relevant screen size. The most common screen size for today's smartphones is 320 × 480, with some mild variations between iOS and Android devices. However, the actual addressable screen real estate is much smaller. On the iPhone's native email client, for example, you must allow 20 pixels for the status bar and 44 pixels each for the tool bars at the top and bottom of the screen. So your actual addressable area is 372 pixels. This will differ from device to device and email client to email client, but assume 372 pixels is a good benchmark.

Position the good stuff above the fold. The important elements—your logo, your main message—should be front and center. Don't worry about making the layout perfectly mirror your desktop version, but rather focus on showing mobile users the valuable stuff first.

Keep it short and skinny. Limit line length to 70 characters or less to make for nice even breaks, and map your one-column design using a grid system that allows users to scale up and down as needed.

Don't skew too small with the text. The ideal font size for headers is considered to be 30 points, and 14-point fonts work best for body copy.

Plan for mis-tapping. Each text link and button should be bolstered with at least 10 to 15 pixels to negate the possibility of mis-tapping. Apple guidelines actually specify padding for all clickable areas.

Friday: Outline Your Campaign Management, Tracking, and Analysis Approach

Like any other media, mobile advertising is useless if you can't track and measure the results. Let's review your options.

Analytics Options

It's a given that most of your mobile advertising campaigns will ultimately drive to a mobile web page of some kind. In Chapter 4, we discussed your options for tracking mobile websites, but let's do a quick recap to refresh your memory. Most likely, your current web analytics solution offers mobile tracking; most of the top options do so including:

- Google Analytics
- Omniture Site Catalyst
- webtrends
- IBM Coremetrics
- Yahoo! Analytics

So, tracking activity on your mobile websites and landing pages will be relatively straightforward. The trick will be to track the flow of clicks from ad content to these final destinations. Maintaining the connection between the two can be challenging.

The ad network you work with will have its own set of tags that will be included in the ad creative and destination pages. They should help facilitate tracking clicks on ads to post-click actions. However, we recommend a couple of additional options:

DoubleClick for Advertisers (DFA) for Mobile Dynamic Advertising, Tracking and Reporting for Advertisers from Google's DoubleClick, commonly known as DART, has been available for mobile for some time now. We recommend it as a cross-check to the ad tracking tags your network puts in place. Checking the discrepancies between reporting from both sets of tags will help you fine-tune your campaigns.

Third-Party Click Tracking As efficient as DART can be, other third-party click-tracking services have evolved specifically for mobile. These services have been designed with mobile in mind from the start and can be another valuable tool in optimizing your campaigns performance.

For Kiwi Market, an option like DFA mobile or some other third-party mobile ad tracking option would provide an impartial third-party benchmark between their own analytics and their mobile ad network's tracking, which could be used to track discrepancies.

Establishing KPIs

The most obvious key performance indicator (KPI) in general will be clicks, but there are a few others to consider for both your mobile SEM and mobile display efforts. The first being actions that happen within the ad:

- Clicks to call
- Clicks to a map or store locator
- Click to offer
- Clicks to a landing page or microsite
- Clicks to an app download
- Clicks to a screen within an app
- Time spent within the ad experience
- Actions completed within the ad experience (these may be the same as the post-click actions outlined here)

Then, of course, there are the post-click actions that happen at the destination, which are far more varied and might include:

- Orders placed
- Coupons or offers redeemed
- Mobile online purchases
- Requests for information
- Email or SMS signups

- Likes, Shares, and +1s
- Videos viewed
- Polls or surveys completed

In short, your mobile ad KPIs will be much the same as any you would set for a desktop campaign. Kiwi Market would be looking at the obvious metrics such as unique users, top entry and exit pages, time on site, bounce rate, shopping cart abandonment—all segmented out and compared to their desktop counterparts to discover variations desktop versus mobile user behavior.

Measuring Success

AdWords enables you to consistently track your mobile campaigns hands-on and measure performance in real time. Many of the mobile ad networks offer the option to view your campaign performance via a web-based reporting system or, in some cases, to import your metrics into your own dashboard.

Apply Results to Ongoing Campaign Development

In the case of mobile SEM, you will optimize on a daily basis and tweak your spend, keywords, and copy to maintain optimal page position for your ad to maximize the click-through rate and conversions. For mobile display, the optimization process will mostly be led by the ad network and will be considerably more complex. The iterative refinement will be less about spend and more about refining placement of your ad from less effective publishers to more effective ones, as well as making changes to creative, copy, and call to action.

In Conclusion

Ads are only one piece of the puzzle, but one that is growing in importance as mobile web usage and app consumption skyrocket. Mobile SEM and Display will be instrumental in driving traffic to your websites and apps, but they're also evolving to become significant drivers to real-world experiences that send traffic into stores and trigger all kinds of real-world behaviors offline. So, while mobile activity still far outweighs mobile ad spend, don't expect it to stay that way for long. This point in time is a golden opportunity to test and learn before the demand for mobile ads inevitably begins to exceed the supply of mobile inventory.

Week 6: Leverage the SoLoMo Nexus

The ability to marry where your customers are (location) *with what they're doing* (context), *and what they want* (intent) *is often referred to as marketing's holy grail. Mobile-enabled social networking platforms are fast becoming the conduit for not only peer-to-peer interactions about interests and intent but also consumer-to-marketer conversations. If you can succeed in tapping into mobile location-based services and data without overstepping that often fine line between delivering value and seeming intrusive, you will be onto something extremely powerful and potentially transformative. In this chapter, we show you how to navigate the fast-evolving geo-social ecosystem without succumbing to the many latent pitfalls.*

7

Chapter Contents

Monday: Understand the Opportunity

If you think about it, mobile devices are inherently social because their primary function is communication, and communication is an innately social function. Likewise, because we carry our mobile devices with us wherever we go, they are also inherently about location. The ability to broadcast location on omnipresent, mobile-enabled social networking platforms, often with the goal of zeroing in on place-specific offers and deals, forms the basis of the social-mobile-location (SoLoMo) nexus.

It's a potent mix that's rife with potential. As we outlined in Chapter 1, "Map the Mobile Opportunity," the closer your target audience is to purchase, in terms of both timing and context, the more important location becomes—and the more directly you can insert yourself into that equation, the more relevant you will be. So let's look at how you can achieve that goal.

In this chapter, we'll again share our own expertise as well as what we learned from talking with the following experts:

- Alistair Goodman, chief executive officer (CEO) of Placecast (`www.placecast.net`), a location-based marketing firm
- Greg Sterling, founding principal of Sterling Market Intelligence and contributing editor for the online publication *Search Engine Land* (`www.searchengineland.com`)
- Jack Philbin, cofounder, president, and CEO of Vibes Media (`www.vibes.com`), a mobile marketing and technology company
- Jim Lecinski, vice president of U.S. sales and service at Google and author of the e-book *Winning the Zero Moment of Truth* (`www.zeromomentoftruth.com`)
- Nihal Mehta, cofounder and CEO of LocalResponse (`www.localresponse.com`), an ad network that targets consumers based on social network data

You'll hear from Alistair, Greg, Jack, Jim, and Nihal throughout this chapter.

Note Changing Mobile User Behaviors

First off, you need to understand the extent of the opportunity. By one estimate, it's pretty extensive. Cisco Systems (`www.cisco.com`), the company we usually associate with the infrastructure side of networking, predicts the number of mobile social network users worldwide will more than double from nearly 950 million in 2012 to 2.4 billion in 2016 (see Figure 7.1). That would be equal to roughly half the total mobile user population by mid-decade.

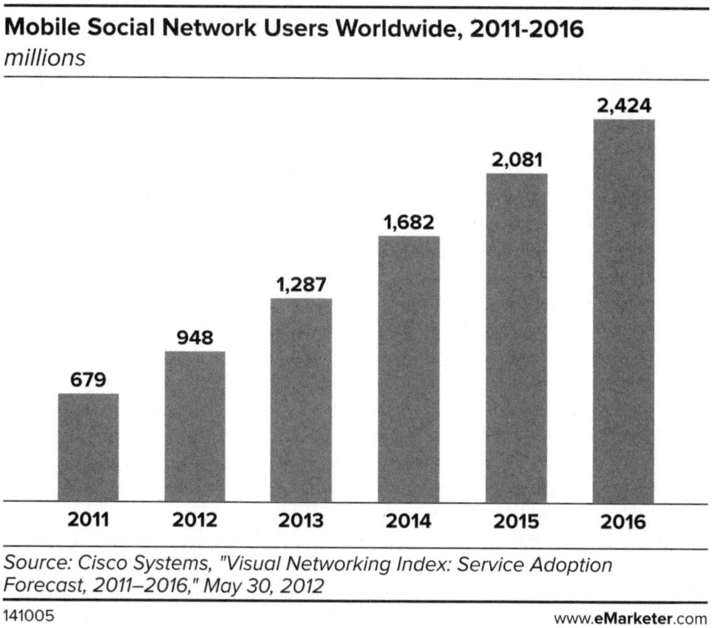

Figure 7.1 Mobile social networking predictions

Be advised: in the United States as well as other developed markets, social networking, like many mobile activities, is far more extensive among smartphone owners than feature phone owners. (By this point, you're probably sensing the trend here.) In other words, there are more mobile social networkers toting smartphones than feature phones at this point. The inverse is likely to hold true in developing regions, at least for the next few years. In short, social networking is becoming a core activity among mobile users. For example, the Google-sponsored "Our Mobile Planet" study (a great resource available from `www.thinkwithgoogle.com/mobileplanet/en/`) has found daily social network access among mobile users to be increasing not only in the United States, but the world over. To give you a sense, "Our Mobile Planet" found that 60 percent of U.S. smartphone owners log into social networks *every day* from their phones; in Latin American countries such as Mexico and Argentina, daily usage tops 70 percent. As this process advances, the platforms social networkers use likewise will assume importance as a meeting point between consumers and marketers.

Facebook, as the 800-pound gorilla of the social networking space, naturally dominates the conversation, whether on the desktop or mobile devices. According to comScore (`www.comscore.com`), a leading digital audience measurement firm, it enjoys by far the greatest reach of any social network. As detailed in Figure 7.2, users also spend longer than seven hours per month there, more time than on the remaining top-six networks combined.

US Smartphone Usage Metrics of Select Social Networks, March 2012

	Unique visitors (millions)	% reach	Average minutes per visitor
Facebook	78.0	80.4%	441.3
Twitter	25.6	26.4%	114.4
LinkedIn	7.6	7.9%	12.9
Pinterest	7.5	7.7%	52.9
foursquare	5.5	5.7%	145.6
Tumblr	4.5	4.6%	68.4

Note: ages 18+ via iOS, Android and RIM platforms; includes app and browser usage
Source: comScore Mobile Metrix 2.0 as cited in press release, May 7, 2012
140154 www.eMarketer.com

Figure 7.2 Mobile social networking and Facebook are practically synonymous.

Adoption of geo-location services is also on the rise. As part of its May 2012 "Visual Networking Index: Service Adoption Forecast, 2011–2016," Cisco projects that nearly 2.1 billion consumer mobile location-based service users around the world by 2016, nearly triple the number in 2012. Granted, Cisco uses an expansive definition that comprises personal navigation, point of interest (POI), friend-finder, and family-tracker services, but the forecast nonetheless speaks to rapid uptake (Figure 7.3).

Consumer Mobile Location-Based Service Users Worldwide, 2011-2016
millions

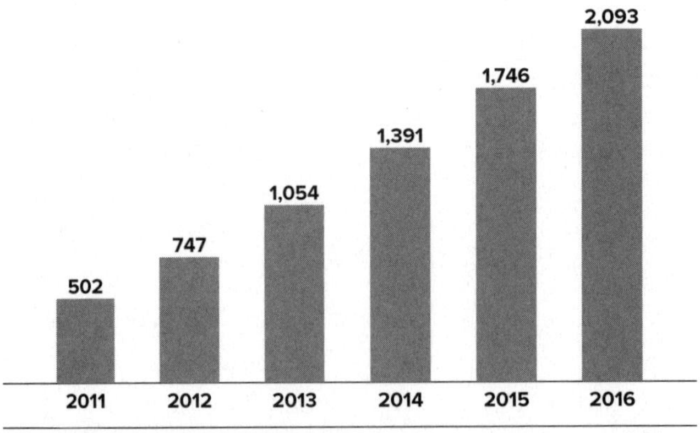

Note: includes services such as personal navigation, point of interest (POI), friend-finder and family-tracker services
Source: Cisco Systems, "Visual Networking Index: Service Adoption Forecast, 2011–2016," May 30, 2012
141003 www.eMarketer.com

Figure 7.3 Adoption of mobile location-based services is expected to soar.

In the United States, as elsewhere, mobile consumers are more likely to use features like navigation (Google Maps, for example) and local recommendations (like Yelp) than geo-social services such as foursquare, which enable them to share their location with friends and discover what's in their vicinity (e.g., places of interest or commerce opportunities). According to a May 2012 study by the nonprofit Pew Research Center's Internet & American Life Project (`www.pewinternet.org`), 41 percent of U.S. mobile owners use *some kind* of location-based service, but just 11 percent use geo-social services.

Among smartphone owners, predictably, usage for both is more than 50 percent greater, as shown in Figure 7.4; but among both mobile phone user populations, adoption of all types of location-based services is accelerating rapidly from a small base. As you'll see on Tuesday, the real value for marketers comes from the intersection of features like mapping and services that allow consumers to share interests and intent.

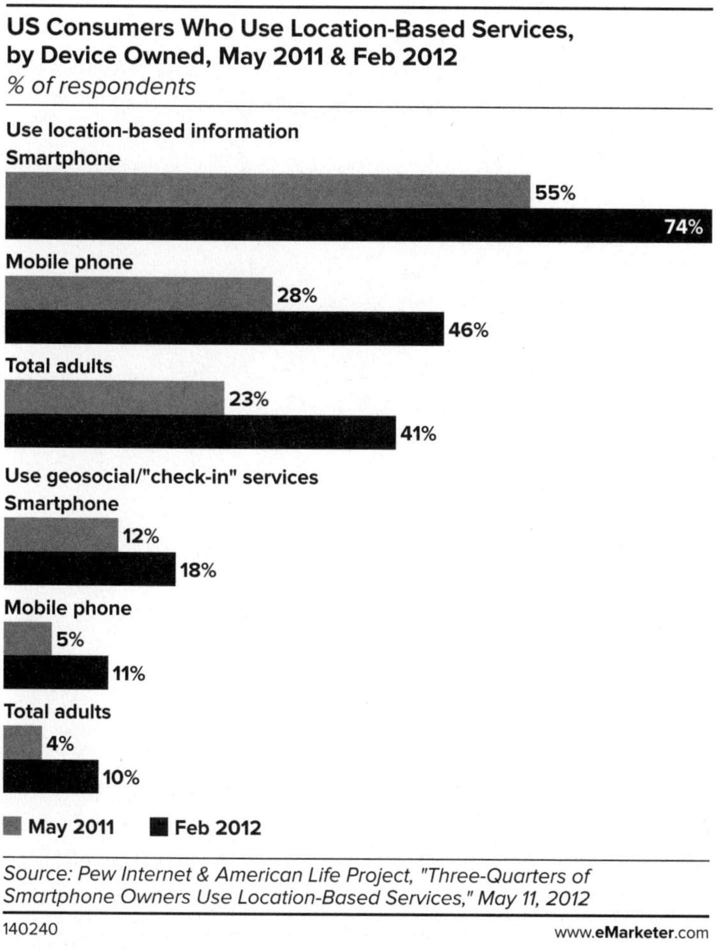

Figure 7.4 Use of geo-social services is accelerating but not yet mainstream.

Part of the challenge for geo-social services may come from lack of awareness and understanding of how they work. For example, according to a December 2011 study by JiWire (`www.jiwire.com`), a location-based mobile advertising company that targets audiences on Wi-Fi networks, 27 percent of U.S. mobile users do not understand check-in services. (The report also found that 30 percent don't care about them, which is a separate issue, compared to 35 percent who love or like them.)

The important characteristic for you to keep in mind is that *proximity increases intent*. As Alistair Goodman, CEO of location-based marketing firm Placecast put it in a June 2012 interview with the online trade publication *Mobile Commerce Daily*, "A consumer near a mall on a Saturday morning has their phone and their wallet and is in a mindset to make a purchase." We know that because a large body of survey data indicates a strong correlation for search for local information and taking action locally.

For example, Google's "Our Mobile Planet" study found that:

- Half of U.S. smartphone owners visited a store after searching for local information on their phone.
- Just over one-quarter bought a product in the store (Figure 7.5).

So if you can insert yourself into that process, you stand a good chance of influencing a purchase.

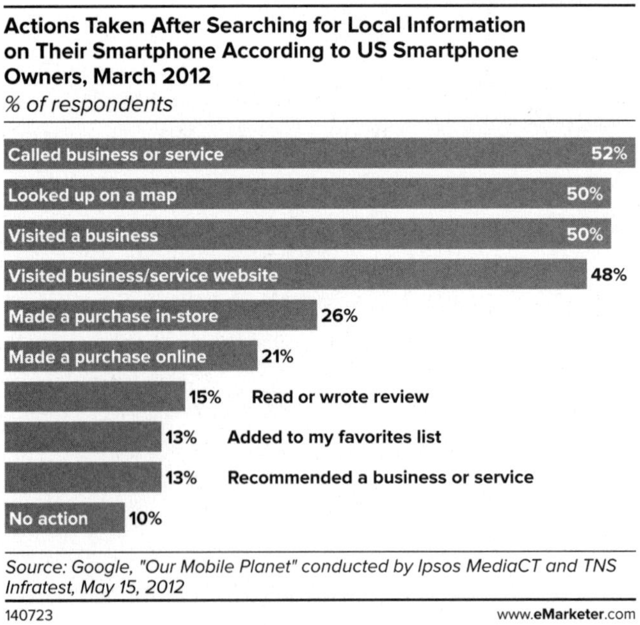

Figure 7.5 Local searches on mobile often lead to purchases.

Bear in mind that the majority of search queries—today—still come from the desktop. But as mobile effectively becomes the new desktop for more consumers, the volume of searches coming from mobile devices will eventually surpass the desktop.

As noted in Figure 7.6, local media and advertising-focused research firm BIA/Kelsey (www.biakelsey.com) predicts the inflection point will take place in 2015.

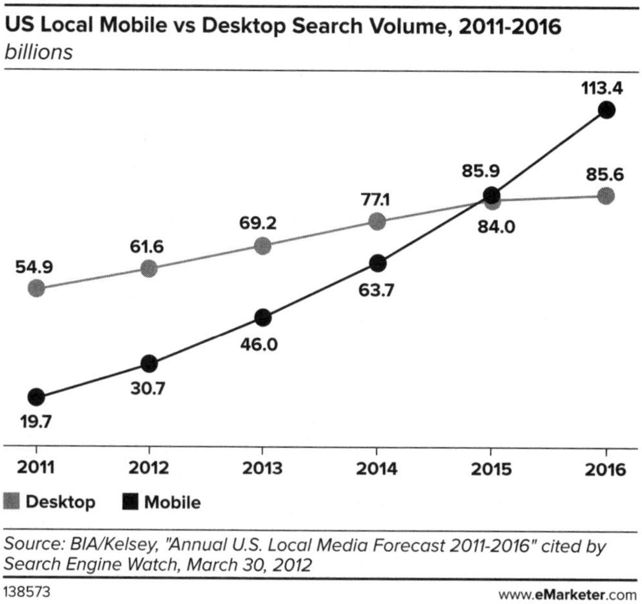

Figure 7.6 Mobile will eventually surpass the desktop in search volume.

> **Nussar Ahmad, Founder and CEO of Mobile Advertising Technology Company Addictive Mobility, on the Growing "Socialization" of Search**
>
> "Consumers increasingly look for information through their trusted network of friends. The way people search is changing from a traditional Google search to asking for input via open-ended questions on social networks such as Twitter. A person's trust in their social network influences their decision, be it a movie critique or a suggestion about a vehicle. Consider that 78 percent of people who want to buy a car list mobile as an influence on their purchase. This figure will only continue to grow. Social has a revealing truth to it, as it is more relevant when someone you know says something. Mobile is simply where it all begins."

Beware the Privacy Pitfalls

As much as SoLoMo promises potential, it is also replete with potential pitfalls. We alluded to the privacy challenges in Chapter 1, but they warrant more exploration. To be blunt, there is a fine line between using location data to provide benefits and using location data in a way that makes consumers uncomfortable. Privacy and security concerns abound here, and they are easily excited by marketers who overstep their boundaries to the point of seeming invasive. Figuring out just where that line is can be tricky. The consumer decision-making process isn't always rational in this regard. On the one hand, consumers like the benefit of more targeted ads and offers. But on the other, they worry about the kinds of personal information they have to give up in order to receive more personalized marketing messages.

A March 2012 poll of U.S. mobile app users by global security association ISACA (Information Systems Audit and Control Association, `www.isaca.org`) illustrates the complex and often vexing nature of the privacy issue relative to mobile location-based services. According to the survey, which included those with smartphones, tablets, and laptops who use any app:

- Fifty-four percent feel there is an acceptable balance between the risks and rewards offered by location-based services;
- But one in five (22 percent) still feel the risks outweigh the benefits.

The big concern for consumers? As shown in Figure 7.7, nearly one-quarter fear having their information used for marketing purposes. Of course, this concern isn't stopping people from using location-based services. The ISACA study found nearly one-third (32 percent) of respondents had increased their usage in the past year.

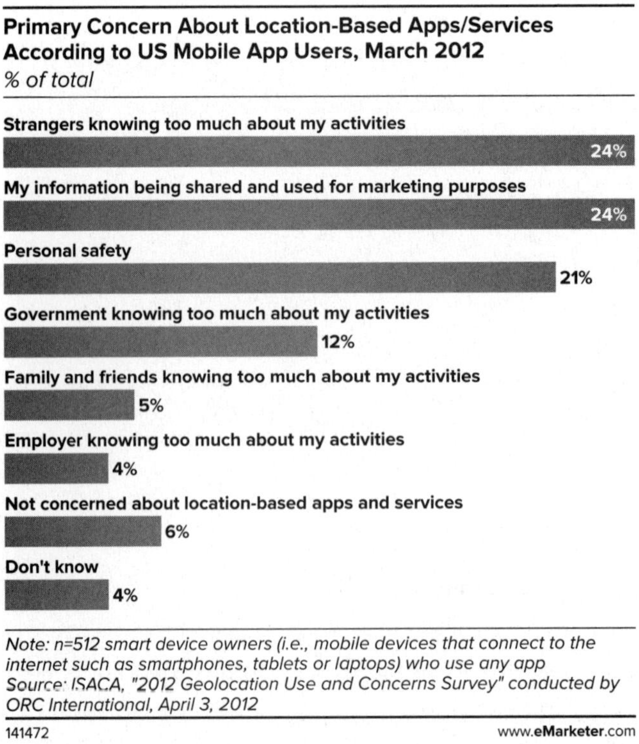

Figure 7.7 Privacy issues around mobile location-based services are complex.

Location: There's a Lot at Stake with Place

You need to remember that there's a lot at stake here. As Rip Gerber, president and CEO of Locaid Technologies (`www.loc-aid.com`), a provider of location-enablement services for brands and developers, told the online trade publication *Mobile Marketer* in June 2012: "The mobile device feels very private, and location services or push messaging can seem intrusive. It isn't just the medium; it's the medium combined with the message and moment—if you screw up any of these elements in relation to the other, it can become not just an effectiveness issue for the marketer but a privacy issue for the consumer."

Here's one way to think about it: We live in an increasingly user-centric world. Consumers are savvier than ever about the marketing programs in which they participate and are apt to use every means at their disposal to evaluate the ROI *they* can expect from participation—not unlike the assessment you will make as a marketer. With something as potentially costly as personal security at stake, your simultaneous challenges include:

- Delivering relevant and useful content
- Demonstrating transparency about data collection and usage
- Proving privacy concerns are being addressed

Taking these steps can help build trust and ward off easily excited fears about privacy and security.

Tuesday: Determine Use Cases

By now, you should have a good sense of the opportunities for reaching your audience using location-based services and marketing parameters. Today, we're going to focus on some specific use cases and best practices. As we've done throughout the book, we refer you back to the roadmap we developed in Chapter 2, "Week 1: Develop Your Mobile Strategy." This will be your guide for incorporating any new tactic into your larger strategic objectives.

In essence, the SoLoMo options at your disposal map to the purchase funnel shown in Figure 2.9. Says Jack Philbin, cofounder, president, and CEO of mobile marketing and technology company Vibes Media: "You always want to be advancing consumers from one stage to the next. If you fail at that, it means you haven't truly engaged that person all the way to being a repeat buyer." Let's illustrate how this might work using our fictional Kiwi Market as an example.

Recall from the research done by Kiwi Market that the supermarket chain's target audience is composed of fairly sophisticated, avid mobile users with high-end smartphones. So, in order to reach Michelle, the sample persona profiled in Chapter 2 (see Figure 2.10 for her customer journey map), the Kiwi marketing team will have marshaled an array of tactics, from mobile search marketing to display advertising to working with geo-social apps to literally putting the supermarket's various locations on the map—the one on your phone, that is.

Search and Discovery

For a category like groceries, convenience and proximity are important factors for prospective shoppers. As a retailer with multiple stores, Kiwi will want to take steps to enable customers like Michelle to find the nearest location. Michelle's journey map indicates that search plays an important role in first getting to know the Kiwi Market brand. Consequently, Kiwi needs to ensure that its website is optimized not only for mobile devices but also for local search.

The importance of search in relation to location is not to be underestimated. Google, for example, stated in October 2011 that 40 percent of mobile searches on its network carried local intent. That percentage has climbed steadily in conjunction with rising smartphone adoption, and there's little reason to expect the upward trend will not continue.

As part of its local search optimization effort, Kiwi will want to build out its presence across local search and directory venues such as Yelp, Google+, Bing, and YellowPages.com. A free tool such as GetListed (`www.getlisted.org`) can help you evaluate your company's local visibility (although bear in mind it's designed for the small business owner, not national chains). Given that reaching out to peer networks for recommendations on social platforms is becoming an important way consumers make choices about where they go, what they buy, and how much they pay for it, Kiwi will also want to build profiles on Facebook, Twitter, foursquare, and others to ensure that it is covering its social discovery bases.

Remember, the name of the geo-social game is participation—the give-and-take between you and your customers that platforms like Google+, Facebook, foursquare, and others facilitate—but it's up to you to take the initiative, claim your pages on key platforms, and make the most of them! We'll go into how you do that in more detail on Wednesday and Thursday.

Google+ Local: Evolution in Progress

In May 2012, Google folded Google Places for Business (`https://support.google.com/places/bin/answer.py?hl=en&answer=142902&topic=1660711&parent=1656746&rd=1`), the company's free listing service that enables businesses to create pages that show up on Google.com and Google Maps, into its Google+ social platform and rebranded Places as Google+ Local (a sample Google+ Local page appears in the following screenshot).

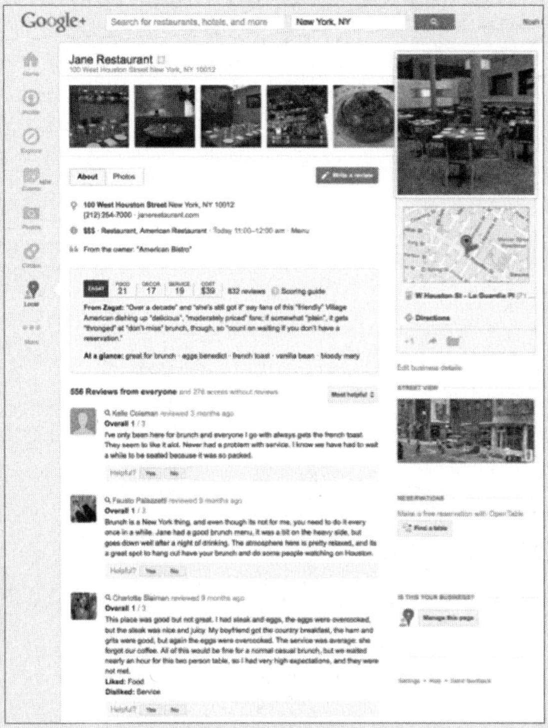

This shift has yielded many benefits, including the integration of Zagat (www.zagat.com, a Google-owned company) reviews and Zagat's 30-point rating scale (in lieu of Google Places' 5-point scale), more opportunities for business owners to have dynamic social interactions with customers, and another venue for local businesses to appear in search results. Unlike Google Places pages, Google+ Local will be indexed, which will bring search engine optimization (SEO) rewards for businesses that use Google+ to their best advantage.

At the time of writing, the external rebranding of Google Places for Businesses to Google+ Local was complete, but Google had not yet migrated the back-end listing management to the new platform. We expect this integration will take place soon.

Kiwi Market can complement these efforts with mobile search advertising. We outlined some sample paid search scenarios on Tuesday in Chapter 6, "Week 5: Promote Your Message with Mobile Advertising," including search ads with a link to a local map, as pictured in Figure 6.8.

Display and Awareness

Social discovery is undeniably an important emerging marketing trend, and you'll want to take steps to ensure you're getting the most out of it. But you'll also want to complement those efforts by building awareness for your brand and product in other ways. That's where advertising comes in. The saying goes that "all politics is local." Increasingly, that's true of advertising as well. As shown in Figure 7.8, local media and advertising-focused research firm BIA/Kelsey (`www.biakelsey.com`) predicts the balance of U.S. mobile ad campaigns will tip in favor of local instead of national in 2013. A rise in geo-targeted campaigns will help drive this shift.

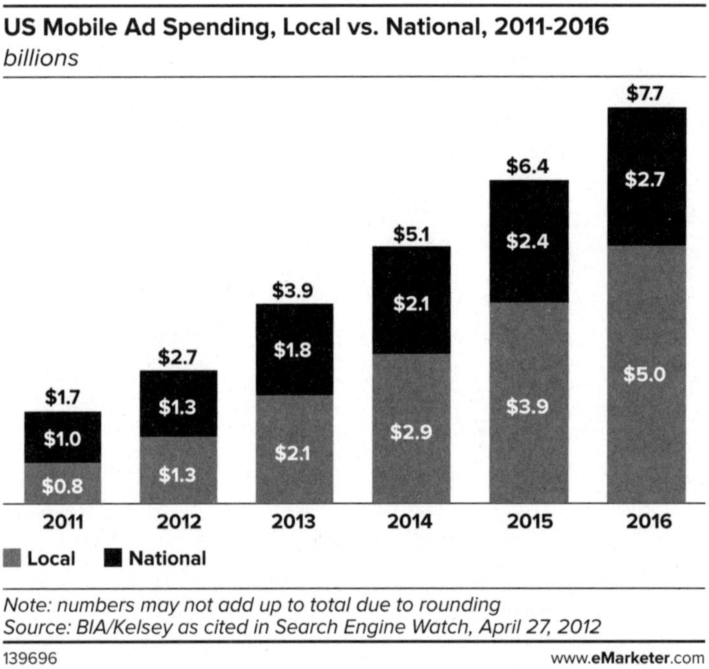

Figure 7.8 Local will soon surpass national advertising as the focus of mobile campaigns.

When it comes to capturing audience attention, a business like Kiwi Market has a lot of options to consider. One is mobile display advertising. We reviewed the range of mobile display ad possibilities in Chapter 6. Targeting by geo-location on the mobile web and in apps is one of the many routes you can take by working with a mobile ad network either directly or via an agency partner.

From a mobile advertising perspective, observes Nihal Mehta, cofounder and CEO of ad network LocalResponse, "Location has become a complete commodity. It's no longer super-sexy or premium because there's so much inventory that can be location-targeted. Because scale is here, you have the two things marketers want—reach and frequency—so you can do things like branding that weren't previously possible with location-based data. And branding can even be the primary goal, for example, 'Let's brand specific retailers in this particular area.'"

Nihal offers the following example: "You leave your office every day at 1:00 PM to grab lunch and fire up CNN.com on the mobile web and there's an ad for a nearby burger place you've never been to before. By doing an ad buy that combines location and daypart, the burger place is betting it can get customers in the door. That's an example of using location parameters for customer acquisition."

Another way for Kiwi to target customers potentially interested in what's around them is by placing ads on Wi-Fi networks. Companies like JiWire (`www.jiwire.com`), which maintains an ad network that reaches over 30,000 Wi-Fi locations, can help Kiwi (and you) connect with in-market customers. According to JiWire's own "Mobile Audience Insights Report: Q2 2011," 53 percent of U.S. Wi-Fi users are willing to share their location in return for relevant content. Although that particular data point is a little dated, we believe it to be directionally valid, and it indicates interest on which marketers can capitalize. The closer a customer is to a location, the more important sales and promotion information becomes, JiWire has found (see Figure 7.9), so Kiwi can take advantage of proximity to highlight what's on special at a local store.

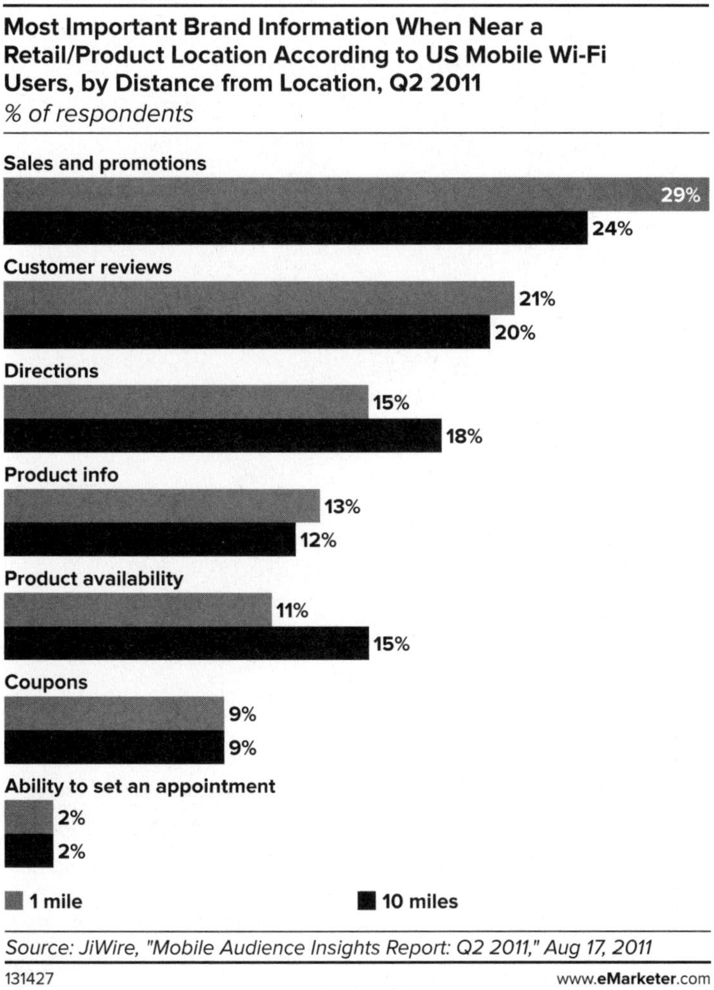

Figure 7.9 Proximity to a store heightens the appeal of sales for in-market shoppers.

However, Nihal cautions that location alone isn't necessarily the decisive parameter in every instance. "If someone is outside a Babies-R-Us, do you serve a diapers ad just because that person is outside the store? It may not be that relevant." In other words, location constitutes one element important for contextual targeting, but it should be combined with other contextually relevant information, such as intent. "Consumers are going to demand more context in their ads. It's kind of like the iPad," Nihal says. "None of us knew that we needed it, because we didn't have it, but now we want it. That's what true contextual advertising, of which location is a facet, will become—like the iPad."

You also need to think what happens beyond the click: Where is that going to lead consumers and how is it going to advance them on their journey? Jack says, "Anybody can create an ad buy and dispense the dollars, but what are you doing to engage consumers when they click on a banner ad and what's the experience they have along the customer journey? That's why location is paramount, because you can serve different ads based on where people are, but the post-click experience, which brings in the social factor *and* location, is so critical to what experience you're going to provide. And that experience is going to differ depending on where your audience is. Based on what's around people, you can tailor that experience to what they're doing."

Alerts and Engagement

Social discovery mechanisms and geo-targeted ads can work equally well for prospective shoppers and existing customers. But, for customers who have already purchased at Kiwi Market and opted in to receive SMS alerts or email offers from the company, push alerts can heighten engagement with the brand and drive people into stores. To reach these customers, Kiwi Market may want to establish a geo-fence around select store locations.

What Is a Geo-Fence?

A geo-fence is virtual perimeter created around a physical location—a retail store, for example—at a distance chosen by the retailer (such as one mile) for the purposes of sending text or push notifications to customers who have opted to receive alerts on their mobile devices when they enter the geographic area defined by the geo-fence.

According to a study sponsored by location-based marketing company Placecast, which specializes in geo-fencing campaigns, the number of U.S. shoppers interested in receiving promotional texts has risen in recent years. As of February 2012:

- Thirty-one percent of U.S. mobile phone owners not already receiving SMS message-based marketing said they were at least somewhat interested in this type of alert
- Ten percent said they were extremely interested in SMS messages.

Time, Location, and Interaction: The Keys to Offer Relevance

A lot of variables go into making an offer relevant to a potential customer. Jack Philbin, cofounder, president, and CEO of Vibes Media believes the three key factors are time, location, and interaction.

Time "You want to think about time: When is someone receiving this opportunity? What is the engagement? Assume you react differently in the morning than you would at night, or around, say, mealtimes if you got an offer from a quick-service restaurant."

Location "You don't want to send an offer for something in Chicago when someone is traveling in New York that day."

Interaction "What's the compelling engagement? Are users clicking on a trackable URL so you can start to gather profile data? If the URL is unique, you can track individual performance and determine specific preferences, likes, and dislikes."

For those already receiving location-based alerts, a notification can be a powerful purchase motivator. A look back at Chapter 3, "Week 2: Start Simple—SMS" reveals why. By opting into a program, customers express an interest in receiving messages, and hence are more predisposed to act on them because they are presumably more targeted at their specific interests. The Placecast study found nearly one in three consumers that opted to receive text alerts visited a physical store and more than one in four purchased the product promoted in the message (see Figure 7.10).

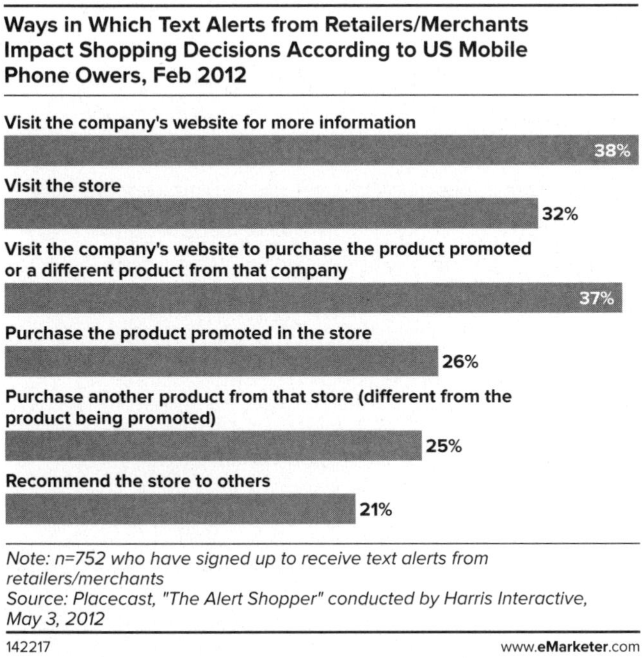

Figure 7.10 Opt-in SMS alerts can drive shoppers into stores and trigger purchases.

Kiwi can also push alerts to its smartphone customers who have the Kiwi Market app on their devices. The ability to target customers in this way requires users to activate the notification feature in the Kiwi Market app, so the company will want to remind customers about that using its other customer contact channels (such as email).

Revisiting the Benefits of Opt-In Marketing with Placecast CEO Alistair Goodman

Location-based marketing firm Placecast runs campaigns on behalf of brands and mobile carriers, all on the basis of opt-in messaging. CEO Alistair Goodman explains why.

"We've shifted more toward opt-in and that's been driven by the effectiveness of those programs, the yield for marketers and brands, and a strong point of view that all of mobile marketing is going to head toward opt-in. The keys are opt-in, consumers being able to set preferences, providing transparency about what data is collected and how it's used, and then giving consumers a lot of control over what they get inside that experience. We believe that's the direction the market is headed."

As a follow-up, we asked Alistair whether presenting consumers with choice and giving them the ability to configure preferences help to alleviate privacy concerns. Here's what he had to say:

"It alleviates an enormous amount of those concerns. We have been big believers in using location data solely to send consumers relevant offers. What we've seen is when you're clear and transparent with consumers, they understand why they're getting certain things on their phone, and they are more likely to stay in programs for longer periods of time. They also have a much higher comfort level with those programs. For example, 18 percent of consumers who have been in one our programs six or more months feel the programs are getting more valuable because they've come to expect offers based on location, and 31 percent of them feel the programs are getting more valuable over time because the perception is the program is learning what they like. At the end of the day, privacy is not a hurdle if you're driving value for both the brand and the consumer."

The takeaway is the opt-in and the ability to set preferences drive trust, and these qualities help to build value over time. In the best case, exemplified by the scenario Alistair outlines, consumers come to see the marketer as a trusted partner who understands their likes and dislikes and presents offers accordingly.

Ambient Media and Conversion and Loyalty

Getting customers in the door is an important step in bringing them closer to purchase. But once they are in a location, you can take additional steps using ambient media to move them farther down the funnel and toward the end of their journey.

> **What Are Ambient Media?**
>
> *Ambient*, in the strictest definition, means "Of, or relating to, one's immediate surroundings." In the context of this book, we use the term *ambient media* to refer to touchpoints and triggers external to the customer's mobile device, including: Wi-Fi nodes, quick response (QR) codes, augmented reality, geo-fences, near-field communication (NFC), surface technology, motion-sensitive and digitally enabled objects and locations, and a host of other media that we'll explain in further detail in Chapter 9, "Week 8: Drive Awareness with Ambient Media."

We'll go into more detail about ambient media in Chapter 8, "Week 7: Check Out m-commerce," and Chapter 9. For now, we want to focus on a couple of options that link specifically to location. For example, Kiwi Market could join the ranks of leading retailers that use shopkick (`www.shopkick.com`), a technology that recognizes and rewards customers as they enter a store. A physical sensor installed in the store triggers the shopkick app on a customer's device, funnels offers, and rewards shoppers with points upon entry. It's kind of like thanking them in advance for their business.

Farther on the horizon are services that will enable marketers to send highly targeted messages to shoppers based on their movements around a store. Companies such as Micello (`www.micello.com`), Point Inside (`www.pointinside.com`), and Aisle 411 (`www.aisle411.com`), for example, maintain indoor map databases. If that information were combined with the kinds of opt-in messaging or alerts we described in the preceding section, you can imagine how it could help marketers chart the path to purchase in a very literal way. You may not see that put into common practice immediately, but as mapping capabilities become a contested area for digital and mobile giants like Google, Apple, and Microsoft, you can be sure indoor space will become just as contested as the outdoors.

Wednesday: Define Your Partners

On Tuesday, we outlined a number of different ways you can market to your audience using a combination of social, mobile, and geo-location parameters. SoLoMo is, for the moment, less technical than say, the highly rigorous steps we showed you in Chapter 3 for SMS marketing. But bear in mind that the landscape is somewhat fragmented and many companies in the SoLoMo ecosystem have offerings that are more robust in one area than another (Google is stronger in local search than it is in social, for example), so you'll still need to work with a roster of partners to bring a mobile location-based campaign to fruition. Broadly speaking, you'll need to consider the following: social networks and geo-social apps, local search and mapping providers, ad networks and technology platforms, and, to a certain extent, the mobile carriers.

Social Networks

In the past few years, the social network landscape has exhibited a pattern of expansion and contraction typical of an emerging medium. First came innovation, witnessed by a proliferation of services, some that began on the desktop and extended to mobile (such as Facebook and Twitter), and others that began as mobile-first platforms (such as foursquare). Expansion was followed by the land-grab stage, in which many small services jockeyed for market share, a process complicated by the meteoric growth of Facebook both in the United States and worldwide. Consolidation and contraction were the inevitable outcome.

We will spare you the full complexity of the roadmap needed to track shifts in the mobile social landscape and focus on the most prominent platforms. One word of caution: the social networking space continues to evolve at a relatively rapid pace, and networks and apps often make changes to existing marketing programs or experiment with new ones, so you have to be prepared to monitor developments pretty regularly.

Facebook

The world's largest social network also has the largest number of active mobile users—543 million monthly active users (MAUs) worldwide as of the end of June 2012. That's over half (54 percent) of Facebook's total 901 million MAUs, although as Facebook stated in its April 2012 Amendment No. 4 to its S-1 filing, "While most of our mobile users also access Facebook through personal computers, we anticipate that the rate of growth in mobile usage will exceed the growth in usage through personal computers for the foreseeable future, in part due to our focus on developing mobile products to encourage mobile usage of Facebook." In plain English, that means Facebook expects the majority of future activity on its platform to come from mobile devices.

In terms of reach, Facebook is the social networking equivalent of TV. It also has the added benefit of high engagement. The challenge with Facebook is users go there to socialize first and entertain themselves second. Engagement with marketers and follow-on activities such as purchasing are certainly rising, but still fall lower on the list. For example, in a June 2012 study from Reuters and research firm Ipsos, just 20 percent of U.S. Facebook users said they had bought products because of ads or comments they saw on the social network.

Facebook has experimented with location-sharing and location-based deals since Fall 2010, but without seeming to fully commit to the effort. Now that it is a public company, however, Facebook's ability to generate revenues for itself and brands using its platform has achieved heightened importance. Simply put, Facebook is getting more serious about commerce. It has moved away from encouraging check-ins as an isolated action and toward incorporating location as an integral element of every action users take on Facebook, from tagging photos to sharing where they're having dinner. If anything, location has become more central to everything we do on Facebook, even if the trigger no longer necessarily comes from a check-in.

With the centrality of location in mind, you can—and should—claim a page for your business. Facebook offers guidelines and FAQs for doing so in its Help Center (`www.facebook.com/help/location/claim`). This will help you interact with an audience that may already be searching for you and enable you to message them with relevant information and offers.

For example, when Facebook users "like" your page and you then post an offer, that offer will show up in their newsfeed, and in turn, they will be able to share it with their friends, even if those people haven't yet liked your business. Moreover, in an effort to expand the reach of its deals program, Facebook has actually decoupled claiming deals from the mobile check-in, which allows users to claim a deal on the desktop *or* mobile device, regardless of their proximity to the business offering the deal. The net result is local businesses can potentially reach a far wider audience than before. Facebook also lists Offers guidelines and best practices in its Help Center (`www.facebook.com/help/offers#admins`).

Twitter

Twitter is not a geo-social network per se, but it does enable users to share location data—and because consumers often use Twitter to broadcast intent and location either by tweeting directly (such as "Stopping by Kiwi Market to buy supplies for tomorrow's BBQ") or via other social platforms that link to Twitter (foursquare being a prime example), it can be a good platform for communicating location-based offers.

You have a few different options for doing so. One is simply by monitoring mentions of your brand and responding to individual comments or in bulk if your listening reveals a confluence of activity around a specific place. This is obviously a very labor-intensive endeavor. Using social media monitoring software and tapping into Twitter's *application programming interface (API)*, which contains latitude and longitude (lat-long) data, can help. But in order to respond in a timely, relevant fashion, someone still needs to be "listening" and able to analyze the incoming data stream.

A second option, best used in conjunction with the first, is Promoted Tweets, one of Twitter's advertising products. Promoted Tweets enable you to target your message to specific geographies. So, an airline, for example, might want to target winter Caribbean getaway specials only to audiences in the Northeastern United States. You can find more information about Promoted Tweets in Twitter's Help Center (https://support.twitter.com/articles/142101-promoted-tweets).

A third option is to work with an ad network like LocalResponse, which captures and filters vast amounts of data publicly broadcast on Twitter and responds with relevant content on Twitter in a matter of seconds. We'll talk more about LocalResponse in the section on ad networks and technology platforms.

Geo-Social Apps

As one of the pioneers of the check-in, foursquare set the pace in terms of bringing gaming dynamics to SoLoMo. But even the pioneers must evolve when the space they helped inaugurate starts to pass them by. Here's what foursquare cofounder Dennis Crowley said to the TechCrunch blog after foursquare revamped its location-based app and launched version 5.0 in June 2012:

"People have pigeonholed us into, 'Oh it's that silly game about points and mayors and badges.' Yeah, that's part of foursquare. But that's not what we're doing with all the amazing check-in data that we're getting from the 20 million users we have. We have well over 2 billion check-ins at this point, and that allows us to predict what's going to be going on in downtown Manhattan two hours from now..."

To put it another way, the games are still there, but they run in the background, so the emphasis can be about what happens beyond the check-in, like using location as a mechanism for discovering local businesses (and recommendations about them) and nearby offers. That's where the value lies for marketers. Industry expert Greg Sterling, founding principal of Sterling Market Intelligence and contributing editor for the online publication *Search Engine Land*, views foursquare as a leading indicator of how consumers are using SoLoMo. He says: "What's going on in mobile is more the foursquare model, where people are leaving tips or star ratings or other short-form content."

As on Facebook, foursquare enables businesses to "claim their venue." Whether you're sole proprietor or operate a chain of stores, you'll want to do this, because it allows you to update relevant data about your business, gives you access to real-time analytics (who's checking in, at what time, how frequently, and so on), and enables you to offer patrons Specials. These can be designed to target new or repeat customers, so the options run the length of the purchase funnel, from customer acquisition to retention.

You can find more information about how to make the most of foursquare and a step-by-step guide on how to claim your venue, offer specials, and use the analytics dashboard on foursquare's Merchant Platform site (https://foursquare.com/business/merchants).

Local Search

In the local search arena, Yelp and Google+ Local are two of the big players you need to consider.

Yelp

Like Google+ Local, Yelp is more a local search service than a social network. But it does have a similarly social element to it: users flock to Yelp to read and post reviews of local businesses and seek out time-sensitive deals. The platform also enables businesses to interact directly with customers, via either public or private responses to posted reviews. Yelp says it had an average 78 million monthly unique visitors in Q2 2012 and users have posted over 30 million reviews of local businesses, so it has scale.

As with some of the other partners we've listed, Yelp gives business owners the opportunity to manage their page (referred to as unlocking in Yelp parlance), which means keeping business information up-to-date (description, history, photos, and the like), and tracking stats about how many people have viewed your page. You'll also be able to offer your customers Yelp Deals, which appear on the desktop site as well as the Yelp mobile app. More information can found in Yelp's support center for business owners (`https://biz.yelp.com/support/what_is_yelp`).

Google+ Local

We talked a bit about Google+ Local, the evolution of Google Places for Business, on Tuesday, but here's some more background. Remember that Google's stated mission is to "organize the world's information and make it universally accessible and useful." Fulfilling this mission depends on Google's ability to *access* the world's information. Competitors like Facebook, which walls off all non-publicly shared activity, represent a serious challenge to Google's mission. In the case of Facebook, there are nearly 1 billion people trading information about likes and dislikes and interacting with content in ways that are mostly beyond Google's reach.

So, think of Google+ as Google's response to this challenge—a way for the search giant to build its own rich store of consumer data so it can continue its mission, maintain the appeal of its ad-serving capabilities, and bolster its marketing and commerce initiatives. In effect, Google+ is Google's attempt to combine the reach of its local search platform with the stickiness and engagement typically associated with social platforms, particularly Facebook and foursquare. It remains to be seen whether Google will succeed in social to the same extent it has succeeded in search. Facebook still dwarfs Google+ in popularity and most key usage metrics (see Figure 7.11). Still, we believe Google+'s ability to piggyback on the popularity of other Google services means it cannot be ignored.

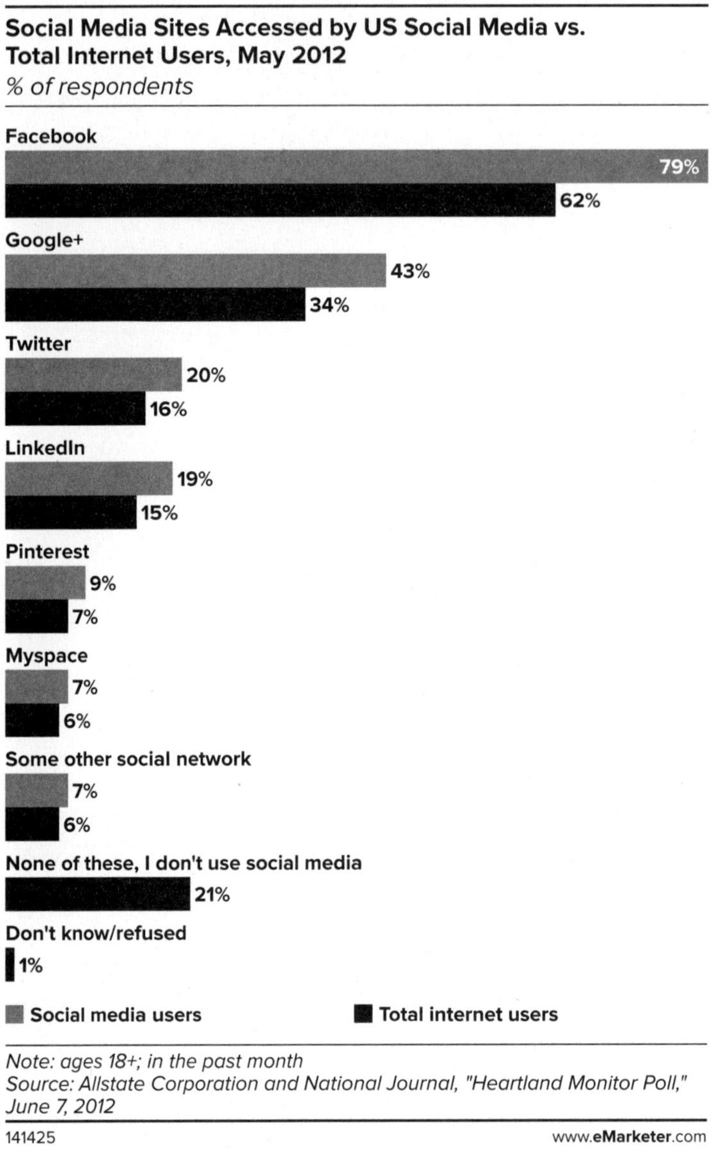

Figure 7.11 Google+ has grown quickly, but still trails Facebook in popularity.

Like Facebook and foursquare, Google+ Local allows you to claim and manage a page for your venue or business. As with Facebook and foursquare, we absolutely encourage you to do this, largely for the same reasons. It's another case of "the more you put in, the more you will get out of it." In the case of Google+ Local, you have the not-insignificant additional SEO benefits of having your business's page index in search results as well as another large venue within Google for your audience to discover your brand. Given the importance of search as a discovery mechanism for everything from brand information to deals, those benefits are hardly trivial.

Thankfully, the process for setting up your Google+ Local listing is relatively simple and you can get started right here: `http://support.google.com/plus/bin/topic.py?hl=en&topic=2566084&parent=1710599&ctx=topic`. Be prepared to provide Google with essential information about your business, including address, type of business, products sold, locations, supported methods of payment, and even images of your establishment (optional but highly recommended). Once you've submitted your data, you'll receive a confirmation from Google by snail mail (yes, really!) within one to two weeks with a unique pin number that you will enter online to confirm your listing. Log into your Google account, enter your pin, and your listing will be live!

Mapping

The ability to determine where you are, what's around you, and how to get where you want to go is in some way intrinsic to the mobile experience. Whether through specific map apps you use to find directions or mapping capabilities that function in the background of other apps, placing yourself in relation to the world at large is fundamentally important. Mobile users doing precisely these things drive much of the location-based activity highlighted in Figure 7.4. Consider also the relationship between searching, mapping, and commerce that you can see in Figure 7.5: Fifty percent of U.S. smartphone owners said that after searching for local information, they looked up that business on a map. Taken together, these actions help move customers along their journey to their ultimate destination.

Just as location is a vital attribute for marketers looking to target their audiences, maps are the increasingly valuable mechanism for doing so. All of the digital giants—Apple, Google, Microsoft—want to exercise more direct control over maps, especially on mobile devices, so they can determine how location information gets deployed and implemented. Of the emerging map wars, Peter Farago, the vice president of marketing for app analytics firm Flurry we encountered in Chapter 5, "Week 4: Maximize Engagement with Mobile Apps," told *Fast Company* in June 2012: "It's just a key thing you have to control. It's like countries protecting their food source. I don't want to have to import all my food in case we ever go to war." As smart devices become progressively more capable, you can bet the richness of maps will only increase, helping transform map apps into graphical search engines.

Google, for example, already offers a wealth of place information, including reviews, if applicable, in its map results. This is another reason why having an up-to-date Google+ Local listing is so important, as that listing information drives what appears in Google Maps results.

Note that other search engines have similar procedures. We emphasize Google because of its importance relative to other search platforms and the role it plays in powering the mapping functionality on so many other sites and services.

Ad Networks and Technology Platforms

Drawing up a comprehensive list of ad networks and technology platforms that can help you hone in on your audience based on where they are and what they are doing could easily fill its own chapter. The list here is far from exhaustive, but it does include companies that are tackling challenging pieces of the SoLoMo puzzle in innovative ways.

LocalResponse We alluded to LocalResponse in the discussion of Twitter. It is an ad network that targets customers based on intent expressed publicly on Twitter and other social networks that feed status updates into a user's Twitter profile. Says LocalResponse cofounder and CEO, Nihal Mehta: "If you tweet that you're at Walgreens, you get a message back from Walgreens' Twitter account, and you get that pretty much within a minute of you tweeting that you're at Walgreens." Because many status updates include lat-long data, a retailer like Walgreens can focus the response to a specific location, such as a store with a time-sensitive special offer. "We deal only with public data," notes Nihal. "Ninety-nine percent of Facebook data is private, so that's off the table. But the majority of Twitter content is public, so we can leverage all that data and retarget against it. We make sure there's no PII [personally identifiable information]. We don't think a Twitter user name is PII because it's public. But we want to make sure we're delivering really good ads. We've seen less than a 0.1 percent opt-out rate and 10 times the industry standard in terms of performance because the ads are so targeted." LocalReponse has another service, which it calls intent retargeting, that enables marketers to buy display ads against the same types of expressed customer intent. "For us at LocalResponse, it's all about the social context. You just tweeted that you're hungry, and now you see a banner ad for Pizza Hut. That has location as a subset, because we want to send you to a Pizza Hut near you. The trigger is having broadcast some type of intent and expressed it across any type of social media, followed by going to a website where you see an ad that's highly targeted and relevant," notes Nihal. LocalResponse employs the same basic underlying data stream, but repurposes it in two different but complementary ways and targets it at different points in the customer journey.

Placecast Placecast is a location-based marketing company that specializes in the kind of geo-fencing campaigns we discussed on Tuesday. For customer acquisition campaigns, Placecast fields ShopAlerts—SMS offers—for brands via the mobile carriers (it has worked with AT&T in the United States and O2 in the United Kingdom). Consumers who opt to receive messaging from their carrier might receive an offer from, for example, a local quick-serve restaurant. Placecast also works directly with brands on loyalty programs that present customers (those who have opted into receiving brand messages via SMS) with location-targeted offers and deals designed to drive them into stores and make purchases.

shopkick Here's a quick refresher on shopkick, which we mentioned on Tuesday: The company has developed a technology that recognizes customers as they walk into a store and presents them with rewards before they reach the checkout counter. This inverts the usual order of things, but you can imagine how it could be a powerful loyalty driver. Cyriac Roeding, shopkick's cofounder and CEO, explained how the technology works in a February 2012 interview with eMarketer. "We've developed a box that emits an inaudible audio signal at 21,000 Hz, which stores plug into a power outlet," he said. "When a consumer walks into the store, their smartphone microphone detects this signal and decodes it to determine the store at which you are located. This allows retailers to only reward those consumers who actually step into their store." The app notifies that shopper of in-store specials and awards them points (called "kicks") redeemable for gift cards, music, and other items at more than 4,000 participating U.S. retailers. "You can earn kicks everywhere and spend them anywhere," Roeding said. "So, essentially, shopkick is the idea of a mall on your mobile phone."

Thursday: Realize Location-Based Marketing Opportunities

Now that you have a sense of the SoLoMo landscape and what the potential opportunities are, let's imagine some scenarios that follow the customer journey.

The first step is to ensure that Kiwi Market shows up when someone like our sample persona Michelle, the super-connected mom, performs a search looking for organic supermarkets. This involves:

- Submitting relevant business information (name, address[es] and phone number[s], URL, store hours, etc.) to directories like the Yellow Pages. These populate online databases that in turn feed search results. As we discussed in Chapter 4, "Week 3: Maximize Reach with Mobile Websites," having a mobile-optimized presence on the other side of the search result is crucial for making a positive first impression on customers.
- Developing a profile on Google+ Local, Yelp, Bing Local, and other local search destinations. Building these profiles will help improve organic search equity for Kiwi Market. They also will be especially important for reaching someone like Michelle, who, although a mobile power-user, hasn't really experimented with geo-social apps.

Still, maximizing Kiwi Market's presence on prominent geo-social destinations such as foursquare by claiming its page is worthwhile in terms of covering the bases and a precursor for offering deals later on. In fact, using assets like Google+ Local, Yelp, and foursquare pages to display special offers is a good way to induce a first-time buyer like Michelle to visit her local Kiwi Market. These can also give existing customers a reason to come back.

The second step is to build a presence on Facebook. Michelle, as we know from her persona profile in Chapter 2, uses the social network daily. So it's quite likely she will reach out to her friends and family to determine whether Kiwi Market is a good match for her goal of eating as much organic food as possible and providing her family with high-quality meals. For similar reasons, Facebook is a good place to post offers, because Michelle's peer network is likely to pass along the deals (or she will see them in her newsfeed).

Kiwi Market will want to complement these efforts by placing targeted display ads to reinforce the messages Michelle may have seen in her searches or when browsing on Facebook. Reviewing the internal market research findings, customer segmentation, and technographics we discussed in Chapter 2 can help determine the types of sites and apps Kiwi will want to target with ads. As we noted in Chapter 4, mobile display ad networks can target ads by app and site category, so Kiwi can easily reach popular recipe apps like Epicurious that fit with Michelle's love of cooking and her interest in fresh food. The ads might highlight seasonally available produce in Michelle's nearby Kiwi Market. Clicking through leads to a 10 percent off coupon. The combined impact of these tactics helps get Michelle in the door. The positive in-store experience inspires Michelle to sign up for Kiwi's loyalty program. The idea of getting SMS alerts with coupons is appealing to Michelle, a frequent texter.

Now that Michelle has opted into Kiwi Market's loyalty program, the supermarket decides to invest in a geo-fencing campaign. Working with its agency and technology partners, Kiwi establishes a geo-fence around select store locations in Michelle's city. It also makes the strategic decision to set up a handful of geo-fences around several of its competitors' nearby locations under the theory that it may be able to lure away shoppers who are interested in other organic specialty markets.

Combining different forms of media can have a powerful effect on in-market consumers. Placecast CEO Alistair Goodman notes, "One of the things we've seen is when you combine other forms of marketing with location-based alerts, you get a substantial lift in purchase behavior. For example, we've run programs with a combination of out-of-home and then alerts in proximity of the store, and in the case where consumers were exposed to both alerts, 70 percent were more likely to make a purchase. Location and time are very predictive of what a consumer is going to be interested in and intends to do, but when combined with other media, you get an even more dramatic lift."

The social component that enables sharing can also work in Kiwi Market's favor here. Because Michelle has converted into a loyal shopper, she is more inclined to promote the store to *her* friends, family, and coworkers. Michelle is not a frequent Twitter user, but she finds it convenient to tweet the link to the coupon for discounts at her local Kiwi location. That action triggers a response from a grateful Kiwi Market and a subsequent banner ad further deepening her engagement the next time she logs onto the mobile web or opens one of her preferred apps.

The bottom line is you need to be engaging at every step of the customer journey in order to get consumers to move to the next stage. "You always try and advance people through the funnel," says Jack Philbin, cofounder, president, and CEO of Vibes Media. "And your mobile engagement and mobile activity should be trying to drive purchase and trying to drive loyalty."

An example of a good retailer to emulate is Starbucks. Jack affirms, "Starbucks does this really well. They have the app, which is very engaging. You can load money into it and scan your barcode and buy. That's transaction. And then loyalty, if you click on the rewards icon, a little star drops into your cup every time. It's a cyclical experience that drives you to engage further, gets you to transact, and makes you a more loyal customer. It's astonishing that more retailers haven't followed suit." It's a virtuous cycle for the customer—and also for Starbucks, because it encourages customers to buy more.

Advice from Google Vice President of U.S. Sales and Service, Jim Lecinski, Author of *Winning the Zero Moment of Truth*

In his 2011 e-book, Google's Jim Lecinski defines any consumer online decision-making moment as a "zero moment of truth" for marketers. In the e-book's forward, Dina Howell, CEO of agency Saatchi & Saatchi X, writes: "The Zero Moment of Truth influences which brands make the shopping list, where shoppers choose to buy, and with whom they share the results. It's up to us to join the conversation at this new moment where decisions are being made, and to provide the information that shoppers naturally crave, in all the ways that they crave it."

We asked Jim what the single most important thing brands can do to connect with consumers in the Zero Moment of Truth from both a content and channel perspective. Here's his advice:

"The biggest piece of advice I'd give? Be there. People looking for information online are raising their hands and saying, 'I would like to know more about this topic.' At the Zero Moment of Truth, there's a chance to make a brand impression and give people the information they're looking for, when they're looking for it."

For marketers looking specifically at a geo-location context, Jim adds: "Brands can most effectively link consumers' checking-in activity to their digital encounters with brands by using all the research and data at their disposal to measure the impact on both online sales and interactions, and on in-store interactions with brands."

Friday: Define Key Analytics

As outlined in Chapter 1, location sharing started life quite literally as a game. The goal was to encourage users to participate in exchange for imaginary status or virtual rewards. But, enabling bragging rights for the person who checks in the most frequently at his or her local coffee shop offers little in the way of rewards to the owner of that establishment—unless all that activity can in some way be connected to commerce. Again, you have to think about where and how different SoLoMo actions can be linked to the purchase funnel and customer journey. At the top of the funnel and beginning of the journey, where branding and awareness-building are at a premium, metrics like shares, Likes, tips, and recommendations can be valuable, particularly to the extent that they help your audience market your brand and products for you. That is the true benefit of working with social platforms. If you can maintain an active voice in the discussion, in effect steering the conversation with timely responses to customer questions or issues or problems that arise, you can achieve a lot in terms of raising your company's profile. For the most part, this will cost you more time than money.

As eMarketer Principal Analyst Debra Aho Williamson put it in her December 2011 "Social Media Measurement: Getting to the Metrics That Matter" report, "Don't count fans. Count what they do for you." She added: "While friends, followers, and 'likes' are an easy benchmark, what is more important is the ways they share, respond, and interact in social media. And tracking influencers is even more important."

In other words, numbers have little value unless they have activity behind them—activity that will help you realize more sales. Once you start to look at post-click activity—the actions your audience takes after seeing a geo-targeted ad or receiving a location-based alert, that's when you can more closely connect to purchase intent. Look for a correlation between ad impressions, click-throughs, and visits to either your company's website (or purpose-built landing pages) or a physical location. If your systems will allow it, track offers from distribution to redemption to the point of sale. Go the extra mile to get to the last mile of commerce.

You also have to look at the success of individual SoLoMo marketing mechanisms, as well as the success of a whole campaign in terms of it adding up to more than the sum of its parts. For example, Kiwi Market needs to examine whether its geo-targeted mobile ad campaign highlighting seasonally available items enjoyed a high click-through rate (CTR). It's great if CTRs are high—that means the ad is engaging and shoppers are gaining exposure to the Kiwi brand. But positive branding metrics alone are not sufficient if Kiwi's ultimate goal is to drive more people into its stores. So, Kiwi needs to track CTRs against a rise in store traffic and purchase activity. In other words, generating offer awareness is good, but generating sales is better—and ultimately preferable.

Nihal puts the ROI question in the following perspective: "We want to get to the point when a brand spends a dollar with us, it produces $2 in return. We're starting to do that by connecting the purchase funnel all the way down. So when you tweet you're at Walgreens, you get a tweet back from Walgreens that has a link to a landing page where you can get a coupon, you redeem that coupon at the register, and that signals that the coupon has been used, and boom, you've converted that customer." Although challenges remain, particularly at the point of sale, you have to strive to tie the success of your SoLoMo marketing efforts to the bump in sales they deliver. "Ultimately," Nihal says, "ROI is dictated by the lift in bottom line from the campaign."

In Conclusion

You want your audience to check in because that action indicates a combination of context, timing, and interest. But you also want your audience to check out, with either an in-store purchase or an e-commerce transaction. So, when an interested customer raises his or her hand, that's the signal for you to present your best offer and guide that customer toward the checkout.

Here's some expert perspective on the rapid evolution of SoLoMo and where it is headed:

Nihal Mehta, LocalResponse Cofounder and CEO "Because there's scale in location-based marketing, you can not only retain customers who are broadcasting their location or presence, but also acquire new customers. That's a big change."

Greg Sterling, Founding Principal of Sterling Market Intelligence and Contributing Editor for Online Publication *Search Engine Land* "Models combining geo-targeted offers, payments, and the analytics that come with them are really powerful and uniquely suited to mobile devices in way you can't do on a PC for obvious reasons." He adds: "I have a sense these are the kinds of unique mobile opportunities that may emerge as the most potent vehicles for marketers."

Think of the SoLoMo nexus this way: Because of the combination of data your audience shares via social networks (location, context, intent, interest), it's a more refined mechanism for targeting prospective shoppers. In effect, it tees them up to make a purchase, which leads to the subject of our next chapter: mobile commerce and payments. Follow along with us as we move toward the end of the customer journey and the bottom of the purchase funnel.

8

Week 7: Check Out M-Commerce

Mobile is changing the way we do everything, but it's probably having a bigger impact on the way we purchase than anything else. In previous chapters, we touched lightly on how our growing attachment to mobile devices is changing the way we shop; in this chapter, we'll look more deeply into the shopping process and how mobile devices are helping us actually buy. From mobile coupons to mobile wallets, we'll examine your options for monetizing mobile and getting your customers to the virtual checkout counter.

Chapter Contents

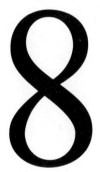

Monday: Understand the Opportunity

At the beginning of this book, we pointed out three essential items you never leave home without: your wallet, your keys, and your mobile phone. In "Chart the Future Forward," we'll talk about how your mobile phone is likely to replace your keys, but we believe it will also replace your wallet in due time. Just as plastic slowly supplanted paper money, we predict that mobile currency will eventually become the main means of paying for goods and services.

From our observation of the U.S. marketplace, the number of customers actually completing a purchase via mobile is still rather low. As you'll see in Figure 8.1, financial transactions on smartphones still add up to a pittance compared to desktop transactions. According to a joint report released in July 2012 by the Interactive Advertising Bureau (IAB) (`www.iab.com`) and research firm ABI (`www.abiresearch.com`), a scant 5 percent of smartphone owners have actually completed an online purchase via their device. Tablet users, on the other hand, execute a significantly higher percentage of mobile sales at 35 percent, a pattern we've seen validated by the site and campaign analytics of many brands. In fact, it's interesting to note that more tablet shoppers end up buying online than at an actual cash register (34 percent).

Activities that US Smartphone and Tablet Users Have Done via Their Device While Shopping, 2012
% of respondents

	Smartphone	Tablet
Contacted friend/ relative—about product purchase	37%	45%
Used internet—check prices/availability	35%	55%
Found product info—while in-store	31%	-
Access social media	30%	46%
Scanned barcode to check prices/availability in-store	30%	46%
Acquired/ redeemed coupons/offers	23%	50%
Location-based search	22%	54%
Use mapping/nav websites/apps	21%	41%
Bought a product/ service in-store at regular checkout	12%	34%
View video	7%	29%
Bought a product/service online using device	5%	35%
Bought a product/ service in store-without using checkout line	4%	28%
Internet communication	-	51%

Note: in the past 3 months
Source: Interactive Advertising Bureau (IAB) Mobile Marketing Center of Excellence, "Mobile's Role in a Consumer's Media Day: Smartphones and Tablets Enable Seamless Digital Lives" conducted by ABI Research, July 16, 2012

143017 www.eMarketer.com

Figure 8.1 Shopping still trumps buying on mobile devices.

If you think about it, it stands to reason that tablet owners would be the bigger spenders—a bigger screen naturally leads to greater usability, making it easier to gather the details required to make a final decision and execute the actual purchase. In most cases, minor usability issues aside, it's pretty much as simple to buy from a website on your tablet as it is on a desktop machine. A study of mobile shopping behavior conducted by online payments provider PayPal (`www.paypal.com`) and research firm Ipsos Insights (`www.ipsos.com`) in 2011 confirms this, with the tablet owners surveyed citing that the larger screen and keyboard and touchscreen functionality provide a better shopping experience. Yet according to a June 2012 report from trade publication Multichannel Merchant (`www.multichannelmerchant.com`), only 29.5 percent of U.S. retailers have an m-commerce web site, so it's clear that a smartphone owner is up against some usability hurdles when he or she wants to buy. Of course, those hurdles won't last for long. Given the growing awareness of the need for mobilized websites and increasing adoption of responsive design techniques, the average smartphone user will no doubt be buying more via their device in the future as it gets easier to do so—but m-commerce via mobile browsers is only part of the story.

M-Commerce versus M-Payments

Before we start our discussion in earnest, we want to draw a distinction between m-commerce and *m-payments*. Dictionary definitions of m-commerce tend to be broad. For example, Merriam-Webster describes m-commerce simply as "business transactions conducted by using a mobile electronic device (such as a cell phone)." For this book, we will group all shopping and purchasing activities that happen on a mobile device under the rubric of "m-commerce." This includes, but is not necessarily limited to, finding and redeeming coupons, price-checking, comparison-shopping, and purchasing. As a subcategory of m-commerce, "m-payments" refer to actual payment transactions that are conducted via mobile devices, whether through the browser, in-app, and SMS or via more future-forward channels such as near-field communications (NFC).

The U.S. and Global Market for M-Commerce

The mobile shopping aspects of m-commerce have taken off in a noticeable way in the United States. It's become increasingly commonplace to see people standing in store aisles and staring down at their smartphones as they search for product information, look for deals, and read reviews. Actual m-payments have been a bit slower to catch on, but they are ramping up fast with the increasing availability of high-speed data, smartphones and tablets, and the advent of advanced payment systems like *mobile wallets*. Let's start off by taking a look at the U.S. and global perspective for m-commerce overall.

Mobile Shopping

Mobile shopping, once relegated to a small, digitally advanced segment of the population, is now a fairly commonplace activity, even if the actual purchase still lags behind. In the May 2012 "Mobile Phone Shopping Diaries," the IAB stated that 73 percent of U.S. consumers claim to have used their smartphones in a store for a variety of shopping-related purposes. For the most part, their activities still revolve around qualifying an in-store purchase, with 28 percent of respondents saying they used their devices primarily to find product and service information.

Yet, these same mobile shoppers also express a keen awareness of how they would like their mobile shopping options to evolve. As shown in Figure 8.2, the ability to actually pay with their phone is a strong point of interest.

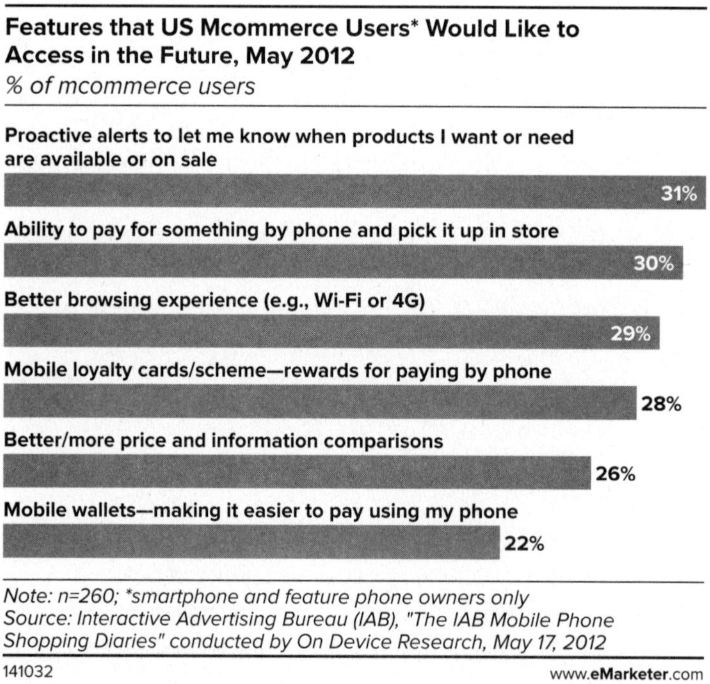

Figure 8.2 Mobile shoppers express a strong interest in mobile payments and rewards.

For marketers, it's essential to understand what smartphone users are doing now as well as what they'd like to be doing in the future. These are the elements that will inform a successful m-commerce strategy and, therefore, drive mobile assisted in-store sales as well as actual m-payments.

Tablets are a slightly different story. While it's true that some tablet owners use their devices in-store, they are in the minority, at least at this point in time. Tablets seem to lend themselves more to home use and shopping during moments of leisure. And, although tablet purchases tend to be of higher monetary value than those made on a smartphone, they also tend to be fairly straightforward, happening through a desktop e-commerce site or through a shopping app. That's not to say that tablet users won't develop their own unique mobile shopping behaviors—the larger screen size of the iPhone 5 and the future uptake of smaller tablet devices, such as the iPad Mini and Galaxy Tab, represent a new family of user interfaces somewhere between the smartphone and the tablet in terms of UI and, therefore, behaviors. But at present, there isn't a great deal of demonstrable difference between how tablet and desktop purchases are conducted. To make a long story short, you'll be focusing most of your m-commerce efforts on figuring out how to support in-store commerce and drive online sales via smartphone.

Mobile-Assisted Commerce and Showrooming

As we've established, much of smartphone m-commerce activity focuses on qualifying a purchase such as looking for coupons, reading reviews, getting product info, and looking for competing prices. Quite often, these activities lead to an in-store purchase or an online purchase conducted via the desktop at a later point in time. We refer to these purchases where mobile supports the process but the actual transaction happens via a non-mobile channel as mobile-assisted commerce.

Quite often, these activities lead to a purchase from a competing retailer or brand—a process known as *showrooming*, where the customer uses their mobile device to find a better product or offer than the one they are currently considering. Showrooming is striking fear into the hearts of brick-and-mortar brands who see their in-store sales slipping away as their customers go elsewhere or buy from online destinations like eBay or Amazon. For this reason, many are hesitant to support or encourage the mobile activities of their customers at all—but avoiding mobile isn't the answer. For these and for all retailers, it's crucial to understand how mobile can be used to strengthen the connection between a brand and its customers and to drive conversions both online and off.

Mobile Marketing and Merchandizing

"Marketing" includes all the activities you conduct, both online and offline, to help drive awareness and desire for your brand and/or products. "Merchandizing" includes all of the activities you conduct that actually get the customer to buy your product or service once they are in the store. In essence, marketing gets your customer into the store, virtual or otherwise. Merchandizing gets them to the register, whether the physical one in the store or the digital one on their smartphone or tablet.

Mobile marketing and mobile merchandizing are integral elements of the m-commerce ecosystem; together, they are the key drivers of m-payments. But our efforts as marketers in these areas are currently falling far short of the opportunity. Remember that IAB report we referenced earlier? It states that while 73 percent of smartphone owners use their device in store while shopping, 53 percent of those shoppers actually walked away from an in-store purchase due to information they retrieved from their device:

- Thirty-eight percent found a better price from another store.
- Thirty percent simply found a better price online.
- Twenty-one percent found a better item online than the one they were considering.
- Thirteen percent found that the product was unavailable.
- Eleven percent read a negative review.
- Eleven percent found a similar item that was preferable and bought that instead.
- Eleven percent couldn't find enough information to sway them to buy the in-store item.

So it's clear that as marketers, we need to pay much more attention to engaging our customers via their smartphone, especially in the context of the in-store experience. However, as illustrated in Figure 8.3, very few retailers are investing in mobile on even a moderate basis.

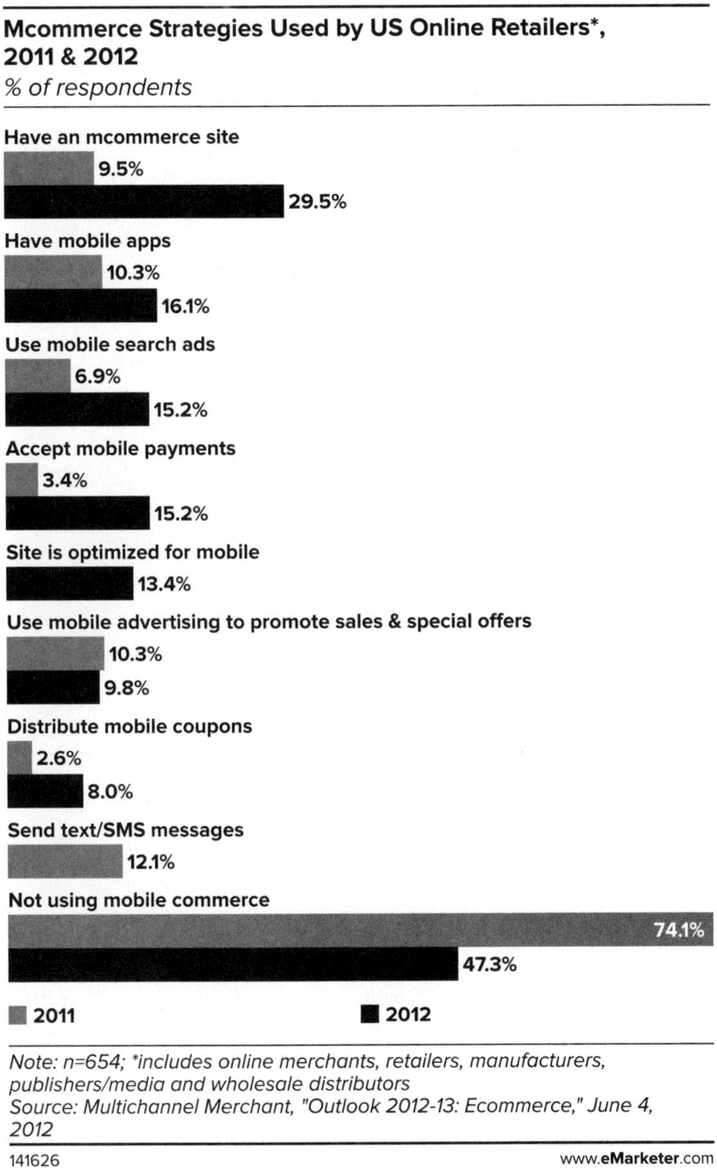

Figure 8.3 As of June 2012, only slightly more than half of U.S. retailers use m-commerce tactics.

There's been a marked increase between 2011 and 2012 in the uptake of certain m-commerce tactics—for example, having an m-commerce-enabled site—but the playing field remains fairly level. There's plenty of opportunity for retailers who understand the landscape and the options for using mobile marketing and merchandizing to draw customers into the m-commerce funnel and drive them toward m-payments.

Mobile Payments

The February 2012 "Mobile Commerce – Reinventing the Way Consumers Shop report from the Consumer Electronics Association" (CEA, www.ce.org) claims that 37 percent of mobile users in the United States are engaging in m-commerce and that the average U.S. consumer will spend $575 via mobile payments in 2012. The report goes on to describe the most popular categories for these purchases as being:

- Music (43 percent)
- Movies (38 percent)
- Tickets (37 percent)
- Apparel (36 percent)
- Books (35 percent)

Interestingly enough, the consumers surveyed also report that they expect to increase their use of mobile coupons in the coming year. One in three (32 percent) plan to actively search for them via mobile and 30 percent plan to actually use mobile coupons on their device—a good indicator that we can expect m-commerce and m-payments to continue to grow. So, while we may be using smartphones to help qualify in-store and offline purchases, it's clear that we're also using them to actually buy.

Most experts predict mobile payments soon will generate big money. According to May 2012 projections from Gartner (www.gartner.com), a well-known research firm with its eye on the mobile market, global mobile payments will soar beyond $171.5 billion in 2012, an increase of 62 percent ($106 billion) from 2011. Gartner predicts 448 million people worldwide will be using mobile payments by 2016. In developing markets—particularly India, Pakistan, and Africa, where smartphone penetration is still quite low—SMS payments will continue to dominate, but large unbanked populations mean these methods will be widespread. By contrast, Gartner predicts that in North America and Western Europe, the mobile web is expected to account for roughly 88 percent and 80 percent, respectively, of the mobile payments market. The jury is still out on purchases made via NFC, but in general we expect to see m-payments really begin to take off in more advanced markets by around 2015/2016.

Gartner also tells us that while Africa and Asia-Pacific (APAC) are currently the biggest mobile payment markets, Eastern Europe is the fastest growing. Right now, Africa and APAC own 60 percent of the mobile payments market and that's expected to hold steady until 2016. In these markets, mobile payments have gained traction by necessity; they provide rural and unbanked communities where there's little or no high-speed data infrastructure with a means for making transactions, both online and in the real, physical world, that would be otherwise impossible. KPMG (www.kpmg.com), a prominent global tax and advisory services firm, predicts global mobile payments will reach $930 billion between 2012 and 2015, growing at an astonishing clip of nearly 100 percent per year. But, it's a phenomenon that is expanding fast outside of the emerging markets where it began.

In wealthier, more digitally advanced societies, mobile payments aren't about necessity as much as convenience. Why carry small change for the soda machine at work when you can simply buy a Coke by text? Why carry around a subway pass when you can simply tap and go? And really, why print or clip a paper coupon to take to the store when you can simply download one to your phone and flash it at the register or get one sent to you based on volunteered preferences and your current location? In the United States, mobile payments may have seen slower growth up until now because we simply didn't need them. But now that we've begun to see the potential of linking payments with other marketing mechanisms, we're going to want them in a big way.

Security and Privacy Concerns

If m-commerce has so much potential, what's the holdup? Well, it's pretty clear that concerns about security have something to do with it. In the aforementioned February 2012 CEA survey, half the respondents expressed that worries about the security of their payment information were their primary reason for not buying via mobile—only an estimated one-quarter of the respondents actually felt comfortable about buying via their mobile device.

It's an understandable concern, but perhaps an unfounded one. We see the current fears about security as being similar to concerns about online commerce in the mid-to-late 1990s and suspect they will fade quickly, just as they did with e-commerce. The biggest concern seems to surround using mobile wallets and other NFC-enabled devices, a topic we'll discuss in greater detail on Thursday. Another report released in May 2012 by JiWire (`www.jiwire.com`), a location-based mobile advertising company that releases quarterly studies on mobile activities and behavior, notes that 37 percent of U.S. mobile device owners (smartphone and tablet) have used some form of mobile wallet service in the previous three months. We think you should always approach third-party research with a grain of salt; but at the same time, all third-party reports we've assessed seem to point to the fact that the way we shop and buy is changing.

So, there is incredible opportunity to use your customers' mobile behavior to drive commerce—both online and in–store—yet few merchants taking advantage of it. Let's look at how you can get started.

Tuesday: M-Commerce Approaches

Like any other aspect of mobile, there's no one-size-fits-all approach to m-commerce. Rather, there are many different paths to purchase. A May 2012 study by research firm

Nielsen (www.nielsen.com) states that consumers use smartphones to shop in very different ways depending on the store they are in. For example:

- Mobile coupons are most popular in grocery stores (41 percent of grocery shoppers actively use them), department stores (41 percent), and clothing stores (39 percent).
- Shoppers in electronics stores are far more likely to use their mobile device to read reviews (73 percent), compare prices (71 percent), and scan quick response (QR) codes for additional information (57 percent). They may still use their mobile device to help them buy or even complete a purchase, but in different ways.

The point being, there are diverse ways to get your customers to the register, and you're going to need to tailor your approach based on a number of criteria including your brand and products. Like any other aspect of mobile, fragmentation is the name of the game.

For a business-to-consumer (B2C) brand like our fictional Kiwi Market, m-commerce presents myriad opportunities. Mobile devices will not only be a direct shopping conduit, but will also play a big role in accelerating in-store sales. Let's look at a few examples in which Kiwi Market tailors its m-commerce approach to customers and context.

The Smartphone Purchase

In Chapter 2, "Week One: Develop Your Mobile Strategy," our clients at Kiwi Market determined that a smartphone-optimized mobile site would be the cornerstone of their mobile strategy. Their research, pulled from a May 2012 report published by research firms eDigital Research (www.edigitalresearch.com) and PortalTech Reply (www.portaltech.co.uk), showed them that 64 percent of smartphone owners use their mobile devices to shop online. The 1.0 mobile site that launched after they developed their strategy was created with limited m-commerce support; the goal was to watch how customers used it and build additional functionality over time.

Michelle, our persona character from Chapter 2, is glued to her smartphone 24/7. In the early days of her customer relationship with Kiwi Market, she relies heavily on the smartphone site to look up info on products in-store and add them to her weekly delivery list. Outside the store, she uses it to check on the status of her weekly grocery delivery, obtain coupon offers, and to contact the customer service department via click-to-call. Let's look at a few scenarios in which mobile plays a fundamental role in getting customers like Michelle to the register.

The Tablet Purchase

Like any busy working parent, Michelle gets her household tasks done between breaks at work and her very limited downtime at home. Once a week, after the kids go to bed, she curls up on the sofa to watch TV and update her weekly shopping list on her iPad.

The Kiwi Market desktop site, optimized to work seamlessly on a tablet, enables her to browse weekly specials and new items and update her standard weekly grocery delivery. But it also enables her to do more, including creating customized catering menus, adding specific instructions and details regarding her guests and events, and place her orders—complex activities she would be very unlikely to engage in via smartphone.

Michelle's behavior is not unique. According to the study from PayPal and Ipsos that we referenced earlier, more than 60 percent of mobile shoppers who buy via their mobile device do so within the comfort of their own home, a trend PayPal has dubbed "couch commerce."

The Mobile-Assisted In-Store Purchase

Many in-store sales begin on a mobile device—but end at a cash register. It's an incredibly challenging attribution model, because there's no clear way to connect the dots between the smartphone and the brick-and-mortar purchase unless some kind of redemption code is used. Yet countless studies from the many research firms cited in this book tell us that smartphone and, to a lesser extent, tablet users, depend on their mobile devices to make brick-and-mortar purchase decisions. In Michelle's case, the smartphone-assisted purchase comes into play in the early days of being a customer when she stops by the store a few nights a week to pick up prepared meals to take home. Inevitably, she spies some additional treat that she thinks her husband or kids would enjoy and has to quickly determine whether it's worth purchasing. Rather than search Google for each product individually, not knowing whether she'll find mobile-friendly content, she chooses to use the Kiwi Market site on her smartphone to look them up, reading reviews from other Kiwi Market shoppers that help her finalize her decision.

The In-App Purchase

After being a regular Kiwi customer for a few weeks, Michelle graduates to downloading the mobile app, which she then uses to provision her weekly shopping list. Often, she finds herself updating her list when she stops by the store on weeknights to pick up prepared meals. While waiting for her takeout to be packaged, she browses the aisles and picks out various treats and staples for that week's order, scanning them via the Kiwi Market QR code stickers affixed to the packaging (an excellent example of mobile merchandizing) to automatically add them to her list. In this instance, the native Kiwi Market app on her phone provides her with functionality that enhances the shopping experience in a way that the mobile web simply can't (at least at this early point in the evolution of HTML5).

Wednesday: Select Appropriate M-Commerce Channels

Investment in mobile is gaining steam: 19 percent of U.S. retailers will invest $100,000 or more in mobile marketing in 2012, says research firm the eTailing Group (`www.e-tailing.com`) in its April 2012 report on m-commerce. Of the retailers interviewed, 85 percent added that mobile commerce was a primary focus in 2012 (versus only 68 percent in 2011). So, how can you choose the right m-commerce channel for your brand and customers—ones that will lead to actual m-payment transactions?

Mobile Web-Based Transactions

For most brands, the mobile browser will be the most logical extension of desktop e-commerce. It's a practical choice since advances in browser-based web technologies have grown by leaps and bounds in the past several years. Theoretically, the transactional elements of your e-commerce website will be fully functional from a technical perspective in the browsers of the most up-to-date smartphones and tablets. The question is, will the user be able to get to the checkout point quickly and easily? In most cases, nuances in support for JavaScript and general usability barriers imposed by touchscreen devices—especially smartphones—will make it a challenge for your site to succeed unless you make some modifications.

If your goal is to mobilize an e-commerce site, any of the directions we reviewed in Chapter 4, "Week 3: Maximize Reach with Mobile Websites," are a valid option. Many, if not most, hosted mobile web vendors now offer basic m-commerce support, and there are some that specialize in it. If you have sufficient technical resources at your disposal, you can probably trade up to a cloud service or integrated CMS-driven approach to building your m-commerce mobile website. Or, assuming your customers are mostly high-end device users, you can skip ahead to a responsive, HTML5 approach if you're ready for it.

Native Application Transactions

We know that consumers are spending a lot of money on apps—a projected $26.1 billion globally in 2012, according to research firm Strategy Analytics (`www.strategyanalytics.com`). But, we also know that they're spending a lot *through* apps, as well. As we discussed in Chapter 5, "Week 4: Maximize Engagement with Mobile Apps," apps cement a bond between your brand and your most loyal consumers. At this stage in the evolution of m-commerce, a first-time or casual, occasional customer is most likely to complete a purchase via your mobile site, but the most dedicated customers are more likely to buy through your mobile app, assuming you've provided them with that option.

Both Apple and Google Play take a 30 percent commission off the top for any premium applications you sell through their channels: sell an app for $1.00 and prepare to surrender $0.30 to the app store. The same 30 percent fee structure applies to in-app purchases for *intangible goods*—for example, points, virtual currency, or digital editions of print publications. *Tangible goods*—in Kiwi's case, groceries—would not be subject to the same terms. Brands selling tangible goods can integrate their existing online payment option into their app and many household names find it well worth the effort to do so. Mobile websites might get the highest volume of consumers, but native mobile apps win with the most engaged consumers—the ultimate spenders. According to a 2011 study from gadget blog Retrevo (`www.retrevo.com`), 43 percent of mobile consumers have downloaded a mobile shopping app, and it's a trend we expect to continue.

One of our favorite examples of in-app payments is the Starbucks Card mobile app that was rolled out to markets worldwide in 2011 after a brief, highly successful pilot period. The Starbucks model of app-based payments recently took on an even more interesting dimension with the integration of mobile payments provider Square into the equation. In the spring of 2012, Starbucks announced plans to begin using Square to process all credit card and debit card payments in its all stores. The Square model has fascinating long-term implications because it enables *proximity payments* without any effort whatsoever on the part of the users other than saying their name. The way it works is ingeniously simple: A customer with the Square app on his or her phone enters the store and Square detects their presence via GPS and relays their info to Starbucks. The user then simply has to say their name at the register and the Starbucks employee will confirm their identity via their name and photo, which will pop up on the cashier's screen. For all the excitement over NFC, which we'll discuss later in this chapter, we think the effortlessness of the Square model has the most promise of all for users.

SMS Payments

SMS payments are probably the most common form of digital commerce globally. In developing regions, micropayments by text are an everyday occurrence; in the United States and Western Europe, they were once a popular channel for selling mobile content such as games and ringtones, but are now mostly relegated to charitable donations and voting for television reality programs. Don't let the last sentence fool you. Using SMS for nonprofit donations and TV voting is hugely lucrative; it's just not a mainstream opportunity for most brands to sell actual products and services. In the United States, the widespread availability of smartphones and tablets has made it far easier to conduct transactions online.

Near-Field Communications

So at this early stage of the game, what do you, as a marketer, need to know about *near-field communications (NFC)*? Well, first and foremost you need to understand the current consumer enthusiasm, as depicted in Figure 8.4, for the technology when it comes to purchasing and payments.

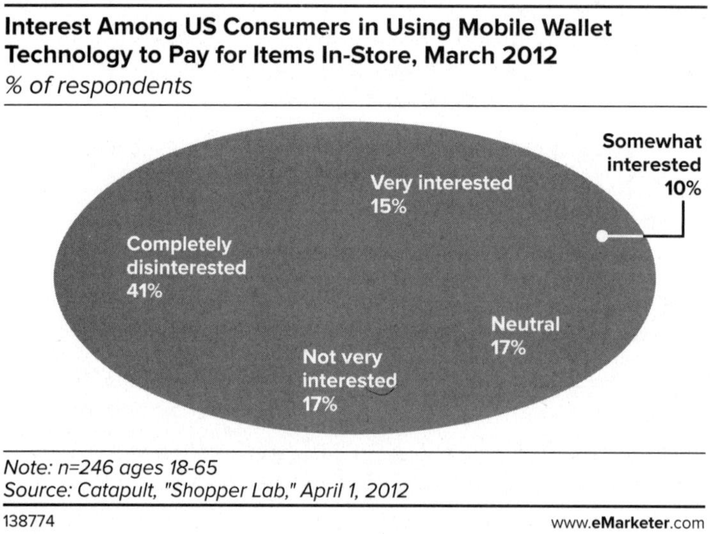

Figure 8.4 U.S. consumer interest in using mobile wallets to pay for in-store purchases is limited but on the rise.

While this might look disheartening at first glance, you have to consider the fact that very few U.S. consumers have seen NFC in action. That can and will change over the next 12 to 18 months. Google is making a strong push for its NFC-enabled Google Wallet technology—signs for which are appearing at retailers across the country. Google has partnered with MasterCard, one of the pioneers of NFC payments here in the United States—and any of the more than 200,000 PayPass-enabled payment terminals in the country can now accept Google Wallet. In fact, at present, most of the devices currently in circulation in the United States with embedded NFC chips are Android smartphones running the Gingerbread operating system or later. But the opportunity isn't just relegated to the latest Android users. Isis (`www.paywithisis.com`), a joint venture between AT&T, T-Mobile, and Verizon that counts most major credit card companies and payment processors among its partners, hopes to bring scale to NFC-based payments. All three carriers plan to begin rolling out enabled devices in late 2012. As you can see in Figure 8.5, those who are aware of the technology have a growing sense of how it might make their lives easier.

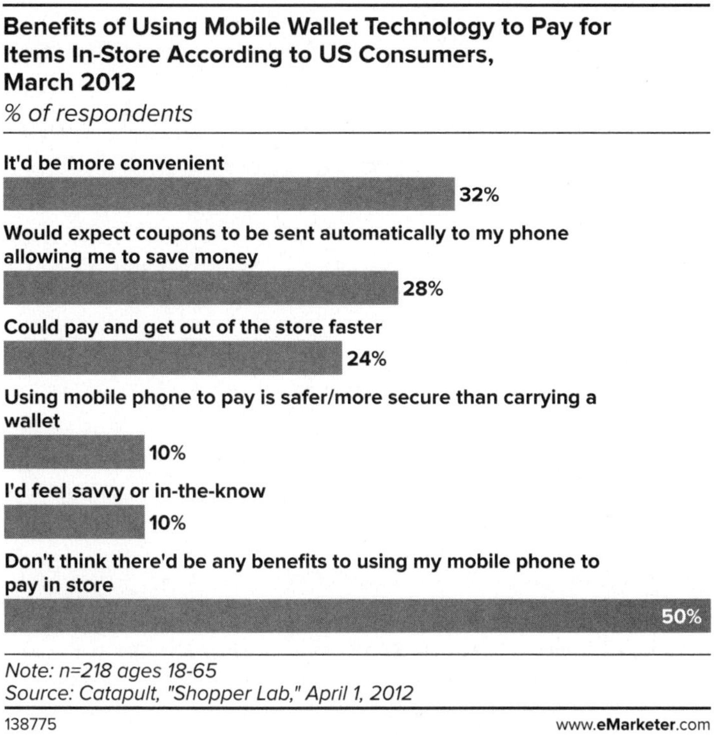

Figure 8.5 Fifty percent of U.S. consumers can see the potential benefit to mobile payments.

One of the more interesting things about NFC-enabled mobile payments is that they aren't strictly relegated to mobile devices. In the United States, MasterCard was one of the first financial services brands to pilot contactless payments with its PayPass services. NFC-enabled credit cards and keychain fobs that could be used on public transportation systems and at select retailers were distributed to customers. At this year's SXSW, Isis (the cross-carrier joint venture) showed off a snap-on NFC-enabled sleeve for the iPhone that adds instant NFC capabilities to the device; and global bank Barclays (`www.barclays.com`) has debuted an NFC sticker for its Visa customers that can be affixed to one's phone. So, while it may take a while for NFC-enabled smartphones—and tablets—to enter the mainstream, there are other ways that the technology can and will filter out to the general populace.

Right now, fears surrounding privacy and security seem to be slowing the process of uptake. While Google has moved full steam ahead with Google Wallet and Microsoft has its own mobile wallet that is due to launch with Windows Phone 8, Apple, notoriously reticent to add new and unproven technologies to its devices, chose not to include on-board NFC in the iPhone. When iOS6 arrived in September 2012, it came equipped with Passbook, an integrated app that aggregates concert tickets, boarding passes, and other types of payment confirmations—but it lacks the ability (for now, at least) to link your credit card and use the app for contactless payments. It's most likely a simple case of Apple's wait-and-see approach to investing in a new technology. In any case, we have no doubt contactless payments will come to the iPhone and all other mobile devices in some form within the next few years. So, let's do a quick overview of how this technology works. This will help you better understand just how valid privacy fears are (or aren't).

When you have an NFC chip on your smartphone, it is able to transmit payment information stored on it to a reader terminal or sticker across a distance of no more than 10cm—basically, you have to be super close to a reader for the info to be passed. So, while it's becoming standard for NFC systems to allow tap-and-go payments of $25 or less without signing or entering a PIN code, the odds of someone being able to virtually pick your pocket with another NFC device are slim to none. That said, standard NFC does support security measures, which enable the user to set a PIN that must be entered for even the smallest amounts. In the event of theft, the credentials on an NFC-enabled device can be canceled as quickly and easily as a lost credit card.

We believe the hold-up has more to do with the small number of NFC-enabled *point of sale (POS)* terminals in retail establishments here in the United States. But, we're seeing Google Wallet stickers in more and more stores and, as the technology becomes more widely supported, we'll begin to see NFC being used for a number of m-commerce and marketing purposes including:

- Payments
- Transmission of loyalty points
- Delivery of coupons and special offers
- Ticketing and access passes
- Transmission of all sorts of marketing content, including but not limited to maps, images, music, and videos
- Transmission of social cues and currency—for example, Twitter follows and Facebook Likes and Shares.

From our perspective, it's really not a question of whether the general public will adopt NFC in support of payments and many other aspects of the brand/consumer relationship, but rather how long it will take. However, we also think NFC will share the market with truly contactless forms of payment such as Square.

RFID versus NFC

You'll often hear the terms "radio frequency identification (RFID)" and "NFC" used interchangeably, which causes no small amount of confusion. While both utilize radio waves to transmit information wirelessly, there are distinct differences. RFID has been standardized for many years and is in active use worldwide, mainly as a mechanism for tracking product inventory. RFID tags, tiny electronic components containing an antenna and memory chip, can be stored in everything from stickers to product packaging and are read with a special RFID reader device.

An important point to understand is that RFID is a one-way technology. Information can be delivered from the tag to the reader, but the reader can't deliver information back to the tag. RFID also works across fairly long distances. Active RFID tags (deemed *active* because they contain a battery that enables them to proactively send a signal to a reader) can send signals up to 300 feet. Passive RFID tags have no battery and rely on the reader to transmit their information; therefore, they are limited to distances of several feet. Because passive RFID tags don't contain a battery, they tend to be smaller and less expensive, which increases their theoretical appeal for potential use in consumer applications. In practice, however, RFID is limited when it comes to consumer use. It's a one-way technology; it can't be used to send and receive information like tickets and payments. This explains the appeal of NFC, a shorter-range technology, where two-way information can be transmitted in a range of up to four inches.

NFC, also referred to as a form of contactless payment and *proximity payment*, is possibly the most anticipated innovation—not just in mobile, but in digital marketing in general—in at least a decade. At present, NFC remains a bit of a mystery to the average marketer because so few NFC devices are in circulation. KPMG (`www.kpmg.com`), the tax and advisory firm we referenced earlier in this chapter, tells us that an estimated 650 million NFC-enabled devices will ship over the next three years, a marked increase over the 44 million that shipped globally in 2011, but that's a drop in the bucket. For NFC payments to really take off, retailers will need to invest in the infrastructure to accept them, and for that to happen, we predict the market for NFC-enabled devices will need to match up to the current penetration rate of smartphones in the United States. That's not going to happen right away. A 2012 report from the nonprofit Pew Research Center's Internet & American Life Project (`www.pewinternet.org`) predicts the global penetration rate for NFC will be roughly 65 percent by 2020.

Thursday: Establish Your Mobile Couponing Approach

In Chapter 6, "Week 5: Promote Your Message with Mobile Advertising," we explained that mobile is not so much a *surf* medium as it is a *search* medium. Well, our observation of the market tells us that a lot of us are searching for deals. In a letter to investors sent in May 2012, Groupon CEO Andrew Mason shared that 30 percent of all transactions on the Groupon platform are executed on mobile devices. What's more, Mason stated that the average U.S. mobile Groupon user spends an average of 50 percent more than average the desktop-only user of the service. It's just one small indicator of how much opportunity is promised by mobile couponing. Consider these insights from a series of recent Mobile Audience Insights Reports, quarterly studies released by JiWire (`www.jiwire.com`) that further illustrate the opportunity.

- Fifty-three percent of U.S. mobile users expressed willingness to exchange their location in return for more contextually relevant content, including deals, coupons, and incentives (Q2 2011).
- Eighteen percent of mobile shoppers redeemed a coupon via their device in the 90 days prior to the survey (Q1 2012).
- Twenty-one percent had searched for a coupon on their mobile device while in-store (Q1 2012).
- Eighty percent prefer locally oriented and contextually relevant mobile ads and are 75 percent more inclined to act on the offers they see if they are local in nature (Q1 2012).

Suffice it to say, the average mobile user is very open to deals, which helps prime the mobile commerce pump. GfK (`www.gfk.com`), the well-known global research firm, claims that:

- Forty-four percent of high-end device owners are actively seeking coupons via their smartphone or tablet.
- Seventeen percent have already made purchases via mobile, making them a very attractive customer indeed.

A growing community of mobile device users is ready and willing to buy if you give them an incentive.

Coupon Formats and Delivery Channels

There are diverse methods for delivering mobile coupons, but the actual coupon format itself will most commonly be:

Alphanumeric Coupons: These are combinations of letters and/or numbers that can be entered into a website (desktop or mobile) or mobile application, or presented at point of sale for redemption.

Image Coupons: These might be graphical images that include an alphanumeric code that can be entered manually or a *1D barcode* or *2D barcode* that can be scanned at point of sale.

So, the formats themselves are actually quite simple—it's the means of delivering the coupon to the mobile device that are a bit more complex.

SMS: Alphanumeric codes can be easily delivered via text for online entry or be presented for redemption at point of sale. SMS can also be used to deliver an image coupon via a clickable link that delivers the user to a mobile web page from which the coupon can be obtained.

MMS: Image coupons can also be delivered using MMS, although this is a slightly less popular option as a delivery channel given the challenges brands face in using MMS consistently, as discussed in Chapter 3, "Week 2: Start Simple—SMS."

Barcodes: There is often some confusion here; many marketers think that the barcode is the coupon itself, but it's really a delivery mechanism. A 1-D (commonly known as UPC) barcode or 2D barcode (commonly known as QR codes) scanned at point-of-sale delivers the embedded coupon info, whether it be an alphanumeric code or a link to some other form of digitally stored information.

Mobile email: Emails received via mobile can contain alphanumeric or image codes that can be entered or scanned at point of sale and/or redeemed online.

Direct mail: Direct mail pieces can be tagged with short codes or with barcodes that can be scanned via mobile device to deliver an alphanumeric or image coupon.

Mobile web: Alphanumeric codes encountered via a mobile web page can be copied and saved to be input later at point of sale and/or redeemed online.

Geo-fenced: Opt-in messages can be sent via SMS or push alert according to a preset list of criteria and the recipient's location. This delivery option is essentially the same as SMS, but with an additional layer of targeting criteria added.

Wi-Fi: Public Wi-Fi networks are a highly popular touch point for mobile users and a key distribution point for download and email or text-to-self coupons and offers.

Bluetooth: Content distribution via Bluetooth (aka *Bluecasting*) has seen little uptake in the United States. Due to low consumer awareness of this marketing channel, it probably won't play into any of your efforts in the near term. There are rumors, however, that Apple is investing heavily in further development of the current standard, Bluetooth 4, so it's possible that our opinion of its potential will eventually change.

Redemption Hurdles

For all its promise, mobile couponing is not without its challenges. For branded brick-and-mortar retail establishments with a standardized POS system, entering a coupon code will be relatively straightforward. However, for consumer packaged goods brands, the redemption process gets much more complicated. There's no guarantee that every retailer selling your product will have the infrastructure or proper employee training to redeem your mobile coupons, and smaller establishments may have antiquated POS systems unable to scan a barcode or may still require collection of paper coupons as proof of redemption. So unless you are doing small, targeted tests or your brand has a consolidated nationwide POS system, it's quite difficult to ensure that redemption will be possible for everyone.

Tracking, Targeting, and Loyalty

There are clearly plenty of hurdles, so why invest in mobile coupons? Well, for one thing, they can be more cost effective—a single digital mobile coupon can often be distributed for a far lower cost than the same offer distributed via print or direct mail. But they can also be far more targeted and, therefore, more effective.

A mobile consumer can obtain a coupon as a one-off in a number of ways—by scanning a QR code or sending a text message to a brand's short code, for example. But, delivering mobile coupons in such an ad hoc fashion is a missed opportunity. Ideally, your mobile coupon strategy should be tied to your CRM and loyalty programs and there are a number of ways to make that work.

The most advantageous way to track coupon redemption is to link unique coupon codes to customer profiles. For example, a new Kiwi Market customer signing up for an online shopping account is encouraged to offer up her mobile phone number in return for special offers, which can be customized according to several criteria, such as:

- Catering offers
- Daily prepared foods specials
- Seasonal specials
- Vegetarian/vegan

Upon signing into their accounts, existing customers are prompted to update their profiles with their mobile number for the same purpose. The customers can then choose to receive their coupons by text or via download to their Kiwi Market app. Each code is unique to that specific user and can be matched back to that unique user upon redemption. This provides the option of distributing coupons according to consumer-specific preferences and making offers more targeted, but it also allows for monitoring of redemption behaviors and enables you to determine which offers resonate with which customers.

If, on the other hand, the customer is proactively requesting a coupon by sending a text message to a short code, the process is somewhat different. The text message that delivers the coupon can encourage the user to opt in for further offers by texting back a keyword in reply—for example: "Text the keywords 'Kiwi deals' back to this message to opt in for future offers." Alternatively, the message delivering the coupon can include a link to an opt-in page where the user can sign up for more offers from the vendor by setting up a customer profile or logging in to an existing account.

Theoretically, customers receiving coupons via mobile email, QR, or any number of other distribution channels can be routed through a similar process. Tying your mobile couponing campaign into customer profiles and loyalty programs will enable you to do a granular level of A/B testing, sending different types of ads based on location, customer profiles, and other personal data. But it also adds an additional step into the process; by making users go through the tedium of an extensive sign-up, you run the risk of some dropping off in the process. Some customers may just want to scan a QR code and go, so you'll have to gauge the potential value of making the process more complicated.

Friday: Define Payment Processing Options

We've established that while mobile shopping is a widespread phenomenon, actual mobile payments are still in their infancy, although they are catching on. Certain small purchases—event tickets or digital downloads such as e-books, MP3s, movies, and apps—have become commonplace. Bigger items—clothing, household articles, travel tickets—are beginning to catch on via tablet. Odds are that, with a little bit of tweaking, your existing e-commerce site will function just fine for tablet users. But smartphones—and the advent of the NFC and contactless payments—present a whole new world of considerations. So let's look at a few of the opportunities you have for processing mobile payments.

SMS Payments

As we established earlier, SMS is the most egalitarian means of mobile payment; literally everyone who has a mobile device can use it. Of course, not every customer who has SMS is going to gravitate toward making purchases this way. It has evolved as a popular payment channel in countries with poor broadband infrastructure where feature phones still dominate. However, it has seen less uptake in parts of the world where users have the option of paying via the mobile browser or app store accounts such as iTunes. In the United States, SMS is usually relegated to smaller purchases such as tickets or mobile content, but the process is the same regardless of the amount spent.

The way SMS payments work is quite simple. The consumer sends his or her payment request via text to a brand's short code and, in most cases, receives back a confirmation request. Once the consumer sends back a confirmation text, a charge is applied to his or her wireless bill via a deal between the brand, the wireless carrier, and, in most cases, a third-party SMS payment provider (a type of specialized SMS aggregator). The content is then delivered, usually via direct download by the user's phone.

SMS payments have the benefit of reach and accessibility, and they're secure because SMS data is encrypted. But for many brands, the cost outweighs the benefit. There's a high price tag in terms of leasing and maintaining a short code, and the wireless carriers and the SMS payment provider each take a share of the payment price as well.

Direct Carrier Billing

Direct carrier billing is very similar to the SMS payment option. In this case, the customer enters a pin number in the checkout process and the purchase is added to their wireless carrier bill. Like SMS, it's a convenient, encrypted payment mechanism that has the benefit of the "out-of-sight, out-of-mind" factor. When customers don't actually enter an amount and credit card info, odds are they're just a bit more likely to spend, at least for small purchases. In the United States, we don't see a great deal of direct carrier billing outside of mobile content like games and ringtones, most likely due to the complexities of dealing with the wireless carriers.

Mobile Web

Mobile web payments are becoming a much more commonplace option as mobile browsers mature. Free shopping carts, notably those offered by Google and PayPal, have mobile support baked in. More advanced shopping cart options, whether hosted or licensed, offer mobile support on a case-by-case basis. If your current desktop shopping cart software doesn't offer mobile support out of the box, your next best option might be to have your m-commerce website built by a mobile vendor that specializes in m-commerce. This narrows your options for development partners, but going with a mobile site vendor experienced in m-commerce will ensure that you offer the best possible user experience in the checkout process.

In-App

We touched earlier on in-app payments, and we think they're one of the most promising options for brands that are looking to build ongoing customer relationships. If the success of the mobile Starbucks Card is any indication, customers who make ongoing incremental payments for tangible goods sold by a brand to which they feel closely connected will jump at the chance to do so via a branded app. There are various options for processing purchases within your mobile app, from integrating your existing online shopping cart to working with a mobile payment provider that specializes in apps.

External Readers

A more recent innovation is credit card readers like Square (`www.squareup.com`) or ProPay (`www.propayjak.com`) that can be appended to a mobile device and work in conjunction with a native app, enabling smaller and/or mobile merchants to take payments via credit card swipe. In-app payments via readers like Square are becoming highly popular with smaller merchants and enable them to accept credit cards anytime, anywhere, and at a lower cost per payment (only 2.75 percent per swipe in the case of Square!). Square has proven to be particularly innovative on the consumer side, as well. Mobile users can verify their identity to merchants via their photograph in the Square app—the shopper simply walks to the checkout counter, says his or her name, and the merchant can verify the shopper's identity by their profile picture, which pops up on the payment system screen. Square is becoming especially popular in the foodtruck scene of U.S. cities—customers simply say their name, get their snack, and receive their receipt via email—the truest form of contactless payment yet!

Digital Wallets

A digital wallet is an account in which payment info is stored. The payment process for digital wallets is pretty simple from the user's perspective. For online payments, the user simply enters a PIN number to confirm a purchase. On NFC-enabled devices, he or she can simply tap and go for smaller amounts and enter a PIN for larger purchases. From the merchant's perspective, it's a bit more complex. Online, they can add support for PayPal, Google Wallet, and any of the other virtual wallet services fairly simply. In-store, it's a matter of installing payment processing systems that support NFC. First Data (`www.firstdata.com`), one of the world's biggest payment-processing providers, has partnered with Google to present merchants with NFC-enabled payment terminals that support Google Wallet.

What's a Mobile Wallet Anyway?

The term "m-payments" encompasses a lot of different behaviors, from buying through a secure shopping cart in a mobile web browser to buying in-app credits in your favorite mobile game. Mobile wallets are a unique and important aspect of this complex ecosystem. In the strictest definition, a mobile wallet is a payment account in which credit is stored, either physically on one's device or virtually in the cloud, and payment is delivered to merchants from that stored account. Increasingly, mobile wallets are also being used to deliver and store other payment-related information, such as loyalty cards and coupons.

In Conclusion

Some pundits believe mobile is actually killing the in-store experience, that as we become more and more wired in real time, we'll simply bypass physical retail altogether. It's a typical marketer's mindset to expect the new medium to supplant the old, but we don't believe this will actually happen. We expected digital to make TV irrelevant, but instead, it's enhanced the way we watch television and even the way we experience films. We expected tablets to kill print, but the magazine and newspaper industry is still alive with revenue supplemented by mobile applications. TV didn't destroy the movies, and the radio industry is still alive and kicking. CDs did pretty much kill vinyl in terms of overall consumption, but the original medium survives and in some ways, thrives in the hands of purist audiophiles.

We could go on and on, but you get the point. What's true is that technology changes human behavior and the customer experience, most often for the better. We firmly believe people won't lose the desire to see and examine an object prior to purchase but, like everything else, how they have that experience may well look very different in the near future. In Chapter 9, "Week 8: Drive Awareness with Ambient Media," we'll examine how the concept of mobility is beginning to influence the physical world and the opportunities this new wave of change presents to marketers.

Week 8: Drive Awareness with Ambient Media

The ubiquity of mobile devices has started to influence how we experience the physical world around us. As we discussed in Chapter 7, "Week 6: Leverage the SoLoMo Nexus," part of the opportunity for marketers lies in the ability to marry location, context, and intent. Part of it also derives from technologies that trigger a connection between a consumer's mobile device and the non-digital world—what we call ambient media. *Think of it as a way to add a layer of interactivity to traditional media, places, and objects that in the past were completely static. In this chapter, we'll discuss how you can use ambient mobile channels, including 2D barcodes, augmented reality, near-field communications, and mobile broadcasting to render the physical world, digital.*

9

Chapter Contents

Monday: Image Technologies

We've spent the past eight chapters delving into very concrete, highly actionable elements of mobile marketing in a step-by-step fashion. As we move into the final two chapters of the book, we enter more prospective territory containing less familiar ground. New technologies continue to stretch the boundaries even as mobile strives to become a mainstream marketing channel. Part of the future of both mobile marketing and marketing in general will be defined by the growing links between mobile, social, and geo-location, which we covered in detail in Chapter 7. Another key piece is ambient media, the subject of this chapter.

We touched briefly on ambient media in Chapter 7, but a quick refresher on what we mean is in order. In the strictest definition, *ambient* denotes "Of, or relating to, one's immediate surroundings." In the context of mobile marketing, the term *ambient media* refers to touchpoints external to the customer's mobile device that trigger interactions on the device or external touchpoints with which the user can interact using a mobile device. These include, by level of adoption for mobile marketing purposes:

- 2D barcodes, such as quick response (QR) codes
- *Augmented reality* (AR)
- *Near-field communications* (NFC)
- Wi-Fi nodes and Bluetooth hotspots that enable the delivery of marketing messages
- Mobile-enabled digital signage and surface computing technology (motion-sensitive and digitally enabled objects and locations)

In short, ambient media is all about using your smartphone to activate—and render interactive—the physical world around you.

In this chapter, we'll again share our own expertise, as well as what we learned from talking with the following experts:

- Adam Broitman, chief creative strategist at digital agency Something Massive (`www.somethingmassive.com`)
- David Berkowitz, vice president of emerging media at digital agency 360i (`www.360i.com`)
- Steve Smith, editor of online publication *Mobile Marketing Daily* (`www.mediapost.com/publications/mobile-marketing-daily/`)

You'll hear from Adam, David, and Steve throughout this chapter, but first from Steve, who puts forth an expansive vision.

"The real promise of mobility," he says, "is the way in which it ties the physical world to digital interactivity and two decades of data we have been building online. Leveraging the full multimedia capabilities of the mobile device offers an unprecedented creative cocktail of interactivity, contextual relevance targeted down to a precise object, the audio/visual capabilities of every mass medium that came before it, and the 'radical' marketing notion that instead of pestering and interrupting the customers during their busy day, we can actually improve their existence."

We happen to agree, so let's look at some ways you'll be able to make that happen using the leading-edge technologies we will discuss over the next five days.

2D Barcodes

We discussed mobile barcodes in relation to couponing in Chapter 8, "Week 7: Check Out M-Commerce." But we're looking at them in a different context in this chapter, so the topic merits a brief review. Remember that mobile barcodes come in a number of formats, including 1D codes (the UPC symbols you commonly see on product packaging) and 2D codes. The major differences are that 2D codes permit a larger amount of encoded data than 1D, allow for faster scanning capabilities, and are less prone to errors. 2D codes can render a range of information, including, but not limited to:

- Links to any website URL (including video content)
- Geographical coordinates (map-based)
- Scan-to-call
- Send a text message or email
- Create an address card or calendar item
- Downloadable coupons or offers
- Social network activation (such as a "like" or "follow")
- Initiate an app download

2D barcodes have been traditionally more popular in mobile marketing due to the amount of information they can pack compared to a 1D code. However, 1D codes are becoming more popular in certain instances, such a mobile coupon delivery, because 1D scanning systems are still dominant at the point of sale. So, as a rule, in your general mobile marketing activities, you'll probably opt to use 2D codes for the variety and flexibility they offer, but you might want to use 1D codes as well, especially if you're distributing offers and incentives that will be redeemed in-store.

Scanning the Differences Between 2D Mobile Barcodes

2D barcodes are two-dimensional graphical images encoded with information that can be read with a specific scanner device or by using a scanner application installed on a mobile device.

QR codes, a 2D barcode format originally developed by Toyota parts subsidiary Denso Wave in 1994 to assist in tracking vehicle production, have emerged as the Kleenex or Xerox of mobile barcodes—the brand name that becomes the generic term for an entire product category. Outside of QR, other well-known 2D barcode formats include:

DataMatrix: The first 2D code standard; developed in Europe in 1989; allows for 2,335 alphanumeric characters.

Continues

Scanning the Differences Between 2D Mobile Barcodes *(Continued)*

Microsoft Tag (`http://tag.microsoft.com/home.aspx`): Four-color high-capacity barcode launched by Microsoft in 2009; allows for 1,000 alphanumeric characters; popular with print publications because of its greater visual appeal.

SnapTag (`www.spyderlynk.com/`): A proprietary, image-based format created by SpyderLynk; can be activated via camera or SMS short code; customizable with brand logo.

These formats are the ones you are likely to run into with the most frequency, and each will have its unique benefit or appeal depending on your objectives and campaign. That said, many other proprietary and open-source 2D code formats are available for experimentation. We're fans of QR for the simple ubiquity factor; numerous reader applications are available for this standard. This raises the odds that your customers will have an app installed on their phone, which in turn increases the likelihood they will scan your code and engage with your campaign.

User Demographics and Projected Uptake

As with many technologies we've covered in this book, mobile barcode usage has been increasing rapidly due to the rise in smartphone adoption. Research firm Yankee Group (`www.yankeegroup.com`) predicts that the number of 2D barcodes users worldwide will increase six-fold between 2012 and 2016, rising from 18 million to 104 million. Usage is currently at its highest in Japan, where QR codes originated, but interest is relatively high in many other countries, as shown in Figure 9.1.

Use/Interest in QR Codes Among Mobile Phone Users in Select Countries, Jan 2012
% of respondents

	Currently use	Are interested	Not interested
Japan	60%	8%	32%
UK	26%	30%	44%
Russia	26%	30%	44%
Canada	25%	32%	52%
Italy	24%	36%	40%
US	24%	30%	46%
Spain	23%	29%	48%
Mexico	21%	36%	43%
Germany	21%	29%	50%
Australia	19%	31%	50%
France	17%	31%	52%
Brazil	16%	40%	44%
China	6%	49%	45%
India	1%	24%	75%

Note: numbers may not add up to 100% due to rounding
Source: TNS, "Mobile Life," April 24, 2012

141737 www.eMarketer.com

Figure 9.1 Interest in QR codes outpaces usage in most countries.

In the United States, barcode scanning tends to be most concentrated among mobile users ages 18 to 49 (Figure 9.2). That conforms to the demographic breakdown of the bulk of the smartphone-owning population.

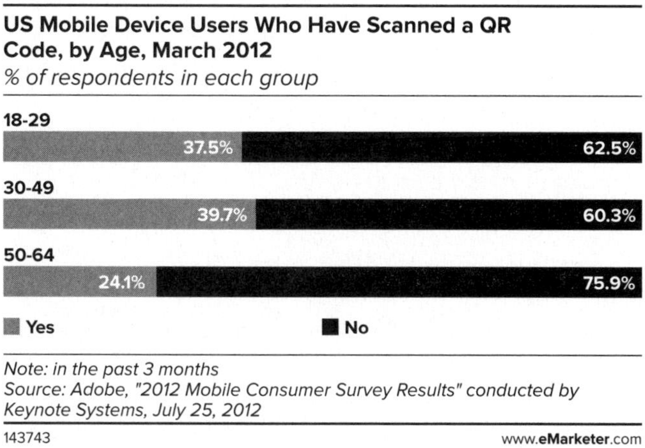

Figure 9.2 Younger mobile users are more willing to experiment with QR codes.

Enthusiasm for mobile barcodes is high among marketers and agencies as well. Globally, roughly 50 percent of marketers use 2D barcodes, and QR codes rank high on the list of mobile technologies marketers and agencies expect to implement in 2012. Figure 9.3 summarizes the results of a study of 163 marketers and 185 agencies by Econsultancy (`www.econsultancy.com`) and Experian Marketing Services (`www.experian.com/marketing-services/marketing-services.html`).

Mobile Channels/Technologies Marketers and Agencies Worldwide Plan to Use in 2012
% of respondents

	Marketers	Agencies
Mobile applications	57%	67%
QR codes	48%	44%
Mcommerce	34%	37%
Mobile advertising	31%	37%
Mobile-optimized emails	31%	30%
Mobile search marketing	28%	31%
SMS	25%	23%
Mobile coupons	10%	15%
Near field communications (NFC)	7%	10%
MMS	4%	7%
Mobile instant messaging	3%	8%
Bluetooth	2%	3%
Other	3%	2%

Note: n=163 marketers; n=185 agencies
Source: Econsultancy and Experian Marketing Services, "Marketing Budgets 2012," Feb 1, 2012
136756 www.eMarketer.com

Figure 9.3 QR codes are high on marketer and agency to-do lists.

Says David Berkowitz, vice president of emerging media at digital agency 360i, "QR codes are becoming more pervasive, and carriers, handset makers, and others are making it easier to scan the barcodes, so in the near term, QR will only get more popular." But much of the responsibility for driving consumer adoption lies with marketers, specifically in making certain the codes are used strategically and that they create positive and useful experiences. Unfortunately, as anyone who has scanned a QR code can attest, this is not the norm.

A study by Vancouver, Canada-based mobile marketing company Mobio (`www.mobio.net`) underscores this point. It found that 60 percent of North American consumers who scanned QR codes in the third quarter of 2011 did so only once. Lack of relevance most likely lies behind this "try once" behavior. According to an October 2011 survey from custom research firm Chadwick Martin Bailey (`www.cmbinfo.com`), 57 percent of U.S. smartphone users who scanned a QR code went on to do nothing with the information.

It stands to reason: If you've scanned a QR code more than once, you've doubtless ended up on a site that is unusable on your smartphone, a 404 error page, or some other destination that is unusable or irrelevant, meaning you went through a lot of trouble for little or nothing in return. In a May 2012 interview with eMarketer, Yankee Group senior analyst Nick Holland offered this assessment: "Marketers were abusing the capability as a quick way to add a call to action with a very disappointing end-user experience. They are still being abused and overused by marketers today in a way that's wholly inappropriate and badly executed."

To prevent this kind of dead-end activity, heed David's words of warning: "There's still a lengthy learning curve, and most brands and publishers using the codes haven't put enough thought into the user experience of what happens after the scan." The takeaway here, as with many tactics we've discussed throughout this book, is to put in the up-front time to understand how QR codes can help you achieve your brand's objectives *and* satisfy your audience's needs before rushing to implement them. If you do decide to use QR codes in your marketing, make sure you spend as much—if not more—time focusing on the post-scan experience as you do trying to get your audience to scan your barcode in the first place.

Use Cases

Much like SMS short codes, which we covered in Chapter 3, "Week 2: Start Simple—SMS," mobile barcodes hold promise as a mechanism for activating static media such as print and outdoor ads, in-store displays, and product packaging. In short, barcodes represent another way for mobile to bridge the physical and digital worlds.

We've seen mobile barcodes truly work for brands in three primary use cases:

Campaign activation: A code is affixed to traditional media, such as print, product packaging, outdoor media, direct mail, or in-store displays as a means of adding a digital layer to a campaign that draws users in and engages them in some way.

Information delivery: A code affixed to any of the aforementioned offline touchpoints triggers an informative experience designed to help a user learn more about a product, service, or topic.

Purchase assistance: A code affixed to offline media—usually product tags, packaging, in-store displays, or direct mail pieces—delivers content that drives consumers toward purchase activities by linking to product reviews, price comparisons, coupons, and discounts.

There are certain types of industry verticals where QR codes have caught on more than others and appear to be delivering more promise. In publishing, for example, many brands seek to get more mileage from their magazine ads by adding scannable codes that link to content designed to further engage readers. According to mobile technology firm Nellymoser (`www.nellymoser.com`), which both tracks this activity in the top 100 U.S. magazines and develops campaigns for marketers using barcodes, as of first quarter 2012, 99 percent of the top 100 publications contained at least one code. Overall the percentage of total ad pages containing a barcode had risen into the 8 to 9 percent range as of March 2012, which was up 4 percentage points year-over-year. In that same timeframe, QR codes emerged as the dominant format, accounting for over 80 percent of the barcodes appearing in magazine ads, up from just over half a year earlier (see Table 9.1).

▶ Table 9.1: QR code growth in magazine ads

Barcode Format	March 2011	March 2012
QR codes	53%	82%
Microsoft Tag	46%	12%
Others	1%	6%

Source: Nellymoser, "Mobile Action Codes in Magazine Advertising," May 2012

In fact, companies in four consumer-oriented industries—beauty, health, home, and fashion—accounted for 45 percent of all mobile barcodes that appeared in magazine ads in the first quarter of 2012, Nellymoser found. These four industries led in deployment of barcodes in-store, as well. That's not to say the QR codes won't work in other areas, of course, but these four are leading the pack.

In terms of implementations, marketers tend to focus on using barcodes to deliver enhanced brand messaging. A September 2011 survey by the Association of Strategic Marketing (ASM, `www.associationofmarketing.org/`) found that among U.S. marketers who used QR codes, two-thirds of the codes linked to product information. Nellymoser's tracking studies indicate print advertisers have long favored using barcodes to showcase videos, such as product demonstrations, how-to content, and behind-the-scenes looks (see Figure 9.4).

Type of Engagement Prompted by Mobile Barcodes Used in the Top 100* US Magazines, Q4 2011 & Q1 2012

% share

	Q4 2011	Q1 2012
Video	44%	35%
Ecommerce	19%	21%
Opt-in/sweeps	23%	20%
Social media	16%	18%
Store locator	11%	11%
Coupon	9%	8%
Photo gallery	8%	7%
Downloads	5%	7%
Recipes	4%	2%

*Note: numbers may not add up to 100% due to barcodes leading to more than one engagement; *ranked by circulation*

Source: Nellymoser, "Mobile Action Codes in Magazine Advertising," May 15, 2012

140376 www.eMarketer.com

Figure 9.4 Video is the top mobile experience launched by mobile barcodes in print ads.

Using barcodes to showcase product demonstrations can be effective for more than branding purposes in certain circumstances. Retail giants such as Sears and Home Depot, for example, have added QR codes that link instructional videos and product reviews to their in-store displays because they know these types of information can trigger a purchase. Macy's, as part of its Backstage Pass program, which we mentioned in Chapter 3, introduced QR codes to in-store displays that linked to videos containing fashion and makeup tips. Again, this is the kind of information that can influence a sale as well as prompt deeper engagement with the brand. In a May 2012 interview with eMarketer, Martine Reardon, chief marketing officer at Macy's, said: "The idea was to offer consumers a sneak preview as to what goes on behind the scenes at Macy's. We wanted to engage consumers with exclusive content. You could snap the QR codes to unlock videos with fashion tips and other content."

As tempting as it is to link barcodes to experiences that will enhance your branding efforts or impart more information about your products, we do want to remind you again to think about how to use barcodes to best serve your customers' needs as well as those of your brand. So, we'd steer you in the direction of the Purchase Assistance use case, in no small part because it is in line with consumer demands. Many surveys indicate that what consumers most want—and even expect—from scanning barcodes is access to deals. You can find the results of one such survey in Figure 9.5.

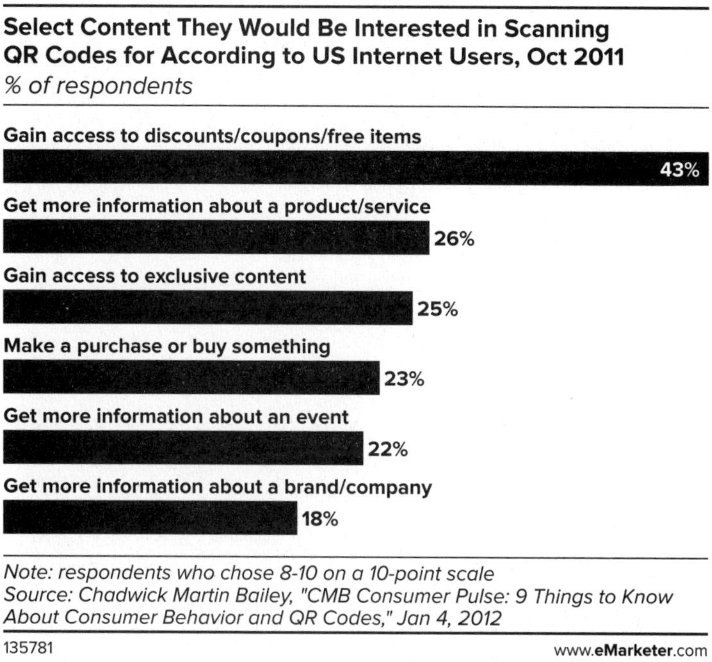

Figure 9.5 Consumers demonstrate strong interest in discounts obtained via QR code scans.

Yet, most marketers do not connect barcodes to deals; less than one-quarter of the codes in the ASM study linked to discounts. No doubt that ratio has evolved somewhat since the survey was fielded, but the low percentage connected to deals and coupons is emblematic of the kind of disconnect you want to avoid when implementing emerging technologies in your campaigns. As long as you're trying to change consumer behavior (and you are with mobile barcodes), you need to offer your audience a compelling reason for making the shift. Providing an incentive or reward for taking the action you want them to take is a tried-and-true technique.

Of course, adding barcodes to in-store displays and product packaging does present a degree of danger to brick-and-mortar retailers. In Chapter 1, "Map the Mobile Opportunity," we alluded to the issue of *showrooming*, the practice of researching a product in a store and then buying it elsewhere—online, by phone, or from another brick-and-mortar business. In December 2011, at the height of the holiday shopping season, Amazon ran a one-day promotion offering consumers up to $5 off a purchase if they compared prices using the Amazon Price Check app, which enables shoppers to find the lowest prices by scanning a barcode, taking a picture of a product, or initiating a text or voice search. That may sound like a cutthroat move, but it is really better-informed, more-empowered, and smartphone-toting shoppers who are driving this level of competition.

Execution Considerations

Consumers are becoming more familiar with mobile barcodes as they grow increasingly commonplace, but you still face the challenge of a "try once" mentality. You need to think about how you can get your audience to do more than experiment with snapping a code: You want this activity to become a regular feature of how your audience engages with your brand.

Barcode Solutions

As we mentioned earlier in this chapter, you have two basic options for 2D barcodes:

Standard 2D Barcode Formats Actually, there are several standard 2D code formats internationally, but if you are doing mobile marketing in the United States, you'll probably want to opt for QR because it's the most popular format here. QR is a sound choice because it's an open standard and can be scanned by a wide variety of free barcode reader apps. If you go this route, you'll have one additional decision—whether to go with a free code generator or use a vendor that offers a commercial 2D barcode service.

> **Free 2D Barcode Generators** Many free code generators are available online. Like any free service, some are better and more full-featured than others. A few of them can be a good first step for small tests; but if you plan to make 2D barcodes a standard component of your marketing strategy, you'd be wise to consider a commercial 2D barcode service.
>
> **Commercial 2D Barcode Services** Why pay for QR when it's open source and you can create codes for free? Well, there are a few practical reasons. For one, if you're going to use QR extensively, you're going to want the support, analytics, and ability to mass-produce codes that a managed solutions vendor can provide. Another appealing reason is that these commercial platforms enable you to quickly and easily change the call-to action behind a code already in circulation as well as plug in certain supporting functions, such as landing pages and SMS.

Proprietary 2D Barcode Formats There are numerous proprietary 2D barcode formats. Microsoft Tag and SnapTag are among the best known, but there are many others. The proprietary formats are appealing in that they allow you to modify the visual appearance of your code to a much greater degree than you'd be able to do with the standard QR format. Many proprietary barcode formats also offer an advanced level of tracking and analytics that make them very appealing to marketers. Some, like Microsoft Tag, enable you to generate standard QR codes in addition to their proprietary codes—the best of both worlds. But proprietary formats also have a few drawbacks. Many require proprietary readers, meaning your customers may be required to download a new app before they can scan your code. In our experience, the extra, added step of downloading a new app to simply scan a code can be a deal breaker for the average user. Others enable the user to email or text a photo of the tag, which is an appealing option if you're dealing with users who have older smartphones or feature phones. However, that detracts somewhat from the immediacy factor that makes 2D codes so appealing in the first place.

The type of solution—and vendor—you choose will be based on your needs and your budget. Although there are many free tools online that enable you to create 2D barcodes, doing so at scale and with the appropriate analytics in place is a task best relegated to a professional vendor. Fortunately, many cost-effective options are available. The more challenging question is, how customized do you really want to get with your codes? If you need a code that looks just like your company logo, you may want to trade up to a more specialized, proprietary solution.

Best Practices for Executing Your Campaign

Most of the implementation failures we see on a daily basis—the QR code on the TV screen, the QR code on a subway car poster—can be directly attributed to faulty execution. Follow these tips to make sure your campaign works smoothly.

Make it visible. First, make sure your barcode is clearly visible to the eye on whatever medium you use to deploy it. Don't make it so small that it might be missed or hidden within other visual elements of an ad. Place it clearly and obviously within the user's line of vision. Likewise, make the call-to-action associated with the barcode obvious and transparent. Nellymoser's study found that 64 percent of all codes in print ads were accompanied by information indicating what would happen after the scan, so this practice is becoming widespread.

If you expect to make barcodes a feature of your media campaigns, consider placing them in most if not all your advertising, so your audience comes to expect barcodes from you. Of course, you can use barcodes that link to different content depending on the medium (print versus outdoor, for example) and your objective with each. Our fictional Kiwi Market might use a barcode on an outdoor ad to link to a store locator, or if the ad were located in close proximity to a store, it might link to a coupon usable at that particular location. A barcode in a Kiwi Market print ad, on the other hand, might help build awareness for the supermarket's catering business or online ordering system.

You may also want to experiment with using different barcodes on different media so you can track whether one medium or code placement outperforms the others. For example, you might find that QR codes placed on outdoor signage generate a very high scan rate versus the same code placed on a direct mail piece. Even if—make that especially if—the content the code generates is the same, using unique codes for different placements will add a level of attribution modeling you wouldn't get otherwise. Understanding where QR codes perform best will help you use them more successfully over time.

Make it possible. People can't scan your QR code if they don't have a scanner app on their mobile device. Most smartphones do not have this capability preinstalled as part of the operating system, so don't assume your target audience has the reader they'll need to read your code. Make it easy for users who don't have a scanner app to get one by including a URL in your ad copy—or, better yet, a text-to-download link for a free scanner app.

Make wise placement choices. How often have you seen a QR code on a subway poster, where you have no data connection to complete the action? Or on a digital scoreboard at a sporting event where you have no real hope of lining up the image from afar and capturing it accurately? Or, worst of all, flashed on the screen during a television commercial, giving you a scant 30 seconds to grab your phone, open your scanning app and...you get the point. When you decide to use a QR code, be wise about where you choose to put it. QR codes are at their most powerful when used as a trigger for offline media and physical objects. But remember: users still need to be able to scan a code clearly, so place it within a realistic line of vision.

Make it compelling. A key consideration, and one that will keep your audience coming back, is linking barcodes to compelling content—and content that is accessible from a mobile device. The call-to-action needs to pique your targets' interest, and the follow-through needs to deliver on the promise you set, from both a technical and a substantive perspective. (This might be a good time to review the recommendations in Chapter 4, "Week 3: Maximize Reach with Mobile Websites.") In short, make sure the links behind the code actually work and test to confirm the content renders properly on multiple devices. You don't want the first time your audience tries your barcode to be the last.

Make it pay off. Last of all, but arguably most important, make sure your code campaign actually delivers value. It can be an experience, a special offer, a piece of information, or any other of a number of interactions, but think it through and be certain that it meets the needs of your users and provides real value. Barcodes fall within that realm of mobile marketing where we've seen shiny new object syndrome take over time and again—don't fall victim to it!

The Road Ahead

Some experts see QR codes as an interim technology that will ultimately be superseded by NFC once NFC-equipped devices and point-of-sale hardware become more pervasive. Research firm Yankee Group, for one, predicts this scenario will begin to take hold around 2014 (see Figure 9.6). Part of the thinking here is that unlike barcodes, which require users to open an app and have Internet access to see the linked content, connecting to NFC-enabled content is easier, requiring users only to tap their smartphone against the item to receive the associated message or discount.—Of course, that presupposes users have their NFC capabilities turned on and not off to preserve their battery.

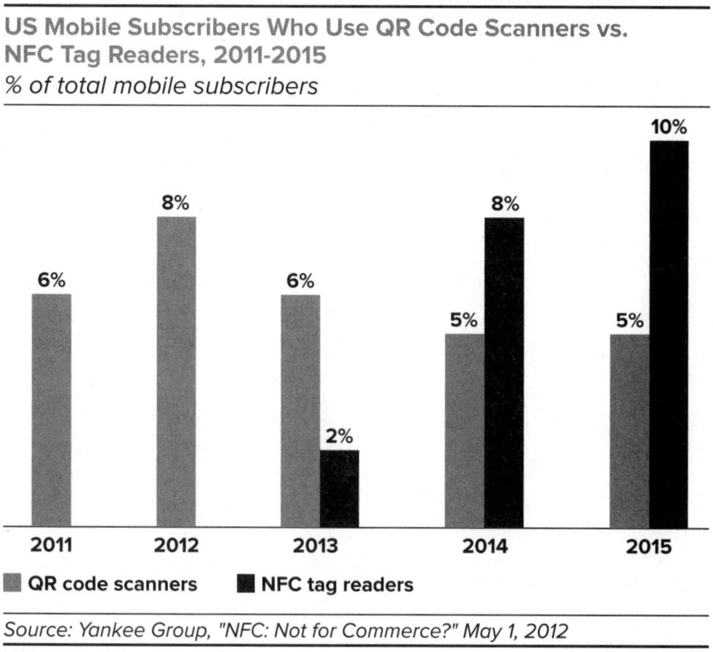

Figure 9.6 Some forecasters predict NFC will supersede QR codes.

We'll talk in more detail about NFC on Wednesday; but suffice it to say, the reality is that many if not most of the emerging technologies we're covering in this chapter will be complementary, not exclusive. Collectively, they will form pieces of a larger puzzle. David explains: "NFC isn't going to replace QR. The carriers' NFC alliance, Isis (`http://paywithisis.com`), for example, includes support for QR. People might tap their phones on in-store displays, but scan QR codes printed in magazines and newspapers. There are still far too few handsets with NFC, and then consumers need to be educated on the value proposition. That's going to take years. There are some benefits for consumers, but that's not enough to overcome inertia."

Image Recognition

We'll touch very briefly on image recognition, as it is something that hasn't yet gained much of a foothold in the marketplace. If you're not familiar with what we mean by image recognition, the best and easiest place to start might be with Google Goggles (`www.google.com/mobile/goggles`), a feature built into Google's Android and iPhone search apps. It enables users to search by taking pictures of objects and places rather than inputting text. Currently, it's limited to a number of categories:

Text: You can, for example, snap a picture of a menu in a foreign language and Google will offer to translate it for you.

Landmarks: Take a picture of the Eiffel Tower and Google will return information about it.

Books: Take a picture of a book cover and Google will provide additional information, as well as links to sites where you can order the book, including Google Books.

Contact information: Photograph a business card and Goggles will create an address card for you.

Artwork: Take a picture of a painting (that is, if the museum staff will let you get away with it) and you'll see links to a Wikipedia page about the artist.

Wine: Photograph the label of a wine bottle and you'll get information and links to Google Product Search to buy the wine.

Logos: Snap a company logo and you'll presumably see links to that company's website.

The Android version of Google Goggles also scans barcodes, a feature not present in the iOS version of the app.

From the user's perspective, image recognition technologies function similarly to barcodes in that users still need to open an app and take a picture in order to get a result. But as a marketer, you currently have a lot less control over what the user sees—it's more a form of visual search. The results are more dependent on the types of search engine marketing and optimization best practices covered in Chapter 6, "Week 5: Promote Your Message with Mobile Advertising," than they are with mobile barcodes, where you get to select the content to which a barcode is linked.

Even if image recognition has yet to move to the mainstream, it is something worth keeping your eye on. As the Web becomes progressively more visual and more mobile, optimizing your brand imagery for visual search is likely to emerge as an important factor in your brand's visibility sooner or later.

Tuesday: Augmented Reality

Augmented reality (AR) has long been heralded as one of those "next big things," and for good reason: The prospect of enhancing the physical world using digital technologies is tantalizing.

What Is Augmented Reality?

Augmented reality is a way of enabling a mobile user to "see" a virtual overlay to the physical world by combining and maximizing on-board mobile device features such as the camera, GPS, compass, accelerometer, and broadband connectivity.

Computer vision and overlays are the two main components to AR, explains Adam Broitman, Something Massive's chief creative strategist. Says Adam, "Computer vision, which is the detection piece, looks for vectors and objects, and says 'that is a building' [if you happen to be pointing your phone toward a properly marked building] and on top of that you can layer on GPS and other information. The computer vision piece is central to augmented reality technology. Then, there's the overlay piece, which is the digital infusion of information into a video feed" [meaning the information about the physical object or environment you happen to be viewing that is projected, in effect, onto the smartphone camera].

Users can experience AR through dedicated smartphone browsers, such as Layar (`www.layar.com`), Junaio (`www.junaio.com`), or Wikitude (`www.wikitude.com`), and similarly through search apps like Yelp, whose Monocle feature superimposes reviews of local establishments onto the smartphone camera's view. There are also marketer-specific apps. For example, Amazon and Ikea are two brands that offer AR shopping companions. We predict that many more will follow suit in due time. The implications for not only brands and marketers but also consumers are extremely exciting.

"The world becomes clickable. Objects and places are activated with deeper data and even purchase opportunities pour in straight from the cloud," says *Mobile Marketing Daily* editor Steve Smith. "These moments are easily shared in multiple ways. You not only get to show to others where you are and what you are doing but you can also leave traces for others who follow you physically. Tagging a space is a kind of virtual and nondestructive graffiti."

Projected Uptake

United Kingdom-based Juniper Research (`www.juniperresearch.com`), a respected forecaster of digital trends, predicted in February 2011 that global augmented reality revenues would soar from just $1.5 million in 2010 to $1.5 billion in 2015. That's an astounding hundred-fold growth.

The vantage point in 2013 looks a little different. Rather than exploding as a mainstream mobile marketing channel, as was predicted two years ago, AR is emerging in a more cautious fashion, as marketers strive to understand where and how it can enhance their campaigns in a way that adds value rather than gimmickry. At this stage, it's safe to say AR remains in the experimental realm, for marketers and consumers alike.

One possible wrinkle to the technology is that it may not develop primarily on mobile devices as we currently know them. Instead, it's possible that wearable computers, such as the Project Glass eyewear Google demonstrated to great effect at its annual I/O developers conference in June 2012, will take the lead. Google's experimental

AR-enabled glasses feature many of the same components found in today's smartphones, including an accelerometer, gyroscope, and wireless radios for pulling in web-based data. Imagine the Google Goggles visual search we described on Monday, only with the results projected right in front of your eyes. In an August 2012 edition of its weekly *Analyst Insider* newsletter, research firm ABI Research (`www.abiresearch.com`) stated "there is little doubt that the future of AR is not in smartphones or tablets, but in more natural, eyewear-based interfaces."

As with QR codes, which require users to have one or more apps on their phones to scan a code, entering an AR experience involves firing up a dedicated app, something Adam believes continues to hold back the advance of both technologies. He says: "The hardware will need to support an endemic augmented reality experience for it to reach the type of penetration search engines, for example, have reached."

Still, marketers are, at the very least, curious about by AR. Among those polled by the Society of Digital Agencies (SoDA, `http://societyofdigitalagencies.org/`) for the industry association's "Q1 2012 Digital Marketing Outlook," 35 percent characterized themselves as "intrigued" by AR and an additional 22 percent declared themselves "excited" (Figure 9.7). To put these findings in context, the excitement score may have been the lowest among 13 technologies included in the survey, but the intrigue score was tied for seventh. At this point, a likely conclusion is the lack of excitement relative to other emerging technologies is in part a function of a lack of awareness or understanding of AR.

David Berkowitz on the Outlook for Augmented Reality

AR has some significant social implications, for example, allowing people to tag and share information on physical locations—not so much augmented reality as much as it is *annotated* reality. But does that translate into great, untapped potential for marketers? We asked David Berkowitz, vice president of emerging media at leading digital agency 360i, for his perspective. His take suggests AR will add the most value as an underlying technology that is integral to a marketing experience, not something consumers need to activate themselves:

"Augmented reality will never matter to consumers, and that's how it should be. Consider the application GoldRun (`http://goldrungo.com/`), which superimposes digital objects over images to create entertaining photos. It's entirely about augmented reality, and yet has nothing to do with AR.

"AR is a tool developers have to create engaging experiences. What's especially exciting about AR is that with the potential to blend the digital and physical realms, the possibilities are so open-ended that we barely have a sense today of what can be done with it."

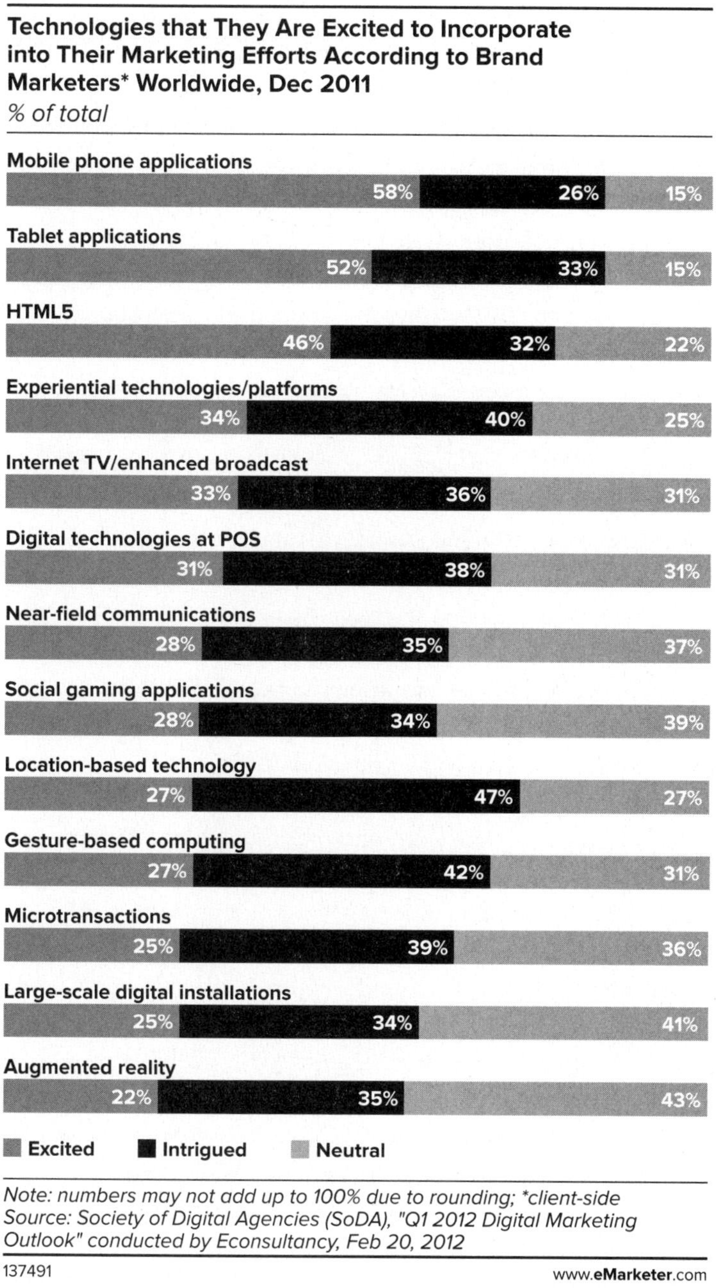

Figure 9.7 Marketers express interest in incorporating augmented reality into their campaigns.

Use Cases

As a new way of literally viewing the world, the initial use case for AR was "the wow factor: things that people hadn't seen before," says Something Massive's Adam Broitman, who began running AR campaigns in 2008. At that time, AR had a certain magical quality, but, he notes, "as with all new technologies, that wears off." Now that the novelty factor has worn off, the marketing case for AR is less about "wowing people and more about uncovering information in everything around you."

Adam compares AR to search marketing: "Much in the same way that search marketers help consumers find a brand using search engines, augmented reality applications, such as blippar (www.blippar.com) and Wikitude, that overlay information on the real world are the beginning stage of utility-based augmented reality."

As with mobile barcodes, activating print ads and product packaging constitute what Adam sees as "the low-hanging fruit." He notes that for consumer packaged goods manufacturers, incorporating AR actually doesn't require any changes to existing packaging, just awareness that the experience is accessible. Of course, even if that conserves resources in one area, it puts an additional item on the marketing department's to-do list, so if you're considering an AR implementation, evaluate first whether AR is really the most effective way to generate the results you want or whether another more proven, less flashy tactic will have better ROI metrics. At this stage, Adam believes AR is "not something on your must-do list; it's not SEO [search engine optimization], for example."

But Adam sees more interesting applications of AR taking shape in the near future. "Moving forward," he says, "we're going to see innovations like Google's Project Glass as another way that people search the world. So having things properly place-marked in Google Places [now known as Google+ Local] will become important, just as you'd have your website with the proper metadata, alt-tags, and copy to optimize for search engines. Actually having your physical locations or place you want to be found properly marked will be critical because people will be looking in augmented space to find them."

Even outside of specialty eyewear that may or may not become commercially available, possibilities exist for marketers to do more than offer enhanced information. Rather, the premise—and the promise—of AR lies in the ability to provide a new level of utility. "Imagine you've just brought home a piece of Ikea furniture," says Adam. "You lay out all the pieces, hold your phone up over them, and it actually shows you, like a visual instruction manual, what to do. The potential here is far richer than simply overlaying information. Conceivably, your phone should be able to detect those objects and overlay an outline of what the end state should look like, and as you bring different parts into view, it should be able to tell you 'that's the right piece,' so it's actually more a digital assistant rather than just information. That's when it gets really exciting, and when you can get people to go the extra mile for an experience like that."

Execution Considerations

From a technical standpoint, AR is less mysterious today than it was a few years ago. The software you'll need is readily available and, in many cases free. To choose the right options, you'll first want to decide what kind of AR campaign you want to conduct:

Marker-based AR: In marker-based AR experiences, the augmented reality is triggered by the user viewing an image through the viewfinder of a mobile device, or, placing an image in front of a desktop or laptop computer's camera. The image, or "marker," is what sets the augmented experience in motion. This type of campaign is a great choice if you want to reach mobile *and* desktop users.

Location-based AR: In this type of AR experience, the augmented reality is triggered by location; therefore, it's only truly effective on GPS-enabled mobile devices.

Many good free or reasonably priced augmented reality *software development kits (SDKs)* are on the market, but their support for marker versus location-based AR varies. Some of the better options include:

- Total Immersion (`www.t-immersion.com/`)
- Aurasma (`www.aurasma.com`)
- Metaio (`www.metaio.com`)
- Wikitude (`www.wikitude.com`)
- String (www.`poweredbystring.com`)
- Zugara (`www.zugara.com/`)
- Qualcomm's Vuforia (`www.qualcomm.com/solutions/augmented-reality`)

In many cases, you'll be satisfied by marker-based AR. Adding location detection as an enhancement to the experience is often possible if the SDK you choose does not supply it. But no matter your goal, you'll need to have the right development skills at hand to execute. With its added nuances, AR is not ordinary software development, so unless you have a crack team of developers in-house, you'd be wise to seek out specialists.

A Word of Caution About AR Content

In some cases, AR is simply annotated reality—that is, text information overlaid onto a real-world vista. But, it's often something much richer, such as animated imagery. This type of rich-media AR is exciting and engaging; but keep in mind that to be successful, it needs to be developed specifically with AR in mind. If you think you can take imagery meant for the Web or for print and reuse it as-is in an AR app, think again. That is to say, you can use the imagery, but it won't have the expected, 3D-like image quality we've quickly come to expect from AR. The best effect will come from creating 3D and 2D images specifically with the AR experience in mind.

The strategic standpoint is where things get more complex. As we've emphasized throughout this book, you need to think about the *why* along with the *what* and the *how* when implementing a new tactic or technology. This is a point Adam underscores as well: "The strategic consideration I always tell clients about when they're considering augmented reality is that they need to be thinking about the augmentation part—so that they're adding a value layer on to what already exists, as opposed to something that's completely separate. You might think of it as mixed reality, where it's the sum of the digital and physical parts. When you bring the physical and digital together, you make something greater." A related and no less important consideration: "You need to make it into an end-to-end experience." That is, don't make AR an appendage of your mobile campaign; integrate it throughout your marketing, so it becomes a marker for your brand.

Overall, Adam's perspective is that "there's been some nice work out of the cutting-edge digital shops, but no one's really taken AR to the point of being a necessity." When asked what it's waiting for, he quips: "It's waiting for Apple. It's waiting for someone to come out and make it obvious and simple. Technology is often presented in a way that it doesn't feel human or doesn't relate to the human experience. But Apple has always been good at focusing on what you gain from the technology, not what it is. We need a company that can speak to the advantages on a large scale in that kind of way, which is easier said than done. It's easy to point to what the formula is, but to combine the software technology with a really elegant hardware solution and then tell that story to the whole world is much more challenging."

For now, standard reality may be enough for most consumers and most marketers. But as more technologies intrude on our daily lives, AR might just prove to be a saving grace. "A personalized AR overlay will help filter signal from noise in any given context. In the best-case scenario, AR won't add to the clutter so much as cut through the clutter to identify the places and objects you really don't want to miss," predicts *Mobile Marketing Daily* editor Steve Smith.

Wednesday: Near-Field Communications

As we noted in Chapter 8, the terms *radio frequency identification (RFID)* and NFC are commonly used interchangeably, in part because both employ radio waves to transmit information between objects. RFID is the more established of two; it has been used in inventory management and asset tracking for over a decade. RFID is also able to transmit data over a longer range, but remember it is a one-way technology, limited to sending information from a tag to a hand-held reader. NFC represents an evolution of RFID in that it allows two-way communication between objects, albeit over a shorter range, and thus is more suitable for ticketing, payments, and marketing campaigns. Although RFID has seen widespread deployment in supply chain management and logistics, we believe the advantages NFC brings in data transmission and interactivity make it the better bet for marketing applications. You should certainly be aware of the distinctions between the two, which we covered in some detail on Wednesday in Chapter 8, but as you start thinking about future-forward ways to incorporate ambient media into your marketing campaigns, our recommendation is to focus your attention on NFC rather than RFID.

Projected Uptake

We talked quite a bit about NFC in relation to mobile wallets and mobile payments in Chapter 8. Remember that if you're one of the lucky few to have an NFC chip on your smartphone, it can transmit information across a range of up to four inches. The current emphasis is on using NFC for so-called contactless or proximity payments. The same technology that allows tap-and-go payments can also be used to transmit all sorts of marketing content, including but not limited to maps, images, music, and videos, not to mention social engagements such as Twitter follows and Facebook Likes and Shares. Built-in hardware makes for a more seamless information exchange than the image technologies we talked about on Monday and augmented reality, which we covered on Tuesday. That explains why many are pinning their hopes on NFC and betting the potential of tap and go will make other technologies obsolete.

Most forecasts for NFC assume that mobile wallets will be the driving force behind adoption; there has been less talk around the purely marketing applications of the technology. That said, once NFC-enabled devices are widely available, there's nothing impinging on the growth of NFC-based marketing as well. As of August 2012, the trade publication *NFC World* (`www.nfcworld.com`) listed just over 60 smartphones and tablets that include NFC functionality, the majority of which are not available in the U.S. market. Yankee Group, the research firm we cited on Monday, estimates the total number of NFC users in 2012 at just over 16 million, over 90 percent of which are located in the Asia-Pacific region (Figure 9.8). Overall, that's still a small number, and especially so in comparison to the total Asia-Pacific population, which is nearing 4 billion.

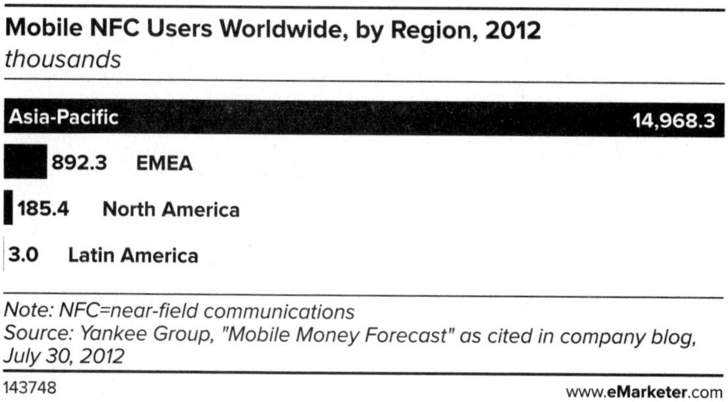

Figure 9.8 Asia-Pacific leads in NFC adoption.

In several years, however, the situation could look dramatically different. Shipments of NFC phones are expected to increase substantially. U.K.-based research firm Informa Telecoms & Media (`www.informatandm.com/`) predicts 630 million NFC-equipped handsets will ship globally in 2015, accounting for 40 percent of total shipments, compared to 3.5 percent of total shipments in 2011 (see Figure 9.9).

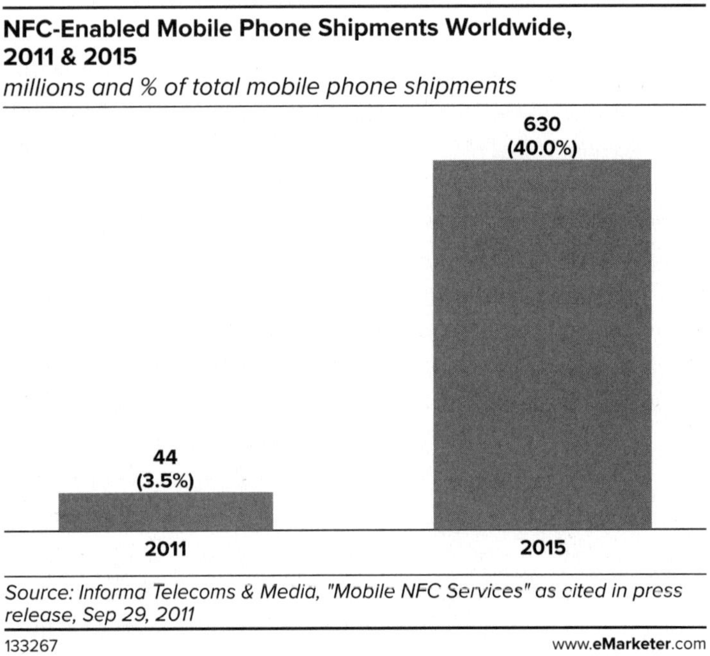

Figure 9.9 Big growth ahead for NFC-enabled devices

Despite the limited availability of NFC-enabled devices, marketers are nonetheless energized by the potential NFC holds. As you saw in Figure 9.7, 63 percent of brand marketers surveyed worldwide are either excited or intrigued about incorporating NFC into their campaigns. Of course, the percentage of marketers and agencies actually doing so on a global level is still far lower, as shown in Figure 9.3. But we expect those figures to climb in line with the adoption of NFC devices. Given the current distribution of NFC users, it's safe to say the Asia-Pacific region and Western Europe will see mainstream deployments of NFC-based advertising before the United States does.

Potential for Marketers

As with QR codes and AR, activation of print and out-of-home campaigns, information delivery, and purchase assistance represent the low-hanging fruit for NFC. Experiments from major brands have focused on precisely these avenues. Some examples follow.

Reading, United Kingdom In March 2012, 13 major brands, including supermarket chain Morrisons, fashion retailer H&M, Universal DVD and Universal Special Projects, car maker Mercedes, TV channel ITV2, energy drink Lucozade Sport, game maker EA Games, and Unilever's Lynx, Toni & Guy, Magnum, and Vaseline brands signed onto a project spearheaded by out-of-home advertising company JCDecaux (`www.jcdecaux.co.uk/`) to blanket the city of Reading with over 300 NFC-enabled outdoor ads. The advertisers pledged to update the content of their ads weekly, including rotating special offers, vouchers, games, and music. The ads also featured QR codes to maximize reach.

Lexus The Japanese luxury automaker ran an ad for the Enform infotainment app suite available in its 2013 GS model in the April 2012 issue of *Wired* magazine that featured an embedded NFC tag. The tag activated video demonstrations of each app.

H.I.S. In May 2012, the Japanese-based global travel agency ran ads incorporated into the straps of a number of Tokyo subway lines, giving straphangers something new to do on their daily commutes.

John Lewis The U.K. department store chain ran an NFC-enabled out-of-home campaign in June 2012 across 100 London bus shelters. The ads were designed to raise awareness for the store's Click & Collect order online, pick-up-in-store service.

Granted, these campaigns represent early tests. More proof points are needed to move the needle from "good in principle" to "good in practice."

The great benefit of built-in hardware, of course, is that it offers the potential for a more seamless user experience—it removes one or more steps required to actually reach the activated content. We can expect more of the kinds of implementations noted here. In theory, NFC offers the promise of activating just about any surface, so everything but the sky is really the limit once the number of NFC-capable devices reaches a critical mass!

Execution Considerations

Given the potential, you're probably wondering what you can do with NFC now. Realistically, the answer is, not a whole lot—at least at this point.

If you're a retailer, you're most likely already investigating the NFC point-of-sale payment processing mechanisms we discussed in Chapter 8. If you're outside the sphere of physical payments, you can still take advantage of NFC. The tags are relatively cheap and NFC readers can be had for a reasonable cost. With some custom coding, it would be fairly simple to run very small-scale tests with NFC-embedded objects. Kiwi Market, for example, could embed NFC chips into customer loyalty cards and enable shoppers to tap their card against an in-store reader to rack up points for each purchase.

However, if you are relying on scale, you may have a bit more of a wait. The number of mobile devices with embedded NFC is still limited, and the market continues to await drivers for mass adoption.

Thursday: Mobile Broadcasting

After the still-emerging channels we discussed on Tuesday and Wednesday, we now turn to two technologies that are far more pervasive—pretty much every smartphone and tablet on the market is Wi-Fi and Bluetooth-enabled. Yet, despite the ubiquity of these technologies in the devices we carry, they are far less widely used for mobile marketing purposes than QR codes and NFC. We think of Wi-Fi and Bluetooth as mobile broadcasting in the sense that these technologies allow you to transmit your message to large, albeit localized audiences. Wi-Fi and Bluetooth both enable the delivery of the same kinds of marketing messages and content we've talked about throughout this chapter, including, but not limited to, coupons, contextual or location-based advertising or offers, downloads (apps, images, music, video, games) and social interactions. Both function on the basis of hardware built into your mobile device, but they are quite different in terms of underlying technology.

Wi-Fi is fundamentally an access mode that enables your smartphone or tablet (or laptop for that matter) to connect to the Internet, often at higher speeds than you'd achieve on your mobile carrier's network (and without cutting into your monthly data allotment). Wi-Fi networks typically operate at a range of 100 to 300 feet, hence their technical designation as wireless local area networks (WLAN).

Bluetooth, a proprietary standard developed by telecommunications equipment manufacturer Ericsson (`www.ericsson.com`) in 1994, was designed for secure, short-range data exchange. Today, the Bluetooth Special Interest Group (`www.bluetooth.org/`), a trade association with over 16,000 members, manages development specifications, protects the trademarks, and oversees standards qualification programs for new devices that incorporate Bluetooth technology. Unlike Wi-Fi, which connects you and your device to a network of many, Bluetooth establishes a direct, secure connection between two Bluetooth-equipped devices (such as a phone and headset or a phone and a computer), hence its designation as a personal area network (PAN). This process generally requires a password exchange—if you've ever tried to pair your phone with your car's Bluetooth system, you're probably familiar with the routine.

Given the technological differences between Wi-Fi and Bluetooth, you could think of Wi-Fi as enabling one-to-many proximity marketing. Bluetooth, on the other hand, functions on more of a one-to-one basis, albeit with the potential to reach many people within range of the Bluetooth network. Another distinction to keep in mind: Bluetooth follows opt-in permission-based guidelines similar to those we covered in Chapter 3 for SMS, whereby the recipient of a Bluetooth-activated message or offer needs to positively affirm willingness to receive marketing messages from whatever brand is transmitting them.

Wi-Fi

As mobile device users, we spend an increasing amount of time on Wi-Fi networks, whether at home, work, or in places such as cafes, airports, malls, and hotels. Usage of Wi-Fi among smartphone and tablet owners is nearly universal, especially for tablets, a much lower percentage of which feature cellular data connections, as shown in Figure 9.10.

Installed Base of US Tablets, by Connection Type, Q1 2012
% of total

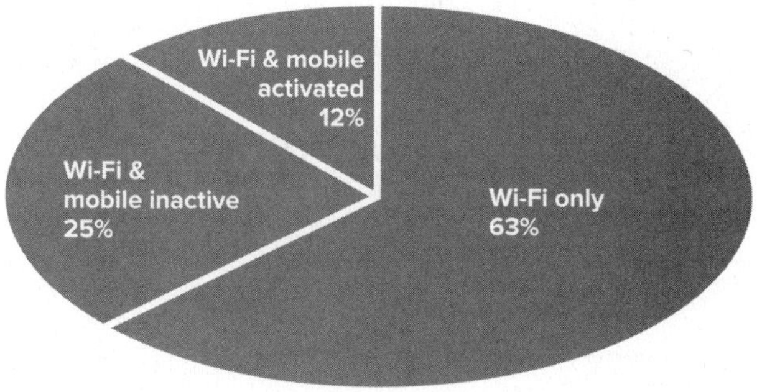

Source: Chetan Sharma, "State of the Global Mobile Industry: Annual Assessment 2012", April 30, 2012

139898 www.eMarketer.com

Figure 9.10 Wi-Fi connections are dominant among tablet owners.

According to Informa Telecoms & Media, the U.K.-based research firm we cited on Wednesday, 70 percent of smartphone data traffic worldwide was transmitted over Wi-Fi networks as of January 2012. In some European countries with high data tariffs, that figure rose over 80 percent (see Figure 9.11). As mobile carriers around the world implement monthly data caps designed to alleviate pressure on overburdened cellular data networks, you can expect those percentages to keep going up. (Trust us. Your carrier will thank you.)

In North America, in another sign of the advance of post-PC computing, JiWire (`www.jiwire.com`), the location-based mobile advertising company we cited in Chapter 7, found that smartphones and tablets accounted for 52 percent of total Wi-Fi hotspot usage (35 percent for smartphones and 17 percent for tablets), compared to 48 percent for laptops. A year earlier, laptops represented 70 percent of total usage, compared to 21 percent for smartphones and 9 percent for tablets.

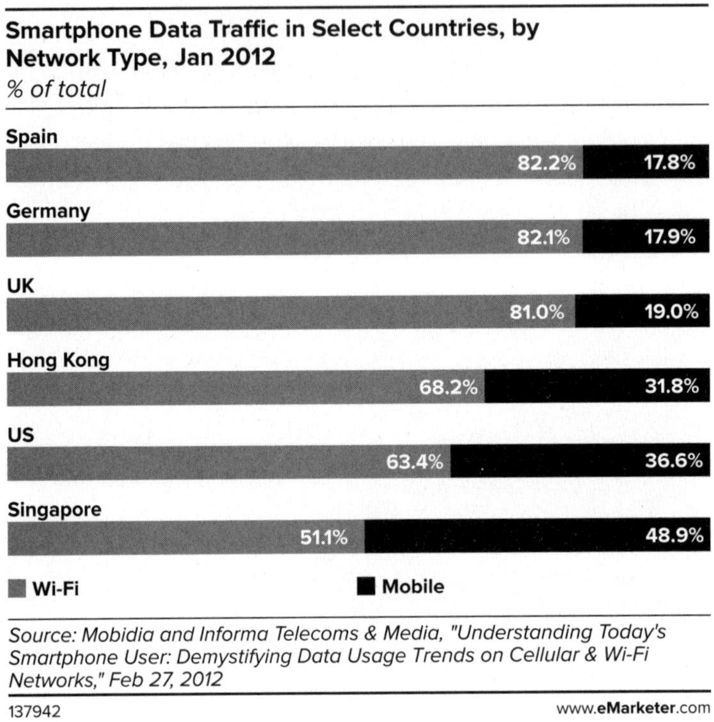

Figure 9.11 Wi-Fi accounts for a high percentage of smartphone data traffic.

Of course, the growing availability of Wi-Fi networks is also a major factor behind the explosion in Wi-Fi-based data traffic. According to JiWire, the number of public Wi-Fi locations worldwide totaled nearly 777,000 as of Q2 2012, up 35 percent from Q1 2011, and more than triple the total from 2008. Take a look at the numbers reported in JiWire's "Mobile Insights Audience Report: Q2 2012."

2008: 237,507

2009: 289,476

2010: 414,356

2011: 682,929

2012: 776,556

Another interesting development to monitor is the difference in business models behind Wi-Fi hotspots in the United States compared to the rest of the world. According to JiWire, the breakdown as of Q2 2012 was as follows:

Worldwide: 79.9 percent paid versus 20.1 percent free

U.S.: 76.0 percent free versus 24 percent paid

In other words, the United States is almost diametrically opposed to the rest of the world. But consider this: where there's free, there's also an opportunity for ad-supported, so keep that in mind as you think about use cases.

Use Cases

As we noted in Chapter 7, JiWire research indicates that over half of U.S. Wi-Fi users are willing to share their location in exchange for relevant content. So, if you combine pervasive usage of Wi-Fi with a high percentage of free hotspots and consumers' general receptiveness to relevant location-based offers, you have the recipe for proximity marketing. Consumers who log into Wi-Fi networks are primed for learning and engaging with what's around them. You should bear in mind how device usage differs by venue, however. For example, JiWire finds that the majority of North American Wi-Fi usage in places like restaurants and cafes comes from smartphones. Tablets, as you might expect, see higher usage in malls and lean-back venues like hotels than they do in dining establishments.

If you want to reach users on Wi-Fi networks, your best bet is to work with a dedicated ad network that has a presence across many hotspot locations, such as JiWire or Cloud Nine (`www.cloudnine.com/`). You may also want to consider large carrier-based Wi-Fi networks, such as AT&T, which maintains over 30,000 hotspots in the United States alone, including in numerous hotels, airports, and retail locations, or perhaps the ultimate in mobility—the increasingly ubiquitous in-flight Wi-Fi networks maintained by the likes of Gogo (`www.gogoair.com/`).

Depending on your business, be sure to take a close look at the retail sector. Major retailers, including Macy's and Sears in the United States and the U.K. supermarket chain Tesco, increasingly offer free Wi-Fi to customers (see Figure 9.12) because they know

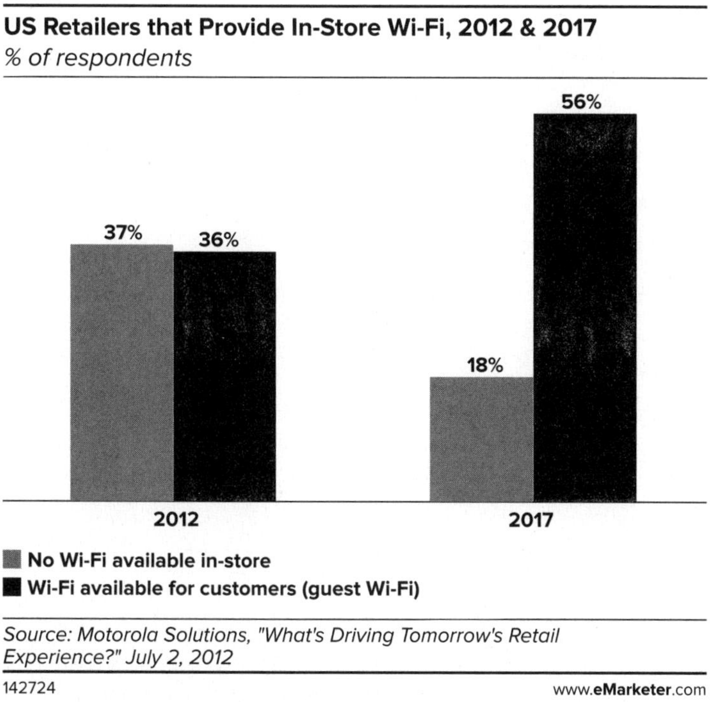

Figure 9.12 In-store Wi-Fi looks to become a common feature for U.S. retailers.

shoppers are using their smartphones to find reviews, compare prices, watch product videos, and connect to social networks. Offering the perk of free Wi-Fi is one way retailers can control and even track that activity, which can provide insights they can use it to keep shoppers' purchasing in-store.

If you're a marketer, especially if you sell your products in a Wi-Fi-enabled retail location, consider the benefits of using the store's Wi-Fi network to offer incentives. Consumers who sign on will certainly be in-market and likely receptive to your message in that context. The retailer will benefit as well, as such an offer may be just the inducement a consumer needs to prevent a showrooming incident that results in the consumer making a purchase elsewhere.

Bluetooth

Bluetooth is pervasive; it is embedded in nearly every mobile device currently on the market, as well as most laptops, many other peripheral devices, and, increasingly, in-car infotainment systems. Yet, it has seen little or no usage for marketing purposes. Digital agency 360i's vice president of emerging media, David Berkowitz, offers an explanation, "Bluetooth is stuck in this unfortunate realm of being so pervasive that it's so established that it's boring. And still, so few people understand it. It has all of the mystery without the mystique. Most people don't know what it does and don't want to know. A big challenge for Bluetooth is that people are becoming especially sensitive about battery life, so if people need to turn on something that isn't already on, that's a big hurdle."

The password authentication exchange between two Bluetooth-enabled devices likewise presents ease-of-use issues. If you've ever tried to pair your phone with another Bluetooth device, you've no doubt experienced the frustration of not knowing the right passcode to enter. Consumers will keep trying if it means being able to make hands-free calls in their car, but they will not be as tenacious if the only thing at stake is receiving a marketing message.

Use Cases

Could the situation David describes change? The short answer is, yes…but. In theory, you can use Bluetooth to accomplish many of the objectives we listed on Monday, including campaign activation, information delivery, and purchase assistance. In theory, Bluetooth offers some intrinsic advantages relative to the other technologies we've covered in this chapter, namely a highly secure, permission-based link between consumer and marketer. That said, there are substantial hurdles to using Bluetooth to do what those other technologies might be effective at doing.

First, you have the awareness challenge, as David's comments underscore. It's not that Bluetooth can't be a viable marketing delivery mechanism—it's that you have to educate consumers about the possibility and then get them to use it as such. That takes time, resources, and persistence, precisely at a moment in which you're likely using all three to build awareness of delivery mechanisms like QR codes, NFC, and perhaps AR. Here's some data that illustrates this challenge: CBS Outdoor and consumer insights firm Kantar Media (`www.kantarmedia.com`) did a study among European consumers in France, Ireland, Italy, the Netherlands, Spain, and the United Kingdom in November 2011. The results, shown in Figure 9.13, demonstrate far higher rates of awareness—and usage—of QR code and SMS short code-enabled outdoor ads than for Bluetooth-activated ads. Granted, that's but one example, but we feel it reflects the broader challenges you'll encounter when implementing Bluetooth-based marketing campaigns.

Awareness and Usage of Select Outdoor Ads According to Internet Users in Europe, Nov 2011
% of respondents

	Awareness	Usage
QR codes	39.79%	13.34%
Promotional text code in an ad	34.21%	14.53%
Touchscreen billboard advertising	20.37%	7.48%
Ad image recognition	15.53%	5.33%
Online check-in/location-based vouchers	13.98%	4.89%
Tweets/Facebook updates on digital ads	13.72%	4.43%
Augmented ads	13.69%	4.20%
Bluetooth-enabled advertising	13.13%	4.47%
Motion & gesture interaction	6.64%	1.70%
NFC	5.76%	1.40%

Note: n=9,024 ages 18-54; UK, Ireland, France, Spain, Italy and Netherlands
Source: CBS Outdoor, "Interactive Europe: The Outdoor Media Landscape is Changing" conducted by Kantar Media, March 21, 2012

140616 www.eMarketer.com

Figure 9.13 Consumers have limited awareness of Bluetooth-enabled ads.

Second, and related to the first, much as we've encouraged you to shy away from shiny new object syndrome, shiny objects do benefit from a lot of exposure (some might say hype) and consequently generate a lot of interest, some of which may lead to actual traction in the market. Bluetooth has always been seen in a more utilitarian light, which may explain its pervasiveness in applications outside marketing. It's vital, for example, for linking your smartphone to your car's infotainment system. With considerable momentum behind QR codes and NFC, in particular, from a wide array of sources (handset manufacturers, mobile carriers, banks, credit card and payment processing firms, advertising agencies, and technology giants, just to name a few), our feeling is that Bluetooth will remain a niche technology when it comes to mobile marketing.

Friday: Digital-Out-of-Home

Remember Steven Spielberg's 2002 film *Minority Report*? Like many future-looking science fiction films, it was meant to be a cautionary tale about the role technology plays in our lives. At the same time, because the film was expertly made, it also made some of that technology look pretty cool. And wouldn't you know it, some of the technology portrayed in the film is slowly but surely moving out of the realm of science fiction and into the realm of daily reality. For the last section of this chapter, we'll try to sort through what's still fiction and what you can really do with the two technologies we've broadly classified under the rubric of digital-out-of-home (DOOH): interactive signage and surface computing.

The first development, interactive signage, includes the kinds of digital billboards you commonly find in malls, movie theaters, office buildings, and transit hubs. It is far more prevalent than surface technology. Some digital signage is actually mobile in the literal sense, namely, the screens you find atop taxi cabs or on the side of buses or metro railways. Some of it is merely mobile-enabled, much in the same way that it triggers interactions that take place on our devices. In the realm of out-of-home advertising, digital signage is to traditional roadside billboards what the Web is to print.

The second development still falls mostly in the "coming soon" category. To wrap your head around surface computing technology, imagine an entire tabletop or wall featuring the same kind of multitouch screen you currently have on your smartphone or tablet. The big difference is surface technology enables multiple user inputs simultaneously—lots of different people can interact with a surface computing screen at the same time, each doing different things. Chances are, you've witnessed surface computing and didn't even know it. If you've ever watched the news anchors on CNN manipulate images and maps on giant, 82-inch capacitive monitors, you've seen it in action. That's probably the most visible manifestation of the technology to date, but expect to see more large-format, multitouch, interactive out-of-home ads in locations like bus shelters coming soon to urban areas.

Mobile-Enabled Digital Signage

In an age of media saturation, it's tempting to think that digital signage is everywhere, as it was in Ridley Scott's dystopian sci-fi classic *Blade Runner.* In urban areas, that often seems the case. But in fact, digital out-of-home is still a small piece of a much larger advertising pie. Research firm PQ Media (`www.pqmedia.com`) estimates that global spending on DOOH will reach $8.3 billion in 2012. That's a mere fraction of the $542.3 billion in total media ad spending eMarketer estimates for 2012. Per PQ Media, DOOH is most prevalent in the Asia-Pacific region (40 percent of the market), followed by the Americas (35 percent) and Europe (23 percent).

Even though digital signage is far from ubiquitous, many marketers consider it highly strategic when it comes to transmitting personalized and proximity-based messages. For example, in a global survey by the Aberdeen Group (`www.aberdeen.com`), a research firm owned by direct marketing services company Harte-Hanks (`www.harte-hanks.com`), 47 percent of the retailers characterized as "leaders" and 27 percent classified as "followers" said they use digital signage to deliver personalized offers to customers. As with many of the ambient technologies we've talked about in this chapter, mobile devices are the activation mechanism for those offers.

Context, as we discussed in Chapter 7, is an important element of personalized and proximity marketing. Imagine you're waiting in line at a movie theater on opening night to see the latest superhero blockbuster, and a screen near you offers exclusive content such as an app enabling you to visualize yourself as your favorite character. You are, in effect, a captive audience—you're already primed for the film, and chances are good in that situation that you'd be receptive to engage further while you wait for your seat. Your smartphone enables you to take that step right there. Similarly, if you happen to wander around the mall following the film, you're apt to be interested in eating or doing some shopping. Local merchants can respond by adjusting the messages on digital bulletin boards, displaying interactive menus for local restaurants and targeting consumers with coupons and special offers.

Digital signage can promote further engagement once you enter a business. Imagine a bar that instead of a traditional jukebox features a digital, screen-based version that allows diners to make song requests from their own music libraries as well as vote on songs selected by other patrons. Berkeley, California-based Roqbot (`www.roqbot.com`) is one such startup enabling precisely that. These are the kinds of connections between mobile devices and digital signage that we can expect to see more of in a not-so-distant future. Remember, *Blade Runner* was set in 2019, which is fast approaching.

Surface Technologies

Even more in the realm of science fiction, the notion of motion-sensitive, digitally enabled objects calls to mind the holodeck popularized by *Star Trek: The Next Generation*—a virtual world of simulated objects. Microsoft pioneered the category in 2007 when it introduced Surface—a tabletop computer (not to be confused with the 2012 tablet computer of the same name) designed and priced primarily for commercial deployment. (Most consumers had little use or interest in a $12,000 computer, no matter how cool it looked.)

Outside of regular appearances in sci-fi films, surface computing has slowly expanded, but the actual applications of it we can expect to see in real life are a bit more mundane than what you see in the movies. Imagine the kinds of digital signage we've just described, only with interactive touchscreens. You'll find them in high-traffic areas like malls and airports, where they can help shoppers and travelers navigate option-filled locations. You'll also find them in stores, where retailers want to enable customers to interact with their products, and restaurants, where they can serve as an interactive entertainment platform as well as an eating surface. Naturally, the Surface first surfaced in such a capacity in Las Vegas, the United States' closest approximation of the urban landscape depicted in *Blade Runner* (minus the persistent rain, of course). Increasingly, you're starting to see places such as retail locations, restaurants, and airport lounges equipped with iPads or other tablets. In these instances, the surface technology is not on the same scale as an interactive wall, but the interactive surfaces and the objects on them, namely apps, are also more familiar for the average consumer.

From entire walls or spaces that become digitally and touch-enabled to the steady incorporation of tablets into the retail and eating experience, one thing is safe to say: Wherever you look, there are going to be more screens in your line of sight and at hand. Whether they'll be able to detect your thoughts and desires, as in *Minority Report*, remains to be seen, but ambient digital and mobile media will undoubtedly infuse our awareness of the physical world.

In Conclusion

The technologies and media we've highlighted in this chapter have not seen widespread usage—yet. Something Massive Chief Creative Strategist Adam Broitman and 360i Vice President of Emerging Media David Berkowitz both caution about regarding the challenges associated with changing consumer behavior, specifically, getting consumers to adopt new and often unproven technologies. Similarly, both see Apple as a potential game-changer in this regard.

Says David, "Apple is a wildcard with anything it does. Apple could endorse Bluetooth or NFC, reinvigorate SMS or pink unicorn stickers, and it could change consumer behavior nearly instantly. Apple is just about the only company that can consistently change consumer behavior. Because of Apple, we use touchscreen handsets, listen to portable digital music, and collectively download billions of applications. Whatever Apple endorses has strong potential to go mainstream and ripple far beyond its own devices."

The technologies and media we've discussed in this chapter are, for the most part, waiting for their ripple. But, with mobile effectively becoming the new desktop and emerging as the mainstream computing idiom, they point the way to the future. By the future, we mean not just for mobile marketing, but marketing in general, which we see as defined by three key qualities: mobile, social, and ambient.

In the next and final chapter, we'll map out the road ahead, focusing on what we see as the new four Ps you need to integrate into your marketing—Portability, Preferences, Presence, and Proximity—and **mobile innovations** to watch.

Chart the Future Forward

Over the past nine weeks, we've taken you from the basics of mobile right through some of the most intricate emerging technologies. We've taught you how to map a strategy and mobilize a .com *website, leverage the social/mobile/local nexus, and plot your plan for mobile payments. So, what's next? At the rate technology is evolving, it's hard for marketers to look too far into the future with any real accuracy. The devices we use today can, and probably will, look different in two years. As we've said, it's not so much the devices that should concern you as it is the way those devices are changing our approach to marketing overall. In this final chapter, we'll discuss some of the more future-forward technologies we are watching. We'll also focus on the way they are affecting how you connect with your customers and discuss ways you can effectively plan to take advantage of them.*

10

Chapter Contents

The New Customer Journey

It might surprise you to hear that we're not big fans of the term "customer journey," especially because we've used it liberally throughout this book. In order to share the insights we hoped to impart, it made sense for us to use the vernacular, but in truth, we'd like to see the term go away altogether. In fact, we'd like to do away with the word "mobile" as well, because both words are misleading. Why? Well, first off, customers don't know they're on a journey. They have little clue that they're traveling through a purchase funnel—and they definitely don't think in terms of mobile web versus desktop web, or native apps versus web apps, to the same extent you do. To them, it's all just media, and they're after relevant content, a great experience, and perhaps some good deals. So, for us to keep bucketing our efforts into silos is more than a little counterproductive. As our favorite advertising industry elder statesman, Alan Siegel, told us in the Introduction, let's not focus on the delivery mechanism, let's focus on the content, and everything else will fall into place.

Of course, that's not as easy as it sounds. We're in the midst of a tremendous shift in the way marketing works, and while change is good, it's also difficult. Surprisingly, the hardest part of the challenge isn't in knowing the technologies involved and how to use them, but in understanding the human element. As consumers, our expectations, our behaviors, and the paths we take to achieve our objectives are evolving very, very quickly—it's no longer a straight point-A-to-point-B trajectory. In truth, it probably never was, but the increasingly ubiquitous digitization of the human experience is making our journey from prospect to customer to advocate more complex and convoluted than ever. Yet as marketers, we tend to apply a very linear, old-school model to doing our jobs.

In Chapter 4, "Week 3: Maximize Reach with Mobile Websites," we discussed the move toward responsive design, an innovation that we believe will revolutionize the way we create digital content. But, we believe that as an industry, we need to take it one step further and apply the responsive approach to marketing as a whole. In this chapter, we'll share our own insights on how the customer journey is evolving and the technologies that are making it happen.

In the introduction to this book, we talked about the simple fact that just like everything else, media evolves. Not only does it evolve, it does so at an increasingly rapid pace. You are probably familiar with the concept of Moore's Law, which posits that the power of computer processors doubles every two years. That concept applies equally to the rate at which consumer behavior adapts to technical innovation. Until the mid-1990s, the customer journey was pretty straightforward (at least to outward appearances). As marketers, we assumed that a potential customer would hear about our brand in one of four key ways:

- Through a print or out-of-home ad
- From a television commercial or movie

- From a radio ad
- From a friend (word of mouth)

The general assumption was that the potential customer would hear about your brand through one of these channels and then visit a store or showroom to check it out. The pivotal moment of decision-making—what Procter & Gamble christened the "Second Moment of Truth"—happened there, at the shelf, as the customer decided whether or not to buy. The "Second Moment of Truth" came post-purchase when the happy customer recommended the product to a friend, creating a virtuous cycle in which satisfied customers create new ones for your brand.

With the advent of the Web, the aforementioned channels didn't go away, but a new, highly powerful dimension was added in the form of branded websites. As marketers, we realized the progression from prospect to customer to advocate wasn't anywhere near as linear as we thought. Purchase decisions were happening in real time before the customer got to the shelf—sometimes without the customer ever setting foot in the store at all. Advocacy was happening directly—and indirectly—across multiple channels and platforms and often occurred before purchase via "likes" and "shares" within the customer's social graph.

All of a sudden, things became way more complex. The customer journey wasn't a simple equation anymore, and we had a whole new set of marketing metrics to figure out. We started to realize that we had to be more present, in more ways, and in more places, and that we had to actually pay attention to who our customers were and what they had to say. Yet, we still had it easier than we realized. When the Web looked like Figure 10.1, your biggest worry really was "Does it work in Internet Explorer on a Mac?"

Oh, how times have changed.

Figure 10.1 The Web in 2000

Now, the Web looks something like Figure 10.2. Most of us have yet to completely figure out digital marketing in general, let alone how to market using mobile devices. It's beyond daunting to tell you that you need to think beyond smartphones and tablets, as well—but the fact is you do.

Figure 10.2 The Web in 2012

The reality is, as the world around us becomes increasingly digitized, the customer journey is becoming infinitely more complex. We're connected now 24/7 via our desktops, smartphones, and tablets. But, as the Web encroaches on physical spaces and objects, those connections can and will become more ambient, more intimate, and more powerful. Consequently, it will become far more difficult for us as marketers to determine when that Zero Moment of Truth, the moment in real time when consumer decisions are made, actually occurs. We'll need to be more nimble, in not only our use of technology, but also our approach to the individual customer.

The light-speed evolution of technology is forcing us to confront the nonlinear customer journey; clearly, you have to understand the technology, or we would not have written this book. Before this chapter ends, we'll discuss some of the most disruptive technologies on the horizon. But, understanding the technologies simply isn't enough. You also need to understand the four Ps of the new customer journey: *Portability*, *Preferences*, *Proximity*, and *Presence*.

The New Guiding Principles of Digital

We'd argue that the most exciting development in digital marketing to date has been the emergence of social media. Facebook, Twitter, WordPress, Pinterest, and the countless other satellites within the social media ecosystem forced the realization that marketing isn't a monologue, but a conversation. People will talk, and it's not really a choice of whether to join the conversation or not. With that, came the realization that those conversations are happening in real time, on smartphones and tablets, via SMS and apps and an ever-growing spectrum of non-traditional channels. Social and mobile may occupy different aspects of your marketing budget, but the reality is that the two are inextricably intertwined—one could not have evolved without the other.

Accepting that marketing is a conversation opened our eyes to the fact that we need to be present in all the situations in which those conversations occur. It has also pushed us to accept the fact that customers are individuals with their own wants, needs, and terms; and while the industry is still largely stuck in a one-size-fits-all model of marketing, we firmly believe we're moving toward a far more customized method of connecting with our customers based on the guiding principles of *Portability*, *Proximity*, *Preferences*, and *Presence*.

Portability

Our jobs were so much easier when we only had to worry about desktops, laptops, and a couple of different browsers. It may have seemed ridiculously complex to us back when it was all so new, but in reality, we had it pretty easy. Now, the content we create has to flow across multiple digital touchpoints—something it was not, in most cases, designed to do. Your site needs be equally useful, usable, desirable, findable, and engaging across desktop, smartphone, *and* tablet browsers; and it needs to provide contextually relevant content, functionality, and experiences for each.

But, it's not just about the browser anymore. Digital experiences are happening through native apps, messaging, geo-social networks, ambient delivery channels, digital surfaces, and social machines of all shapes and sizes. So, making certain the content you create and the data you collect is portable to browsers just isn't enough.

Take our clients at the fictional Kiwi Market, for example. At the end of their mobile strategy, they netted out with a robust, CMS-driven mobile website that will adequately service their customers' needs until they can roll out a responsive website a year or two down the road. But to fully extend their brand and take advantage of all the possibilities mobile presents, they'll work with their agency partners and technology providers to ensure that:

- Their content is *highly extensible* by choosing open design and technology standards and selecting partners, products, and services that support them.
- Their content is *highly accessible* by choosing to use open standard formats and protocols for their APIs.

The only constant is change and, as much as we'd like to offer more meaningful advice on portability beyond what we've already mentioned, we can't. Although we're pretty sure the medicine cabinet in your bathroom will be capable of displaying your Facebook feed by 2015 or so, we can't honestly claim to know what the data format for it will be. However, if you choose open standards, keep your content accessible, and avoid painting yourself into a corner with closed systems and technologies, you'll be more than halfway there—not to mention way ahead of the competition.

Preferences

Preference-based marketing has a long history of starts and stops. In the earlier days of the Web, there were numerous attempts to get people to opt in for ads in exchange for offers and content; to date, the only place this model has truly survived is in the form of opt-in email marketing and SMS. As marketers, we found that it was a lot easier to group customers into segments and make educated guesses as to what they'd respond to than it was to actually *ask* them. However, we think that with mobile, the preference-based model may just have turned a corner. Just as iTunes trained us that it's acceptable to pay for content, the geo-aware capabilities of mobile have begun to train us that it's acceptable to volunteer a small piece of information in exchange for something of value, such as a deal. Google Maps is a great example. Your current location is highly detailed personal information, yet most of us don't think twice about giving it up in exchange for something as simple as an address.

Think of the implications of such technology for our fictional Kiwi Market. Opt-in preferences could enable Kiwi to effectively customize the example persona Michelle's experience every time she sets foot in the store. Based on her shared preferences, Kiwi would know that Michelle is an amateur chef with a passion for classic French cuisine as well as a working mom with two young kids. The site could then tailor the content and offers it presents to her to those specific needs and interests. Rather than casting its nets wide with general offers and broad, general content, Kiwi could begin to tailor its messaging and approach to what's actually meaningful to each consumer at any given time.

Put yourself in the customer's position: Imagine, in the future, that your mobile device includes control panel settings that allow you to publicly broadcast certain preferences and/or targeting criteria to brands and advertisers. That information would enable them to tailor their messages to you, the user. For example, you could broadcast:

- Your age
- Your gender
- Your education level
- Your native language
- Your current location
- Your hobbies, likes, and dislikes
- Brands and product categories from which you are willing to receive communications and on what basis

Then, imagine that a brand's website or app (or digital kiosk, Bluetooth node, NFC point-of-sale module—you get the picture) can tap into these opt-in preferences via an API or some form of proximity technology, and on the basis of what you have shared, understand what is appropriate to offer you, as well as when, where, and how to do it.

Proximity

As we've already referenced, the ability to actually be where your customers are has long been the holy grail of marketing and advertising. Now, thanks to mobile devices and the ever-expanding array of connected and convergent places and objects, you can actually achieve it. Proximity is one the richest and most diverse capabilities that mobile has to offer us, and it goes far beyond store locators and location-based display ads.

Location, in its most basic form, is extremely important for a brick-and-mortar brand like Kiwi Market. As you saw in Chapter 7, "Week 6: Leverage the SoLoMo Nexus," localized Google Search marketing is one of the cornerstones of the chain's mobile strategy, and they've begun to dabble in locally targeted search and display advertising. They've even begun to distribute special offers on a local level via text using geo-fencing and push alerts generated from their mobile app based on location. However, Kiwi realizes that location can be used for more than just marketing—it can enrich the customer experience as a whole.

Here's an example of how that might work: Visit the Kiwi Market website on a smartphone when you're in a store, and upon receiving permission to detect your location, the site will serve you offers and specials specific to that store, show you info on what's in season locally, and tell you what's new and fresh in the catering department. By contrast, visit the site when you are more than a few blocks away from a store and you'll automatically receive higher-level content that introduces you to the Kiwi Market brand and offerings.

End users may not know they're on a customer journey, but just the same, they want to get to their end destination, their end goal, quickly and efficiently with as little friction as possible. Anything you, the brand, can do to make their lives easier in this regard will strengthen the connection between you. It might be as simple as helping to find your closest location via Google on a smartphone or filtering unique content and offers relevant to the spot they're in. It might be as complex as allowing them to pay for your products and services with a tap of a cellphone.

Here's what you need to remember: Layering permission-based on location and personal data over your marketing efforts will enable you to create content and experiences that are highly meaningful—far more so than anything you could do online in the conventional sense. If you know who I am—and *where* I am at right this moment—your chances of connecting with and converting me are extremely high.

Presence

Presence is a concept borrowed from the world of instant messaging (IM); one that we believe will become increasingly relevant as digital technology becomes more ambient and integrated into the physical world. In IM parlance, presence indicates a user's current state of activity as well as his or her ability to engage in conversation—for example, "away from my desk" or "in a meeting"—"please do not disturb." Essentially, presence is what we've come to know as "status" in the age of social media. Presence, however, differs from status in that it indicates what I'm doing but also adds an additional dimension of receptivity. Whereas my Facebook status simply tells you what I'm doing right now, presence indicates what I'm doing and what it means to you if you want to interact with me. Transferred to the broader spectrum of digital marketing and layered on top of portability, preferences, and proximity, it presents far richer and more interesting possibilities than a simple status message ever could.

As we proposed earlier, imagine functionality built directly into the operating system of your smartphone that enables you to continually broadcast a custom presence to people—and brands—throughout the day. For example, you might always be "available" to your significant other for a phone call or text, but "busy" for calls or texts from friends during your working hours. The easiest scenario we can use to illustrate how a brand might leverage presence in this way would be through an app. For example, your smartphone might have a presence API that a brand could integrate into its native app to control how and when the app communicates with you via push messages. Our prototypical Kiwi customer, Michelle, for example, might choose to relay her status to Kiwi Market at lunchtime Monday through Friday as "hungry" in order to receive messages about what's on special that day in the Kiwi café. However, on the weekends as she ferries her kids to soccer and ballet, she might choose to be *out* to "lunch" because her kids prefer to visit their favorite fast food restaurants as a treat.

Preferences, presence, and proximity work together symbiotically to create the most synergistic connection between brand and consumer. What you're open to right now you may not want tomorrow, and what interests you in one location may be of zero interest when you are in another. You may be open to offers from Kiwi Market, but not the fast food franchise down the street. You might only want to hear from Kiwi on Tuesdays and Thursdays when they offer vegan specials. You may want to hear about cooking classes and tastings, but only on weekends when you have time to enjoy them. The layering of presence over location and preferences has the potential to make all our fears about mobile marketing (the worries about privacy and bombarding users with too much unwanted information) a thing of the past. Portability of content—the first and most fundamental piece in the mobile marketing puzzle—makes it all possible.

The four Ps of digital may evolve somewhat differently from the way we've envisioned them here, but there is absolutely no question that, separately and together, they will be the hallmarks of how you connect with your customers in the years to come.

Mobile Innovations to Watch

When we discussed Kiwi's mobile strategy in Chapter 2, "Week 1: Develop Your Mobile Strategy," we mapped out what Michelle's customer journey looked like, from prospect to purchaser to loyal brand advocate, including the many desktop and mobile touchpoints involved. However, flash forward from 2012 to 2015 and Michelle's journey may well look quite different. We're hesitant to make too many predictions about exactly what it will look like, but we have a few ideas about what you should keep your eye on.

Social Machines Odds are you don't feel an overwhelming need to have your refrigerator text you a reminder to pick up the milk or to tell your toaster you'd like your whole wheat a little on the light side this morning. You've probably never wished you could "like" a brand of candy after you bought a snack from a vending machine nor had the opportunity to pay for a soda with a tweet, but none of those scenarios are very far off in the future and some are already a reality. Global brands like Coca-Cola have been tinkering with socially enhanced vending machines for some time now, and we can expect more brands to enter the space as the technology that enables this sort of interaction becomes more accessible. One of the more interesting companies on our radar, BugLabs (`www.buglabs.com`), has been doing some especially interesting work in this space, enabling consumer brands to connect with new and existing audiences via vending machines and other physical interfaces through social cues. We think you'll be seeing more and more of the paradigm they are helping to shape.

Digital Glass Since its debut in early 2011, Corning's "A Day Made of Glass" has become one of the most talked about and widely viewed video series on YouTube (`www.youtube.com/watch?v=6Cf7IL_eZ38`). It showcases the daily lives of average citizens across the globe, enriched by the digitally enabled surfaces of their homes, workplaces, and vehicles. While the world depicted in these videos may seem far in the future, the engineers at Corning, Google, and similar design-technology think tanks may not be that far off from making it reality. Corning's flexible Gorilla Glass and Google's Project Glass are just the beginning. In the very near future, our windshields, bathroom mirrors, countertops, and just about every other smooth surface you can imagine will have the potential to transmit and receive digital information.

Voice Control Siri, Apple's digital voice assistant, is just the tip of the iceberg. Voice control has great potential to go beyond the personal assistant model introduced for the iPhone in 2012. Coupled with voice recognition, which adds an additional level of personalization and security, we foresee voice control infiltrating more corners of the splinternet; users might soon interact with signage and other digital interfaces on an effortless, more personalized level through simple speech.

Facial Recognition If you find remembering and entering passcodes and passwords tedious, just wait! In the future, you may simply have to glance at your smartphone, tablet, or other digitally enabled interface to access content, share info, and even conduct transactions. At least that's what the major players in the mobile world seem to be banking on. In June 2012, Facebook purchased Israeli facial recognition startup Face.com for as yet undisclosed (yet not hard to guess) purposes. Android 4.0 (Ice Cream Sandwich), released in December 2011, came equipped with a facial recognition option for unlocking your device. Meanwhile, patent filings from 2012 indicate that Apple has designs of its own on facial recognition. To make a long story short, the how and when of facial recognition remain to be seen, but there's a very strong possibility that it will become a regular part of your mobile experience in the near future. As with voice, once users have accepted facial recognition for accessing and controlling their mobile devices, the potential for marketers to use it won't be far behind.

Eye Control Eye control is similar to voice control and facial recognition, in that it is a form of non-touch human/computer interaction, but with a twist—eye control is more about navigation than security, access, or preferences. In a multitouch, multiplatform world where we already have our hands full with pinching and zooming every screen in sight, the ability to control interactions with a glance has the obvious potential to help us move more efficiently through our unique customer journeys. Although the marketing usages are still unclear, it's not hard to hypothesize how, coupled with facial recognition technology, eye control could allow for extremely personalized experiences.

In Conclusion

Our goal has been to arm you with an understanding of mobile that will help you plan for your clients, build your brand, and manage your partners and vendors. We hope we have succeeded and have started you on your way. As you continue your own journey as a mobile marketer, you can refer to this book's glossary of terms and the appendices, which list vendors and tools that will help as you move forward. We also encourage you to visit our blog at www.mobileanhouraday.com, where we will continue to analyze the latest trends, technologies and companies in the mobile industry and interview brands and marketers on how they are using mobile to achieve their goals. If you'd like to share your own experiences or ask questions, we'd love to hear from you! You can reach out to us at authors@mobileanhouraday.com.

Appendix A: Research Firms

A

As we discussed in Chapter 2, "Week 1: Develop Your Mobile Strategy," your ability to gather the right data and synthesize it into actionable insights will determine a large portion of your mobile marketing success. Quantitative and qualitative research will constitute the backbone of this effort. Here, we've compiled a list of go-to resources that can help you map out your mobile strategy.

Appendix Contents

Subscription Research Firms

Research firms gather data on market trends, customer demographics, and user behaviors on a much larger scale than you can achieve on your own with focus groups, customer interviews, or surveys. As a paying subscriber, you can access this data and use it to compile custom reports. Most of these firms also publish syndicated research reports on a variety of topics related to digital and mobile marketing. Many firms in the following list offer advisory and consulting services in addition to research.

ABI Research `www.abiresearch.com`

BIA/Kelsey `www.biakelsey.com`

comScore `www.comscore.com`

eMarketer `www.emarketer.com`

Forrester Research `www.forrester.com`

Gartner `www.gartner.com`

International Data Corporation `www.idc.com`

Juniper Research `www.juniperresearch.com`

Kantar `www.kantar.com`

Nielsen `www.nielsen.com`

Ovum `www.ovum.com`

Pyramid Research `www.pyramidresearch.com`

Strategy Analytics `www.strategyanalytics.com`

TNS Global `www.tnsglobal.com`

Yankee Group `www.yankeegroup.com`

Research Resources

Working with primary research firms and survey vendors can provide custom insights into consumer attitudes and behavior.

Primary Research Firms

Following is a short list of primary research companies with expertise in mobile that can help you gather information about your target audience.

DynamicLogic `www.dynamiclogic.com`

InsightExpress `www.insightexpress.com`

Wave Collapse `www.wavecollapse.com`

Survey Vendors

Customer surveys are a vital building block in the strategy development process. They can yield a wealth of information on common user behaviors and attitudes.

Crowd Science `www.crowdscience.com`

Crowdtap `www.crowdtap.com`

Qualtrics `www.qualtrics.com`

SurveyMonkey `www.surveymonkey.com`

WorldAPP KeySurvey `www.keysurvey.com`

Appendix B: SMS Aggregators

As noted in Chapter 3, "Week 2: Start Simple—SMS," SMS aggregators are specialty businesses that have established technical integration and business relationships with the wireless carriers. These relationships enable aggregators to perform two key tasks: buy SMS messages from the carriers in cost-effective bulk, and send SMS messages quickly and efficiently across the wireless carriers' networks. These are tasks you cannot do yourself, neither as an individual nor as a major corporation.

Per the Common Short Code Administration (CSCA) website (`www.usshortcodes.com/`*), SMS aggregators are categorized into tiers based on their capabilities and relationships with the carriers. Note that the following lists of aggregators, drawn from the CSCA site, are current as of this writing, but be aware that the roster may shift; check* `www.usshortcodes.com/csc_aggregators.html` *for the most up-to-date lists by tier.*

B

Appendix Contents

Tier 1

Tier 1 SMS aggregators maintain direct short-message peer-to-peer (SMPP—an industry protocol for exchanging SMS messages) connections and premium settlement agreements with at least four of the five major U.S. wireless carriers (AT&T, Sprint, T-Mobile, US Cellular, and Verizon). They support carrier-grade SMS and MMS capabilities and provide a high-level 24/7 service agreement. They publish content only where the rights to that content are clearly owned by the customer (e.g., they won't knowingly plagiarize or spam).

Ericsson `www.ericsson.com`

mBlox `www.mblox.com`

Mobile Messenger `www.mobilemessenger.com`

Motricity `www.motricity.com`

Openmarket `www.openmarket.com`

Sybase 365 `www.sybase.com`

Velti `www.velti.com`

Vibes Media `www.vibes.com`

Tier 2

Tier 2 SMS aggregators maintain direct SMPP connections with at least three of the five major U.S. wireless carriers, and settlement agreements with two of the five. Unlike Tier 1 firms, they support only carrier-grade SMS capabilities, but they still provide the same type of high-level 24/7 service agreement. Similarly, they publish content only where the rights to that content are clearly owned by the customer (e.g., they won't knowingly plagiarize or spam).

Syniverse `www.syniverse.com`

3CInteractive `www.3cinteractive.com`

Tier 3

Tier 3 SMS aggregators are not aggregators in the truest sense of the word, but rather mobile marketing companies that specialize in SMS and run their campaigns on the backbone of a Tier 1 or Tier 2 provider. They tend to mark up the costs of their services beyond what a Tier 1 or Tier 2 provider would charge. On the other hand, they also offer a full-service model that the larger Tier 1 and Tier 2 aggregators often do not, including managing your campaigns for you from short code acquisition to analytics.

Aerialink www.aerialink.com

4INFO www.4info.com

i2SMS www.i2sms.net

Mobile Accord www.mobileaccord.com

Moonshado www.moonshado.com

Netpace www.netpace.com

Netsmart www.netsmart.eu

Nokia www.nokia.com

Single Touch www.singletouch.net

TeleMessage www.telemessage.com

Txtwire www.txtwire.com

Appendix C: Mobile Web Resources

C

Ensuring that your mobile site functions effectively across multiple devices and platforms involves a lot of testing. These services and tools can help you determine whether your content is optimized for the mobile environment.

Appendix Contents

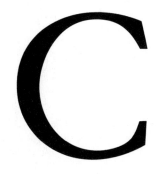

Device Detection

As noted in Chapter 4, "Week 3: Maximize Reach with Mobile Websites," when a browser sends a request to your site for a page, it also sends along an identifier known as a *user agent*. A script on the website detects that user agent and returns the right content for the particular device. The following device detection tools can assist in that process.

Device Atlas `www.deviceatlas.com`

Mobiforge `www.mobiforge.com`

WURFL `wurfl.sourceforge.net`

Test Tools

These tools can help you test whether (and to what degree) your website is mobile-friendly.

Adobe Edge Inspect `http://html.adobe.com/edge/inspect/`

Google Mobilizer `www.google.com/gwt/n`

Modify Headers (Firefox Add-on) `https://addons.mozilla.org/en-US/firefox/addon/modify-headers/`

W3 mobileOK Checker `http://validator.w3.org/mobile`

The iPhone 4 Simulator `http://iphone4simulator.com/`

The iPhone 5 Simulator `http://iphone5simulator.com/`

Appendix D: Mobile App Resources

D

App development is a highly complex process, requiring both technical and marketing expertise. These resources can help you at key junctures of the development process.

Appendix Contents

App Development Resources

The following app development resources offer detailed guidelines, software development kits (SDKs), tools, and other content specific to each platform that can help you start building your app.

Android Developer Resources `http://developer.android.com`

BlackBerry Developer Resources `http://developer.blackberry.com`

iOS Developer Resources `http://developer.apple.com/devcenter/ios`

Windows Phone Developer Resources `http://msdn.microsoft.com/en-us/library/ff402535(v=vs.92).aspx`

Test Services

Ensuring that your app is functioning properly across multiple devices and wireless carriers involves a significant amount of testing. The following vendors can help you test your app and work out any technical bugs before you submit it to any of the app stores.

Belatrix `www.belatrixsf.com`

BSquare `www.bsquare.com`

Compuware Gomez `www.compuware.com/application-performance-management/gomez-apm-products.html`

Infostretch `www.infostretch.com`

Keynote Device Anywhere `www.keynotedeviceanywhere.com`

Mobile Labs `www.mobilelabsinc.com`

Perfecto Mobile `www.perfectomobile.com`

Smartbear `www.smartbear.com`

Tosca Test Suite `www.tricentis.com`

uTest `www.utest.com`

App Marketing Resources

As we noted in Chapter 5, "Week 4: Maximize Engagement with Mobile Apps," marketing your app can be as big a job as building it in the first place. The following resources can help you with your prelaunch and post-launch earned media planning.

Press Release Services

Many apps get a big bump in downloads from a good old-fashioned press release. The prMac (`www.prmac.com`) Apple-specific wire service can be effective at garnering coverage.

App Review Sites and Directories

We recommend focusing your prelaunch and post-launch earned media efforts on reaching out to key influencers. The following lists of app reviews, blogs, and directories can help you determine which sites you will want to target.

148Apps `www.148Apps.com`

app.itize.us `www.app.itize.us/wp`

AppAdvice `www.appadvice.com`

AppCraver `www.appcraver.com`

AppSafari `www.appsafari.com`

AppStoreApps.com `www.appstoreapps.com`

AppStorm `www.appstorm.com`

Appvee `www.appvee.com`

Frackulous `www.frackulous.com`

FreeiPadApps.net `www.freeipadapps.net`

I Use This App `www.iusethisapp.com`

iFanzine `www.ifanzine.com`

IntoMobile `www.intomobile.com/apps/ipad`

iPad Apps Review Online `www.ipad-apps-review-online.com`

iPhone App Review `www.iphoneappreview.com`

iPhoneAlley `www.iphonealley.com`

iSource `www.isource.com`

iusethis `www.iphone.iusethis.com`

Macworld `www.macworld.com/appguide/index.html`

Smokin Apps `www.smokinapps.com`

TapCritic `www.tapcritic.com`

TechSpheria `www.howsmyapp.com`

The APPera `www.theappera.com`

The Daily App Show `www.dailyappshow.com`

The iPhone App Review `www.theiphoneappreview.com`

TheTopAppPreviews.com `www.thetopapppreviews.com`

Today in iOS `www.todayiniphone.com`

TouchArcade `www.toucharcade.com`

TUAW `www.tuaw.com/hub/app-reviews`

Twittown www.twittown.com

What's On iPhone www.whatsoniphone.com

Android-Specific Sites

The following sites may be useful when developing Android apps.

AndGeeks www.andgeeks.com

Android App Review Source www.androidappreviewsource.com

Android AppDictions www.androidappdictions.com

Android Apps www.androidapps.com

Android Community www.androidcommunity.com

Android Rundown www.androidrundown.com

AndroidGuys www.androidguys.com

Androidmarketapps.com www.androidmarketapps.com

AndroidTapp www.androidtapp.com

Androinica www.androinica.com

Ask Your Android www.askyourandroid.com

Aviator Android Apps www.aviatorandroidapps.com

Best Android Apps Review www.bestandroidappsreview.com

Droideo www.droideo.com

Planet Android www.planetandroid.com

TalkAndroid www.talkandroid.com

Game-Specific Sites

Consider reaching out to these sites if you're developing gaming apps.

AppGamer.net www.appgamer.net

Slide To Play www.slidetoplay.com

The Portable Gamer www.theportablegamer.com

TouchGen www.touchgen.com

App Analytics Firms

As noted in Chapter 5, app-specific analytics solutions currently offer the most robust level of detail about app usage. If you are serious about investing in apps, you may want to consider one of the following firms.

App Annie www.appannie.com

Flurry www.flurry.com

Google Mobile Analytics www.google.com/analytics/features/mobile.html

Localytics www.localytics.com

MixPanel www.mixpanel.com

Mobilytics www.mobilytics.net

Appendix E: Mobile Ad Networks

If you're planning to advertise on the mobile web or in mobile apps, you'll need to engage the services of a mobile ad network. As discussed in Chapter 6, "Week 5: Promote Your Message with Mobile Advertising," mobile ad networks are vendors that purchase inventory from publishers—usually mobile websites and mobile apps—and resell this inventory to advertisers. We've classified mobile ad networks according to three primary models: premium, premium blind, and blind. Bear in mind that these categorizations do not constitute any sort of value judgment about any of the companies that appear in this appendix; they are meant to be representative, not exhaustive.

E

Appendix Contents

Premium

Premium mobile ad networks limit their inventory to a select number of premium publishers, which tend to be the mobile websites and apps that are household names and command a huge number of eyeballs. They generally allow you to cherry pick inventory and select only the apps and mobile websites on which you want your campaign to run.

Advertising.com `www.advertising.com`

Microsoft Mobile Advertising `advertising.microsoft.com/international/mobile-advertising`

Mobile Theory `www.mobiletheory.com`

NAVTEQ `www.navteq.com`

Premium Blind

These are premium networks that utilize a blind segmentation model. They offer the same top-notch inventory as a regular premium network, but don't allow you to choose where your ad will appear.

Greystripe `www.greystripe.com`

HUNT Mobile Ads (Latin America) `www.huntmads.com`

Jumptap `www.jumptap.com`

Madhouse (China) `www.madhouse.cn`

Millennial Media `www.millennialmedia.com`

Velti `www.velti.com`

Blind

Blind networks aggregate a vast quantity of inventory among less-trafficked mobile sites and apps. Their costs are often much lower than premium mobile ad networks, the catch being that you have very little control over where your ad will run. The networks usually bundle their publishers into virtual segments that fit certain demographic targets—for example, sports fans or business travelers. Your ads will run within mobile websites and apps in segments that match your budget and targeting criteria, but you won't know exactly where you ad is appearing.

AdColony `www.adcolony.com`

Admob `www.google.com/ads/admob`

Admoda `www.admoda.com`

Adfonic `www.adfonic.com`

BuzzCity `www.buzzcity.com`

InMobi www.inmobi.com

Leadbolt www.leadbolt.com

madvertise www.madvertise.com

Mojiva www.mojiva.com

Rhythm NewMedia www.rhythmnewmedia.com

TapJoy www.tapjoy.com

Appendix F: Blogs, Online Publications, and Twitter Feeds

Online resources—particularly blogs, industry publications, and Twitter feeds—are vital assets for staying current. Blogs and online publications offer deep dives into a range of topics from breaking news to product reviews to company announcements, while Twitter provides continually updated, at-a-glance snippets on a similar range of topics, with a healthy dose of individual personality added to the commentary. Here, we've assembled lists of resources that span many aspects of the mobile ecosystem.

F

Appendix Contents

Blogs

To keep up-to-date, we follow numerous thinkers and doers, plus a handful of blogs that have blossomed into media properties in their own right. Some of these resources focus specifically on mobile, while others cross multiple platforms. This list is just a handful of our favorites. An extended and continually updated blog roll is available on `www.mobileanhouraday.com`.

AllThingsD `www.allthingsd.com`

AndroidGuys `www.androidguys.com`

Android Official Blog `http://officialandroid.blogspot.com`

BGR `www.bgr.com`

Carnival of the Mobilists `http://mobili.st`

C. Enrique Ortiz `http://weblog.cenriqueortiz.com`

Communities Dominate Brands `http://communities-dominate.blogs.com`

Daring Fireball `http://daringfireball.net`

Engadget `www.engadget.com`

Ethan Marcotte `http://ethanmarcotte.com`

GigaOM `www.gigaom.com`

Gizmodo `www.gizmodo.com`

Jan Chipchase `http://janchipchase.com`

London Calling `http://londoncalling.co`

LukeW Ideation + Design `www.lukew.com`

Marketers Studio—David Berkowitz's Marketing Blog `www.marketersstudio.com`

Mashable `http://mashable.com`

Mobhappy `http://mobhappy.com/blog1`

MobileGroove `www.mobilegroove.com`

Mobile Industry Review `www.mobileindustryreview.com`

MobileOpportunity `http://mobileopportunity.blogspot.com`

Mobileslate `www.mobileslate.com/blog`

Musings of a Mobile Marketer `http://technokitten.blogspot.com`

Open Gardens `http://opengardensblog.futuretext.com`

PandoDaily `http://pandodaily.com`

Pogue's Pages `www.davidpogue.com`

ReadWriteWeb `www.readwriteweb.com`

SmartMobs `www.smartmobs.com`

TechCrunch `http://techcrunch.com`

Textually.org www.textually.org

The Mobile Marketing Review www.themobilemarketingreview.com

The Pondering Primate http://theponderingprimate.blogspot.com

The Verge www.theverge.com

Online Publications

Beyond the mainstream business media (*Bloomberg Businessweek, Fast Company, Forbes, Fortune,* the *New York Times, The Wall Street Journal,* Wired, et al.), online publications, many focused partially or entirely on mobile developments, are indispensable resources for staying up-to-date on new products, companies, and other industry developments. A short (and by no means exhaustive) list of relevant publications follows. Check out the book's companion website, www.mobileanhouraday.com, for a more extensive list.

Ad Age www.adage.com

Adweek www.adweek.com

FierceMobileContent www.fiercemobilecontent.com

FierceWireless www.fiercewireless.com

MobiAD News www.mobiadnews.com

Mobile Entertainment www.mobile-ent.biz

Mobile Marketer www.mobilemarketer.com

Mobile Marketing Daily www.mediapost.com/publications/mobile-marketing-daily

Mobile Marketing Watch www.mobilemarketingwatch.com

mobiThinking www.mobithinking.com

paidContent www.paidcontent.org

VentureBeat www.venturebeat.com

Wireless Week www.wirelessweek.com

Twitter Feeds

For those of you not in the know, Twitter was originally conceived as a mobile-first service allowing users to microblog via SMS (you didn't think that 140-character limitation was a coincidence did you?). These are just a few of our favorite mobile influencers on Twitter. You can find more by following us at @themobilebook.

Brian Fling @fling

C. Enrique Ortiz @ortiz

Chetan Sharma @chetansharma

Daniel Appelquist @torgo

Eric Y Lai @ericylai

Ethan Marcotte @beep

Om Malik @om

Greg Sterling @gsterling

James Pearce @jamespearce

Jeff Hasen @jeffhasen

John Gruber @gruber

Joy Liuzzo @joyliuzzo

Luke Wroblewski @lukew

Peter Paul Koch @ppk

Rick Mathieson @rickmathieson

Rudy De Waele @mtrends

Russell Buckley @russellbuckley

Stephanie Rieger @stephanierieger

Appendix G: Conferences, Events, and Organizations

G

Staying up-to-date with a fast moving industry such as mobile can be challenging. Attending conferences and participating in industry organizations are two ways you can keep current with the latest trends and best practices.

Appendix Contents

Conferences and Events

As mobile progressively becomes a hotter topic, new events are springing up seemingly overnight. We could probably fill a whole chapter with conference listings so we've just tried to include the most prominent events here. You can find a more exhaustive and continually updated list on `www.mobileanhouraday.com/digitalindustryevents`.

Apps World: Apps World is the principal annual event devoted to native mobile applications (`www.apps-world.net`).

Digiday Mobile: Put on by the Digiday online trade magazine, Digiday Mobile is held annually in New York (`http://digidaymobile.com`).

International CTIA Wireless and MobileCON: Put on by CTIA—The Wireless Association (`http://ctia.org`), these annual events focus on the general mobile market (`www.ctiawireless.com`) and mobile-centric IT and enterprise concerns (`www.mobilecon2012.com`), respectively.

MMA Forum: The Mobile Marketing Association runs several national and international events throughout the year that are excellent networking opportunities for newbies and seasoned mobile marketers alike (`www.mmaglobal.com/events`).

Mobile Insider Summit and OMMA: The online trade publication MediaPost runs several mobile-focused events throughout the year, including the OMMA Mobile conference held in New York during Advertising Week and the biannual Mobile Insider Summits (`www.mediapost.com/events`).

Mobile Marketing Strategies: An annual event devoted to all things mobile for agency and brand-side marketers (`www.mobilemarketingstrategiessummit.com`).

Mobile World Congress: The premier global mobile technology and media conference is held each February in Barcelona (`www.mobileworldcongress.com`).

SXSW: Although not exclusively mobile, the SXSW Interactive festival held each March in Austin, Texas, is a hotbed of cross-platform workshops and ideas that are invaluable to anyone planning to integrate mobile into their marketing mix, as well as an increasingly important venue for the debut of mobile-focused companies (`www.sxsw.com`).

The Mobile Media Upfront: The annual mobile ad upfront event is sponsored by various online and mobile agencies (`www.mobilemediaupfront.com`).

Industry and Professional Organizations

Several major industry organizations are focused entirely on different aspects of the mobile ecosystem. But with mobile now crossing industry lines, many other trade and professional organizations have mobile-focused committees and resources designed to educate their members. Here, we've listed the primary organizations relevant to marketers.

CTIA—The Wireless Association: This nonprofit organization serves the needs of the wireless communications industry. It is an excellent resource for industry insights (www.ctia.org).

Interactive Advertising Bureau (IAB): Although not exclusively a mobile organization, the IAB has several task forces devoted to helping advertisers make the most of mobile. It is an excellent resource on topics related to mobile advertising and tracking (www.iab.net).

Mobile Marketing Association (MMA): The Mobile Marketing Association is the main professional organization serving mobile marketers around the world. It supports numerous working groups and committees devoted to research and standardization of best practices. It also provides numerous educational benefits and networking opportunities to individual and company members worldwide (www.mmaglobal.com).

Mobile Monday: Known to members as MoMo, Mobile Monday started in Helsinki in 2000 as a casual gathering of designers, developers, and other assorted mobile geeks convening on the first Monday of every month to share ideas and works in progress. In the intervening years, MoMo has grown to over 140 chapters in cities across the world and continues to expand as a grassroots community of mobile enthusiasts. It's one of the best networking opportunities we know of and odds are there is a chapter in your city; if not, you can always start one (www.mobilemonday.net).

The Direct Marketing Association (DMA): The DMA is the main professional organization serving the needs of the direct marketing and advertising community, for which mobile is an increasingly vital component (www.the-dma.org).

WOMMA: The Word of Mouth Marketing Association is primarily devoted to social media but will become a more relevant resource for mobile marketers as mobile, social, and local marketing converge (www.womma.org).

Glossary

accelerometer An embedded sensor that measures acceleration, tilt, and overall orientation, making the screen shift from landscape to portrait as you tilt or rotate your device. The accelerometer was first used by Apple in the iPhone, but is now a standard component of most tablets and high-end smartphones.

aggregator (SMS) Organizations with the technical infrastructure and business relationships required to send and receive SMS/MMS messages across the wireless carrier networks. The organizations function as middlemen between wireless carriers and brands. Any business or individual wanting to use SMS in the United States must procure the services of an aggregator. The aggregator provides the brand with hosting for their code, connection to the wireless carriers, bulk rate messaging, and, in some cases, campaign planning and management or access to a self-service campaign management portal for an extra monthly fee.

AJAX Asynchronous JavaScript and XML, or AJAX, is a combination of web technologies, including HTML, XHTML, CSS, JavaScript, XML, XSLT, the Document Object Model, and the XMLHttpRequest. Together, these technologies allow developers to create websites and web applications that update immediately as a user performs an action, without requiring a reload of the entire page.

alt-tags Alt-tags are text descriptions that are displayed while an image is being loaded or in lieu of an image when a user has images turned off on a mobile device. Because images often take longer to load via mobile and some users turn off images altogether, alt-tags are considered a best practice for mobile SEO.

ambient Marketing that combines various non-desktop digital interfaces and media (such as mobile devices, surface technology, Bluetooth, augmented reality, and the like) to create real-time user experiences. Ambient media use your smartphone to activate—and make interactive—the physical world around you.

anchor text The clickable text in a web link that is visible to the user; an important element of SEO.

Android Google's native operating system for smartphones and tablets. Android versions to date have all been nicknamed after desserts and include: Cupcake (1.5), Donut (1.6), Éclair (2.0/2.1), Froyo (2.2), Gingerbread (2.3), Honeycomb (3.0), Ice Cream Sandwich (4.0), and Jelly Bean (4.1).

app definition statement A document that contains an app's purpose, users, and high-level features and content.

app extensions A form of paid search-engine marketing offered by Google that enables an advertiser to promote native mobile applications by including a download link for an app within the body of search ads on mobile devices.

application (native) An application (app) designed to be downloaded and installed on a user's mobile device. Native apps differ from web apps in that they can tap into the device's native functions and features, such as the camera or near-field communication (NFC) chip, and allow the user to save information and access some or all content and features offline. Native apps are usually designed using compiled programming languages such as C++ or Java, or, in some cases, a combination of compiled code and a front-end markup language such as HTML5. See also *native mobile app*.

application (web) An app designed to enable a user to perform a specific function or set of functions within a web browser; in the case of mobile apps, usually designed with HTML5. See also *mobile web app*.

application programming interface (API) An API is a set of technical specifications that enable one type of system to interface with another, facilitating the exchange of digital information.

app store A destination (in both website and native application form) from which free and paid native mobile applications can be discovered and downloaded. The best-known app stores are the iTunes App Store and Google Play, but numerous others exist, including native app stores for Windows and BlackBerry, versions particular to wireless carriers worldwide, and various independent storefronts such as GetJar.

augmented reality (AR) The overlay of digital information onto real-world objects and locations, as viewed through a digital interface such as a smartphone or web cam. AR experiences are triggered via geo-location, reading, or scanning of some kind of physical marker or through a combination of both.

beta testing Performing tests of an early, working version of a website or native application to assess functionality and usability.

blind ad network An ad network model in which advertisers have no insight into where their ads run; often composed largely of remnant inventory (impressions that publishers are unable to sell). Ads are placed in "channels" of sites categorized together according to content type or intended audience.

Bluecasting The use of Bluetooth to distribute marketing messages and content such as coupons, videos, and offers. Bluecasting is usually an opt-in service in which users agree to receive messages when they are in the proximity of a Bluetooth hotspot.

Bluetooth A two-way, short-range, wireless protocol for data transmission operating on the 2.4GHz spectrum. The most familiar and common uses of Bluetooth are in wireless phone headsets, wireless mice and keyboards, and in-car systems, but the technology can also be used to distribute content from a Bluetooth hotspot to end-use mobile devices (see *Bluecasting*).

click-to-call A link placed in a mobile ad or on a mobile web page that automatically initiates a phone call between the advertiser and user when it is clicked.

click-to-download A search-engine marketing format containing a link to an app store download page.

click-to-offer A search-engine marketing format that enables a user to click to obtain a special offer or deal.

cloud platform (mobile) A service provider that offers cloud-based tools that can be used to mobilize an existing desktop website for multiple device types.

.com A colloquial term for a desktop website.

context The situational wants and needs of a user based on his or her position within the customer journey.

cross-platform toolkits A collection of tools, code samples, and APIs that enable developers to use markup code and scripted computer programming languages to develop native mobile applications for multiple platforms at once.

CSS Cascading Style Sheets, a document containing stylistic code that dictates the appearance of a website or web page. Cascading Style Sheets Level 3 (CSS3) is the most recent iteration of CSS used in conjunction with HTML5 to create dynamic cross-platform websites and applications.

customer journey The path taken by a potential customer from the initial stages of discovering a brand to becoming a loyal customer and advocate.

dayparting The practice of placing advertising to be displayed at specific times of day in which it will be most effective.

developer license A license to develop official native apps for a particular platform such as iOS or Android.

device detection The practice of detecting what type of device is requesting a web page and then delivering content that is formatted specifically for that device; usually achieved via some type of server-side script.

double opt-in The practice of requiring a mobile subscriber to opt in twice for an SMS or MMS marketing program; most commonly required for programs involving ongoing messages or premium content.

earned media Buzz gained through editorial content, PR, and word of mouth.

feature phone A mobile phone that does not have a fully functioning web browser and which is used primarily for voice calling and texting. Feature phones are usually smaller in size than smartphones and have lower-resolution non-touchscreens.

firmware A mobile device's native operating system.

fourth generation (4G) The fourth, and most recent, generation of wireless technology standards. There are currently two competing 4G technologies, Long Term Evolution (LTE) and WiMAX. All of the Tier 1 U.S. wireless carriers have committed to implementing LTE.

fragmentation Refers to the vast diversity of devices in the mobile ecosystem with their varying platforms, operating systems, functions, and form factors, and the associated marketing challenges.

freemium Native mobile apps that are free to download but incur charges for updates or certain additional services/content.

fully hosted Mobile websites that are developed and hosted by a third party apart from the brand that owns the site.

fully native mobile apps Mobile apps developed using the app platform's native software development kit (SDK) and making little or no use of external data sources.

global positioning system (GPS) The global positioning system is a satellite navigation system maintained by the United States government.

The signals relayed by the GPS are freely available to businesses and individuals and are used by the wireless carriers to pinpoint the positions of subscribers.

haptics The use of touch as method of relaying information to a user through a digital interface—for example, the vibration a user feels when pressing a touchscreen button; also commonly referred to as haptic feedback.

hosted mobile site Refers to a mobile website hosted by a third party.

HTTP headers Key elements of the request that is made when a device (in this case, a mobile device) requests a page from a website.

HTML5 The latest iteration of the Web's primary markup language, with elements that are instrumental in building touch and geocentric, app-like mobile user experiences.

hybrid mobile apps Refers to native mobile apps that are developed using the native SDK but make use of web-based content and services to provide essential elements of the user experience.

Human Interface Guidelines Guidelines issued by Apple to aid developers in creating mobile websites and applications that fully leverage all the features and functionality iOS devices have to offer.

ideation In mobile parlance, the process of developing a creative concept for an app, mobile website, or campaign.

image technologies Refers to technologies that utilize some form of image recognition, including quick response (QR) and other forms of barcode scanning, as well as true forms of image recognition such as Google Goggles.

index The database in which a search engine stores the web pages indexed by bots.

intent The level of a user's readiness and willingness to engage and/or convert.

intangible goods Refers to digital content sold via native mobile apps such as games, credits, points, and e-books.

interactive voice response (IVR) IVR is a digital system enabling users to interact with a menu of choices by voice command.

iOS Apple's operating system for mobile devices, including the iPod touch, iPhone, and iPad; currently in its 6.0 iteration.

keyword (SMS) In SMS parlance, a keyword is a word or phrase used to identify a unique campaign running on a specific common short code. Multiple keywords can be provisioned for a single short code, which enables that one code to support numerous simultaneous campaigns.

keyword density Keyword density refers to the ratio of keywords to non-keywords within a mobile web page.

latency The lag that occurs between the time content is requested by the user and when it is actually delivered.

Long Term Evolution (LTE) The 4G wireless standard supported in the United States by all of the Tier 1 wireless carriers, LTE promises high-speed data transmission for mobile devices at speeds rivaling those of fixed broadband networks.

machine-to-machine (M2M) Technologies that enable one digital system to communicate directly with another, often using wireless technology.

m-commerce A blanket term for all shopping and buying activities occurring via mobile devices.

media queries A feature of CSS that checks for particular aspects of the device making a page request (for example, screen size) and modifies the page layout accordingly.

media strategy The use of strategic planning processes to inform the development of media campaigns and purchase of media itself.

messaging fees The costs incurred by both the sender and receiver when an SMS message crosses the wireless carrier networks. For brands, these costs usually range from 2 cents to 5 cents on average but can scale lower or higher when bought in volume and depending on the aggregator with which the brand chooses to work.

meta description An HTML meta tag traditionally used to describe the contents of a web page for the benefit of search-engine spiders.

mobile-assisted commerce In mobile parlance, the use of a mobile device to conduct a transaction in some way, usually through researching and qualifying a purchase.

mobile first A design practice, rapidly growing in popularity, in which mobile users are given primary consideration in the design of features and navigation and in the development of content.

mobile readiness A measure of the degree to which a brand is able to connect with its customers via mobile channels, particularly via mobile web.

mobile web app A mobile app designed to run in the mobile browser; most commonly designed using HTML5 and CSS3.

mobile technographics A brand's customer demographics as defined by their use of mobile technology.

m-payments Refers to any monetary transactions conducted using a mobile device as the payment conduit, whether through NFC, mobile wallet, or an external reader.

mobile wallet Applications that store payment and other related information such as loyalty cards and coupon offers in digital format on a user's mobile device.

mobile phone users Refers to all mobile phone owners, including those using feature phones and smartphones.

multimedia messaging service (MMS) A richer form of SMS messaging that supports the sending and receiving of multimedia content such as images, audio, or video to a wireless subscriber.

multitouch A form of input for touchscreen devices in which two or more fingers can be used to manipulate the screen at one time.

native mobile app A mobile app designed to be downloaded to and run on a user's mobile device.

near-field communications (NFC) A short-range, two-way wireless radio frequency ID channel that delivers data using interacting electromagnetic radio fields. NFC differs from other radio transmission standards in that it requires very close proximity (four inches or less) to transmit data, making it more secure than similar technologies such as Bluetooth.

1D barcode Barcodes that present data in a linear, one-dimensional fashion. The most familiar flavor of 1D barcode is the UPC barcode commonly found on product packaging.

open rate Refers to the percentage of recipients who open and view a message. The open rate equals the exposed recipients/messages viewed.

opt-in Opt-in refers to the process by which a mobile subscriber gives explicit consent to receive one or more SMS or MMS messages from a wireless carrier or content provider. Opt-in is required for all commercial uses of SMS/MMS messaging in the United States. In most cases, a user sending a text to a short code is considered permission to send that user a return message. Ongoing messages generally require that a specific opt-in message be sent to the sender—for example, "Text DEAL back to this short code to receive weekly coupons."

opt-out Opt-out refers to the process by which a mobile subscriber revokes his/her consent to receive further SMS communications from a wireless carrier or content provider. The keywords STOP, QUIT, OPT OUT, END, CANCEL, and UNSUBSCRIBE are reserved for generating an automatic opt-out on most carrier networks.

operating system (OS) The native master software that runs the core functions of a computer or mobile device. Common mobile operating systems include Apple's iOS, Google's Android, Research In Motion's (RIM) BlackBerry, and Microsoft's Windows Phone.

owned media Refers to a brand's leverageable assets for marketing, including its `.com` website and branded social spaces, such as Twitter and Facebook.

page view The number of times a web page is viewed by users within a specific time period.

paid media Media purchased for a specified cost per unit; usually refers to display advertising or search-engine marketing. Also commonly referred to as bought media.

personalization The modification of content or a user interface according to customer-specified preferences or observed behavioral patterns.

platforms Types of mobile devices grouped by capabilities and operating systems—for example, Android or iOS.

point of sale (POS) The physical point at which a transaction is processed in-store, usually at a checkout counter.

portability The ability of content to be extended to multiple digital touchpoints.

preferences A user's specific wants and needs, likes and dislikes, as explicitly expressed to a brand.

premium blind A mobile ad network in which a sizable percentage of the publishers are premium, but advertisers still have little or no visibility into where their ads run.

premium content Refers to content, usually of the downloadable variety, for which the content provider charges a fee. Examples include ringtones and native mobile apps such as games and digital magazine editions.

premium SMS SMS messages that incur a fee above and beyond standard message rates, usually charged for delivery of premium content.

presence the availability and willingness of a user to receive content and/or communications from a brand at any given time.

progressive enhancement A design practice used in tandem with mobile first in which content and features are layered on top of a core mobile user experience in layers of progressive complexity.

proximity the physical location of user in relation to a brand.

proximity payments Payments effected via mobile device at the point of sale using a variety of mechanisms, including browser, apps, SMS, or NFC.

pull A process in which a user requests marketing messages from a brand, such as mobile-originated SMS or search-engine queries.

purchase funnel The process through which a prospect becomes a customer and eventually an advocate; traditionally progresses from awareness to consideration to purchase to ownership to loyalty.

push A process in which a brand proactively presents marketing messages to a customer—for example, in-app messages.

quick response (QR) codes The most popular form of 2D barcodes used in the United States.

radio frequency identification (RFID) A wireless technology in which data is transmitted from an RFID tag to an RFID reader via radio frequencies; used primarily in inventory and supply chain management and automated collection of transit tolls.

random short code Refers to a common short code composed of randomly assembled numbers (versus a vanity code, which is explicitly assembled to spell out a word or acronym).

reach The addressable audience for a particular campaign, website, or app.

redirect The practice of automatically forwarding users to a URL different from the one they have clicked. In mobile parlance, it refers to using redirects to send a user to mobile-specific content.

referrer The web page that delivered a user to your website.

relevance In mobile parlance, the ability of content or service to meet a customer's real-time needs.

responsive design The practice of designing a single website that modifies its format in real time to optimize the viewing experience for the capabilities and screen size of the device at hand.

search engine results page (SERP) A single page of search results returned to an end user's device by a search engine.

segments Groups of customers defined by similar personal and/or behavioral characteristics—for example, soccer moms or business travelers.

shared short code The practice of using a single short code to run SMS campaigns for multiple brands (versus licensing a single, brand-specific short code for each). Shared short codes are a popular workaround for brands looking to get to market quickly by bypassing the often lengthy carrier approvals process involved in licensing a unique common short code.

short code A five- or six-digit code that acts as a phone number from which brands can send and receive SMS and MMS messages; also known as a common short code (CSC).

short message service (SMS) SMS is a wireless carrier standard for delivering short, text-only messages, usually limited to 160 alphanumeric characters, from person to person or from a business to a consumer. SMS is universally available on smartphones and feature phones. Commonly referred to as "text messaging."

showrooming The practice by which shoppers use their mobile device in-store to research a potential purchase by looking for competitive information such as pricing, features, and reviews; showrooming sometimes leads to a purchase from an online merchant or another brick-and-mortar retailer.

site links Additional clickable links embedded into a search marketing ad designed to drive consumers deeper into a website, or, in the case of mobile, to click-to-call or drive them deeper into an installed mobile application.

single opt-in The process by which a subscriber opts in to a standard-rate messaging program, usually by texting to a common short code.

smartphone A mobile device that features a high-density, high-resolution color display (typically, a touchscreen interface among the latest generation devices) measuring two or more inches; an advanced, purpose-built operating system; the ability to send and receive email and SMS/MMS; a full-featured web browser that can render standard web pages except those elements built with Flash; access to and the capacity to run applications; a camera that can capture still images and high-definition video; GPS capabilities; and the ability to access both Wi-Fi and high-speed mobile broadband networks.

social machines Refers to objects that are not traditionally connected to the Internet, such as vending machines, that are rendered interactive by including some type of sensor or other digital component.

software development kit (SDK) A collection of tools, APIs, and sample code used to create applications.

splinternet A term used to describe the splintering of the Internet into different standards, channels, platforms, and access devices.

standard-rate SMS An SMS program in which the subscriber is billed according to a wireless carrier's standard messaging rates, usually pennies per message. Standard-rate SMS programs generally require only a single opt-in.

subdirectory A URL structure in which pages are housed in a subdirectory of the main domain—for example, `www.kiwi-market.com/mobile`.

subdomain A URL structure in which pages are housed in a web domain that is a subcategory of a larger web domain—for example, `http://mobile.kiwi-market.com` would be a subdomain of `www.kiwi-market.com`.

tablet A portable, lightweight computer primarily characterized by a touchscreen navigational interface; popular examples include the Apple iPad, Samsung Galaxy Tab, and Amazon Kindle Fire.

tangible goods A term used by Apple to define nondigital content purchased via a native app interface. Examples of tangible goods include apparel, accessories, household items, and collectibles—in essence, something that is an actual, physical object versus a digital one. Tangible goods are not subject to Apple's 30 percent commission fee that is levied on digital content (also known as intangible goods).

targeting A familiar term from online advertising, targeting refers to the available criteria by which a brand can define the audience for a campaign. Gender, age, designated market area (DMA), household income, time of day (dayparting) and geo-location are all examples of targeting.

technical audit In mobile parlance, a process by which a qualified technologist assesses a brand's digital infrastructure to assess how it can be extended to multiple device platforms.

technographics A market research tool used to segment a brand's customers according to their use of technology.

third generation (3G) The blanket term for the third generation of wireless standards, delivering voice and data at rates as high as 2Mbps. 3G standards include UMTS/W-CDMA, CDMA2000, CDMA 1xEV-DO, EDGE, and CDMA 1xRTT.

trafficking (ad) A blanket term for all of the tasks involved in setting up and managing an online advertising campaign including, but not limited to, set up and monitoring of the campaign in an ad serving program.

transcoding Refers to the process of taking an existing website and modifying it on-the-fly to be viewable/usable on a device for which it was not originally intended.

2D barcode A two-dimensional barcode one-ups its 1D cousin by storing information both horizontally and vertically, which enables it to pack in 7,089 characters versus the 20-character capacity of a 1D code. The most commonly used form of a 2D barcode in the United States is QR; the two terms are often used interchangeably, but QR is simply one variety of the 2D barcode standard.

user agent In mobile parlance, a signifier within an HTTP header that tells a website what type of device is requesting a web page from the site.

user interface (UI) The look and feel of a mobile website or application—the navigation, buttons, and overall layout. UI can also refer to the desktop design of a smartphone or tablet.

validate Validation is the process of assessing a design or concept's effect on the end user.

vanity short code A common short code that spells out a word or acronym that ties into your brand, making the code easier to remember.

viewport The actual viewable screen area of a desktop computer or mobile device.

WAP An acronym for Wireless Application Protocol, a very early, open, international set of protocols for the delivery of mobile data. WAP 2.0, released in 2002, opened the door to greater usage of the mobile web by enabling faster, more sophisticated mobile websites.

WebKit A rendering engine developed by Apple for the Safari web browser, WebKit now powers the browsers of most other top operating systems, including those of Android, BlackBerry (OS6+), Windows Phone, and Kindle devices, as well as select Symbian, Samsung, and Nokia devices.

white-labeling The practice of taking an existing piece of content, most commonly a native app, customizing it with a brand's look and feel and redistributing it as part of a promotional or marketing campaign; white-labeling an existing app can be a lot faster and cheaper than creating one from scratch, although generally less successful.

Windows Mobile (Windows Phone) Microsoft's original operating system for mobile devices has evolved through many incarnations from the very earliest versions of the Windows CE operating system in the early nineties to the current Windows Phone version 8 introduced in October 2012.

XHTML XHTML is a markup language based on HTML that conforms to XML syntax, enabling it to share the same cross-standard compatibility that XML supports. All modern smartphone and tablet browsers can read XHTML web pages, and its flexibility makes it an especially popular choice for developers creating mobile web content.

XML Also known as eXtensible Markup Language, XML is a general-purpose markup language designed to facilitate the sharing of data over the Internet between systems that don't share the same internal data structures—a sort of digital Esperanto. Many other current popular document specifications, including XHTML, RSS, and ATOM, are based on XML.

Index

Note to the reader: Throughout this index **boldfaced** page numbers indicate primary discussions of a topic. *Italicized* page numbers indicate illustrations.

A

B

C

D

E

F

G

H

I

J

K

L

M

N

O

P

Q

R

S

U

V

W

Y